Religious Persecution and Political Order in the United States

Religious freedom is a foundational value of the United States, but not all religious minorities have been shielded from religious persecution in America. This book examines why the state has acted to protect some religious minorities while allowing others to be persecuted or actively persecuting them. It details the persecution experiences of Mormons, Jehovah's Witnesses, Catholics, Jews, the Nation of Islam, and orthodox Muslims in America, developing a theory for why the state intervened to protect some but not others. This book argues that the state will persecute religious minorities if state actors consider them a threat to political order, but they will protect religious minorities if they believe persecution is a greater threat to political order. From the beginning of the republic to post-9/11, religious freedom in America has depended on the state's perception of political threats.

David T. Smith is jointly appointed in the United States Studies Centre and the School of Social and Political Sciences at the University of Sydney. He holds a PhD in political science from the University of Michigan.

Cambridge Studies in Social Theory, Religion, and Politics

Editors

David C. Leege, University of Notre Dame
Kenneth D. Wald, University of Florida, Gainesville
Richard L. Wood, University of New Mexico

The most enduring and illuminating bodies of late nineteenth-century social theory – by Marx, Weber, Durkheim, and others – emphasized the integration of religion, polity, and economy through time and place. Once a staple of classic social theory, however, religion gradually lost the interest of many social scientists during the twentieth century. The recent emergence of phenomena such as Solidarity in Poland, the dissolution of the Soviet empire, various South American, Southern African, and South Asian liberation movements, the Christian Right in the United States, and Al Qaeda have reawakened scholarly interest in religiously based political conflict. At the same time, fundamental questions are once again being asked about the role of religion in stable political regimes, public policies, and constitutional orders. The series *Cambridge Studies in Social Theory, Religion, and Politics* will produce volumes that study religion and politics by drawing upon classic social theory and more recent social scientific research traditions. Books in the series offer theoretically grounded, comparative, empirical studies that raise "big" questions about a timely subject that has long engaged the best minds in social science.

Titles in the series

Religious Persecution and Political Order in the United States

DAVID T. SMITH

University of Sydney, Australia

CAMBRIDGE
UNIVERSITY PRESS

CAMBRIDGE
UNIVERSITY PRESS

32 Avenue of the Americas, New York, NY 10013-2473, USA

Cambridge University Press is part of the University of Cambridge.

It furthers the University's mission by disseminating knowledge in the pursuit of education, learning, and research at the highest international levels of excellence.

www.cambridge.org
Information on this title: www.cambridge.org/9781107539891

© David T. Smith 2015

First published 2015

Printed in the United States of America by Sheridan Books, Inc.

A catalog record for this publication is available from the British Library.

ISBN 978-1-107-11731-0 Hardback
ISBN 978-1-107-53989-1 Paperback

To my parents,
Brian and Sue Smith

Contents

Acknowledgments

I have been working on this project in one form or another for eight years. The research and writing was spread across three cities – Ann Arbor, Sydney, and Seattle. I owe a significant debt of thanks to many people in all these places. I will try to be thorough in my acknowledgments.

I begin with the people most immediately involved in the writing and production of the book. Thanks first of all to Margaret Levi, who has provided tremendous encouragement and advice to me over the last four years as my mentor at the United States Studies Centre at the University of Sydney. The manuscript workshop she organized at Sydney in 2013 was a transformative event for the book. James Morone as a discussant saw the theoretical structure of the book in a way that I could not, and I have him to thank for the shape the book is in now. Rebecca Sheehan, Ryan Griffiths, and Niki Hemmer also provided valuable comments that day, and I am grateful to have them as colleagues at Sydney. Thanks very much to Lewis Bateman at Cambridge University Press for his patience and faith in this project, and to Kenneth Wald, David Leege, and Rich Wood for their comments on the manuscript.

In the final completion of the manuscript I have relied on the urgent assistance of several people to whom I will always be grateful. Thanks to Rob Mickey and Neill Mohammad for their readings of the final version of the manuscript and their astute comments on it. They have made the manuscript a lot better, and my respect for them knows no bounds. Thanks to Amanda Corlett of the American Civil Liberties Union for permission to use the beautiful 1936 map, "Compulsory Patriotism in the Schools." Thanks again to Rob for obtaining the final image of that map, and to Paul MacKay for his tweaks. It is thanks to Lizzie Ingleson that this book has a bibliography. Thanks to my editor Elda Granata for all her help, and her patience, and to Sathishkumar Rajendran and Kevin Broccoli for their copyediting and indexing.

I wrote the penultimate draft of the book while on study leave at the University of Washington (UW) in the first half of 2014. UW was the perfect environment in which to finish (and add significantly to) the manuscript. I am grateful to Margaret Levi and Peter May for arranging my stay there, and for making me feel so at home in Seattle. Thanks to Chris Parker for all his hospitality and help. I was fortunate to spend time with Tony Gill, who helped the project along substantially by letting me explain it on his Research on Religion podcast. I benefited a lot from talking to him. I also benefited from presenting the project at the UW Political Science Department colloquium, where I received valuable feedback from Victor Menaldo, Rebecca Thorpe, Peter May, Mark Smith, and Steve Pfaff, among others. Thanks to James Long for letting me discuss my work with his UW graduate seminar. Finally, thanks to Meg Stalcup for talking me through her research, and to Laurie Tazuma.

While the manuscript was still very much a work in progress, I had the unusual opportunity to discuss it on drive-time radio at ABC Sydney in 2013. This was a wonderfully clarifying exercise. Thanks very much to my student Christine Gallagher for making that happen, to Richard Glover for being a gracious host, and to everyone who gave me feedback on it.

Going back to the beginning of the project, I must thank above all the five remarkable people who served as my dissertation committee at the University of Michigan: Bill Clark, Anna Grzymala-Busse, Andy Markovits, Rob Mickey, and Rob Franzese. I assembled this committee before I even knew what I wanted to write about, and I made the right choices – I cannot imagine a more supportive, patient, and insightful group of advisers. They gave me badly needed discipline when I required it (which was all the time) and oversaw numerous episodes of creative destruction. They taught me to think in new ways. I still turn to them for advice. Thanks to them most of all for their friendship.

Many other Michigan faculty showed great generosity toward this wide-eyed Australian student who, as one of them put it, had a tendency toward "thunderous irrelevancies" in seminars. This book borrows heavily from the many things they taught me. For that, I thank Jenna Bednar, Jake Bowers, Ted Brader, Pam Brandwein, Edie Goldenberg, Rick Hall, Ron Inglehart, Don Kinder, Jeanette Kirkpatrick, Ken Kollmann, Dan Little, Danielle LaVaque-Manty, Mika LaVaque-Manty, Jim Morrow, Scott Page, Arlene Saxonhouse, Chuck Shipan, Elizabeth Wingrove, and Bill Zimmerman. Special thanks to Jana von Stein and my fellow Antipodean Rob Salmond, both of whom shared so much with me.

More than anyone else, my fellow graduate students at Michigan shaped my understanding of the country I was in. I will never be able to account for how much I learned from them and how much their friendship meant to me. For everything they gave me, thanks to Richard Anderson, Matias Bargsted, Janna Bray, Sarah Croco (due to whom I am no longer mathematically illiterate),

Allison Dale-Riddle, Anne Davis, Papia Debroy, Charles Doriean, Katie Drake, Kate Gallagher, Cassie Grafstrom, Krysha Gregorowicz-Heavner, Eric Groenendyk, Josh Gubler, Sourav Guha, Brent Heavner, Shanna Kirschner Hodgson, Liz Hudson, Ashley Jardina, Andrea Jones-Rooy, Nathan Kalmoe, Dan Katz, Brad Kramer, Merethe Leiren, Dan Magleby, Shaun McGirr, Erin McGovern, Jane Menon, Jennifer Miller-Gonzalez (who showed me the true meaning of Thanksgiving), Neill Mohammad, Pat O'Mahen, Spencer Piston, Paul Poast, Michelle Pritchett, Michael Robbins, Joel Selway, Khuram Siddiqui, Noah Smith, Derek Stafford, Jess Steinberg, Michio Umeda, Bonnie Washick, Claire Whitlinger, Scott Woltze, Alton Worthington, Jessica Wyse, Rachel Yates, and Jon Zelner. Double thanks to anyone I ever lived with or who let me stay at their house for a prolonged period (Neill, Liz, Jess, Charles, Jen, Dan, Mike, and Kate) and to Krysha and Brent, who were singularly excellent guides to American culture. Finally, all praise to Jules van Dyck-Dobos of Le Dog. People who knew me in Ann Arbor will know how much he means to me.

Since returning to the University of Sydney I have been surrounded by an extraordinary bunch of colleagues. I am grateful to Brendon O'Connor, Rebecca Sheehan, and Geoff Garrett for making feel welcome at the United States Studies Centre from the moment I got here. Brendon and Bec have been the best colleagues and friends I could have hoped for, and I have learned a huge amount from them. Bates Gill has been a wonderfully supportive leader of the Centre. Thanks also to Thomas Adams, Luika Bankson, Jonathan Bradley, James Brown, Nina Fudala, Sean Gallagher, Sarah Graham, Gorana Grgic, Lindsay Gumley, Max Halden, Lauren Haumesser, Niki Hemmer, Jen Hunt, Lizzie Ingleson, Malcolm Jorgensen, Adam Lockyer, Aaron Nyerges, Susan Pond, Craig Purcell, Rob Rakove, Tom Switzer, Cindy Tang, Amelia Trial, Shawn Treier, Meghan Walters, and Shane White.

In my other home in the Department of Government and International Relations, I have the great privilege of having colleagues who taught me as an undergraduate. For all their mentorship over the last four years, I cannot give enough thanks to Ariadne Vromen, Diarmuid Maguire, Rodney Smith, and Graeme Gill. Thanks so much for having me back. I have also benefited immeasurably from conversations, dinners, and drinks with Anna Boucher, Minglu Chen, Peter Chen, Charlotte Epstein, Anika Gauja, Ben Goldsmith, Ryan Griffiths, Michael Jackson, John Mikler, Chris Neff, Pippa Norris, Susan Park, Simon Tormey, and Colin Wight.

Thanks finally to my support network here in Sydney. Since coming back home in 2011 I have relied heavily on the people I knew from my pre-American life. They have helped me in more ways than I can say here. Thanks for everything to Ivan Ah Sam, Dean Bastian, Ben Cameron, Phil Carlon, Saskia Carr, Matt Davis, Gareth Edwards, Dom Knight, Nina Koutts, Gordon McLeod, Sarah Minns, and Tamara Watson. Thanks especially to Stuart Madgwick, Genya Sugowdz, and Matthew Sugowdz-Madgwick for keeping me well fed and my intellectual fire burning. And thanks, finally, to my loving and much-loved family – Sue Smith, Brian Smith, Stephen Smith, Michael Hanus-Smith, and Monica Hanus-Smith. I owe them so much that I will not commit my debts to paper, apart from this: Sue and Brian taught me from the youngest age possible what religious and political tolerance meant, and that it isn't the same thing as agreement. This book is dedicated to them.

I

Introduction

THE PUZZLE OF AMERICAN RELIGIOUS PERSECUTION

In the nineteenth century the Mormons were driven out of four states. In Missouri, the third state in which the Mormons settled, their neighbors declared war on them in 1838 when they seemed close to gaining a numerical majority in three counties. The ensuing skirmishes and massacres only ended when Governor Lilburn Boggs declared Mormons enemies of the state and issued an "extermination order" that forced them to flee to Illinois. In Illinois the state government initially welcomed the Mormons, but the reception soured by 1844, when local militias grew alarmed by Joseph Smith's increasing political and military power in the city of Nauvoo. On the pretext of defending free speech, an anti-Mormon mob lynched Smith when he destroyed a Nauvoo printing press that had denounced him. After the Mormons fled to Utah in 1847, the federal government fought for decades to break Mormon political power in the territory. Republicans had vowed to abolish Mormon polygamy in the west, and in 1883 Congress passed legislation stripping Mormons of the right to vote, hold political office, or serve on juries. Even harsher legislation in 1887 allowed the federal government to seize church property, including temples. The long campaign against the Mormons eased only after their leaders capitulated on the polygamy issue and forcibly realigned Mormon voters to the Republican Party.

In the late 1930s, elementary schools across the United States expelled thousands of children of Jehovah's Witnesses who refused to salute the American flag during the daily pledge of allegiance. In 1940, the Supreme Court ruled that school districts were within their rights to expel Witnesses, whose religious freedom did not include the right to disrupt the national unity the flag salute promoted. The flag conflict escalated into public violence as the Second World War approached and citizens questioned the loyalty of Jehovah's Witnesses. In small towns in every state, mobs attacked Witnesses while they proselytized. There were more than two thousand violent anti-Witness incidents between 1940 and 1942, many of which involved police, sheriff's departments, and other local authorities. Despite the repeated pleas of Jehovah's Witnesses and the ACLU, the federal government took little action to prevent the violence. The attacks only subsided when the draft came into effect and the government began imprisoning large numbers of Witnesses who refused to enter it.

Freedom from religious persecution is a central part of American national identity. It is enshrined in the constitution and the Bill of Rights, and every generation of civics textbooks teaches that early settlers came to the American colonies to escape persecution. The International Religious Freedom Act of 1998 reinforced the global defense of religious liberty as an aim of US foreign policy. But the experience of Mormons and Jehovah's Witnesses shows that religious toleration has not been extended to everyone in the United States. The constitution has not protected the freedom of every religion; in both of these instances the Supreme Court interpreted the constitution in a way that enabled persecution. James Madison and others believed that religious diversity and fragmentation would protect minorities in America because there would be no majority rule or polarization. This religious fragmentation, however, did not help groups that others did not recognize as legitimate religions. The United States may have one of the world's strongest records of religious toleration, but the standard explanations for this toleration are lacking when it comes to explaining important exceptions. These are not "exceptions that prove the rule," but rather exceptions that cast doubt on our understanding of the rules.

The fact that American governments have victimized religious minorities in the distant past may seem like a mundane point with little importance to contemporary religious persecution. American society has changed, generally in a more liberal direction, in every dimension since the Mormons and Jehovah's Witnesses were persecuted. Americans no longer tolerate all kinds of practices, such as slavery and lynching, which were also commonplace during those periods. However, circumstances continue to arise that place some minorities outside the framework of religious protection. After the 9/11 terrorist attacks, the U.S. government subjected Muslims in America to an aggressive program of surveillance, including infiltration of places of worship, that Americans would not tolerate if it were done to other groups.[1] This was not the first time, as I will show, that the state has treated Muslims as a public threat. It is important to examine the historical record of actually existing religious freedom in America to make sense of the present and the future.

The historical persecution of religious minorities, especially Mormons and Jehovah's Witnesses, poses three puzzles. First, the conditions to which scholars attribute non-persecution in America – a tolerant constitutional framework and

[1] Davis, Darren (2007). *Negative Liberty: Public Opinion and the Terrorist Attacks on America.* New York: Russell Sage Foundation, ch. 9.

a religiously diverse society in which no denomination has a majority – have been in place since the 1790s. If these are the institutional and social features that prevent religious persecution, why have they not done so consistently over time? Second, religious persecution has been extremely selective throughout American history. Most religious minorities *have been protected*, and even as it persecuted Mormons and allowed the persecution of Jehovah's Witnesses, the United States justifiably earned its reputation as a place that was unusually tolerant toward other minorities such as Jews and Anabaptists. Religious freedom in the United States is not, as some revisionists have argued, mythological;[2] despite the dominance of political institutions and discourse by white Protestants, a basic norm of religious freedom has prevailed. The puzzle is why some were violently excluded from it.

The third puzzle is that the minorities that were excluded would seem to be among the least likely candidates for religious persecution. The two most serious cases of persecution – those of the Mormons and Jehovah's Witnesses – were inflicted on groups that originated in the United States, were heterodox offshoots of Protestant Christianity, were numerically small at the time of their persecution, and were ethnically indistinguishable from white, mainstream Protestant denominations. The persecution of these two groups is surprising considering major theories about intergroup conflict. Previous studies have suggested that religious divides are most inflammatory when they overlap with other cleavages such as ethnicity, race, class, or nationality.[3] A long-standing body of scholarship also argues that majorities see minorities as more threatening the larger they get.[4] Studies of religious prejudice have found individuals feel more prejudice toward religious groups which are more remote and "other" from their own, such as members of different world religions.[5] All of these things should make it improbable that violence would be visited upon two small, home-grown offshoots of Christianity with no distinctive ethnic characteristics.

---

[2] See Sehat, David (2011). *The Myth of American Religious Freedom.* New York: Oxford University Press.

[3] Allport, Gordon W. (1958). *The Nature of Prejudice* (abridged). New York: Doubleday, pp. 413–426; Kleppner, Paul (1970). *The Cross of Culture: A Social Analysis of Midwestern Politics, 1850–1900.* New York: Free Press; Fox, Jonathan (2004). "Counting the Causes and Dynamics of Ethnoreligious Violence." *Totalitarian Movements and Political Religions*, 4:3, pp. 119–144.

[4] Key, V.O. (1949). *Southern Politics in State and Nation.* New York: Alfred A. Knopf; Blalock, Hubert M. (1967). *Toward a Theory of Minority-Group Relations.* New York: Capricorn Books; Liska, Allen E. (1992). *Social Threat and Social Control.* New York: SUNY Books.

[5] Glock, Charles Y., and Rodney Stark (1966). *Christian Beliefs and Anti-Semitism.* New York: Harper and Row, pp. 19–40. Kalkan, Kerem Ozan, Geoffrey C. Layman, and Eric M. Uslaner (2009). "'Bands of Others'? Attitudes toward Muslims in Contemporary American Society." *Journal of Politics*, 71:3, pp. 847–862; Theiss-Morse, Elizabeth (2009). *Who Counts as an American? The Boundaries of National Identity.* New York: Cambridge University Press, pp. 2–3.

Mormons and Jehovah's Witnesses are not the only religious groups to have been persecuted in the United States. In the 1850s, a national political party devoted to stripping Catholics of their rights took power in several major cities, and street gangs fought to stop Catholic immigrants from voting. Until the 1890s, it was normal for media outlets to claim Catholic immigration was a Vatican plot to seize control of America, and the government considered legislation that discriminated specifically against Catholic schools. In 1915, the lynching of Jewish industrialist Leo Frank in Atlanta heralded a new era of popular anti-Semitism that coincided with the redoubling of WASP efforts to keep Jews out of elite institutions. The reconstituted Ku Klux Klan, which numbered more than two million in the 1920s, led boycotts of Jewish businesses. In the 1930s, Father Charles Coughlin and Gerald K. Winrod warned millions by radio of Jewish schemes to bring American Christians to their knees through their control of the government and finance.

Popular anti-Catholic and anti-Semitic sentiments in the United States were far more widespread than hatred of Mormons and Jehovah's Witnesses, who to most Americans were distant and little-known sects. But in conflicts between Catholics and Jews and their antagonists, the government usually took the side of the religious minority. This was particularly true of the federal government, which suppressed Know-Nothing gangs and thwarted nativist legislation in the mid-nineteenth century, and unleashed the FBI and HUAC against anti-Semitic groups in the twentieth century. Individual Catholics and Jews certainly suffered at the hands of their persecutors, but, as groups, Catholics and Jews ultimately triumphed over them with the help of the government. Mormons and Jehovah's Witnesses had no such victories. When the government intervened, it was on the side of the persecutors. Persecution only ended when these groups were forced into submission on the terms the persecutors demanded.

THE ARGUMENT OF THIS BOOK

In this book, I concentrate on the state's role in and response to religious persecution. Discrimination and violence toward religious minorities can arise in a society for any number of reasons. Theological disputes, struggles over resources, the demonization of outsiders, and conspiratorial rumors have all caused Americans to persecute members of religious minorities, and the relative weights of these factors are difficult to calculate. However, the response of state actors at various levels of government determines the intensity of the persecution, how long it lasts, and the terms on which it ends. When faced with the civic persecution of a religious minority, state actors can respond in one of three ways: they can act to stop it, they can allow it to happen without participating in it, or they can actively join the persecuting effort.

I argue that this response is determined by the imperatives of the state. State actors are primarily interested in maintaining political order. At the federal level in the United States this has meant imposing national authority across a vast, chaotic geographic and political space while defending a liberal economic order. At the provincial level, it has meant creating a safe environment for investment and growth while maintaining the power of local elites and autonomy from federal interference. At the local level, it has meant preserving community cohesion, minimizing disturbances, and peacefully managing conflict between competing interests. State actors will persecute or allow the persecution of a religious minority when they believe that minority is a threat to political order. However, they will act to stop religious persecution when they believe the persecution itself is a threat to political order.

I argue that this logic best explains the pattern of state response to religious persecution in the United States. In the 1830s and 1840s, state governments that had initially welcomed Mormons turned against them when they established rival centers of power, with militias that rivaled the states themselves in terms of military capacity. This dynamic unfolded on a much larger scale from the 1850s onwards, when the federal government sought to break Mormon domination in the remote Utah territory. In these cases, governments sided with non-Mormon neighbors of the Mormons who complained that they were sealing off large tracts of land from the economic, political, and moral norms of the United States.

During the Second World War, Jehovah's Witnesses' refusal to salute the American flag threatened the symbolic political order that linked patriotism with the social status of war veterans in American communities. In small communities where war veterans made up a considerable power bloc, local authorities either acquiesced or participated in the violent repression of Witness efforts to proselytize. While federal officials objected to this treatment of Jehovah's Witnesses, they did little about it. The American Legion and other opponents of the Witnesses used violence to intimidate and expel Witnesses from their towns, often inflicting significant harm, but they stopped short of killing Witnesses or inciting major riots. Officials in the over-stretched Justice Department had little incentive to interfere with this violence perpetrated by respectable citizens, despite Witness complaints that their First Amendment rights were being violated.

In the mid-nineteenth century, on the other hand, governments at all levels consistently refused to give in to demands of anti-Catholic nativists that they restrict immigration or voting rights for newcomers. Although Catholicism was closely linked with anti-American subversion in the popular imagination, from the viewpoint of the state, nativists themselves posed the greater threat. They organized disreputable secret societies, inviting the same complaints about secrecy and subversion that they leveled at Catholics. They were also widely associated with violent street gangs that wreaked havoc around urban elections during the 1840s and 1850s. For these reasons, nativists were more likely to be victims of violent state interventions than the Catholics they targeted, and the political establishment shut the door on nativist legislative agendas even where nativists had overwhelming majorities.

American anti-Semitism peaked between 1915 and 1935, and was prevalent among economic and political elites who barred Jews as members of clubs and students at top universities, and supported restricted housing covenants that kept them out of exclusive neighborhoods. However, anti-Semitism as an organized political force never found support at any level of the state. In mass politics, anti-Semitism had an anti-establishment, populist, and eventually fascist tendency that represented grievances against the ruling class and industrial capitalism. When the likes of Father Coughlin and Gerald Winrod railed against Jewish financial power, they channeled a more general anger with big business and the government. Officials on both sides of politics found this threatening, and took measures to monitor and stigmatize political anti-Semitism. After Hitler came to power in Germany, anti-Semitism widely became associated with Nazism and un-American disloyalty.

The experience of American Muslims has been complicated and varied, but it also fits this general pattern. Throughout most of the twentieth-century immigrant Muslims lived in relative peace, regarded by state actors as a harmless ethno-religious minority deserving of the same protection as groups such as Catholics and Jews. But the FBI regarded the Nation of Islam, made up of African Americans, as a dangerous political "hate group" and attempted to repress it with violence, surveillance, and internal disruption using informants and agents provocateurs. Since 9/11, various state actors have regarded both Islam *and* the persecution of Islam as a threat. While condemning anti-Muslim hate crimes and popular expressions of Islamophobia, the state has also placed large sections of the Muslim population under heavy and intrusive surveillance in the name of countering terrorism and "radicalization."

None of these are settled, binary cases of persecution or non-persecution. Each case involves a dynamic process of social conflict in which religious persecution plays a role. The responses of state actors in these conflicts were not preordained by structural factors, and they did not remain fixed over time. Would-be persecutors could sometimes anticipate how the state would respond, but the response was often unpredictable and acts of persecution tested the state's reaction. State actors' perceptions of threats to political order changed as circumstances changed. The way religious minorities themselves responded to persecution also shaped the course of these conflicts. In some cases when state actors participated in religious persecution, religious actors eventually arrived at explicit bargains with the state to cease the persecution, as in the case of the Mormons. In other cases, as for Jehovah's Witnesses and the Nation of Islam, there were more gradual organizational and doctrinal changes that ultimately allowed for greater state accommodation of them, as well as changes in external circumstances that lessened the state's perception of them as threats. Within Catholic and Jewish communities there were debates over the extent to which these groups should "Americanize" in order to avoid alienating the public or the state.

The argument of this book assumes that actors in the democratic state, from presidents to sheriffs, have a degree of autonomy.[6] They do not simply respond to claims from within civil society, picking the strongest side when conflicts arise in order to ensure their political survival. State actors develop and act on preferences derived from the needs and self-conception of the state as an organization. The most fundamental of these preferences relate to maintaining the state's – that is, their own – authority. This authority – the ability to make decisions that will be followed and respected by the public – rests on widespread public acceptance not just of the state, but of the entire political order that encodes the proper role of the state and its relationship with the nation, individuals, civil society, families, and markets. This political order has elements that are material (e.g., the physical resources of the state), normative (e.g., the rights of individuals and groups vis-à-vis the state and each other), and symbolic (e.g., rituals of loyalty to the nation performed by state and non-state actors alike).

Both state and non-state actors are wary of threats to this order, which may come in the forms of foreign armies, radical political movements, corrupt officials, or deviant behavior. The state assumes responsibility for countering such subversive threats. But state and non-state actors may clash sharply over what constitutes a subversive threat, and how the state should deal with it. Scholars such as David Brion Davis, Richard Hofstadter, Michael Rogin, and others have identified a long-standing "counter-subversive" strain in American political culture that is obsessed with threats to the nation and its way of life.[7] While the state has sometimes joined this counter-subversive cause – as in the Red Scare of the 1950s, for example – it often sees these counter-subversive claims as dangerous. The "paranoid style," as Hofstadter called it, tends to be intolerant of difference and prone to violence. In its most extreme form it accuses the government of being in the hands of the nation's

---

[6] This conception of the state as a distinctive set of actors and institutions with decision-making power autonomous from society was originally developed in opposition to pluralist conceptions of the state as an arena for struggles between competing interests, or Marxian conceptions of the state as the political organization of ruling class interests. As I explain in Chapter 2, my conception of the state in this study retains the idea of autonomous decision-making derived from public authority, but moves away from other "statist" concepts such as the state as an established and unitary actor, or an impermeable boundary between state and society. On "statist" scholarship, see Huntington, Samuel P. (1968). *Political Order in Changing Societies.* New Haven: Yale University Press; Skocpol, Theda (1985). "Bringing the State Back In: Strategies of Analysis in Current Research." In Peter B. Evans, et al. (eds.) *Bringing the State Back In.* New York: Cambridge University Press; and Krasner, Stephen D. (1984). "Approaches to the State: Alternative Conceptions and Historical Dynamics." *Comparative Politics,* 16(2): 223–246.

[7] Davis, David Brion (1960). "Some Themes of Counter-Subversion: An Analysis of Anti-Masonic, Anti-Catholic and Anti-Mormon Literature." *The Mississippi Valley Historical Review,* 47(2): 205–224; Hoftsadter, Richard (1965). *The Paranoid Style in American Politics.* New York: Knopf; Rogin, Michael (1987): *Ronald Reagan, the Movie: and Other Episodes in Political Demonology.* Berkeley, CA: University of California Press.

enemies. Counter-subversives can become subversives themselves when they threaten to take power back from the state in the name of "the people."

Religion, by nature, is a potential threat to temporal political order. Religious adherents recognize a structure of authority and obligation that goes beyond the state or normal social conventions, and they see themselves as in some way different from – if not superior to – non-adherents. Some religions are deeply critical of the existing political order, and advocate elaborate alternatives. Others avoid politics, but place heavy demands on their members that may put them in conflict with social conventions or the law. However, religion may also be supportive of political order. Religions may counsel their members to accept state authority and recognize proper distinctions between ecclesiastical and temporal authority. Those religious groups identified with the majority of the population may bolster nationalism and participate in nation-affirming rituals. Religious groups that enjoy de jure or de facto privileges from the state may wield outsized political influence and will resist any changes to the system from which they benefit.

Members of religious organizations that are invested in the political order are often suspicious of those who are not, or who seem not to be. Throughout American history, counter-subversives from the Protestant religious mainstream have complained that other religious groups are incompatible with the American political order; that they are too clannish, authoritarian, fanatical, chauvinistic, or foreign. Since the late eighteenth century, these accusations have carried far more weight than older quarrels over theological error, blasphemy, or heresy. Sometimes, state actors have agreed with these complaints. They have set aside First Amendment concerns with religious freedom to protect a political order that they believe is under threat from religious groups with no loyalty to it. But at other times, these complaints *are* the threat to social and political order, raising the specters of divisiveness, intolerance, and mob rule. This latter scenario is especially likely when the complainants are tied to broader movements that the state identifies as anti-systemic or subversive.

The struggles of religious minorities have not happened in isolation from the broader politics of the United States. Throughout the book, I will show that the fates of religions have been intertwined with some of the largest, most formative political conflicts in American history. The "Mormon question" was determined by the federal government's quest to establish hegemony across the entire American continent. The place of both Mormons and Catholics in the politics of the nineteenth century was linked to the partisan battle over slavery. The treatment of Jehovah's Witnesses and Jews was informed by the approach of the Second World War and the question of American involvement in it. The war between the government and the Nation of Islam occurred in the context of black insurgency against white supremacist power structures. The Muslim experience in the twenty-first century has been shaped by the post-9/11 national security state.

ALTERNATIVE MODES OF EXPLANATION: PLURALISM, LEGALISM, AND PARTICULARISM

As far as I am aware, this is the first work to address historical variance in the American state's response to the persecution of religious minorities. As such, there are no ready-made alternative explanations to the one offered in this book. However, existing scholarship on relationships between minorities and the state offers three alternative frameworks that could be adapted to this question.

The first framework comes from the pluralist or "society-centric" approach to American democratic politics. In this understanding, the state primarily mediates conflicts between competing interests in society. State actors, especially politicians, are individuals with their own interests and strategies for achieving them, not part of an apparatus with distinctive preferences of its own. While early pluralists such as Dahl argued that every competing group can achieve power by mobilizing diverse political resources, later pluralists such as Lindblom emphasized the structural advantages enjoyed by some groups over others in the political arena, especially those with economic power.[8] Under this framework, especially in its latter version, one puzzle of this book seems to have an obvious solution: Mormons and Jehovah's Witnesses were subject to persecution while Catholics and Jews avoided it because the latter were simply much larger and better connected politically than the former. Jehovah's Witnesses, who numbered about 40,000 nationally at the time of their persecution, further handicapped themselves by refusing to vote, thus giving office-seeking local politicians no incentive to offer them protection.

Throughout the book, I will show that this explanation, while intuitively appealing, has limited use in explaining the experience of religious minorities in America. Mormons, who quickly became a numerical majority in the counties and territories they settled, should have been able to find patronage from one of the major parties. Because Mormons voted as a bloc under the direction of their leadership, pluralist logic suggests they possessed a political resource that could have bought them powerful allies. At several points they made overtures toward the Democratic Party, the party that traditionally resisted aggressive efforts to "Americanize" religious minorities outside the Protestant mainstream. As I will show, however, Democrats in Congress ultimately abandoned the Mormons, voting with Republicans to disfranchise them in Utah. Only those Southern Democrats who had most reason to oppose the Republicans' state-building program sided with the Mormons, who were a significant obstacle to it.

---

[8] Dahl, Robert (1961). *Who Governs? Democracy and Power in an American City*. New Haven: Yale University Press; Lindblom, Charles (1977). *Politics and Markets*. New York: Basic Books. For an overview of pluralist approaches to the American state, see Krasner, Stephen (1984). "Approaches to the State: Alternative Conceptions and Historical Dynamics." *Comparative Politics*, 16(2): 223–246.

When the Republican Party was founded in 1854 there were few Catholic votes available to it and it drew much of its support from the anti-Catholic Know-Nothings. But party leaders banished anti-Catholicism from Republican platforms as they regarded it as a distraction from the more important issue of anti-slavery. Meanwhile, various Democrats at different times embraced anti-Catholic initiatives, despite the party's strong Catholic constituency. A group of Democratic congressmen joined Republicans in 1888 to block the admission of heavily Catholic New Mexico into the Union as a state; in 1924 the Democratic Party narrowly defeated a proposed platform measure that would have denounced the anti-Catholic and anti-Semitic Ku Klux Klan.[9] American political parties, then, have often ignored electoral incentives to support or oppose the rights of religious minorities. Most state efforts to suppress or protect religious minorities have been bipartisan, reflecting a shared ideology around political order.

The second framework, which I term "legalism," has featured in many previous studies of relations between religious minorities and the state in America. From this perspective, the changing fortunes of religious minorities can be explained by the development of legal doctrine around religion. This fits with a more general picture of courts as prime movers in American politics, the ultimate spheres of conflict over basic rights.[10] The key events in the legalist story are Supreme Court cases about the scope of the First Amendment, such as the *Reynolds* decision of 1877 that decoupled the protection of religious beliefs from religious behavior, the *Gobitis* decision of 1940 that found religious expression did not trump national cohesion, and the *Barnette* decision of 1943 that overturned *Gobitis*. These cases certainly appear to have influenced subsequent religious persecutions. Congress voted to ban polygamists from voting in 1882, a few years after *Reynolds* ensured that this would not be considered an infringement of religious beliefs. Violence against Jehovah's Witnesses exploded in the weeks following *Gobitis*, which had found that school districts were within their rights to expel Witness children for refusing to salute the American flag. Many scholars have identified the incorporation of

[9] Stewart, Charles, and Barry Weingast (1992). "Stacking the Senate, Changing the Nation: Republican Rotten Boroughs, Statehood Politics, and American Political Development." *Studies in American Political Development*, 6(2): 223–271; McVeigh, Rory (2009a). "Power Devaluation, the Ku Klux Klan, and the Democratic National Convention of 1924." *Sociological Forum*, 16(1): 1–30.

[10] One of the most striking articulations of this perspective comes in J.P. Nettl's classic article, in which he argues that the law in the United States supersedes many of the roles of the state in other countries. In Nettl's words: "In the United States, the law and its practitioners have perhaps been the most important single factor making for political and social change and have time and again proved to be the normal instrument for bringing it about. Instead of demonstrating a narrow and self-sufficient interpretation of existing rules, which British law shares with that of the Continent, American law has tended to follow closely, and frequently to anticipate, major changes in public attitudes and has provided a vehicle to which the whole proliferation of social thought and action could be hitched. This is too well known to need elaboration here." From Nettl, J.P. (1968). "The State as a Conceptual Variable." *World Politics*, 20(4):559–592.

First Amendment rights at the state level, which did not occur until the 1940s, as the legal events that secured the rights of religious minorities against state and local officials, who were the most frequent violators of them.[11]

Legalist narratives have been particularly important in studies of Jehovah's Witnesses, who went to the Supreme Court thirty-nine times between 1938 and 1946 to secure their rights to proselytize and refuse the flag salute. Scholarship on the Witnesses' struggles has overwhelmingly focused on these cases, which generated thousands of pages of documents and had significant implications for First Amendment jurisprudence.[12] But as important as these and other First Amendment cases were, they did not develop in isolation from politics.[13] They also have relatively little explanatory power over patterns of violence and discrimination; conditions on the ground for Jehovah's Witnesses did not change much in response to their legal victories. Indeed, the court case about police harassment of Witnesses that led to the state-level incorporation of the right to the free exercise of religion (Cantwell v. Connecticut) was decided a month before the greatest surge of public violence against Witnesses, which often involved law enforcement agents. As I will show in Chapter 6, while Jehovah's Witnesses frequently invoked the constitution to defend themselves from persecution, constitutional law had little relevance to the political actors responsible for their persecution. The attacks on Witnesses were fundamentally assertions of local order. While sheriffs, police, and mobs violated numerous laws in their efforts to keep Witnesses out of their towns, the federal government made almost no effort to intervene on the Witnesses' behalf.

A third perspective, which I call "particularism," is not so much a theoretical framework as an epistemological convention in the study of religious persecution. While there have been some notable recent exceptions, nearly all studies of religious persecution focus on the experiences of a single group, and treat those experiences as *sui generis*.[14] They examine the deep historical roots of tension and intolerance, and trace sequences of events that lead to the violent expression of intolerance. In these studies, the causes of persecution are found in the particular circumstances of historical relations between the persecutor and

---

[11] The incorporation of the anti-establishment clause, however, was led by jurists with well documented anti-Catholic prejudices who wanted to "protect" public money from Catholic schools. See Drakeman, Donald (2007). "'Everson v. Board of Education' and the Quest for the Historical Establishment Clause." *American Journal of Legal History*, 49(2): 119–168.

[12] See, e.g., Manwaring, David (1960). *Render Unto Caesar: The Flag Salute Controversy.* Chicago: University of Chicago Press; Newton, Merlin Owen (1995). *Armed with the Constitution: Jehovah's Witnesses in Alabama and the U.S. Supreme Court, 1939–1946.* Tuscaloosa: University of Alabama Press; Peters, Shawn Francis (2000). *Judging Jehovah's Witnesses.* Lawrence: University Press of Kansas.

[13] On the role of political struggle outside the courts in the judicial development of civil liberties, see Kersch, Ken (2004). *Constructing Civil Liberties: Discontinuities in the Development of American Constitutional Law.* New York: Cambridge University Press.

[14] The most important exception is Brian J. Grim and Roger Finke's groundbreaking comparative study, *The Price of Religious Freedom Denied: Religious Persecution and Conflict in the 21st Century* (New York: Cambridge University Press, 2011).

the persecuted. There have been few attempts to compare the experience of different persecuted and non-persecuted groups with a view to establishing common causal patterns.

There have, for example, been no comparative studies of the experiences of Mormons and Jehovah's Witnesses in the United States, despite obvious similarities that observers noticed at the time the Witnesses were being persecuted. Instead, studies of both groups have emphasized the singularity of their experiences. Indeed, the persecuted group's uniqueness (particularly in the case of the Mormons) is often taken to be an important causal factor in their persecution. Spencer Fluhman's recent book *A Peculiar People* joins a long line of work that shows how Mormons crafted such a distinctive identity – reinforced by exaggerated stereotypes held by non-Mormons – that, by the mid-nineteenth century, Mormons came to be seen as a quasi-ethnic group. Many historians have argued that this "peculiarity" laid the groundwork for persecution because it enabled Americans to see Mormons as a foreign entity rather than an American religion.[15]

While these ideographic studies contain great insight into the dynamics of religious persecution, we need a comparative perspective to more fully understand the causal mechanisms involved. Every religious minority and religious conflict may be unique, but the repertoire of state responses to them is not. Even as the American state has changed over time, the decisions state actors at all levels of government face remain similar. To those charged with maintaining social and political order, what is a threat to that order? How do they balance the demands of the mainstream with the rights of those outside it? When do counter-subversive campaigns in civil society support political order, and when do they undermine it?

Each of these alternative perspectives has some value. In accordance with the pluralist viewpoint, antagonists toward religious minorities tend to be more successful when they petition the state if they have more political resources at their disposal. The legalist framework is particularly useful when we examine the constraints that one part of the state may impose on another. And the conflicts and hostilities that lead to religious persecutions are certainly historically contingent, rooted in particular circumstances of time and place. In this book I do not ignore these insights, but I seek to integrate them into a theoretical framework of state action that makes patterns of religious persecution intelligible over time and space.

[15] O'Dea, Thomas F. (1957). *The Mormons*. Chicago: University of Chicago Press; Moore, R. Laurence (1986). *Religious Outsiders and the Making of Americans*. Oxford: Oxford University Press; Mauss, Armand (1994). *The Angel and the Beehive: The Mormon Struggle with Assimilation*. Champaign: University of Illinois Press; Givens, Terryl L. (1997). *The Viper on the Hearth: Mormons, Myths, and the Construction of Heresy*. New York: Oxford University Press; Marr, Timothy (2006). *The Cultural Roots of American Islamicism*. New York: Cambridge University Press, ch. 5; Fluhman, J. Spencer (2012). *"A Peculiar People": Anti-Mormonism and the Making of Religion in Nineteenth-Century America*. Chapel Hill: University of North Carolina Press.

METHODS AND DATA

This book is a comparative case study of the experiences of five different American religious minorities: Mormons, Jehovah's Witnesses, Catholics, Jews, and Muslims. I have selected these cases primarily because of their historical prominence, their continuity as religions and their shared experiences of persecution coupled with considerable variance in how the state responded to that persecution. In the conclusion I briefly address the potential bias of limiting this study to prominent, surviving religions as opposed to groups such as the Branch Davidians or MOVE, which were extinguished by state violence.[16]

The book uses both primary and secondary historical research, and I use a variety of methods across cases to establish causal narratives. When examining the rise of Mormonism, I use qualitative analysis of newspaper sources to look at the discourse surrounding Joseph Smith. When I turn to the federal government's response to Mormon dominance in Utah, I use qualitative analysis of congressional speeches and quantitative analysis of house voting on the Edmunds Act to test hypotheses about why the anti-Mormon and anti-Edmunds coalitions formed. To tell the causal story of state acquiescence to violence against Jehovah's Witnesses, I use both quantitative and qualitative analysis of hundreds of affidavits that Witnesses submitted to the Civil Rights Section of the Justice Department, detailing their experiences.

For the case studies of the Catholic, Jewish, and Muslim experiences I rely mostly on large bodies of existing historical research, though my analysis of the Muslim experience since 9/11 also makes extensive use of recent media sources. Some cases in this book are much better known than others. Of necessity I spend more time, and undertake more original research, on cases that are not as well known in scholarship or in popular understanding. The chapters on Mormons, and especially Jehovah's Witnesses, are substantially longer, for example, than the chapters on Catholics and Jews, because there are many more basic facts about the former cases that still need to be established, both for the benefit of the reader and as a matter of historical record.

---

[16] I have not included black Christianity as a case in this book, despite the fact that sociologists of religion regard black American Christians as a distinctive religious grouping, and that black Christians have been subject to very high levels of violence over several centuries. The Civil Rights era alone could make for a case study, featuring the bombing of black churches and the assassination of black Christian leaders. However, I exclude black Christianity from this study because the persecution of black Christians has been part of a much broader campaign of racial oppression in which religious identity has usually been incidental to racial identity in the eyes of persecutors. The reason white supremacists targeted specifically religious institutions and leaders in the Civil Rights era was because of their prominent role in the Civil Rights movement, which had fundamentally secular objectives. As I show in Chapter 9, the persecution of the Nation of Islam was also intertwined with a broader campaign against black nationalism and black power, but in this case the chief antagonists regarded the religion itself as particularly dangerous and in need of eradication.

PLAN OF THE BOOK

This book will proceed as follows. In Chapter 2 I elaborate the theory of this book, grounded in the logic of the state's defense of political order. I place this in the context of existing understandings of religious freedom and persecution in the United States, which stress the tolerant framework of the constitution and the incentives for tolerance that arise from religious fragmentation. In this chapter I also briefly explore the general conditions under which state actors come to see religious minorities as threats to political order.

In Chapters 3 and 4 I examine the experience of the Mormons in the United States. Chapter 3 details the rise of the Church of Latter-day Saints, from their founding by Joseph Smith in 1828 to the murder of Smith in 1844. I show how, in these early years of growth, the Mormons were initially welcomed, but then violently rejected by state governments when their communities grew too economically exclusive and militarily powerful. In Chapter 4 I analyze the federal government's campaign against the Mormons after their move to Utah, and in particular attempts by Congress, which were ultimately successful, to strip Mormons of their rights to vote or hold office. I show how this was related to the national Republican Party's program of state-building, and why Southern Democrats alone resisted the disfranchisement of Mormons.

Chapters 5 and 6 address the treatment of Jehovah's Witnesses, the clearest case of where state inaction was the dominant response to persecution. Chapter 5 explains the origins of the Witnesses as a particularly vigorous, and often antagonistic, proselytizing sect. It shows how Witness children resisted the increasingly popular flag salute in public schools, and why this particularly aroused the hostility of the American Legion, one of the most important groups in the history of American civil society. Chapter 6 explores patterns of violence against the Witnesses and the acquiescence of local officials to it. Using hundreds of affidavits filed by Witnesses who suffered assaults, I show how this violence fitted into a long-standing repertoire of "establishment violence" in America, in which local elites assert order in the face of a perceived subversive threat.

Chapters 7 and 8 contain cases in which the state acted decisively to stop religious persecution. Chapter 7 shows why, despite the rapid and explosive rise of nativism as a political movement, various levels of the state successfully snuffed out political anti-Catholicism in the mid-nineteenth century (at least in its most severe manifestations). Chapter 8 shows how the state, especially at the national level, came to treat anti-Semitism as a subversive threat linked to foreign enemies of the United States, despite the continuing prevalence of anti-Semitism in American public opinion.

Chapter 9 examines the multifaceted Islamic experience in the United States. The state has often made distinctions between threatening and non-threatening forms of Islam, persecuting the former and protecting the latter. In this chapter I show how the state drew a sharp contrast between "authentic" Islam and the

Nation of Islam, which it regarded as a political movement rather than a legitimate religion. I also show how, after 9/11, various levels of the state have acted to stop the mass persecution of Muslims while maintaining their own apparatuses of surveillance and repression within Muslim communities.

I conclude in Chapter 10 by revisiting the comparative lessons of the book, and testing the robustness of my theoretical framework against the cases of MOVE and the Branch Davidians. I also consider how the experience of persecution, and the state response to it, changed and shaped the religious groups in this study. As I stress throughout the cases, religious persecution is a dynamic process in which the outcome is rarely completely settled. Religious adherents and leaders make conscious decisions about how they resist or acquiesce to persecutory pressure. Incidents of persecution play a major part in the collective memories of religious minorities, and sometimes the lessons of persecution become part of religious doctrine. The relative religious peace currently prevailing in the United States is the cumulative product of an often-violent struggle over the question of the degree to which society and the state should accommodate unpopular religious minorities. That struggle is far from over.

2

Religious freedom and persecution in America

A *theoretical overview*

INTRODUCTION

The central argument of this book is that in the United States, the protection of religious minorities from persecution has been contingent on state actors and their perceptions of threats to political order. If they regard religious minorities as a threat to political order, state actors are more likely to allow civil society to persecute them, or to join in the persecution. If, however, state actors see a greater threat in the persecution itself, they will act to protect religious minorities.

This explanation is at odds with the two dominant conceptual approaches to religious freedom in the United States. One approach sees religious freedom in America as preordained either by the constitution or by the conditions of religious pluralism that have existed since the colonial period. In this explanation, incidents of persecution have occurred throughout history, but these have ultimately expanded the legal conception of religious freedom that is always changing in the direction of greater inclusiveness. The other approach sees "religious freedom" as ideological cover for white, Protestant majoritarianism and views the persecution of religious minorities as normal, part of a broader system of social domination of all racial, ethnic, religious, and sexual minorities.

I argue that religious tolerance, enforced by the state, has frequently prevailed in America because state actors see religious intolerance as a threat to their own authority, or to the greater legitimacy of the order on which their authority rests. While this usually secures the long-term physical safety and political rights of religious minorities, breakdowns in religious tolerance have been frequent enough and violent enough to show the contingency of minority well-being on the threat perceptions of state actors. Sometimes the state sees them as the threat to be countered. Neither the constitution nor structural pluralism can protect religious minorities on their own; protection depends on which side the state takes in political conflicts.

In this chapter I construct and elaborate on this theory and suggest some likely conditions under which civic actors may succeed or fail in persuading state actors that a religious minority is a political threat. First, however, I contextualize this approach by outlining the strengths and weaknesses of existing approaches to religious freedom and persecution in the United States.

NARRATIVES OF RELIGIOUS TOLERANCE AND INTOLERANCE IN AMERICA

Existing literature on religious freedom in the United States has emphasized two main mechanisms that protect religious minorities: a tolerant and non-discriminatory constitutional framework, and a long-standing religious diversity that has encouraged cooperation and prevented domination by any single group. This section explores the workings of these mechanisms, and also how they might break down: Even with a tolerant constitution and a fragmented religious scene, how does intolerant religious majoritarianism arise to threaten religious minorities?

Conditions for the protection of religious minorities, I: religious freedom in law

The First Amendment to the US constitution reads, "Congress shall make no law respecting the establishment of a religion, or prohibiting the free exercise thereof; or of abridging freedom of speech, or of the press; or the right of the people peaceably to assemble." The power of these forty-six words to protect religious minorities from persecution has long been at the heart of the official narrative of religious freedom in the United States.

In 1790, while several states were still debating ratification of the Bill of Rights, the leaders of numerous religious minorities wrote to President George Washington to congratulate him for his government's affirmation of religious freedom in the First Amendment. Washington's most famous response was to the Jewish congregation of Newport, Rhode Island. He wrote that the government "gives to bigotry no sanction, to persecution no assistance," and wished "the children of the stock of Abraham who dwell in this land to continue to merit and enjoy the good will of the other inhabitants – while everyone shall sit in safety under his own vine and fig tree and there shall be none to make him afraid."[1] Washington believed the new constitution would establish the United States as a non-persecuting nation – a rarity at that time.

More than two centuries later, Congress mandated that the United States take increasing responsibility for preventing religious persecution abroad. The

---

[1] Washington, George (1790). "Letter to the Jews of Newport." *Washington Papers*, 6: 284–285. Available at www.tourosynagogue.org/index.php/history-learning/gw-letter, last accessed June 2, 2013.

International Religious Freedom Act of 1998 established an Office of International Religious Freedom within the State Department, whose job is to monitor and report on violations of religious freedom around the world, with serious violations meriting automatic sanctions.[2] The text of this legislation explicitly links America's global mission for religious freedom with its origin as a haven from persecution:

> The right to freedom of religion undergirds the very origin and existence of the United States. Many of our nation's founders fled persecution abroad, cherishing in their hearts and minds the ideal of religious freedom. They established in law, as a fundamental right and as a pillar of our nation, the right to freedom of religion. From its birth to this day, the United States has prized this legacy of religious freedom and honored this heritage by standing for religious freedom and offering refuge to those suffering religious persecution.[3]

At a 2011 address to the UN Office of the High Commissioner for Human Rights, Suzan Johnson Cook, the US Ambassador-at-large for International Religious Freedom, urged other countries to adopt the American model of religious freedom to combat religious intolerance, discrimination, and violence. She framed the proper role of the state in Washington's terms, offering "to bigotry no sanction, to persecution no assistance." While emphasizing the government's responsibility to develop and enforce robust legal protections against discrimination and violence, Cook argued that "laws seeking to limit freedom of expression in the name of protecting against offensive speech are actually counterproductive."[4] In other words, the protective value of religious freedom requires other First Amendment freedoms as well, especially freedom of speech. Religious freedom remains a live and volatile political issue in the United States, and legislators as well as courts are vigilant about the non-establishment and free exercise clauses.[5] In 1993, Congress passed the Religious Freedom Restoration Act, which specified it was impermissible for even a religiously neutral law to burden a person's freedom of religious practice.[6] This act featured prominently in the

---

[2] See Farr, Thomas F. (2008). *World of Faith and Freedom: Why International Religious Liberty Is Vital to American National Security.* New York: Oxford University Press.

[3] H.R. 2431 (1998), Sec. 2.a.1.

[4] Cook, Suzan Johnson (2011). Remarks at Office of the High Commissioner for Human Rights Panel on "Combating Intolerance and Discrimination Based on Religion or Belief." Geneva, June 14, 2011. Available at www.state.gov/j/drl/rls/rm/2011/166097.htm, last accessed June 2, 2013.

[5] Louis Fisher argues that Congress, not the Supreme Court, has been the most important branch of government for protecting the rights of religious minorities, acting to safeguard these rights when the courts ignore or contradict them. Fisher, Louis (2002). *Religious Liberty in America: Political Safeguards.* Lawrence: University Press of Kansas.

[6] The RFRA was a response to the 1990 Supreme Court decision in *Employment Division, Department of Human Resources v. Smith*, a case related to the ceremonial use of peyote by Native Americans in Oregon. The court's finding that the burdens placed on religious practice were irrelevant as long as a law was religiously neutral outraged many observers, including both religious liberals and religious conservatives. Some legal observers were shocked by the way the

2014 case of *Burwell v. Hobby Lobby*, in which the Supreme Court found that the Affordable Care Act substantially burdened business owners with a religious objection to providing contraception to their employees through federally mandated insurance plans.[7]

Legal scholarship has emphasized the success of the First Amendment in protecting religious freedom; Stephen Feldman describes it as the "standard story." He cites the declaration of a Pennsylvania court in 1989 that the First Amendment guarantees "religious liberty and equality to 'the infidel, the atheist, or the adherent of a non-Christian faith such as Islam or Judaism.'"[8] This view is also emphasized in civics textbooks, which retell the familiar narrative of how immigrants came (and continue to come) to the United States to enjoy its constitutionally protected religious freedom.[9] The same story has regularly featured in presidential speeches, and has found some of its strongest expressions in the words of presidents who themselves have come from outside the white, Protestant majority.[10] Barack Obama neatly encapsulated the importance of religious freedom to American national identity during an address at the annual White House Iftar Dinner, celebrating Ramadan, in 2010: "This is America, and our commitment to religious freedom must be unshakable. The principle that people of all faiths are welcome in this country, and will not be treated differently by their government, is essential to who we are."[11]

ruling overturned decades of precedent considering the impact of laws on religious practice. Congress sought to restore pre-*Smith* requirements. See Berg, Thomas C. (1994). "What Hath Congress Wrought – An Interpretive Guide to the Religious Freedom Restoration Act." *Villanova Law Review*, 39(1): 1–70.

[7] See the majority opinion in *Burwell v. Hobby Lobby*, authored by Samuel Alito. Available at www.law.cornell.edu/supct/pdf/13-354.pdf, last accessed February 26, 2015.

[8] Feldman, Stephen M. (2003). "Religious Minorities and the First Amendment: the History, the Doctrine, and the Future." *Journal of Constitutional Law*, 6(2): 222–277.

[9] Schwille, John and Jo-Ann Amadeo (2002). "The Paradoxical Situation of Civic Education in Schools: Ubiquitous and Yet Elusive." *New Paradigms and Recurring Paradoxes in Education for Citizenship*, 5: 105–136. Whether students actually absorb these lessons is a different matter. According to one study, only 52% of high school students could correctly identify amendments to the Constitution as the legal source of religious freedom in the United States. Niemi, Richard G. and Jane Junn (1998). *Civic Education: What Makes Students Learn*. New Haven: Yale University Press, p. 31.

[10] See, e.g., John F. Kennedy's famous speech on religious tolerance before the Greater Houston Ministerial Association on September 2, 1960. Kennedy explicitly drew on Article VI of the Constitution, prohibiting a religious test for office, and mentioned the struggles against established religion that had created religious freedom in the United States: "For while this year it may be a Catholic against whom the finger of suspicion is pointed, in other years it has been, and may someday be again, a Jew—or a Quaker—or a Unitarian—or a Baptist. It was Virginia's harassment of Baptist preachers, for example, that helped lead to Jefferson's statute of religious freedom." Available at: http://millercenter.org/scripps/archive/speeches/detail/3363, last accessed June 3, 2013.

[11] Available at www.nytimes.com/2010/08/14/us/politics/14obama.html, last accessed June 3, 2013. This speech was given in the context of the controversy over the construction of an Islamic center near the site of the 9/11 attacks, which came to be known in the news media as

As well as having an honored place in America's narrative of itself, the idea of the constitution as protector of religious minorities fits with recent scholarship on the causes of religious persecution. In particular, Brian Grim and Roger Finke have shown that countries with less regulation of religion tend to have much less violent persecution of religious minorities. The only way to put religions on an equal footing, for these authors, is to guarantee religious liberty for all. If the state privileges one religion over another, the favored religion will be likely to use its temporal power and influence to repress other faiths. They argue strongly against alternative models of religious regulation, such as restrictions on proselytism, which are designed to keep religious peace by creating and maintaining separate religious communities. Such restrictions create religious grievances and help to license persecution.[12] The United States is arguably the least regulated religious environment on earth, and by this logic we would expect it to have some of the lowest levels of religious persecution because the constitution explicitly makes no attempt to regulate religion.[13]

This liberal and legalistic theory of non-persecution is widely accepted in both its scholarly form and its folk narrative form. When religious persecution has occurred in the United States, it has not dented America's self-conception as a constitutional haven from religious persecution. Even persecuted minorities themselves have invoked the power of the Constitution and sought remedies through the courts, as we shall see in the case of the Jehovah's Witnesses. But for religious minorities seeking the kind of freedom that America promises, the question remains: Why does this legal protection sometimes fail? Who does it fail? Could it happen again?

Conditions for the protection of religion minorities, II: Religious fragmentation

Another approach to the protection of religious minorities goes beyond legal and political institutions, and looks to the conditions under which those institutions may be created. When do governments have an incentive to create a robust system in which religious freedom will be respected and protected for all? Several major Enlightenment thinkers arrived at similar conclusions on this question. They believed religious tolerance would prevail where there were many religions and none was a majority. Voltaire observed Jews, Muslims, and Christians doing business together in London's Royal Exchange and concluded that while a single religion could lead to government

---

the "Ground Zero Mosque." Obama supported the construction of the center. The White House Iftar, as the *Times* article points out, is a tradition extending back to Thomas Jefferson, and which was maintained on an annual basis by George W. Bush.

[12] Grim and Finke (2011), pp. 70–87 and 169–194.

[13] It is the only country to receive a score of 0 on Jonathan Fox's authoritative index of governmental regulation of religion. Fox, Jonathan (2008). *A World Survey of Religion and the State*. New York: Cambridge University Press.

tyranny and two religions would set people at each other's throats, "as there are such a multitude, they all live happy, and in peace."[14] Adam Smith argued the zeal of religious teachers would only be "dangerous and troublesome" where either a sole religion was tolerated or where society was divided into two or three large religious groups. That same zeal would be "altogether innocent" in societies consisting of hundreds or thousands of sects as they would be obliged to learn "candour and moderation" when "surrounded on all sides with more enemies than friends."[15] James Madison famously linked religious and political pluralism in *The Federalist*. In both cases, he argued, the fact of multiplicity provided the mechanism by which civil rights would be secured:

> In a free government the security for civil rights must be the same as that for religious rights. It consists in the one case in the multiplicity of interests, and in the other in the multiplicity of sects. The degree of security in both cases will depend on the number of interests and sects; and this may be presumed to depend on the extent of the country and the number of people comprehended under the same government.[16]

For Madison, the number of sects and interests is a function of population size, which is why he favored a large federal system in America. For all three of these very different liberal thinkers, the connection between pluralism and freedom is primarily about numbers. None of them suggests that any one religion is naturally more tolerant or predatory than any other; it is the numerical distribution of religions that determines how they will behave.

In *The Political Origins of Religious Liberty*, Anthony Gill gives a theoretical and empirical account of how religious pluralism gave rise to institutions of religious freedom in colonial America, among other places. Gill argues that religious preferences are naturally pluralistic in any society, an axiom of the "supply side" approach to religion also taken by Grim and Finke. He proposes that in order to maximize their market share under these conditions, the dominant religions in all countries prefer government regulations that subsidize themselves and restrict minority religions. Minority religions, which could not hope to obtain such preferential treatment from the government, always favor unregulated regimes that put all groups on an equal footing. When no religion has a majority of adherents, all religions seek religious freedom. Governments are likely to create regimes

---

[14] Voltaire, François Marie Arouet de ([1778] 1910). *Letters on the English*. Vol. XXXIV, Part 2. New York: P.F. Collier & Son, 1909–1914. Available at www.bartleby.com/34/2/, last accessed June 4, 2013.

[15] Smith, Adam ([1776] 1987). *The Wealth of Nations*. bk. 5, ch. 1, pt. 3, art. 3. Available at http://press-pubs.uchicago.edu/founders/documents/amendI_religions31.html, last accessed June 4, 2013.

[16] Madison, James (1787–1788). *The Federalist Papers*, No. 51. Available at www.ourdocuments.gov/doc.php?flash=true&doc=10&page=transcript, last accessed June 4, 2013.

of religious freedom when they do not need to secure the political support of one dominant sect.[17]

In this account, the making of America as a society of competing religious minorities was a natural result of its origin in a series of settler colonies. For the economic survival of the colonies, colonial governments needed to do whatever they could to encourage immigration. For some, this meant allowing settlers from many different religious backgrounds to settle the colonies, and under the condition of equal political rights.[18] Although Puritan colonies such as Massachusetts were notoriously intolerant, others such as Rhode Island, Pennsylvania, and eventually Virginia developed strong codes of mutual religious toleration among their fragmented populations. High levels of internal migration and then the Revolutionary War necessitated further religious freedom across America: in Gill's words, "the necessity to form a united front against the British motherland required that all denominations get along if only through mutual disregard."[19] When the colonies formed a new republic, creating a very large and inescapably diverse polity, it was natural that the framers of the constitution adopted the model of religious freedom pioneered by the large, diverse colonies such as Virginia and Pennsylvania.

Recently, Robert Putnam and David Campbell have traced the long-term consequences of religious heterogeneity in America. Putnam and Campbell argue that a very deep form of religious tolerance exists in the United States – most Americans believe, even against the teachings of their own churches, that believers in other religions can also go to heaven.[20] This kind of acceptance of religious difference is unusual in a society with such high levels of religiosity. Putnam and Campbell posit that the most important reason for it is that "most Americans are intimately acquainted with people of other faiths." Religious fragmentation means that, even with relatively high levels of religious homogeneity in some communities, most Americans have family or close friends with different religious beliefs. It is hard for them to believe that their loved ones are not going to heaven just because of religious differences.[21] This is an important religious extension of social contact theory – the idea that contact between members of different groups can reduce group tensions if that contact

---

[17] Gill, Anthony (2008). *The Political Origins of Religious Liberty*. New York: Cambridge University Press, pp. 41–55.

[18] Ibid., p. 92.

[19] Ibid., p. 109.

[20] Putnam, Robert D. and David E. Campbell (2010). *American Grace: How Religion Divides and Unites Us*. New York: Simon & Schuster, pp. 534–540.

[21] Ibid., p. 526. In Putnam and Campbell's vivid telling: "We call it the 'Aunt Susan' principle. We all have an Aunt Susan in our lives, the sort of person who epitomizes what it means to be a saint, but whose religious background is different from our own. Maybe you are Jewish and she is a Methodist. Or perhaps you are Catholic and Aunt Susan is not religious at all. But whatever her religious background (or lack thereof), you know Aunt Susan is destined for heaven. And if she is going to heaven, what does that say about other people who share her religion or lack of religion? Maybe they can go to heaven too."

takes place under the right circumstances. It also, however, implies that insular religious groups that do not assimilate socially are less likely to find tolerance.

The overall picture that emerges from these theoretical accounts is that religious fragmentation brings about religious peace in several stages. Initially, many competing sects may distrust each other, but when they are forced to live together with none having a majority, they are likely to devise institutions that encourage religious equality and freedom, if only for their own security. These institutions enable religious heterogeneity to continue in peace, and over time a much deeper form of tolerance will develop thanks to prolonged contact under favorable conditions. The history of the United States seems to embody this theoretical narrative, but again we are left with questions about the exceptions to the rule. When is heterogeneity heresy?

Seeds of exclusion?

Each of these conditions for protecting minority rights has some potential weaknesses. These weaknesses emerge from the question of religious identity: What counts as a "legitimate" religion? Who decides? And when do religious minorities come to see commonalities between themselves – such as a shared Protestantism or Christianity – which can transform them from a collection of mutually vulnerable sects into a religious majority, aggressively asserting its rights over those who do not share its identity? These questions may shed some light on why and how a government, or a society such as the United States, can persecute some religious minorities without damaging its self-perception as a protector of religious minorities.

The seeds of religious exclusion are present in one of the foundational texts of liberal religious tolerance: John Locke's 1689 *Letter Concerning Religious Toleration*. In the mid-eighteenth century Locke's thought dominated American liberalism, and it is hard to overstate his ideological influence on the American Revolution.[22] Locke attributed religious toleration to the Gospel of Jesus Christ as well as "the genuine reason of mankind." He was appalled by the spectacle of Christians persecuting each other in the name of salvation and professed not to understand how they could misread the New Testament so badly. One's personal relationship with God is an inward matter, and no magistrate could possibly coerce true religious faith – if faith is coerced, it cannot be faith. It follows that civil authority should not be entangled with religious belief. Locke believed nobody's rights should be jeopardized on the grounds of his religion, "whether he be Christian or Pagan," but he had some important qualifications.

Locke argued against tolerating any group that attributed to itself "peculiar privilege or power above other mortals," or that refused to recognize authorities

---

[22] Bailyn, Bernard (1968). *The Ideological Origins of the American Revolution*. Cambridge: Harvard University Press; Hartz, Louis (1955). *The Liberal Tradition in America*. New York: Harcourt Brace.

outside of its ecclesiastical community. Such a group, he warned, was likely to harbor destructive secret agendas. No church had the right to toleration if "all those who enter into it do thereby ipso facto deliver themselves up to the protection and service of a foreign prince." This would amount to letting in a foreign army. "Lastly," wrote Locke, "those are not at all to be tolerated who deny the being of a God. Promises, covenants and oaths, which are the bonds of human society, can have no hold upon an atheist."[23]

For Locke, religious toleration depended on respect for the boundary between inward beliefs and outward responsibilities to civil society. The temporal authorities needed to observe this boundary, but so too did religious groups. Because certain religious groups notoriously did not, the civil authorities should not tolerate them lest they endanger the whole social compact that made toleration possible. While Locke explicitly mentioned "Mahometans" who were "bound to yield blind obedience to the Mufti of Constantinople," his seventeenth-century readers would also have recognized Roman Catholics among the groups who were "beholden to foreign princes." Many other religious sects were also open to charges of excessive secrecy, separateness, and disrespect for civil authority.

Locke's criteria for who deserved religious tolerance left room for relatively few groups apart from the various Protestant denominations and sects. Even persuading these groups to tolerate each other was something of an achievement. As Chris Beneke has documented, seventeenth- and eighteenth-century churches in the American colonies were obsessed with the idea that other churches were in error, and that the eternal lives of souls were at stake in doctrinal quarrels between denominations. Mutual acceptance only came after a gradual shift in attitudes and norms, especially among the clergy, toward a state of civility and political cooperation. This normative shift was a result of the realization that so many small religious groups could not lead completely separate lives in a unified polity. By the time of the Revolution, "[s]omething had indeed changed in America. In the generally expressed preference for piety over theology, in the generally expressed disdain for restrictive creeds, in the easy mixing of America's sects in voluntary societies and constitutional conventions, Crèvoceur's claim that America was growing indifferent to the particular forms its religion took rang true."[24]

---

[23] Locke, John (1689). *A Letter Concerning Toleration.* Available at http://etext.lib.virginia.edu/ toc/modeng/public/LocTole.html, last accessed June 5, 2013.

[24] Beneke, Chris (2006). *Beyond Toleration: The Religious Origins of American Pluralism.* New York: Oxford University Press, pp. 174–175. In the "preference for piety over theology" described here is a notable echo of the devout but theologically indifferent religious pluralism that the Eisenhower administration actively promoted in the early Cold War as a means of uniting a divided population against Communism. Eisenhower's formulation of this principle was "our form of government has no sense unless it is founded in a deeply-felt religious faith, and I don't care what it is." Henry, Patrick (1981). "'And I Don't Care What It Is': The Tradition-History of a Civil Religion Proof-Text." *Journal of the American Academy of Religion,* 49(1): 35–47, p. 36. See also Herzog, Jonathan P. (2011). *The Spiritual-Industrial Complex: America's*

The flipside of this newfound mutual respect was that Americans were wary of groups that could upset the balance. Locke's warning against those who attributed a "peculiar privilege" to themselves, and those who were insufficiently respectful of civil authority, delineated clearly political criteria for religious toleration. Unity out of diversity – *e pluribus unum* – was a hard-won achievement for the early American republic. There would always be concern that the wrong kind of diversity could threaten this fragile arrangement. Tolerance would not be extended easily to groups that did not recognize other groups as equal to themselves or which gave more weight to their own ecclesiastical authorities than to common political institutions. As I will show in the following chapters, attempts at religious persecution often began with the accusation that a certain group was implacably hostile to others or did not respect American democracy.

A new era of brotherhood and ecumenicism among Protestant churches also undermined the second mechanism by which minority religions were protected – the fact that no group had a majority. As groups such as Congregationalists and Presbyterians developed a shared sense of identity as American Protestants, the groundwork was laid for a Protestant majoritarian nationalism that would become more acute as non-Protestant immigrant populations grew.[25] David Sehat argues that the Protestant majority created a coercive "moral establishment" that, at least until the 1920s, used the courts to persecute dissidents and imposed suffocating limitations on political reformers of all kinds. "Proponents of the moral establishment," according to Sehat, "claimed that religion was necessary to reinforce the moral fabric of the people, which was, in turn, necessary for the health and preservation of the state. But their understanding of religion was decidedly narrow.... Religion usually meant Protestant Christianity."[26]

While the boundaries of the Christian "mainstream" have continuously expanded throughout American history, those outside the boundaries have often been denied full recognition of their American nationality.[27] In *Hellfire Nation*, James Morone offers a parsimonious account of how religion has drawn stark boundaries between insiders and outsiders in the United States. An astonishingly diverse range of political causes began with a common preoccupation: sin. Outsiders threatened the fabric of American communities because they were seen as lazy, violent, drunk, promiscuous, or otherwise morally deficient. The parameters of sinfulness were defined by America's

---

Religious Battle against Communism in the Early Cold War. New York: Oxford University Press.

[25] On this point see Flake, Kathleen (2011). "An Enduring Contest: American Christianities and the State." In Brekus, Catherine A., and W. Clark Gilpin (eds.) *American Christianities: A History of Dominance and Diversity*. Chapel Hill: University of North Carolina Press, pp. 491–508.

[26] Sehat (2011), p. 8. See also Flake (2011).

[27] Hutchison, William R. (2003). *Religious Pluralism in America: The Contentious History of a Founding Ideal*. New Haven: Yale University Press; Theiss-Morse (2009), pp. 2–3.

puritan heritage and Protestant identity, and successive waves of newcomers (beginning with Germans, whom Benjamin Franklin hated) were the subjects of jeremiads about the imminent downfall of America unless something was done about them. The public policy consequences were enormous, from the Northern evangelical crusade against Southern slaveholders (who fulfilled the quadrella of sin by being lazy, violent, drunk, and lecherous) to the formation of the FBI in the wake of a "white slavery" panic over Jewish-run prostitution rackets.[28]

Americans, then, despite their confessional fragmentation, have not seen themselves as a collection of mutually vulnerable religious minorities. Instead, they have seen themselves as a Protestant nation, or a Christian nation, or a Godly nation. However inclusive these categories might have been in terms of population percentages, they could make life grim for those outside them. As we have seen, even the most universalistic conceptions of American identity – the United States as a land where every individual conscience is sacrosanct – contain proscriptive warnings against groups who are too insular or fanatical to respect that sanctity.

For all of these reasons, the American religious scene has never been an entirely inclusive one, despite the absence of a denominational majority and a constitutional framework guaranteeing religious freedom and equality. Prejudice against various religious minorities has been rampant at certain points in American history, and this prejudice has often been justified in the name of religious freedom itself. This brings us to the central question of this book: When does the state allow prejudice to turn into persecution?

THEORETICAL BUILDING BLOCKS: PERSECUTION, CIVIL SOCIETY, AND THE STATE

What is persecution?

"Persecution" in this study refers to violence or discrimination against members of a religious minority because of their religious affiliation. Persecution involves the most damaging expressions of prejudice against an out-group, going beyond verbal abuse and social avoidance.[29] It refers to actions that are intended to deprive individuals of their political rights and to force minorities to assimilate, leave, or live as second-class citizens. When these actions happen persistently

---

[28] Morone, James A. (2003). *Hellfire Nation: The Politics of Sin in American History.* New Haven: Yale University Press.

[29] Grim and Finke define "violent religious persecution" as "physical abuse or displacement of people because of religion" (2011, p. xii). I supplement this definition with discrimination, partly because this fits with the ordinary language definition of persecution and also because some discrimination is intimately associated with violence. Those who are denied civil and political rights will be violently restrained when they try to exercise those rights, either by the state or with state complicity. Discrimination, physical harm, and extermination are the latter stages of Gordon Allport's five-stage sequence of prejudiced expression toward outgroups, following antilocution (verbal attacks) and avoidance (Allport 1958, pp. 14–15 and 48).

over a period of time, and include large numbers of both perpetrators and victims, we may refer to a "campaign" of persecution that usually has the goal of excluding the targeted minority from the polity. These campaigns, as I explain below, usually begin within civil society in secular democracies.

In this study I am particularly concerned with the state *response* to campaigns of persecution. How do those legally charged with maintaining social and political order react when members of a majority try to excise or subordinate a minority? The state reaction is critical to the intensity, duration, and outcome of a persecutory campaign. If state actors intervene on the side of the persecuted minority, they may limit the damage to isolated incidents and ensure that minority members continue to exercise their civil and political rights. If state actors fail to intervene, the minority may sustain serious damage and be forced to flee or intimidated into abandoning religious activities that the majority deems offensive. If the state intervenes on the side of the persecutors, minority members may face forced removal, legal subordination, imprisonment, or death, with little in the way of recourse.

This study seeks to explain the variance in the state response to religious persecution throughout American history. When does the state defend religious minorities from persecution, when does it allow persecution to happen, and when does it actively persecute? Before laying out the theoretical framework for an answer, I will clarify what "the state" means in the American context, and how the state interacts with civil society during religious persecutions.

The state in America

The American state has changed substantially over the two centuries this study covers. It may seem to make little sense to talk about the "postal state" of the 1820s and the burgeoning "warfare state" of the 1940s as the same entity.[30] Stephen Skowronek has argued influentially that the development of national administrative capacities took place around the turn of the twentieth century, and prior to that the United States had a qualitatively different political order that was far from the modern, industrial bureaucracy that underlies traditional definitions of the state in social science.[31]

Other scholarship, however, has challenged the idea of American "statelessness" before the twentieth century. William Novak documents an

---

[30] On the centrality of the postal service to the national state in the nineteenth century, see John, Richard (1995). *Spreading the News: The American Postal System from Franklin to Morse.* Cambridge: Cambridge University Press; and Carpenter, Daniel (2000). "State Building Through Reputation Building: Coalitions of Esteem and Program Innovation in the National Postal System, 1883–1913." *Studies in American Political Development,* 14: 121–155. On the development of the extensive the Second World War national state, see Sparrow, James (2011). *Warfare State: World War II Americans and the Age of Big Government.* New York: Oxford University Press.

[31] Skowronek, Stephen (1982). *Building a New American State: The Expansion of National Administrative Capacities, 1877–1920.* Cambridge: Cambridge University Press.

extensive nineteenth-century regulatory state, created mainly at the local and state levels, which empowered an active officialdom and touched every aspect of Americans' lives.[32] Jerry Mashaw shows that at the federal level too, Congress from the beginning delegated broad authority and coercive powers to administrative officials who operated independently of the executive.[33] Brian Balogh argues that the importance of foreign policy during the nineteenth-century expansion across the continent meant Americans regularly turned to the "general government" for solutions to problems, though its role remained "hidden in plain sight," displaced in the popular imagination by heroic settlers and entrepreneurs.[34] Even though a national administrative state actually has been present throughout American history, the "state" in that sense has been mostly absent from American political vocabulary, which is dominated by the language of government and the law.[35] This may make the language of "state response" unfamiliar, but it is entirely warranted in this book.

The coherence of the American state and its centrality to the story of religious persecution become clear when we consider the core of nearly all definitions of the state: the actors and institutions who monopolize coercive control over a given territory.[36] However idiosyncratically and inconsistently the American state has been organized, it has always endowed actors with public authority over delimited geographic spaces and areas of competence. As Skowronek notes, "after all the European comparisons have been made, the extreme features of American government in the nineteenth century are still best appreciated as distinguishing a particular organization of institutions, procedures and human talents that asserted control within the national territory."[37]

"The state" in the American context does not refer to a single unitary, intentional actor or a static, established entity. Rather, it refers to actors who exercise public authority and the institutional arrangements that grant and

---

[32] Novak, William (1996). *The People's Welfare: Law and Regulation in Nineteenth-Century America.* Chapel Hill: University of North Carolina Press.

[33] Mashaw, Jerry (2012). *Creating the Administrative Constitution: The Lost 100 Years.* New Haven: Yale University Press.

[34] Balogh, Brian (2009). *A Government Out of Sight: The Mystery of National Authority in Nineteenth-Century America.* New York: Cambridge University Press.

[35] Nettl, J.P. (1968). "The State as a Conceptual Variable." *World Politics,* 20(4): 559–592.

[36] Most definitions of the state in social science are descended from Weber's definition in *Politics as a Vocation* (1919): the organization that claims "the monopoly of the legitimate use of force within a given territory." Some later definitions have abandoned the idea of legitimacy, instead emphasizing effectiveness in the use of force (as in Mancur Olson's "stationary bandit" model). However, these later definitions may also be compatible with more recent understandings of legitimacy that stress rational or "quasi-contingent" consent. See Olson, Mancur (1993). "Dictatorship, Democracy and Development." *The American Political Science Review,* 87(3): 567–576; Rogowski, Ronald (1974). *Rational Legitimacy: A Theory of Political Support.* Princeton: Princeton University Press; Levi, Margaret (1988). *Of Rule and Revenue.* Berkeley: University of California Press.

[37] Skowronek (1982), p. 8.

maintain that authority. In this study we are concerned with authoritative actors at all geographic levels of the state – national, provincial, and local – especially those whose area of competence is keeping the peace, enforcing the law, and ensuring the free exercise of civil and political rights. This obviously involves the state's security apparatus, which in the United States has included various armies, militias, police forces, sheriff's departments, and intelligence agencies. It also includes executive actors who deploy the security apparatus, legislators who make laws about rights, and courts that interpret and validate those laws.

The American state has been a dynamic entity. Over the last two centuries, the geographic scope of its authority has expanded vastly. The national state has gradually assumed new functions, often bringing it into conflict with state actors at other levels. The boundary between state and society, as I will explore further below, has usually been permeable rather than fixed. The constant changes in the American state – the expansion and sometimes contraction of authority, conflict between different levels and organs of the state, and the fluid border between state and society – are an important part of any story of the decision-making of state actors, including their response to the persecution of religious minorities.

State actors are, for the most part, deeply invested in the existing political order on which their authority rests. By "political order" I refer to both the institutional arrangements of the state and the web of conventions, symbols, rituals, and rules that create the sense of a shared polity in which citizens and the state are mutually loyal to each other. State actors at different levels naturally take different views of the polity, and so have different priorities in their maintenance of the political order. At the national level, state actors have fought to establish control of continental territory and to preserve a liberal economic order. Over time, the national state has assumed and maintained the functions of taxation and conscription which characterize modern states, and which rest on an acceptance among citizens that the state is acting in the interests of the people and exercising its powers fairly.[38]

At the level of states, which have established territorial boundaries, state actors have sought to promote economic development by attracting outside investment and (in many cases) immigration. This often means negotiating compromises between new immigrants and investors and established residents and economic interests. They have also sought to protect their own authority from encroachment by the national state. At the local level, state actors are concerned with community cohesion and protecting the interests of local elites, insofar as this is compatible with maintaining their own authority and keeping the peace. At all levels, state actors are concerned with preventing and quelling disorder. State actors, as I explain below, will

---

[38] Levi (1988); Levi, Margaret (1997). *Consent, Dissent and Patriotism.* New York: Cambridge University Press.

only tolerate non-state violence when they believe it bolsters the political order rather than subverting it.

Civil society and the state

In secular democracies, state actors rarely initiate religious persecution of their own accord. Democratic states are in general much less likely than authoritarian regimes to use repressive violence against their own citizens, and this norm of non-violence is particularly strong where robust institutions exist for holding governments accountable to the populace.[39] Secular democratic states, though they come in a variety of forms, have a shared Westphalian conception of moral and political order that casts individuals as "autonomous consenting selves" and states as entities that govern according to material and strategic interests, not the advancement of a religion.[40] These states may regulate religious life to some extent, but state actors do not see it as their role to intervene in religious disputes. In long-standing secular democracies, different religious groups tend to enjoy formal equality of legal rights (if not equal distribution of state resources), and different democracies have developed a wide range of institutional arrangements for peacefully managing religious pluralism.[41]

The persecution of religious minorities instead originates in civil society. "Civil society" refers to a country's organized associational life outside of the market and the state. The groups that make up civil society include clubs, churches, political parties, cultural associations, business associations, and unions. Mass media, which informs citizens about civic life and the workings of the state, is also part of civil society.[42] Civil society carries positive connotations for most social scientists. Robert Putnam emphasizes the Tocquevillean features of civil society: its horizontally organized nature, its independence from the state, and the way it fosters habits of democratic participation, which strengthens the institutions of the democratic state.[43]

Even in America, civil society is not completely separate from the state. The government has nourished voluntary civic associations, which in turn have played important roles in reforming the government and shaping public policy.[44] The nature of civil society often depends on national context; Polish

[39] See Davenport, Christian (2007). *State Repression and the Domestic Democratic Peace*. New York: Cambridge University Press.

[40] See Hurd, Elizabeth Shakman (2008). *The Politics of Secularism in International Relations*. Princeton: Princeton University Press, pp. 21–45.

[41] See Monsma, Stephen V. and J. Christopher Soper (1997). *The Challenge of Pluralism: Church and State in Five Democracies*. Lanham: Rowman and Littlefield.

[42] See, e.g., Loizos, Peter (1996). "How Ernest Gellner got mugged on the streets of London, Or: Civil Society, the Media, and the Quality of Life." In Dunn, Elizabeth and Chris Hann (eds.) *Civil Society: Challenging Western Models*. London: Routledge.

[43] Putnam, Robert (2000). *Bowling Alone*. New York: Simon & Schuster.

[44] Skocpol, Theda (1997). "The Tocqueville Problem: Civic Engagement in American Democracy." *Social Science History*, 21(4): 455–479.

scholars and activists, for example, have conceptualized civil society as a force of political organization, often with vertically organized components, that provides resistance to a repressive state apparatus.[45] Elisabeth Jean Wood has shown how a vibrant civil society emerged from conditions of civil war and repression in rural El Salvador.[46] Across all of these different understandings of civil society, there remains a core idea that civil society is vital to participatory politics. These participatory politics, however, need not be liberal or democratic.[47]

In the United States there is a long tradition of groups of citizens making contentious claims on the government in the name of "the people."[48] Citizens believe the government needs to be made more directly responsive to the people, or that the people need to exercise their collective, Lockean rights against government intrusion and overreach. Often, however, these claims are accompanied by an understanding of "the people" that excludes large numbers of citizens, sometimes with violent implications.[49] Civil society can be dangerous for unpopular minorities when it harnesses majoritarian claims that the state must act to protect the people from undesirable outsiders. Even a very widespread prejudice against a group may be relatively harmless if it lacks a political voice and an organizational structure to transform it into a claim for state action.[50] It is civil society that begins the process of making prejudice into persecution.

Which kinds of claims from civil society can mobilize the state's coercive monopoly against a religious minority, or at least persuade the state not to intervene in episodes of violent persecution? The identities of the claimants are important. A large body of scholarship in political science and sociology has shown that even in a pluralistic system in which all citizens enjoy formal legal

---

[45] Arato, Andrew (1981). "Civil Society against the State: Poland 1980–81." *Telos*, 47: 23–47; Ekiert, Grzegorz, and Jan Kubik (1999). *Rebellious Civil Society: Popular Protest and Democratic Consolidation in Poland, 1989–1993*. Ann Arbor: University of Michigan Press.

[46] Wood, Elisabeth Jean (2003). *Insurgent Collective Action and Civil War in El Salvador*. New York: Cambridge University Press, ch. 6.

[47] Berman, Sheri (1997). "Civil Society and the Collapse of the Weimar Republic." *World Politics*, 49(3): 401–429; Foley, Michael W., and Bob Edwards (1996). "The Paradox of Civil Society." *Journal of Democracy*, 7(3): 38–52.

[48] Morone, James A. (1998). *The Democratic Wish: Popular Participation and the Limits of American Government* (revised edition). New Haven: Yale University Press.

[49] Kirkpatrick (2006). Kirkpatrick, Jennet (2008). *Uncivil Disobedience: Studies in Violence and Democratic Politics*. Princeton: Princeton University Press.

[50] I take the vocabulary of "claim-making" from Charles Tilly. In Tilly's words: "We might think of collective claim-making as an interactive performance. Like veteran members of a theatrical troupe, political actors follow rough scripts to uncertain outcomes as they negotiate demonstrations, humble petitions, electoral campaigns, expulsions of enemies, hostage taking, urban uprisings, and other forms of contention. Such performances link pairs or larger sets of actors, the simplest pair being one claimant and one object of claims. The actors in question often include governmental agents, polity members, and challengers as well, with challengers sometimes newly mobilizing from the regimes previously unmobilized subject population." Tilly, Charles (2003). *The Politics of Collective Violence*. New York: Cambridge University Press.

equality, some groups are inevitably far more powerful and politically effective than others. The rich are more powerful than the poor, ethnic and racial majorities are more powerful than minorities, men are more powerful than women, and the old are more powerful than the young.[51] This basic social fact of inequality and stratification has important effects on contentious claim-making. Prejudice is most likely to succeed as persecution when it originates from a position of social power. Civic actors in well-established networks with close links to institutional power are more likely to have their prejudices taken seriously than those who are socially and politically marginal.

The form that a persecutory claim takes is also important. What are civic activists demanding that the state "do about" a religious minority, and how are they making those demands? As I will explain in more detail below, claims are most likely to succeed when they are framed in terms that do not attack religion itself, but instead target a group behavior that is seen as dangerous or disorderly. In the United States, campaigns against religious minorities have taken the form of crusades against drinking on the Sabbath (targeting Catholics), programs to eliminate polygamy (targeting Mormons), demands for government action against racketeering (targeting Jews), jeremiads against the dangers of bloc voting (targeting both Catholics and Mormons), and community outrage over refusals to salute the American flag (targeting Jehovah's Witnesses).

One recurring claim leveled against many religious minorities in the United States is that they imprison women. Nativists charged that Catholic priests lured innocent women to convents and then subjected them to sexual slavery. Similar captivity narratives were a staple of anti-Mormon literature, and feminists joined Christian conservatives in arguing that Mormon women needed to be liberated from their polygamous husbands. In the twenty-first century, the claim that Muslim men routinely abuse their wives was at the heart of a campaign to ban Sharia law from state legal systems. As I will show in the case studies, these crusades to "liberate" the women of religious minorities have had varying degrees of success in eliciting a response from the state. While captivity narratives often play on deep anxieties about racial mixing dating from first contact between Europeans and Native Americans,[52] they are most politically successful when framed in liberal terms, as a fight to ensure the rights to which American women are entitled. I will show that anti-polygamy campaigns were more successful than anti-Sharia campaigns because the former had support from the feminist movement that the latter has never found.

---

[51] In the famous words of E.E. Schattschneider, "The flaw in the pluralist heaven is that the heavenly chorus sings with a strong upper-class accent." See Schlozman, Kay Lehman (1984). "What Accent the Heavenly Chorus? Political Equality and the American Pressure System." *The Journal of Politics*, 46(4): 1006–1032.

[52] See Morone (2003); and Rogin, Michael Paul (1975). *Fathers and Children: Andrew Jackson and the Subjugation of the American Indian*. New York: Knopf.

Often anti-minority claim-making occurs within the accepted rules of democratic politics, in the form of petitions, demonstrations, editorials, party platforms, and legislative agendas. Sometimes, however, it takes forms such as vandalism and violence.[53] These approaches are much riskier and less likely to succeed in democracies, but occasionally they have been fruitful.

THE LOGIC OF STATE ACTION: DEFENDING POLITICAL ORDER

This brings us to a major theoretical point which is applicable beyond the United States, but is particularly useful for explaining the American experience. State actors in democracies usually see intergroup prejudice as a threat, especially when it is associated with violence. *They will only tolerate the political expression of prejudice when they see it as supportive of the existing political order rather than subversive of it.* This makes most religious persecution intolerable to state actors in liberal democracies. For reasons discussed above, discrimination on the grounds of religious beliefs violates deep norms in modern secular states. When state actors victimize one religious group, or allow it to be victimized, they run the risk of creating a system of religious privilege that would undermine their own secular authority.

Violence is even more problematic; if the state tolerates violence by non-state actors, it endangers its own monopoly on the legitimate use of force. Actors in a relatively weak state, however, may allow extra-state violence that they see it as supportive of the established order, especially if the state itself cannot enforce that order. Many episodes of vigilantism in American history have fitted the pattern of what H. John Rosenbaum and Peter Sederberg call "establishment violence," in which privileged groups use extra-legal force to protect the status quo where the state is unable to do so.[54] The persecution of religious minorities, I argue, has occasionally fallen into this category, and when it has the state has been more likely to tolerate it.

One of the most underappreciated factors stopping the persecution of unpopular religious minorities in America is that expression of popular religious prejudices has often been associated with subversive political

---

[53] Tilly explains how regime types affect the repertoires available to contentious actors. There is considerable room for violent political expression in low-capacity democratic regimes in which the state lacks the ability to enforce order. Throughout much of its history the United States has been a "weak state," and throughout all of its history it has been an unusually fragmented and incoherent one. Under these circumstances, it is to be expected that we would see contentious actors resort to violent repertoires. It is less clear under what circumstances violent action would actually secure desired policy outcomes. Tilly (2003), pp. 44–54.

[54] Rosenbaum, H. Jon, and Peter C. Sederberg (1974). "Vigilantism: An Analysis of Establishment Violence." *Comparative Politics*, 6(4): 541–570; see also Brown, Richard Maxwell (1976). "The History of Vigilantism in America." In H. Jon Rosenbaum and Peter C. Sederberg (eds.), *Vigilante Politics*. Philadelphia: University of Pennsylvania Press, pp. 79–103; and Ingalls, Robert P. (1987). "Lynching and Establishment Violence in Tampa, 1858–1935." *The Journal of Southern History*, 53(4): 613–644.

movements. As I show in Chapter 7, anti-Catholicism in the mid-nineteenth century was organized by secret societies with bad reputations and violently prosecuted in the streets by gangs of disaffected young men. State actors, and the middle classes from which most of them came, found this combination of secrecy and thuggery distasteful and frightening, even when they shared the same prejudices. When anti-Catholic Know-Nothings entered state and federal legislatures, they faced crippling institutional resistance to their programs even when they commanded impressive majorities. Anti-Semitism, despite its huge popularity from the 1910s to the 1940s, was even more politically toxic. In the South and Midwest it was tied to mutant forms of populism that harbored bitter grievances against industrial capitalism, the federal government, and north-eastern elites. While the Protestant upper classes practiced their own social discrimination against Jews, they were appalled by the spectacle of anti-Semitic rabble-rousing, which targeted them as much as it targeted actual Jews. Anti-Semitism had no serious political sponsorship from either party, and the rise of Hitler sealed its fate as a subversive fringe movement that would be watched rather than listened to.

Prejudice against religious minorities was only allowed to take on a discriminatory and violent political form in America when it had the backing of powerful networks, was tied to mainstream political agendas, and was controlled in such a way that state actors did not see it as a threat to secular and democratic political order. State actors weigh the political costs and benefits of repression. In the sections below I outline two recurring, causally important political processes that make state actors more likely to tolerate religious persecution – the delegitimization of religious minorities, and boundary control of religious conflicts.

Delegitimization of religious minorities

The protection a state gives to a religious minority depends on that group's perceived legitimacy as a religion. As Arthur Greil has argued, religion is "a *claim* made by certain groups and – in some cases – contested by others to the right to the privileges associated in a given society with the religious label."[55] In most countries, governments maintain criteria for state recognition of religions, and may require religious groups to register with a government agency. This recognition entitles them to tax and customs privileges, and allows them to build structures where large numbers of people may congregate to worship. In many countries, the right of conscientious objection to military service is tied to religious recognition. Just as importantly, violent attacks motivated by religious identity are treated as a serious threat by the state when the victim is a member of an officially recognized religious group. Groups that fail to obtain official

[55] Greil, Arthur L. (1996). "Sacred Claims: The 'Cult Controversy' as a Struggle over the Right to the Religious Label." In Bromley, David G., and Lewis F. Carter (eds.), *The Issue of Authenticity in the Study of Religions.* Greenwich: JAI Press. p. 46.

recognition have a much harder time. They may not gain permission to build houses of worship, and may be subject to punitive taxation. Their members may be thrown in prison for refusing military service. The state may regard their worship services as political gatherings. Both state and non-state actors may violently prey on them with relative impunity.[56]

Throughout American history there has been no official registration of religious groups, and neither state nor federal governments have maintained legal criteria for religious recognition.[57] While this reflects norms of religious tolerance, it has left decisions about the de facto legitimacy of religious groups in the hands of a wide range of state actors confronted with various situations in which this legitimacy has come into question. Some have argued that this absence of a definitive standard has disadvantaged minorities outside the Christian and Protestant mainstream.[58] It has certainly made state actors

[56] These observations are based on extensive reading of congressional *International Religious Freedom* reports from 1999 to 2008, available at www.state.gov/j/drl/rls/irf/.

[57] An exception is the Internal Revenue Service, which is responsible for determining whether organizations can be exempt from taxation, and must decide whether organizations "operate exclusively for religious or charitable purposes." This occasionally requires it to make judgments about whether an organization's activities should be considered "commercial" rather than "religious" or "charitable." The most famous example of this is a long-running series of disputes between the IRS and the Church of Scientology. In the late 1960s, the IRS denied Scientology tax-exempt status, determining that it operated mainly to enrich its founder, L. Ron Hubbard. After Scientology regained tax-exempt status, there were further questions over whether expensive "auditing" exercises for members could be tax deductible (this was eventually resolved in favor of Scientology). See Eaton, Alison H. (1996). "Can the IRS Overrule the Supreme Court?" *Emory Law Journal*, 45: 987–1034.
 This is different from the kinds of decisions that other countries have made about Scientology, which involved qualitative judgments about whether it could be considered a religion at all. In 1965, the parliament of the Australian state of Victoria issued a lengthy report on Scientology determining that it could not be called a religion, based on what was known of its teachings. According to the report, "Except for the purpose of deceit, scientology has not been practised in Victoria on the basis that it even remotely resembles a religion.... The attitude of Hubbard towards religion is one of bitter cynicism and ridicule, which gives the lie to his directive 'change no man's religion'. In a warped and sneering fashion he snipes at all things sacred in much the same way he attacks the medical profession, though there is generally less venom in his tone when he is dealing with religion. Scientology is opposed to religion as such, irrespective of kind or denomination. The essence of Hubbard's axioms of scientology is that the universe was created not by God, but by a conglomeration of thetans who postulated the universe. Sometimes God is referred to as the Big Thetan. Many of the theories he propounds are almost the negation of Christian thought and morality." On the basis of this report, Scientology was prohibited in Victoria, South Australia, and Western Australia until the 1980s. See Anderson, Kevin (1965). *Report of the Board of Inquiry into Scientology*. Melbourne: Parliament of Victoria. p. 149.

[58] Feldman, Stephen M. (2000). "A Christian America and the Separation of Church and State." In Feldman, Stephen M. (ed.) *Law and Religion: A Critical Anthology*. New York: New York University Press. See also Sehat (2011). This was particularly evident in the nineteenth century; during the twentieth century a series of Supreme Court cases began to establish more explicit and also more relaxed definitions of "religion" that, since the 1960s, have referred to belief in an "ultimate concern" rather than belief in God. See Introvigne, Massimo (1999). "Religion as

susceptible to pressure from civil society over questions of religious legitimacy.[59] I argue that religious groups are much more likely to be persecuted when there is a prevailing, powerful discourse in civil society that represents them as something other than a genuine religion.

Civic opponents of a religious minority will often deny that the group in question is an actual religion entitled to the protection of the state. This accusation can take many forms. One of the most common claims is that a religion is simply fraudulent, a pretext to swindle its converts and enrich its leaders. The claim of fraudulence suggests that the group's leaders are involved in a criminal activity, which demands a response from the state. New religions are particularly vulnerable to allegations of fraud. While all religious beliefs seem implausible to non-believers, major world religions enjoy a credibility that comes with longevity and global influence. People do not doubt the sincerity of their leaders or adherents; their opponents are more likely to accuse them of fundamentalism or fanaticism – forms of excessive and blinding religiosity – rather than not being real religions. The beliefs of new religions always seem less plausible. Being recent creations, their origins are far more open to scrutiny and skepticism. As Mormon historian Patrick Mason has pointed out, "Americans don't think twice about Jesus walking on water or God sending Jews manna from heaven, because those age-old stories have become part of the culture.... the story of Jesus' resurrection is now accepted by the vast majority of Americans, but the story of Joseph Smith digging up gold plates or seeing angels is subject to scrutiny."[60]

A closely associated claim is the accusation that a group is a cult. The term "cult" has technical and non-pejorative meanings in the sociology of religion, describing either a religious group held together by devotion to a living charismatic leader, or a religious group that exists in a particularly high state of tension with surrounding society.[61] In popular use, however, the term "cult" denotes an authoritarian, totalistic group that recruits members aggressively and maintains their loyalty through systematic indoctrination. This popular understanding of "cult" has significant political and legal ramifications; as James Richardson notes, "the term has such negative connotations that for it to be allowed in court proceedings is a major victory for those opposing groups

claim: Social and legal controversies." In Platvoet, Jan G., and Arie L. Molendijk, *The Pragmatics of Defining Religion: Contexts, Concepts and Contests.* Leiden: Brill. pp. 44–45.

[59] Ibid., pp. 46–47.

[60] Quoted in Hagerty, Barbara Bradley (2012). "Mormonism: A Scrutinized, Yet Evolving Faith." National Public Radio, November 28, 2012. Available at: www.npr.org/2012/11/28/166022894/mormonism-a-scrutinized-yet-evolving-faith, last accessed June 26, 2013.

[61] Zablocki, Benjamin, and Thomas Robbins (2001). "Introduction: Finding a Middle Ground in a Polarized Scholarly Arena." In Zablocki, Benjamin, and Thomas Robbins, *Misunderstanding Cults: Searching for Objectivity in a Controversial Field.* Toronto: University of Toronto Press; Stark, Rodney, and William Sims Bainbridge (1985). *The Future of Religion: Secularization, Revival, and Cult Formation.* Berkeley: University of California Press.

being referred to as cults."[62] Since the 1970s many countries, including the United States, have seen civil court cases over allegations that cult members have been brainwashed, as well as criminal cases over attempts to forcibly retrieve family members who have joined cults.[63] "Cult" also denotes something apart from genuine religion, at least as understood in terms of the major world religions.[64] Anthony Hoekema, in a book which remains popular in some evangelical American circles, disparaged Christian Science, Jehovah's Witnesses, Mormonism, and Seventh-Day Adventism as "The Four Major Cults" and warned true Christians to stay away from them.[65] The French government monitors and produces annual reports on groups identified as having "cultic deviances."[66]

Another potentially damaging accusation is the claim that a religious group is actually a political movement masquerading as a religion. Religion is a major force in politics around the world; constitutional separation of ecclesiastical from temporal authority does not prevent religious organizations from openly involving themselves in political life.[67] Even smaller and more separatist religious bodies with little interest in broader political issues will lobby government actors to protect their own political interests. This political activity can make nearly any religious group vulnerable to arguments that they are undermining constitutional divisions between church and state. While these arguments usually have little traction, they can sometimes become salient and powerful. They are particularly useful for opponents of a religion who do not want to be seen as opposing freedom of religion. In 2010, Tennessee Lieutenant Governor Ron Ramsey, in the midst of a primary campaign, warned supporters at a rally about the impending threat of Sharia

---

[62] Richardson, James T. (1993). "Definitions of Cult: From Sociological-Technical to Popular-Negative." *Review of Religious Research*, 34(4): 348–356, 354.

[63] Richardson, James T. (1991). "Cult/Brainwashing Cases and Freedom of Religion." *Journal of Church and State*, 33: 55–74, 55; Robbins, Thomas (2001). "Combating 'Cults' and 'Brainwashing' in the United States and Western Europe: A Comment on Richardson and Introvigne's Report." *Journal for the Scientific Study of Religion*, 40(2): 169–175.

[64] See Brinkerhoff, Merlin B., and Marlene M. Mackie (1986). "The Applicability of Social Distance for Religious Research: An Exploration." *Review of Religious Research*, 28(2): 151–167, 153–154.

[65] Hoekema, Anthony A. (1963). *The Four Major Cults: Christian Science, Jehovah's Witnesses, Mormonism, Seventh-day Adventism*. Grand Rapids: William B. Eerdmans Publishing Company. See also Martin, Walter (1996). *The Kingdom of the Cults*. Minneapolis, MN: Bethany House Publishers.

[66] The agency responsible for this is the Mission interministérielle de vigilance et de lutte contre les dérives sectaires (MIVILUDES), translated as "Interministerial Mission for Monitoring and Combating Cultic Deviances." See Beckford, James A. (2011). "Religion in Prisons and in Partnership with the State." In Barbalet, Jack, Adam Possamai and Bryan S. Turner (eds.) *Religion and the State: A Comparative Sociology*. London: Anthem Press, pp. 46–47.

[67] See Philpott, Daniel (2007). "Explaining the Political Ambivalence of Religion." *American Political Science Review*, 101(3): 505–525; Grzymala-Busse, Anna (2012). "Why Comparative Politics Should Take Religion (More) Seriously." *Annual Review of Political Science*, 15: 421–442.

law in the United States. After assuring them that he "is all about freedom of religion," he stated that:

> But you cross the line when they start trying to bring Sharia Law into the United States. Now you could even argue whether being a Muslim is actually a religion, or is it a nationality, a way of life or cult, whatever you want to call it? We do protect our religions, but at the same time, this is something that we are going to have to face.[68]

In response to a request for comment from a reporter, Ramsey also said that "my concern is that far too much of Islam has come to resemble a violent political philosophy more than peace-loving religion."[69]

As I will explore further in Chapters 3, 4, 5, and 6, Mormons and Jehovah's Witnesses were subject to all three of these delegitimizing accusations, often at the same time. From the moment the Book of Mormon appeared, detractors accused Joseph Smith of being a fraud and peddling lies. As he began to gather followers, newspapers painted a picture of Mormonism as a fabulous scam to enrich Smith, while irate clergy complained he was tricking their former parishioners into handing over their life savings to him. With Smith's followers numbering in the thousands, his neighbors increasingly began to fear Mormon political power and Smith's seemingly limitless influence over the lives of Mormon communities. Anti-Mormon literature of the mid-nineteenth century depicted Mormons as helpless, indoctrinated captives serving the ambitions of Smith and other Mormon leaders; when Smith ordered the destruction of a printing press, his enemies in Illinois took it as a sign that he needed to be eliminated, which occurred with the complicity of the Illinois government. After Smith's death and the Mormon exodus to Utah, revelations that the surviving Mormon leadership was practising polygamy further cemented the popular image of Mormonism as a lawless theocracy that needed to be brought back into the fold of American civilization.

Jehovah's Witnesses were a little-known sect even at the height of their persecution in the 1940s. They were frequently referred to as a cult – in the words of the *Chicago Tribune*, a "freak cult that hates everything!" Their extensive proselytism did not familiarize Americans much with their theology, but rather antagonized the numerous enemies who believed they were harboring other agendas. Rumors circulated that they were a Nazi fifth column and that their literature was printed on German paper. The powerful American Legion accused Witnesses of being un-American because of their refusal to salute the flag. The impunity with which Witnesses were beaten in

---

[68] Quoted in Cass, Michael (2010). "Tennessee politician's remarks on Islam raise uproar." *USA Today*, July 28, 2010. http://usatoday30.usatoday.com/news/nation/2010-07-8-islam-remarks-furor_N.htm, last accessed June 26, 2013.

[69] Quoted in Mackey, Robert (2010). "Tennessee Official Says Islam May Be a 'Cult.'" http://thelede.blogs.nytimes.com/2010/07/27/tennessee-official-says-islam-may-be-a-cult/?_r=0, last accessed June 26, 2013.

the streets of small towns suggested that local lawmen did not regard Witness proselytism as an expression of religion that deserved protection.

The Nation of Islam experienced the most explicit state challenge to its legitimacy as a religion. As I show in Chapter 9, in 1955 the FBI produced a lengthy document charging that the Nation was a "political cult" rather than a genuine religion. Drawing on the religious authority of other American Muslims, the FBI warned that the Nation of Islam was not to be confused with authentic Islam. Among other things, the FBI argued that members of the Nation had no sincere belief in Allah, which to them was "just another name to be memorized." The group, according to the FBI, existed purely to propagate hatred of whites and the United States rather than to serve any spiritual purpose.

Other unpopular religious groups – Catholics, Jews, and Anabaptists – did not suffer from the same level of delegitimization. Certainly, both Catholics and Jews were also rumored to be subversive political forces. One popular nineteenth-century theory held that Catholic immigrants were agents of the Austro-Hungarian Empire, while Jews in the twentieth century were constantly accused of pushing the United States into war for the benefit of Jewish financiers. But these suspicions had their limitations. Nobody could deny that Catholicism and Judaism are religions, whatever else they might be. As large, well-established groups that had been in America since before the revolution, both religions had powerful political allies (especially in the Democratic Party) and could successfully invoke appeals for religious tolerance in their defense. Anabaptists (the Amish and Mennonites), despite the strangeness of their customs and the exemptions they sought from civic life, also benefited from the unquestioned acceptance that they were legitimate religious groups, and that their conscientious objections to military service and some forms of taxation were grounded in a genuine Christian faith.

Boundary control

Federalism is a key element in the way religious conflicts have developed in the United States. Different levels of the American state – federal, state, and local – have different organizational imperatives, and have frequently been in conflict with each other over the boundaries of their respective areas of authority. Maintenance of law and order usually devolves to the most local level. Higher-level agencies may intervene, however, where more local authorities are incapable of enforcing the law, or where they violate state or nationally prescribed individual rights while performing their duties. Local authorities will occasionally invite higher-level intervention, but often they will resist it. These boundary conflicts between state actors often play a role in the outcome of conflicts between religious minorities and their antagonists. Actors at different geographic levels of the state may take different sides in these conflicts, perceiving different kinds of threats. The outcome of the conflict may depend on which side can mobilize its allies.

E.E. Schattschneider identified control of the scope of conflicts as one of the core activities of politics. In any fight, the outcome is likely to be determined by the onlookers, who may decide to join the fight and alter the balance of power. It will often be in the interests of the weaker side to expand the scope of the struggle and persuade others they should join. As Schattschneider shows, an entire vocabulary exists to expand the scope of conflict by framing it in universal terms. The language of basic rights implies universal significance: if my rights are endangered, then everybody's rights are potentially under threat, so my struggle is also yours. On the other hand, the stronger side may deliberately try to restrict the scope of conflict in order to prevent others from joining and tipping the balance. They employ the opposite vocabulary of privacy, local autonomy, and personal responsibility: this is not the business of anyone else.[70]

This dynamic of scope control is highly relevant to the study of religious persecution. Persecution often begins in local intergroup conflict in which a powerful majority uses its numbers to oppress, expel, or eliminate a minority. While the victimized minority will appeal to the outside for help – either from higher authorities, or from outside allies – the persecuting majority will try to prevent "outside interference." Persecution may also result from a near-opposite situation, when a local minority that is part of a national majority believes it is being oppressed by the local majority. The locals may try to nationalize the conflict, complaining that they are becoming second-class citizens in their own country and calling for the nation to forcefully reassert itself over the tyrant minority. The locally dominant majority may fight back by claiming that it, like any other group, has the right to exercise political power where it is the majority. Whether persecution succeeds often depends on who is able to expand or restrict the conflict.

This is particularly important in large, federal polities such as the United States. Edward Gibson and Robert Mickey have recently shown in separate studies how regional governments in Mexico, Argentina, and the American south were able to maintain authoritarian enclaves in democratic countries. They denied political rights to their local opponents, and prevented national authorities from intruding in their jurisdictions and enforcing democratic rule. A key to this local "boundary control" (Edward Gibson's term) was that autocratic state rulers maintained party ties with national legislators that allowed them to mobilize the legislature against federal intervention, often using the justification of "states' rights" or local autonomy. Maintaining local authoritarian rule became much more difficult if the national party turned against the local party, as the Democrats did in the United States in the early 1960s.[71]

---

[70] Schattschneider, E.E. (1960). *The Semisovereign People: A Realist's View of Democracy in America*. New York: Holt, Rinehart and Winston, p. 7.

[71] Gibson, Edward L. (2012). *Boundary Control: Subnational Authoritarianism in Federal Democracies*. New York: Cambridge University Press; Mickey, Robert W. (2014). *Paths Out of Dixie: The Democratization of Authoritarian Enclaves in America's Deep South, 1944–1972*.

In the nineteenth century, the various opponents of Mormons expanded the scope of their conflict from local disputes over land, elections, and business deals into a national moral crusade led by the Republican Party. Mormons had antagonists everywhere they became the majority. Their vigorous proselytism, religious and commercial insularity, and bloc voting all created the fear that they were taking over every district in which they settled. Chapter 3 shows how "gentiles" (non-Mormons) mobilized state governments to expel Mormons on the grounds that they posed a threat to state democracy. After being forced from Missouri by an "extermination order" signed by the governor, and from Illinois by state militias that were complicit in the murder of Joseph Smith, the Mormons were forced to travel to Utah, where they could effectively act as a territorial government of their own.

After the Civil War, conflict between Mormons and non-Mormons in Utah became a national conflict. The Republican Party had promised in its foundational platform of 1856 to stamp out the "twin relics of barbarism, polygamy and slavery." Successive Republican administrations, however, had been able to do little about the polygamous Mormon settlement in Utah that had dominated the territory since it was founded in 1845. The U.S. government lacked both the legal authority to break Mormon hegemony in Utah and the physical capacity to project state authority into the remote territory. Throughout the 1870s and 1880s, more radical opponents of Mormonism convinced congressional Republicans that polygamy was such an urgent problem that the government should effectively abolish political rights for Mormons. It was not enough to argue that polygamy was a moral outrage: anti-Mormons in Utah argued it was the pillar of a system of despotic social control that had made the territory into a tyranny. The government had to remove the polygamous Mormon leadership from political power by taking away the rights of polygamists to vote, hold office, or serve on juries. Republicans persuaded many (though not all) congressional Democrats to join the fight, creating an appearance of moral unanimity that was necessary for the extraordinarily rare act of passing legislation to strip a religious group of its political rights.

In the lead-up to the Second World War, the opponents of Jehovah's Witnesses – most importantly, the American Legion – sought to do the opposite. They restricted the scope of their conflict with the Witnesses to the local level, where prominent Legionnaires could dominate small-town law enforcement, using the resources of police and sheriffs' departments to drive Jehovah's Witnesses from their towns. Jehovah's Witnesses were never a majority anywhere, and unlike Mormons they had no interest in getting or exercising political power (they did not even vote). The threat they posed in small towns was not material but symbolic: by refusing to salute the American flag, Witnesses failed to uphold the rituals of American nationalism that also reinforced the high esteem in which war veterans were held. The American Legion, along with other civic associations, found this intolerable.

The campaign against Witnesses was national, but the state was only involved at the most local levels. Witnesses from every state reported violent harassment, often with the acquiescence of local law enforcement, as well as discriminatory measures such as the expulsion of their children from public schools. Witnesses and their allies tried to expand the scope of the conflict. The ACLU and its legal team sought to frame the wave of persecution as a civil liberties issue and called on the federal government to intervene. In the 1930s and 1940s, Witnesses and the ACLU took nearly forty local cases to the Supreme Court in an effort to obtain rulings that would override the myriad city statutes that enabled harassment. The ACLU also sent thousands of pages of affidavits documenting violence against Witnesses around the country to the fledgling Civil Liberties Division of the Department of Justice, hoping that this would prompt federal intervention (it never did). As I will argue, the American Legion carefully controlled the use of local violence precisely in order to avoid the kind of national intervention that the Witnesses and the ACLU wanted.

In contrast, boundary control proved to be a chronic problem for anti-Catholic politics in the United States. Anti-Catholic parties were able to seize control of entire states, but then their planned naturalization reforms were frustrated by federal jurisdiction over immigration rules. National parties did not want to cooperate with nativist agendas, which interfered with both their state-building programs and their electoral prospects. Boundary control problems also thwarted political anti-Semitism, as Jewish advocacy organizations were able to universalize their cause and link it to the broader struggle of democracy against fascism. By the 1940s, political anti-Semitism at any level was closely associated with disloyalty to the United States.

CONCLUSION

This chapter has established the basic theoretical structure of my argument. In secular democracies, religious persecution tends to arise from within civil society. The intensity, duration, and ultimate outcome of this persecution depends on the response of state actors. State actors are predominantly concerned with defending political order and they often refuse to tolerate the violent expression of prejudice, which threatens both social harmony and their own monopoly on the use of force. They will only allow religious persecution, or participate in it, when they believe that a particular religious minority poses a threat to political order. This is more likely to occur where state actors do not believe that a certain group is a "legitimate" religion. However, state actors will intervene on the side of religious minorities when they believe the persecution itself is a threat to political order, which is likely when the agents of persecution are linked to subversive political movements.

This argument is consonant with that of Anthony Gill, mentioned above, who posits that political leaders weigh the costs and benefits of religious freedom to themselves. Under some circumstances they will benefit from making laws that favor a dominant religion, while in others they will benefit more from giving all religions equal rights. In my analysis, the central decision for state actors is about which group – a religious minority, or its antagonists – poses the greater threat to them.

3

Joseph Smith and the rise of Mormonism

The political threat of religious charisma

INTRODUCTION

The Church of Jesus Christ of Latter-day Saints, which Leo Tolstoy called "the American religion,"[1] is also the most violently persecuted religion in American history. Between the appearance of Joseph Smith's *Book of Mormon* in 1830 and Smith's murder in 1844, the Mormons were chased out of New York, Ohio, and Missouri by neighbors enraged at their aggressive proselytism and the extraordinary claims of Joseph Smith. The Mormons' flight from Missouri in 1838 was prompted by a series of bloody skirmishes with well-organized opponents; Governor Lilburn Boggs responded with a quasi-genocidal executive order declaring that the Mormons had "made war upon the people of this state" and "must be exterminated or driven from the state if necessary for the public peace."[2]

A few years after the Mormons had fled to Illinois and established a thriving city, an anti-Mormon mob lynched Smith with the assistance of a local militia. Facing the prospect of more violence and coercion, most of the remaining Mormons undertook a long, hazardous journey to Utah under the leadership of Brigham Young in 1847, believing they would be beyond the reach of their enemies in the United States. The federal government initially encouraged the move, seeing the Mormon exodus as an opportunity to establish an American presence in the western territories newly captured from Mexico. In return for Mormon allegiance to the United States, the Fillmore Administration appointed Brigham Young as governor of Utah Territory. Relations deteriorated as the Mormon leadership became increasingly assertive over the territory, making life intolerable for non-Mormon federal officials and leading to the Buchanan Administration's brief invasion of Utah in 1857.

---

[1] Bloom, Harold (1992). *The American Religion*. New York: Simon and Schuster, p. 97.
[2] The text of the "Exterminating Order" is available from http://contentdm.lib.byu.edu/cdm/compoundobject/collection/NCMP1820-846/id/2834, last accessed January 30, 2013.

The abortive invasion was followed by a series of increasingly aggressive congressional actions designed to force the Mormons to conform to American anti-bigamy laws. These culminated in the Edmunds Act of 1882 and the Edmunds-Tucker Act of 1887, which forbade Mormons from voting, holding elected office, or serving on juries, and authorized the federal government to confiscate Church property, including temples. These last measures induced the Church leadership to abandon polygamy in 1890, though it continued in secret for a while; Congress held up the seating of Senator Reed Smoot for seven years over the issue of whether the Mormon leadership was still allowing plural marriages to take place at the turn of the century.[3]

The story of how a nation of people who prided themselves on their religious liberty came to persecute the Mormons so extensively is controversial and complicated. While revulsion over polygamy has traditionally been understood as the main reason, polygamy alone cannot explain everything. The most violent anti-Mormon actions occurred before the practice was even known by non-Mormons, and other religions that violated nineteenth-century sexual norms were usually left alone.[4] Certainly, polygamy later served as a focal point for anti-Mormon opposition, but it generated as much titillation and amusement as outrage.[5] There was much more at stake in the Mormon conflicts than the morality of plural marriage.

Historical scholarship has emphasized the real and perceived differences between Mormons and other Americans, and how these differences contributed to conflict. One important strand of thinking on anti-Mormonism suggests nineteenth-century Mormons had a quasi-ethnic status as a "peculiar people," even though the differences that separated them from other Americans were greatly exaggerated and reified in public discourse.[6] Many scholars argue that this construction of Mormon "peculiarity" facilitated anti-Mormonism by removing conflict from the realm of religious disagreement – instead of persecuting religious difference, anti-Mormons saw themselves as countering a subversive and foreign "other." J. Spencer Fluhman argues that when accusations of "heresy" finally came to dominate anti-Mormon discourse in

[3] Flake, Kathleen (2004). *The Politics of American Religious Identity*. Chapel Hill: University of North Carolina Press.

[4] Stein, Stephen J. (1992). *The Shaker Experience in America*. New Haven: Yale University Press.

[5] Young, Kimball (1954). *Isn't One Wife Enough?* New York: Holt; and Arrington, Leonard J. (1958). *Great Basin Kingdom: An Economic History of the Latter Day Saints*. Cambridge: Harvard University Press, pp. 238–239.

[6] O'Dea, Thomas F. (1957). *The Mormons*. Chicago: University of Chicago Press; Moore, R. Laurence (1986). *Religious Outsiders and the Making of Americans*. Oxford: Oxford University Press; Mauss, Armand (1994). *The Angel and the Beehive: The Mormon Struggle with Assimilation*. Champaign: University of Illinois Press; Givens, Terryl L. (1997). *The Viper on the Hearth: Mormons, Myths, and the Construction of Heresy*. New York: Oxford University Press; Marr, Timothy (2006). *The Cultural Roots of American Islamicism*. New York: Cambridge University Press. ch. 5; Fluhman, J. Spencer (2012). *"A Peculiar People": Anti-Mormonism and the Making of Religion in Nineteenth-Century America*. Chapel Hill: University of North Carolina Press.

the late nineteenth century, this represented a hard-won achievement for the Mormons, because merely being religiously unorthodox was not grounds for persecution in the United States.

There is disagreement, however, over how the social construction of intolerable difference occurred. In particular, the question of whether Mormons or their antagonists were responsible for creating the myth of Mormon "peculiarity" has led different scholars to very different stories about why Americans persecuted Mormons. In *Religious Outsiders and the Making of Americans*, R. Laurence Moore argues that Mormons themselves were responsible for most of the social construction of Mormon difference. Dismissing the idea that there was any "objective" difference that should have caused conflict between Mormons and other Americans, Moore posits "Mormons were different because they said they were different and their claims, frequently advanced in the most obnoxious way possible, prompted others to agree and treat them as such."[7] Joseph Smith and Brigham Young "advertised deviance." Their promotion of plural marriage and communal property created a distinctive "outsider" status – some form of which, Moore argues, all Americans crave. Mormons deserve Tolstoy's "American religion" label because they embody the American search for an identity grounded in outsiderism.

In Moore's account this aggressive assertion of difference by Mormons and their leaders facilitated both persecution and growth, often in concert with each other. He notes that "the trait most commonly cited to denounce the Mormons, the one that clearly rankled anti-Mormons the most, was arrogance. Smith called God his 'right-hand man' and taught his followers all too well to regard themselves as superior to others."[8] In this respect Mormons resembled Christians and Jews in the early Roman Empire, who attracted persecution in a pluralistic religious environment because they insisted their monotheistic religions were superior to, rather than compatible with, the existing marketplace of cults.[9] Smith was well aware of the parallels, and of the fact that persecution of the early Christians had helped them to prosper rather than inhibiting their growth.[10]

Terryl Givens, in *The Viper on the Hearth*, argues the opposite – that it was the enemies of Mormonism who constructed a quasi-ethnic identity for Mormons. Rather than emphasizing their deviance, Givens claims Mormon leaders tried to downplay it: "Mormons engaged in a quite conscientious 'campaign of superior virtue,' by which they intended to persuade their compatriots that they were *not* social deviants, but rather more American than apple pie."[11] The widespread perception of Mormon deviance was

---

[7] Moore (1986), p. 31.
[8] Ibid., p. 33.
[9] See Stark, Rodney (1997). *The Rise of Christianity*. San Francisco: HarperSanFrancisco.
[10] Moore (1986), p. 35.
[11] Givens (1997), p. 17.

created by a cottage industry of hack writers who told lurid tales of harems and secret rituals.[12] The public devoured shocking stories about Mormon polygamy because these stories both outraged and entertained; they served as socially acceptable pornography in an era of Victorian morality.

Authors constructed Mormon deviance in terms of foreignness, not only through oriental stereotypes about polygamous seraglios,[13] but also by giving Mormon characters dark complexions and East European accents.[14] Timothy Marr also emphasizes this "orientalization" of Mormons, noting that even the territory of Utah came to be seen as "Turkey in our midst."[15] For Givens, it was this construction of Mormons as an ethnicized, separate group that enabled their persecution in a country where religious liberty was a hard-won norm. Even though anti-Mormons were most fundamentally disturbed by Mormon heresy, they could only mobilize public support behind the anti-Mormon cause by moving the issue away from a religious dispute and into the more familiar territory of ethnic conflict.

Though they disagree on key points, both of these accounts share an emphasis on the radical difference of the Mormons from other Americans, whether real or perceived. For Moore, this difference came from social deviance, while for Givens it took on a quasi-ethnic form. While this may explain conflict and hostility between Mormons and their neighbors, we need to go further to explain why the state, at all levels, consistently sided with anti-Mormons against Mormons when conflicts arose. The Mormons' communal organization, insularity, and tendency to concentrate in large numbers made them seem like a threatening presence to their non-Mormon neighbors, and certainly contributed to conflicts, as I will show. However, social difference and deviance was not the main factor that allowed Mormons' opponents to mobilize the state against them. Indeed, too much emphasis on the distinctiveness of Mormons might have encouraged the idea that they were a distinctive people, entitled as such to recognition and protection of their unique customs as other intentional communities and foreign religions enjoyed.[16] The fact that Mormons were perceived as

---

[12] The role of fiction writers in creating a picture of Mormon decadence that came to be widely regarded as true has an interesting parallel with the career of *The Protocols of the Elders of Zion*, which also began as a novel. See Cohn, Norman (1967). *Warrant for Genocide.* London: Eyre and Spottiswoode.

[13] In reality Mormon polygamy usually involved men marrying destitute widows or the aging unmarried sisters of their current wives. See Young (1954).

[14] See especially chapter 7 of Givens (1997). Mormons in reality were almost entirely descended from New England puritans and English and Scandinavian immigrants.

[15] Marr (2006), ch. 5.

[16] Marr notes about Islamic stereotypes of the Mormons that "Transposing islamicist observations to define the moral boundaries of the community of the United States enabled a comparativist critique of the direction of domestic polity, but it also at times had the ironic effect of promoting the social prominence and worldly significance of the fledgling Mormon church." Marr (2006), p. 186.

different was less important than the ways in which they were seen as a political threat.

There were two rhetorical devices that opponents of Mormonism used, sometimes successfully, to mobilize the state against the Mormons. The first was to claim Mormonism was not an actual religion. This charge was particularly prominent during the lifetime of Joseph Smith, and it generally revolved around the allegation that Smith was a fraud. This claim, as I will show by examining media accounts of the time, was intimately linked to Smith's status as a charismatic prophet. Religious charisma is a polarizing phenomenon. It generates devoted followers among those who perceive the divine gifts of the charismatic leader, and especially those who believe that they benefit from those gifts. However, others see religious charisma as fraudulent if they do not see any divine gift or fail to benefit from it themselves. If Smith was not the prophet he claimed to be, this naturally led to suspicions that his real aim was either personal enrichment or political power.

The second claim was that the Mormon form of authority – a hierarchy led by a theocratic prophet – threatened the democratic culture that allowed religious freedom to exist in the United States. This argument made its way to the highest levels of the government. Anti-Mormons employed a muscular liberal rhetoric, strongly resonant with the Republican Party, equating Mormonism with slavery, a system antithetical to American liberties that had to be broken by force if necessary.[17] Mormon women, in particular, were portrayed in muscular liberal rhetoric as hapless victims of the Mormon hierarchy and sometimes of their own husbands, prisoners who needed to be freed. Although most Mormons were converts who had freely chosen the theocratic life, popular understanding of Mormons was shaped by "captivity narratives" in which women were lured into polygamous harems by spellbinding rogues. In Congress, this kind of rhetoric prevailed over objections that Mormon difference should be respected legally (if not morally), and that the persecution of a religious minority set a dangerous precedent.

Neither of these rhetorical devices – Joseph Smith as charismatic fraud or the Mormon hierarchy as theocratic slave-drivers – depended on the idea of radical Mormon difference. Indeed, justifying the political repression of Mormons required anti-Mormons to show there was nothing distinctive about Mormons that justified giving their leaders any special rights or leeway. The Mormon people were to be regarded as "deluded fanatics" (prior to Smith's death) or helpless captives (during the Utah period). To delegitimize the Mormon religion, Smith's detractors denigrated him as an illiterate farmhand whose only special talent was persuading the credulous to hand over their money, not as the leader of a distinctive community of faith. While later

---

[17] Philip Hamburger shows a similar phenomenon in the nineteenth-century anti-Catholic discourse, a fundamentally repressive position framed as a defense of American liberties. Hamburger, Philip (2001). "Illiberal Liberalism: Liberal Theology, Anti-Catholicism, & Church Property." *Journal of Contemporary Legal Issues*, 12: 693–726.

nineteenth-century anti-Mormons grudgingly accepted that Mormonism was an actual religion – albeit a completely misguided one – they nonetheless insisted that Mormons were Americans who could not assume their full political rights until they abandoned the thoroughly un-American system of charismatic theocracy. Polygamy also played a role in whipping up popular outrage against the Mormons, but it was most likely to inspire political action when it was linked to the hated system of charismatic authoritarianism.

The rest of this chapter examines the Mormon experience during the life of the Mormons' founding prophet Joseph Smith, which ended violently in 1844. It shows how Smith's charismatic authority, which was such an important factor in the growth of his church, also created the basis for claims that he was a fraud and a would-be dictator. I show why Mormon social organization caused conflict with the Mormons' near neighbors, and why state authorities sided with anti-Mormon forces in the violent disputes that subsequently erupted. Chapter 4 focuses on the period after the Mormons moved to Utah, and how the federal government responded to Mormon control over a large piece of American territory. In particular, I examine how the determinedly anti-Mormon Republican Party persuaded a majority of Democrats to undertake legislation that damaged not only the religious freedom of Mormons, but also the electoral prospects of their own party.

CHARISMA AND FRAUD

In 1830 Joseph Smith published the *Book of Mormon*, a new body of Christian scripture he claimed he had translated from golden plates given to him by the angel Moroni. Reviewers of the book almost unanimously pronounced it fraudulent; not only did they disbelieve it, they also saw it as a premeditated hoax.[18] One widely reprinted review from the *Rochester Republican* in 1830 concisely summarized all the ways that the book would be described over the coming years: it was a "vile imposition," "an evidence of fraud, blasphemy and credulity, shocking to the Christian and the moralist." Little was known about Smith in those days, but the article describes him as "a fellow who, by some hocus pocus, acquired such an influence over a wealthy farmer of Wayne County, that the latter mortgaged his farm for $3000, which he paid for printing and binding 5000 copies of the blasphemous work."[19] It was not enough for early detractors to call Smith a blasphemer; blasphemy was no longer grounds for persecution or even serious social sanctioning in the United States (another review noted, somewhat regretfully, that the book "smacks pretty strongly of what we used to call blasphemy.") Respectable Americans could no longer sanction conflict over mere religious differences,

---

[18] Cannon, Donald Q. (2007). "In the Press: Early Newspaper Reports on the Initial Publication of the Book of Mormon." *Journal of Book of Mormon Studies*, 16(2): 4–15.

[19] Unsigned, reprinted in the *Rhode Island American*, April 16, 1830.

but the *Book of Mormon* was different – it was an act of fraud, putting Smith outside the realm of religious tolerance.

Despite this hostile reception, Smith rapidly amassed followers. The qualities that repelled so many reviewers of the *Book of Mormon* may also have been what drew so many believers to Smith and to Mormonism. Perceptions of charisma and perceptions of fraud are different sides of the same coin. Max Weber defined charisma as:

> a certain quality of an individual personality by virtue of which he is set apart from ordinary men and treated as endowed with supernatural, superhuman, or at least specifically exceptional powers or qualities. These are as such not accessible to the ordinary person, but are regarded as of divine origin or as exemplary, and on the basis of them the individual concerned is treated as a leader.[20]

These are necessary qualities for anyone claiming to be a religious prophet, and Smith certainly seems to have had them. Weber even mentions Smith as an example of the charismatic type of leader, though with the caveat that he "cannot be classified this way with absolute certainty since there is a possibility that he was a very sophisticated type of deliberate swindler."[21]

Weber's hedged judgment of Smith is unusual; most people evaluate charismatic leaders as *either* genuine or fraudulent. There is no indifferent middle ground, especially if they are explicitly claiming powers of divine communication. Roy Wallis, in his analysis of Children of God leader David Berg, gives an important insight into why this is the case. Charisma, Wallis argues, is a "transactional" phenomenon created by interactions between the charismatic leader and his followers. The personal qualities of a leader, which can be observed neutrally, are not enough to construct genuine charisma. Followers must believe that they are receiving the benefits of that charisma, that the charismatic gift has touched them in a way that has enhanced their own standing. In Wallis's words, charisma "emerges out of a particular structure of social relationships in which an exchange takes place of mutual attribution of status and worth."[22]

Taking all this into account, we can see why it was relatively rare for any non-Mormon to take a position of detached admiration for, or even neutrality toward, Joseph Smith. While in the crowded American religious marketplace one could express polite respect for many religions (especially other Christian denominations) that differed from one's own, Smith made a set of claims that one either bought wholesale or had to denounce. He claimed to be a nineteenth-century prophet who had been given revelations from God calling for a radical revision of Christianity. Accepting Smith's theological claims required accepting Smith and his story, and becoming a Mormon who

---

[20] Weber, Max (1947). *The Theory of Social and Economic Organization*. Translated by A.M. Henderson and Talcott Parsons. Glencoe: The Free Press, p. 358.
[21] Ibid.
[22] Wallis, Roy (1982). "The social construction of charisma." *Social Compass*, 29(1): 25–39.

actively followed him. If one did not, then the alternative explanation was that he was lying on a massive scale.[23]

Contemporary scholars have found ways to overcome this charisma/fraud dichotomy. Harold Bloom, a fervent though non-believing admirer of Smith, stresses his personal magnetism: "no one can study the portraits of Joseph Smith or read descriptions of him by his contemporaries and avoid the sense of mysterious charm. Whatever account of charisma is accepted, the Mormon prophet possessed that quality to a degree unsurpassed in American history."[24] Even such an admiring account as this, however, is not consonant with how a Mormon believer perceives Smith's charisma. Richard Bushman, Smith's most recent and authoritative Mormon biographer, downplays personal magnetism on Smith's part, arguing that his charismatic hold over his followers was purely due to his perceived divine gifts: "Joseph's charismatic authority can easily be misconstrued. He was not the luminous figure he is sometimes made out to be. Attention focused on his gift, not his personality."[25]

In the early nineteenth century relatively few non-believers could take such a detached stance toward Smith, especially if they were in close proximity to him. Members of rival churches in particular were obliged to condemn his pretentions to being a prophet. One article, signed by "A PRESBYTERIAN" who lived close by a Mormon settlement in Ohio, wrote disgustedly of how Smith "pretends to go to the Lord occasionally for advice."[26] Alexander Campbell, leader of the Disciples of Christ, wrote a lengthy review of the *Book of Mormon*, pointing out all the instances in which it disagreed with biblical history and geography, and concluded that Smith was not only a fraud, but also an atheist.[27]

One conceptual problem Smith's detractors faced was explaining how he had actually written the *Book of Mormon*. If Smith was, as they widely agreed, an ignorant charlatan, then how had he crafted this lengthy book, which showed great familiarity with what was then known of the history and geography of the ancient Near East and North America? The question persists in some form to this day; Richard Bushman takes it to be one of the most compelling pieces of

[23] Nobody appears to have made the "lunatic, liar or lord" argument about Smith, allowing for the third possibility that he may have been deluded. None of the hundreds of newspaper articles about Joseph Smith from the 1830s and 1840s (that I have seen) suggests Smith was insane.

[24] Bloom (1992), p. 98. Bloom also sees no need to accept the dichotomy that Smith either genuinely translated the *Book of Mormon* golden plates or made the entire manuscript up: "The genesis of the Book of Mormon is not my concern (though I assume that magical trance-states were involved, so that we can dismiss the literalism both of golden plates and of conscious charlatanry)" (p. 86).

[25] Bushman, Richard L. (2005) *Rough Stone Rolling: A Cultural Biography of Joseph Smith*. New York: Knopf, pp. 111–112.

[26] "The Mormon Delusion," originally in the *New Hampshire Gazette*, reproduced in the *Vermont Chronicle*, June 24, 1831.

[27] "Delusions." Originally in the *Millennial Harbinger* (Bethany) February 7, 1831, reprinted in the *Haverhill Gazette* (Haverhill) September 8, 1832.

evidence that he really did translate the book. There is no historical evidence that Smith, aged twenty-four at the time, had ever read anything beyond "the Bible and perhaps the newspaper," yet he produced a manuscript full of "sermons, Christian doctrine, biblical language, multiple characters, stories of adventure, social criticism, theories of Indian origins, ideas about Meso-American civilization, and many other matters."[28]

For Smith's opponents, however, the answer to the puzzle came in the form of the "Spaulding hypothesis." Philastus Hurlbut, excommunicated from the Mormon Church in 1832, traveled to Ohio and New York collecting disparaging affidavits from people familiar with Smith in order to discredit him. His influential efforts (commissioned by an anti-Mormon committee in Ohio) birthed the claim that the *Book of Mormon* was in fact a reworked version of the manuscript for an historical novel written twenty years earlier by Solomon Spaulding. The manuscript had allegedly fallen into Smith's hands via Sidney Rigdon, his highly educated follower.[29] Despite Mormon attempts to refute them,[30] anti-Mormons took Hurlbut's claims as the truthful explanation of "the unaccountable fact that an ignoramus like him, who could neither read nor write, should have produced so connected a work as the pretended Mormon bible."[31] Thus Smith's enemies added literary theft to the list of charges against him.

For those who saw Smith as an obvious fraud, the willingness of hundreds, and eventually thousands of citizens to join his Church and submit to his prophetic authority provoked a range of reactions from bemusement to horror. Far from seeing Mormonism as a unique phenomenon and Mormons as a distinctive religion, many writers linked the propensity to follow Joseph Smith with what they saw as other religious excesses of the Second Great Awakening. They frequently mentioned Mormons alongside other vigorous sects of the period. Campbell's review, for example, noted that many historical eras had produced large numbers of false Messiahs who had gathered followers, and suggested that the present age was one such period. "The Mormonites" were "the most recent and most impudent delusion" in a religious scene that had included the Shakers and the Campbellites as well as numerous other "Barkers, Jumpers and Mutterers" that barely warranted a mention.[32] The *Boston Courier*, in an article examining both the Mormons and Campbellites, declared "there is no end to trickery and imposture in our land. 'Fools are the game that knaves pursue,' and until the people in some sections of the country become more enlightened, there will be plenty of game."[33] The

---

[28] Bushman (2005), p. 72.

[29] Howe, E.D. (1834). *Mormonism Unvailed*. Painesville: Telegraph Press.

[30] Winchester, Benjamin (1834). *The Origin of the Spaulding Story, Concerning the Manuscript Found*. Philadelphia: Brown, Bicking, and Guilbert, Printers.

[31] In the *Philadelphia Mirror*, reprinted in the *Daily Commercial Bulletin and Missouri Literary Register*, September 9, 1836.

[32] Alexander Campbell, "Delusions." Originally published in the *Millenial Harbinger* (Bethany, VA) February 7, 1831; reprinted in the *Haverhill Gazette* (Haverhill, MA) September 8, 1831.

[33] "Delusion." *Boston Courier*, March 17, 1831.

Vermont Gazette cried "this is emphatically the age of excitement, fanaticism and propagandism."[34]

Many Americans who saw themselves as enlightened, including members of long-established churches, were disturbed by what they saw as an undercurrent of irrationality in the novel religious expressions of the revival movements that were attracting poorer and less educated citizens. Mormonism in the early 1830s shared with these other Christian movements some of the practices that would later come to characterize Pentecostalism, including speaking in tongues and faith healing.[35] An 1833 article in Utica's *Evangelical Magazine and Gospel Advocate*, the largest-circulation Unitarian publication in the United States, said that:

> The world has truly got to a strange pass, when people in numbers and companies can be juggled out of reason and common sense, so far as to give themselves up as the disciples and followers of the miserable scapegoat, Jo. Smith, jr., a juggling knave and a lazy swindler, who, having escaped from prison and the hand of legal justice, has set up for himself in religion, by publishing what he calls his golden Bible, his own wicked invention, filled with a tissue of the most glaring absurdities and nonsensical trash.

However, the article emphasized that Smith was not as dangerous as other revivalists, such as Jedediah Burchard, who had brought spirit-infused preaching to large, mainstream congregations:

> But Jo. Smith jr. is not the only impostor and religious juggler of the present age. It is our honest, serious and deep conviction of mind, that *Jedediah Burchard* and his coadjutors in modern fanaticism, are practicing as great an imposition, as vile an imposture, a worse kind of blasphemy, and exerting a far more extensively pernicious influence in society, than that of the Mormon prophet and his followers. For Burchard and his coadjutors are more enlightened, move in a different circle, and impose on more people than the Mormonites have it in their power to impose upon.[36]

Dozens of similar articles appeared in the magazine over the next ten years.[37]

Still other writers lamented that Mormon "credulity" and "fanaticism" should be unfitting in an enlightened republic such as the United States, but sadly were all too commonplace in the current age. A widely reprinted account of the early Mormon Church from the *Ohio Atlas* in 1833 noted that Mormonism had "spread like a wildfire wherever it obtained a foothold," but

---

[34] "Mormon Religion." *Vermont Gazette*, September 13, 1831.

[35] Smith actually curtailed these practices by the end of 1830s. According to Bushman (2005), this was a part of Smith's attempts to "focus" charisma rather than letting it "run wild." Smith wanted to concentrate on developing doctrine through divine revelation, rather than on manifestations of the spirit (pp. 111–122).

[36] *Evangelical Magazine and Gospel Advocate* (Utica) April 13, 1833.

[37] See Dale Broadhurst's archive at http://www.sidneyrigdon.com/dbroadhu/artindex.htm, last accessed March 24, 2010.

asserted that the Mormon scriptures were so ridiculous that the Church was doomed to fail within a few years. While the *Book of Mormon* was thankfully "free from vulgar obscenities," it was such "an absurd collection of dull, stupid, and foolishly improbable stories" that the next generation will "remember ... only to smile at the credulity of the present."[38] The *U.S. Telegraph* editorialized in 1835 that "Our readers may be surprised to learn that any thing so absured should gain credence in this country; but although our Congress did once declare that we were the most enlightened nation in the world, yet the spirit of Mormonism, and the progress of Jacksonism, are most convincing progress the contrary."[39]

All of this shows that the national discourse around Mormonism during Smith's lifetime was shaped largely by hostile reactions to his claims to charismatic prophecy. He was not seen as totally unique – instead he was a pretentious con artist, an "idle, worthless fellow"[40] accumulating followers who otherwise probably would have gone to some other credulous sect. The fraud and credulity trope had taken hold in the initial reviews of the *Book of Mormon*, even before Hurlbut's reports revealed Smith's previous career as a treasure hunter. While rumors about Smith's treasure-hunting past certainly enhanced the general perception of Smith as a charlatan, in writings denouncing Smith this image remained firmly anchored around the apparent absurdity of his claims. Political scientists have noted a prevalent "prophetic style" in the United States among political and social leaders from William Jennings Bryan to Martin Luther King.[41] However, many Americans were not willing to tolerate the claims of someone who actually claimed to be a religious prophet.

LOCAL CONFLICTS

Mormons were certainly considered a distinctive people by their neighbors, with whom they often had serious material conflicts. Mormon communalism may have been consonant with typical American frontier values such as self-reliance and cooperation, but it also had the effect of economically insulating them from nearby non-Mormon communities, reducing opportunities for interreligious exchanges and creating real separateness. Local opponents of the Mormons often linked their communal economic system to allegations of fraud. They warned that previously solid citizens had been persuaded to hand over their possessions to Smith. The "Mormon delusion" letter by an

---

[38] "The Mormons," from *The Ohio Atlas*, reprinted in the *U.S. Telegraph* (Washington, DC) April 12, 1833.
[39] "Mormonism," from the *U.S. Telegraph* (Washington, DC) March 30, 1835.
[40] Ibid.
[41] Shulman, George M. (2009). *American Prophecy: Race and Redemption in American Political Culture*. Minneapolis: University of Minnesota Press; Morone, James A. (2003). *Hellfire Nation: The Politics of Sin in American History*. New Haven: Yale University Press; Roelofs, Mark (1992). The Prophetic President: Charisma in the American Political Tradition. *Polity*, 25(1): 1–20.

unnamed Presbyterian living in Mormon country in Ohio described a Mormon-dominated town near the author's home, which "is called the 'big family,' where no one says that aught of the things he possesses is his own; they have all things in common." The author describes Joseph Smith as "the head man in the big family," and claims that "There are many, who were once respectable and intelligent, who are now following these wretched impostors – these pretended prophets."[42]

An 1832 article by Joshua V. Hines, editor of the *Haverhill Gazette*, described how Mormons had been active in the area and had converted around fifteen townsfolk. The converts included two "defenceless females," who "had acquired by their hard industry $2300 ... which they have given up to go into the general stock." The other converts

> possess between $3000 and $4000, which they are going to put with the general fund, and which they can never draw out again, should they get sick of Mormonism and wish to return home to their friends.... Thus are our friends swindled out of their property and drawn from their comfortable homes, to endure the perils of a journey of about two thousand miles, by these *ignorant fanatics*; and when arrived at their earthly paradise, to become the miserable dupes of those temporal and spiritual lords.[43]

Kirtland, Ohio, where Smith settled in 1830, was the first large Mormon community. The Mormon population of the township grew from about 10 percent in 1832 to nearly 50 percent in 1836. In what would become a familiar pattern, the local non-Mormon press warned that Mormons were planning to take control of the district by the ballot.[44] Joseph Smith had his first personal brush with near-fatal violence in Kirtland in 1832, when mob of about fifty anti-Mormon Ohioans tarred and feathered him and his adviser Sidney Rigdon on the night of March 24.[45] Later he would narrowly escape castration at the hands of an Ohio mob, and even an impromptu death sentence.[46]

Smith chartered a bank in early 1837 on the basis of a divine revelation, which led many Mormons to believe it could not fail. Accordingly, there was a brief period of unsustainable borrowing and spending in the Mormon community in Kirtland, which led quickly to the bank collapsing. While the Mormon economy was ultimately not too badly damaged, for many the Kirtland bank collapse came to symbolize the pathologies of Smith's rule. In the words of one prominent Mormon dissident: "If we give all our privileges to one man, we virtually give him our money and our liberties, and make him a

---

[42] "The Mormon Delusion." From *The New Hampshire Gazette*, reprinted in *The Vermont Chronicle*, June 24, 1831.

[43] Joshua V. Hines, "Prefatory Remarks." In the *Haverhill Gazette* (Haverhill) September 8, 1832.

[44] Harper, Steven C. (2006). "Dictated by Christ: Joseph Smith and the Politics of Revelation." *Journal of the Early Republic*, 26(2): 275–304.

[45] Bushman (2005), pp. 178–182.

[46] Beam, Alex (2014). *American Crucifixion: The Murder of Joseph Smith and the Fate of the Mormon Church*. New York: PublicAffairs.

monarch, absolute and despotic, and ourselves abject slaves or fawning sycophants."[47]

By the end of the 1830s, disillusioned ex-followers of Smith were adding their voices to the chorus of denunciation. Apostates often come to see their former religions as dangerous shams, and throughout history they have played significant roles in fomenting hostile public opinion against these religions.[48] Opponents of religions place a high value on the accounts of apostates, who bring the authority of insider knowledge. In 1838, the *Waldo Patriot* printed a series of letters by former Mormons accusing Smith of fraud. One of the writers, John F. Boynton, claimed he

> withdrew from the church, after having witnessed the abominations of Joseph Smith Jr. and Sidney Rigdon [Smith's principal counselor], in lying, cheating and defrauding; and also having access to their secret councils, we learned their private sentiments; and we are now fully convinced that they are infidels, while they proclaim Christianity; therefore they are base hypocrites, wolves in sheep's clothing, seeking to devour their flock.[49]

Mormon communalism, and Smith's personal control, became particularly volatile issues for non-Mormons when linked to electoral mathematics. The first of three armed conflicts known as the "Mormon wars" began in Daviess County, Missouri, in 1838 with an election riot in the tiny municipality of Gallatin. Mormons, following Smith's prophecy that they should congregate in Missouri, had been buying land in the sparsely populated county since 1836, and by 1838 they were the clear majority, concentrated in the settlement of Adam-ondi-Ahman. It was well known that the Mormons would vote as a single bloc under the directions of their leader; this political practice would consistently provoke anti-Mormon hostility until they finally abandoned it in 1896 as an implicit condition of gaining statehood for Utah (see Chapter 4). In Stephen LeSueur's account of the Missouri conflict, both candidates in the 1838 election visited the Adam-ondi-Ahman Mormons to seek their votes. When the Whig candidate, Colonel William Peniston, concluded that the Mormons would vote en masse for his opponent, he sought non-Mormon support to prevent them from voting. On election day he gave a speech in Gallatin, claiming that the practice of Mormon bloc voting threatened the democratic rights of non-Mormons and urging them to take forceful action to stop them: "if

---

[47] Hill, Marvin S. (1980). "Cultural Crisis in the Mormon Kingdom: A Reconsideration of the Causes of Kirtland Dissent." *Church History*, 49(3): 286–297.

[48] Richardson, James T. (1998). "Apostates, Whistleblowers, Law, and Social Control" and Hall, John R., and Philip Schuyler, "Apostasy, Apocalypse and Religious Violence: An Exploratory Comparison of People's Temple, the Branch Davidians, and the Solar Temple." In Bromley, David G. (Ed.) *The Politics of Religious Apostasy: The Role of Apostates in the Transformation of Religious Movements.* Westport: Greenwood; Shaw, Brent D. (2009). "State Intervention and Holy Violence: Timgad/Paleotrovsk/Waco." *Journal of the American Academy of Religion*, 77(4): 853–894.

[49] *Waldo Patriot* (Belfast) May 4, 1838.

you suffer such men as these to vote, you will soon lose your suffrage."[50] A riot ensued when Mormons attempted to vote.

In the following months, several armed conflicts broke out in Daviess and the surrounding counties as non-Mormons fought to prevent Mormons from settling and establishing numerical superiority in any jurisdiction. These conflicts were aggravated by the fact Smith had formed a militia that fought back with considerable force, and rumors spread that he intended to take Jackson County by force and was massacring non-Mormons along the way. Governor Lilburn Boggs, convinced the Mormons were engaged in a full-scale insurrection against the state, declared in his notorious "Exterminating order" that the Mormons were enemies of the state and they must leave or be eradicated by force. He gathered a state militia of 2,500 to accomplish the purpose.

These conflicts culminated in the Haun's Mill Massacre of October 1838. A major event in Mormon collective memory, the massacre occurred when a group of Mormon civilians in Caldwell County, fleeing the approach of an oncoming militia, attempted to take shelter in a blacksmith's shop. The militia surrounded the log structure and fired rifle and musket rounds into it, before several of them entered the shop and executed surviving Mormons, including a nine-year-old boy and a ten-year-old boy (an eight-year-old girl was also shot, but survived). In total, eighteen Mormons died. The Sheriff of Livingston County had led the attack, and none of the fifty-five attackers was ever prosecuted.[51]

In local conflicts such as this, perceived Mormon difference was related to real features of Mormon social structure, namely insular economic communalism and the ability to raise a militia under Smith's authority. These differences became salient to social conflict because of the electoral implications of Mormon solidarity, and this provided antagonists with the political rhetoric necessary to enlarge the conflict. Anti-Mormon opponents, beginning in Kirtland and continuing in Missouri, claimed Mormon electoral power, based on geographic concentration and disciplined voting, was itself undemocratic and a threat to the cherished republican rights of non-Mormons. Later in the nineteenth century the Know-Nothings would make similar complaints about Catholic immigrants, who were voting in blocs in major American cities (see Chapter 7). In both cases, it was not enough for a minority to have a distinctive identity, either religious or political. To construct a minority as a political threat, antagonists had to show that their growing numbers and herd-like voting threatened the democratic rights of the American majority.

Smith's charismatic authority was central to the construction of the Mormon political and military threat. One account from the *St. Louis Bulletin* in defense

[50] LeSueur, Stephen C. (1987). *The 1838 Mormon War in Missouri*. Columbia: University of Missouri Press.

[51] Ibid., pp. 162–168.

of anti-Mormon military action describes how Smith's standing as a prophet created the Mormon danger:

> The Mormons believe they are the chosen people of God; that their leader, Joseph Smith, has continual revelations from heaven, and they look upon him as the mouth-piece of the Deity. When he issues orders to his tribe, he always says "the Lord sayeth so and so," and we understand his power is as absolute over this deluded people as is the Emperor's of Russia over his lowest serfs. They denominate us as heathens, and say the time will come when their power will spread over the kingdoms of the earth. At their meetings, some of their men or women always pretend to be inspired, and go on jabbering something unintelligible to us, but some of their chief men pretend to understand us by means of inspiration, and translate it to their people. By such means they work upon the superstition of ignorant men, and as Joe makes them believe that they will immediately go to heaven if they fall in battle, it is probable that they will make pretty good soldiers.[52]

The *Bulletin* certainly emphasized difference and distinctiveness. It refers first of all to the Mormon belief in their status as a chosen people, which Moore identifies as the very root of distinctive Mormon identity. But other terms and descriptions designating Mormons as a distinct group are used in a way that undermines and ridicules any true claim to quasi-ethnic standing. They are described as a "tribe," but in the same sentence as "this deluded people," suggesting their peoplehood is defined by collective credulity. The reason their "jabberings" are "unintelligible to us" is only because they are a result of "pretend inspiration." All of this would be merely ridiculous rather than threatening if it were not for Smith's charismatic hold over his followers, who regard his word as the word of God. The last sentence ominously mentions that he has the power to mobilize a militia composed of men who would be happy to die in battle.

Even in the face of a compelling threat, it is not always easy to sell religious persecution. An unusual wave of editorial comment sympathetic to the Mormons appeared in the aftermath of the Missouri violence. The *St. Louis Republican*, in an observation that was picked up by many other newspapers across the country, noted that the most dedicated opponents of the Mormons in Missouri were now profiting greatly by speculating on the land the Mormons had been forced to abandon. This suggested that the Missouri Mormon War had not been a struggle against a genuine threat, but a dishonorable fight over real estate. According to Cleveland's *Daily Gazette and Herald*:

> Great distress and suffering exists among the plundered Mormons, many of whom were formerly quiet, inoffensive citizens of northern Ohio. They were wild and fanatical in their religious notions when among us, but peaceable, humble, and law-abiding in their deportment. There can be no excuse for the murder and rapine

---

[52] *St. Louis Bulletin*, reproduced in the *Vermont Chronicle* (Bellows Falls) November 28, 1838.

with which they have been desolated since emigrating. The infamy will be as lasting as the name of Missouri.[53]

The *Gazette and Herald* maintained the trope that the Mormons were "wild and fanatical in their religion," but claimed this was not relevant to their relations with non-Mormons, which were "peaceable, humble and law-abiding." Similarly the *Baltimore Chronicle* sided with the Mormons even while calling them "deluded":

> From the accounts which are now received, it now seems to us that the poor deluded Mormons are "more sinned against than sinning" in the matter of this war, and their greatest *error* was settling down on some of the best lands in the State, and that in defense of their right to them, against the avarice of others, they were forced to take up arms.[54]

One could subscribe to the leading anti-Mormon tropes of the day and still object to the persecution of Mormons; this is why any complete account of the causes of anti-Mormon persecution must go beyond the formation of anti-Mormon attitudes, and explore what could politically legitimize suspending religious tolerance in the Mormon case.

THE FIRST POLYGAMY CONTROVERSY AND THE DEATH OF JOSEPH SMITH

Public consciousness of the Mormon practice of plural marriage began in Nauvoo, Illinois, in 1844. It led directly to Joseph Smith's death. Smith had established Nauvoo in 1839 after fleeing Missouri, and had been given permission to charter a city by the Illinois legislature. The state had two reasons to welcome the Mormons; first, it was nearly bankrupt and welcomed an influx of tens of thousands of tax-paying immigrants. Second, Illinois legislators recognized the political opportunities presented by the Mormon voting bloc, and so were willing to court them by granting them a city charter. This charter, crucially, allowed the city to pass any ordinance that did not conflict with state and federal laws, and also allowed the establishment of a militia.[55]

By 1844, Nauvoo's population of 15,000 was the second largest in Illinois and its militia, the Nauvoo Legion, numbered over 5,000, the largest such force in the state. Joseph Smith as mayor of the city stood formally atop a political structure for the first time, as well as maintaining control over the church. Styling himself "General Smith," he announced his candidacy for the Presidency of the United States that year, which gave him (and his speechwriters) a chance to

---

[53] *Daily Herald and Gazette* (Cleveland) December 9, 1838.
[54] Reprinted in the *New Bedford Mercury*, November 23, 1838.
[55] For a good brief overview of the events leading to the establishment of Nauvoo, see Hal Schindler, "Polygamy, Persecution and Power All Played a Role in the Nauvoo Exodus." *Salt Lake Tribune*, June 16, 1996.

articulate the distinctive political philosophy he labeled "Theodemocracy." In Smith's view, only the rule of God could provide the nation with "unadulterated freedom" in which men would conduct their affairs in a state of righteousness.[56] While Smith saw theocracy and democracy as complementary, this contradicted mainstream American political thought. Steven Harper argues that Smith's "dialogic revelations," which invested sovereignty in God, created hostility among Jacksonian Americans who believed in democratization, the transfer of sovereignty to the people.[57]

In surrounding communities there was rising fear about the political, economic, and military power of Smith, and Missouri authorities were still trying to extradite him, along with other Mormon leaders. However, serious trouble for Smith began from within his church. A group of high-ranking Mormons led by William Law had broken with Smith over what they saw as his increasing theocratic tendencies and his instigation of the practice of plural marriage. Smith had told other members of the Mormon hierarchy in secret about the revelation that all Mormon men would one day practice plural marriage (this was related to the need to populate the afterlife), but had so far concealed it from the rank and file of the Church as well as all non-Mormons.[58] Outraged by both the immorality of the practice and the perceived abuse of Smith's power that it entailed, the renegade faction published a single issue of a newspaper, called the *Nauvoo Expositor*, to expose Smith.

As well as accusing Smith of being a fallen prophet and becoming too powerful, the paper included a hair-raising account of how Smith supposedly used his charismatic power to induce women into becoming his "spiritual wives."

> The harmless, inoffensive, and unsuspecting creatures, are so devoted to the Prophet, and the cause of Jesus Christ, that they do not dream of the deep-laid and fatal scheme which prostrates happiness, and renders death itself desirable, but they meet him, expecting to receive through him a blessing, and learn the will of the Lord concerning them, and what awaits the faithful follower of Joseph, the Apostle and Prophet of God, when in the stead thereof, they are told, after having been sworn in one of the most solemn manners, to never divulge what is revealed to them, with a penalty of death attached, that God Almighty has revealed it to him, that she should be his [Joseph's] Spiritual wife; for it was right anciently, and God will tolerate it again.... The Prophet damns her if she rejects. She thinks of the great sacrifice, and of the many thousand miles she has traveled over sea and land, that she might save her soul

---

[56] For a thorough overview of Smith's political philosophy, see Mason, Patrick Q. (2011a). "God and the People: Theodemocracy in Nineteenth-Century Mormonism." *Journal of Church and State*, 53(3): 349–375. Mason notes that Smith was murdered before he could ever fully elaborate or systematize his political views.

[57] Harper (2006), p. 281.

[58] Quinn, D. Michael (1985). "LDS Church Authority and New Plural Marriages, 1890–1904." *Dialogue*, 18:1.

from pending ruin, and replies, God's will be done, and not mine. The Prophet and his devotees in this way are gratified.[59]

There were many issues at stake in the initial polygamy controversy. The violation of traditional morality clearly played a role, but the all-important political framing by the dissident Mormons was in terms of Smith abusing his charismatic power. Polygamy in this narrative was not a relationship into which women would enter consensually; Smith lured devout women into Nauvoo by his prophetic status then coerced them into marriage by threatening damnation. This was the very first of the "captivity narratives" that would later become a staple of sensationalist anti-polygamy literature.

Smith unfortunately seemed to prove the *Expositor*'s point when he ordered the Nauvoo Legion to destroy the paper's printing press a few days later after deliberating with the city council. This gave surrounding anti-Mormons such as Thomas Sharp, editor of the nearby *Warsaw Signal*, the opportunity to provoke armed action against Smith. He had now violated both freedom of the press and property rights, two cornerstones of American liberty, and could no longer be tolerated. Sharp published the following account of the destruction of the *Expositor*:

> I hasten to inform you of the UNPARALLELED OUTRAGE, perpetrated upon our rights and interests, by the ruthless, lawless, ruffian band of MORMON MOBOCRATS, at the dictum that of that UNPRINCIPLED wretch Joe Smith.... They also declared the "Nauvoo Expositor," a *"nuisance,"* and directed the police of the city to proceed immediately to the office of the Expositor and DESTROY THE PRESS and also the MATERIALS, by THROWING them into the STREET!!!!

Following this outrage, there was only one possible course of action:

> We have only to state, that this is sufficient! War and extermination is inevitable! Citizens ARISE, ONE and ALL!!! – Can you stand by, and suffer such INFERNAL DEVILS!! to ROB men of their property and RIGHTS, without avenging them. We have no time for comment, every man will make his own. LET IT BE MADE WITH POWDER AND BALL!!![60]

A lethal series of events followed. Numerous outsiders came to Nauvoo with warrants for Smith's arrest, which the Nauvoo court dismissed. Smith responded by declaring martial law, which the Governor of Illinois considered an act of treason against the state. Smith and fifteen other Mormon leaders were charged with treason, and after negotiations with the Governor Smith agreed to surrender to authorities in nearby Carthage, where he would face trial. The Carthage Greys, an anti-Mormon militia, were assigned to protect that

---

[59] *Nauvoo Expositor* 06/07/1844, p. 2A. For the full text, see: http://en.wikisource.org/wiki/ Nauvoo_Expositor, last accessed March 25, 2010.
[60] *The Warsaw Signal* (Warsaw) June 11, 1844.

Carthage jail;[61] predictably, they allowed a mob (which some of them joined) to storm the jail and murder Joseph Smith and his brother Hyram.[62]

It is unusual for a new religion to survive events such as these. The death of the prophet and the continuing promise of further violence in Illinois prompted the majority of Mormons to flee west to Utah under the leadership of Brigham Young. Young had been the President of the Quorum of the Twelve Apostles, an important governing body of the Church hierarchy. Smith had not designated a successor, and Young had to overcome the claims of several others who saw themselves as his rightful replacement. The only widely agreed legitimate successor, Hyram Smith, had been killed alongside Joseph; Young ultimately prevailed over his rivals to fill the vacuum because he, unlike others, had not had substantial doctrinal disagreements with Smith.[63]

Young increased the power of the Quorum of Twelve, effectively installing it as the leadership of the entire Church, and himself assumed Smith's office of "seer, translator, prophet and apostle of Jesus Christ." Smith had created this office for himself in 1830 in order to consolidate his power. After his early disciples Oliver Cowdery and Hiram Page had begun promulgating revelations of their own that contradicted Smith's, Smith decreed at the 1830 conference that he alone received revelations and commandments, while others such as Cowdery only communicated them.[64] While monopolizing revelation in the hands of a single prophet might seem likely to restrict the longevity of the religion after the death of the prophet, Smith's creation of an office of prophet which could be handed to a successor helped to ensure Mormonism's survival.[65]

CONCLUSION

In this chapter I have shown two things. First, the early persecution of Mormons in the United States occurred mainly because of the political challenge of their charismatic and theocratic leadership. Even in a society in which religious freedom is a foundational axiom, there is an inherently limited tolerance for charismatic prophets. Many Americans doubted Joseph Smith's legitimacy as a religious figure and saw his successors as threats to American democracy and republican government. Opponents of Mormonism always constructed this threat in terms of the control they exercised over their followers. Even polygamy, when it was effectively mobilized as a political issue, was

[61] Hill, Marvin S. (2004). "Carthage Conspiracy Reconsidered: A Second Look at the Murder of Joseph and Hyrum Smith." *Journal of the Illinois Historical Society*, 97(2): 107–134.

[62] Arrington, Leonard J. and Davis Bitton (1979). *The Mormon Experience*. London: George Allen & Unwin Ltd.

[63] Turner, John G. (2012). *Brigham Young, Pioneer Prophet*. Cambridge: The Belknap Press of Harvard University Press, ch. 5.

[64] Bushman (2005), p. 121.

[65] Here, indeed, Smith and the Mormons were following the classic pattern of routinization of charisma described by Weber (1947).

construed in these terms. Thus, the thing that made Mormon leaders charismatic – the fact that their followers accepted their theocratic authority – also put them outside the bounds of religious tolerance.

Second, Mormon "peculiarity" or distinctiveness was most salient to the immediate neighbors and rivals of the Mormons, especially those who were in economic or electoral competition with them. It was reinforced by the Mormon tendency to vote in blocs, which posed a threat to electoral candidates they did not support. More broadly, however, American political actors did not see Mormons as a distinctive "people," but as errant Americans who needed to be brought under control.

4

The federal response to Mormonism

INTRODUCTION

After the Mormon exodus to Utah, anti-Mormonism took on much more ideological and partisan dimensions. It was no longer simply about conflicts between Mormons and their non-Mormon neighbors, or the suspicion that Mormon leaders were perpetrating a fraud. Anti-Mormonism became a foundational crusade for the fledgling Republican Party, which associated polygamy with slavery. Republican Party anti-Mormonism united Whig and nativist demands that religious minorities be "Americanized" with feminist and liberal concerns about the captivity to which Mormon women were supposedly subjected. Just as importantly, the Mormons during this period occupied a vast and otherwise largely unoccupied territory in the west, which brought them into direct conflict with the federal state. From the 1850s to the 1880s, the increasingly autonomous Mormon polity in the west posed a threat to a succession of American state-building projects.

This chapter examines the federal response to Mormonism between 1847 and 1896, with a particular focus on the Edmunds Act of 1882, which I analyze through both congressional debates and voting patterns. There are several reasons for focusing on Edmunds in particular, the most important of which is that it is a rare example of a democratic government voting explicitly to deprive one section of the population of its political rights. The extensive debates around the act allow us to reconstruct the rationale for state repression, while the voting record gives us an idea of the incentives of individual legislators to support or oppose repression. The Edmunds Act also poses an important puzzle: Why did so many Democrats support the Republican anti-Mormon agenda, even when it would hurt Democrats electorally?

The Edmunds debate and vote show the limits of pluralistic and legalistic perspectives on the relationship between religion and the state in America. The Mormons were unable to marshal the support of the Democratic Party, traditionally the party of religious minority rights, despite the political opportunity this would have given the Democrats in Utah territory. And the repression of Mormon rights did not simply reflect a limited nineteenth-century understanding of religious freedom. The arguments used by those Democrats who *did* defend Mormon rights were couched in terms that would be extremely familiar to twentieth- and twenty-first-century civil libertarians. The question is why so many Democrats went along with an alternative ideological agenda, usually associated with the Republican and Whig parties, which instead emphasized cultural consensus – what I term "muscular liberalism." This chapter shows how muscular liberalism became the ideology of the late nineteenth-century American state, fomenting an anti-Mormon legislative agenda that for the most part crossed party lines.

MORMON UTAH UNDER BRIGHAM YOUNG

Mormons regarded Brigham Young, like Joseph Smith, as a prophet. His prophetic standing and his place in Mormon history took on legendary proportions after the epic trip to Utah. Utah at the time was virtually uninhabited and extremely difficult to reach, and Young, citing a revelation from God, chose it as the Mormons' new home before the United States had even established sovereignty there. Beginning in 1846, 70,000 Mormons undertook the 1,300 mile trip, mainly on foot and dragging handcarts with them. The title of Leonard Arrington's 1985 biography of Young, *American Moses*, accurately describes his place in Mormon memory and even the national imagination.[1] An important part of Young's achievement was negotiating with the initially hostile federal government. The Polk administration enabled the passage of the Mormon pioneers by allowing them to winter in Indian lands, and in 1851 the Fillmore government, recognizing Young's role as the "colonizer" of the desolate Utah territory, appointed him governor. Thus, the Mormons enjoyed a brief period of good relations with the federal government despite practicing polygamy more or less openly.[2]

The honeymoon period quickly ended. The non-Mormon territorial representatives appointed by the government left Utah shortly after arriving, accusing the Mormons of "malicious sedition" and taking the congressional appropriation of $24,000 with them. Mormons brawled with non-Mormon soldiers, and rumors began that the Mormons were conspiring with the Pahvant Indians. Conflicts between settlers and federal agents were common in all the western territories, but particularly acute in Utah – or Deseret, as the Mormons christened it – because of the religious divide. Federal officials found it almost impossible to do their jobs in the face of local resistance, which included the alleged destruction of federal offices, and Young rejoiced at their steady exit

[1] Arrington, Leonard (1985). *Brigham Young: American Moses*. Urbana and Chicago: University of Illinois Press.

[2] Arrington and Bitton (1992), pp. 161–166.

from the territory. In 1856, he sent apostles to Washington to petition the increasingly hostile federal government for statehood.[3]

The Buchanan Administration responded by declaring Utah "in a state of substantial rebellion" in May 1857, and ordered 2500 troops to the territory to replace Young with a new governor, Alfred Cumming. Buchanan may have been trying to send a message to would-be secessionists in the South, but the increasing assertiveness of the Mormons, who were apparently making the territory ungovernable, was probably reason enough. Polygamy aggravated the issue, as did the Mormons' supposed military power and their rumored alliances with Indians. Young's defiant rule in Utah was a direct challenge to the sovereignty of the United States in the west, and Buchanan was feeling the pressure of newspaper editorials claiming that the Mormons and their Indian allies were preparing for all-out war.[4]

The war never took place. The military expedition, which came to be known as "Buchanan's folly," did not make it to the Salt Lake Valley. The reactivated Nauvoo Legion harassed federal troops with scorched-earth tactics as they tried to make their way through Wyoming in the fall of 1857, forcing them to change direction. While the expedition was delayed over the winter months, Pennsylvania colonel and attorney Thomas L. Kane offered to mediate between Young and the federal government. Kane, a long-standing ally of the Mormons who had previously helped negotiate their passage to Utah, persuaded Young and the Mormon leadership to accept Cumming as governor. He also persuaded Cumming to complete his journey to Salt Lake without his military escort, though the federal government would be permitted to set up a military outpost in the territory away from any Mormon settlements. Thus, the dispute was peacefully resolved, with Cumming assuming the office of governor but leaving Young as de facto "Governor of the People," the most powerful political figure in Utah.[5]

The "Utah War" had one disastrous consequence, however. In September 1857, as unreliable news about the approach of troops swept the territory, a Mormon militia in Southern Utah attacked and massacred more than 100 migrants in a wagon train traveling from Arkansas to California. Local Paiute Indians also participated in the attack. The role of the Mormon leadership in the Mountain Meadows massacre is controversial. In one of the most thorough historical accounts of the massacre, Walker, Turley, and Leonard (2008) argue it is unlikely that Young or other leaders in Salt Lake knew about in advance or endorsed the attack, led by John D. Lee. But the attack did reflect Young's preparations for war, which had included planned guerilla tactics, alliances with Indian tribes, and warnings to migrants that

---

[3] Walker, Ronald W., Richard E. Turley, Jr., and Glen M. Leonard (2008). *Massacre at Mountain Meadows*. New York: Oxford University Press, pp. 20–27.

[4] Ibid., pp. 29–32.

[5] Poll, Richard (1993). "Thomas L. Kane and the Utah War." *Utah Historical Quarterly*, 61(2): 112–135.

they could not be guaranteed safe passage through the territory. Lee was executed for his role in the massacre in 1877, and the incident deepened the Mormons' reputation for violence.[6]

THE REPUBLICAN PARTY AND THE ANTI-POLYGAMY CRUSADE

Utah Territory was overwhelmingly Mormon, and leading Mormons supported the practice of plural marriage from 1852 onwards. Only about 10 percent of the male population had multiple wives at any given time – sheer gender mathematics would make it impossible for many more to do so – but it had become a part of official Church doctrine and so, at least officially, all Mormons believed in the righteousness of it.[7] In reality it seems likely that many poorer rank and file Mormons were resentful of the practice, which was mainly the domain of wealthier and higher-status Mormons and which depleted the pool of marriageable women. Certainly, when the Church finally renounced the practice in the 1890s there was no shortage of Mormons eager to turn in their neighbors who continued it in secret.[8]

The nationalized anti-polygamy campaign began in earnest in 1856. In 1856, the Republican Party's national platform resolved "it is both the right and the imperative duty of Congress to prohibit in the Territories those twin relics of barbarism – Polygamy, and Slavery."[9] The first legislative attempt to abolish polygamy was the Morrill Act of 1862, which outlawed bigamy (states already had laws against bigamy, but this was the first extension of those laws to the territories). This law proved useless. Some Mormons simply evaded it by having one civil marriage and referring to supernumerary marriages as "sealings." Majority Mormon juries, reflecting the overwhelming numerical superiority of Mormons in the territory, thwarted attempted prosecutions. Brigham Young himself married six more wives after 1862.[10]

The transparent failure of the Morrill Act led to a series of far more punitive proposals in Congress. There were five proposals discussed between 1866 and 1874, only one of which was passed. The Poland Act of 1874 attempted to strengthen enforcement of the 1862 law by giving responsibility for cases in Utah to federal officials and courts, and giving "federal judges considerable leeway in the selection of jurors." As harsh as the Poland Act was in circumscribing territorial authority, other proposals had been much more extensive. The Wade Bill (1866) had proposed barring church officers from solemnizing marriages and requiring extensive reporting on church finances to federal authorities; the Cragin Bill (1867 and 1869) proposed abolishing trial by

---

[6] Walker, Turley, and Leonard (2008), pp. 54–128.

[7] Arrington (1958), p. 238.

[8] Bradley, Martha Sonntag, 1993. *Kidnapped from That Land: The Government Raids on the Short Creek Polygamists.* Salt Lake City: University of Utah Press.

[9] www.presidency.ucsb.edu/ws/index.php?pid=29619.

[10] Quinn (1985).

jury in Utah bigamy cases; the Cullom Bill (1869–1870) would have deprived plural wives of immunity from testifying against their husbands, as well as sending the army to Utah, raising a large militia there, and confiscating the property of any Mormon leaving the state on account of the law; and the Ashley Bill (1869) proposed "dismembering" Utah and transferring portions of it to Nevada, Wyoming, and Colorado.[11]

Although polygamy was, as Kimball Young describes, a "dominant moral issue" of the nineteenth century,[12] for thirty years it failed to arouse any concrete action by Congress. Some individual congressmen were enthusiastic, proposing legislative measures, but most of these were never voted on; party leaders and other legislators simply had more pressing priorities. Richard Bensel notes that, despite polygamy's status as a "prototypical hurrah issue," it rarely featured in state-level party platforms as an immediate problem requiring political action.[13]

A legislative agenda for repressive action against polygamy regained traction in the 1880s when liberals, proto-feminists, and Temperance activists joined a vigorous campaign against it. Advocates of women's suffrage had always condemned the practice of polygamy, but had previously shied away from coercive approaches to the problem in Utah. Instead they had supported federal legislation proposed by Radical Republicans that would have granted the vote to women in Utah and several other western territories. They believed this would effectively end the practice of polygamy, allowing women to liberate themselves from "the bond of degradation."[14]

The federal legislation failed, but the territories themselves embraced women's suffrage in the late 1860s. For Wyoming, this was a ploy to attract new settlers; for Utah, it was a way of coping with new settlers. By granting women the vote, the Mormon-dominated legislature diluted the increasing power of (mainly male) non-Mormons in the territory.[15] It is not surprising that giving additional votes to Mormon women would reinforce Mormon power in the territory, but this was the opposite effect from what pro-suffrage advocates had intended. By the 1880s, proto-feminists and their allies were firmly against women's suffrage in Utah. They believed Mormon women were not ready to participate in consensual government; they voted according to the wishes of their husbands, and thus reinforced their subordinate position in family, sexual, and childbearing relations.[16]

---

[11] Arrington (1958), pp. 356–361.

[12] Young (1954), p. 1.

[13] Bensel, Richard Franklin (2000). *The Political Economy of American Industrialization, 1877–1900*. Cambridge: Cambridge University Press, pp. 182–183.

[14] Gordon, Sarah Barringer (1996). "The Liberty of Self-Degradation: Polygamy, Woman Suffrage and Consent in Nineteenth-Century America." *The Journal of American History*, 83(3): 815–847.

[15] Ibid.

[16] Ibid.

Two powerful strands of anti-Mormon rhetoric were visible at this time. On the one hand, nativist propaganda about Mormons reflected familiar, often outlandish themes about other "un-American" groups such as Catholics and Freemasons. Though the Mormons were relatively small and isolated, nativists saw them as a subversive threat to American nationhood, and they accused Mormon men, especially Mormon leaders, of almost unimaginable acts of sexual depravity.[17] A Thomas Nast cartoon from the 1870s depicted a crocodile labeled "ROMAN CHURCH" and a snapping turtle labeled "MORMON CHURCH" crawling over the Capitol, on which was inscribed "Religious liberty is guaranteed but can we allow foreign reptiles to crawl all over us?"[18] On the other hand, proto-feminist and Temperance groups accused Mormons of keeping women in conditions of intolerable oppression, reinforcing the association between polygamy and slavery that had first appeared in the Republican Party platform of 1856.

One of the leading manifestations of this second form of criticism was the *Anti-Polygamy Standard*, published in Salt Lake City by non-Mormon women. The first issue of this newspaper, which appeared monthly from 1880 to 1883, carried a prologue by Harriet Beecher Stowe:

> To the Women of America:
>
> Let every happy wife and worker who reads these lines give her sympathy, prayers and efforts to free her sisters from this degrading bondage. Let all the womanhood of the country stand united for them. There is a power in a combined enlightened sentiment and sympathy, before which every form of injustice and cruelty must finally go down.

The opening editorial further emphasized both the slavery theme and the idea that Mormon women were incapable of liberating themselves:

> The saying "who would be free themselves must strike the first blow," is undoubtedly true in the majority of cases, yet the questions seem pertinent are all those in bondage so circumstanced that they can or will "strike the blow," and if freedom is not to be theirs, except through their own courage and resistance must they forever remain in fetters? Had the abolition of slavery in the South depended entirely on the slaves striking for freedom, they would have remained in bondage until this day.[19]

The paper contained many stories, purportedly from former Mormon wives, about the horrors of polygamous family life. These stories echoed claims that anti-Mormon novelists such as Alfreda Eva Bell and Maria Ward had been

[17] Davis, David Brion, 1960. "Some Themes of Counter-Subversion: An Analysis of Anti-Masonic, Anti-Catholic and Anti-Mormon Literature." *The Mississippi Valley Historical Review*, 47(2): 205–224; Hofstadter, Richard, 1964. *The Paranoid Style in American Politics*. Cambridge: Harvard University Press.
[18] An image of this cartoon is available at http://tinyurl.com/b3wdkj9, last accessed January 30, 2013. Originally found in Gordon (2002), p. 143.
[19] Both block quotes from *The Anti-Polygamy Standard* (Salt Lake City) vol. 1, no. 1, p. 1.

making since the 1850s, that Mormon wives were held in captivity and subject to endemic violence.[20] Polygamy as a problem was framed not just in terms of Christian morality, but in terms of slavery.

Anti-slavery rhetoric resonated throughout the anti-Mormon coalition. Despite the seeming ideological distance between feminists and nativists – one group was fundamentally committed to political inclusion, the other to political exclusion – both had a political base in the Republican Party, which had absorbed many radicals with proto-feminist leanings following the demise of the Whigs and also the nativist vote after the implosion of the American Party.[21] Both shared a hatred of slavery, and had gravitated to the new party dedicated to its destruction. The Republican Party enabled legislative coordination between the two groups even where they had few other shared aims,[22] and anti-polygamists made effective rhetorical use of the unifying anti-slavery cause. This would the first – but not the last – historical instance of political cooperation between feminists and the Protestant Right on specific policy aims.[23]

THE EDMUNDS BILL

In 1882 Senator George F. Edmunds, a radical Republican from Vermont, introduced legislation that would prevent polygamists from voting, holding office, or serving on juries. On the one hand, the latter provision would enable easier enforcement of anti-bigamy laws, but the first two provisions suggested the top priority of the bill was breaking the political hegemony of the Mormon leadership in Utah.

The Edmunds Act was popular in both houses and was passed with substantial margins. Some Southern Democrats, however, offered resistance

---

[20] Gordon, Sarah Barringer (2003). *The Mormon Question*. Chapel Hill, University of North Carolina Press, pp. 47–49.

[21] Foner, Eric (1970). *Free Soil, Free Labor, Free Men: The Ideology of the Republican Party before the Civil War*. New York: Oxford University Press.

[22] See Aldrich, John (2011). *Why Parties? A Second Look*. Chicago: University of Chicago Press.

[23] Conservative Protestantism and feminism notably made common cause in the prohibitionist movement of the late nineteenth and early twentieth centuries. Both elements were present, along with gospel socialism, in the Women's Christian Temperance Union. See Bordin, Ruth (1981). *Woman and Temperance*. Philadelphia: Temple University Press. See also Gusfield, Joseph (1972). *Symbolic Crusade: Status Politics and the American Temperance Movement*. Urbana and Chicago: University of Illinois Press, pp. 93–96. More recently, the feminist movement split over the issue of pornography in the 1970s and 80s, with some feminists such as Andrea Dworkin and Catherine McKinnon supporting anti-pornography statutes that conservative organizations also supported. See Stansell, Christine (2010). *The Feminist Promise: 1792 to the Present*. New York: Simon and Schuster, pp. 345–347. In the 2000s, feminist and evangelical organizations combined to campaign against transnational sex trafficking. See Bernstein, Elizabeth (2010). "Militarized Humanitarianism Meets Carceral Feminism: The Politics of Sex, Rights and Freedom in Contemporary Antitrafficking Campaigns." *Signs: Journal of Women in Culture and Society*, 36:1.

during debates, arguing that while they hated polygamy as much as the other legislators, the Edmunds legislation endangered religious liberty and represented an unconscionable federal incursion into local democracy. Edmunds derided this defense of Mormon rights, answering it with rhetoric that was at once Christian, Republican, and nationalist:

> No man, North or South, who believes in the Christian religion, who believes in a republican government, can maintain or has maintained in this body that this institution of polygamy is one that can exist consistently with our universal idea of the theory of a republican government. Nobody has pretended such a thing. Then may I not assume that we wish to get rid of it? Everybody says do. How are you going to do it? You say you do not like what we have proposed. Will you propose something else? Oh, no. It is always some other day, some other measure that is not now defined, that is not now brought forward. It is some other day, some other time, some other measure, than the one that is proposed.[24]

For Edmunds, breaking the Mormon hierarchy's power was necessary to maintaining "republican government" in the United States, and complaining about religious liberties in the face of this task was an act of cowardice.

Republican legislators were also motivated by the old problem of Mormon bloc voting. In local elections, Mormons voted almost exclusively for the People's Party, which helped maintain Mormon control of school boards and municipal councils. At the federal level they nearly all voted Democratic, while the 10 percent of Utah citizens who were not Mormons voted Republican. This alignment of the territory's political and religious cleavages gave Republicans a particularly strong incentive to disfranchise the Mormons, and again showed that distinctiveness was most likely to lead to repression when it was combined with electoral mathematics.

The vote on Edmunds, however, did not follow the logic of pluralistic political competition. Democrats in both houses were split, despite the fact that the legislation would obviously hurt their party in Congress. There was a notable regional pattern to the split; Southern Democrats voted against the repressive measures in much greater numbers than Northern Democrats. The Southern Democrats, however, were far from unanimous. On some measures they too were split almost evenly.

Why were Southern Democrats the most likely – indeed, almost the only – group in the 47th Congress to oppose the repression of the Mormons? This question warrants our attention for a number of reasons. Southern Democrats in the late nineteenth-century Congresses were not known to be more supportive of civil liberties than others. Most of them had served in the Confederate army during the Civil War, and harbored deep grudges over Reconstruction efforts to empower African Americans politically. The other major vote that year which involved stripping a group of its civil and political rights was the Chinese Exclusion Act, passed two months later; none of the

---

[24] *Congressional Record*, vol. 11, p. 1213.

TABLE 4.1: *Edmunds Bill, final house vote*

Party	Northern states			Southern states			Totals		
	Yea	Nay	Abs.	Yea	Nay	Abs.	Yea	Nay	Abs.
Republican	120	0	17	7	0	3	127	0	20
Democrat	38	6	6	28	36	22	66	43	28
Other	5	0	0	4	1	1	9	0	1
Totals	163	6	23	39	37	26	202	43	49

Southerners who had opposed Edmunds opposed the Chinese Exclusion Act, and some of them were its strongest supporters, despite their lack of proximity to the Pacific West.[25] Furthermore, Southerners arguably represented the most hostile constituencies for Mormons in the entire United States. While anti-Mormon feeling was generally widespread, the South was the only region in which Mormon missionaries were actually killed during the post-war period.[26] In the absence of polls, public violence should have served as an unusually clear signal to office-seeking legislators that Mormons were disliked.[27]

While these facts should lead us to wonder why Southern congressmen voted against repressing the Mormons, there is another fact that poses the opposite problem. Southern Democrats may have had every personal and office-seeking reason for voting to repress, but they – along with all other Democrats – also had an extremely good strategic reason for voting *not* to disfranchise. If the Edmunds Act was going to disfranchise most Mormons in the Utah territory, then it would also be disfranchising most Democrats. The party cleavage in this territory, as well as in neighboring Idaho, aligned almost perfectly with the all-important religious cleavage. There were good reasons to suspect that, having turned the territory Republican, the Republicans would then press to admit Utah as a state, thus adding a vital extension to their precarious advantage in both houses, and cementing their ability to pursue such projects as the tariff and

[25] See Chin (1998) for an account of congressional debates over the act, which banned all Chinese immigration to the United States for ten years, and would be renewed in 1892 and 1902. Chin, Gabriel, 1998. "Segregation's Last Stronghold: Race Discrimination and the Constitutional Law of Immigration." *UCLA Law Review*, 46:1.

[26] Mason, Patrick Q. (2011b). *The Mormon Menace: Violence and Anti-Mormonism in the Postbellum South.* Buice, David (1988). "A Stench in the Nostrils of Honest Men: Southern Democrats and the Edmunds Act of 1882." *Dialogue: A Journal of Mormon Thought,* 21(3): 100–113.

[27] See Mayhew (1974) for an account of Congressmen as political actors most strongly motivated by election and re-election. An alternative explanation is that violence of all kinds was higher in the South, which would have weakened any anti-Mormon signal in the killing of missionaries. Mayhew, David (1974). *Congress: The Electoral Connection.* New Haven: Yale University Press.

the gold standard.[28] Thus, long-term party strategy should have mandated voting against the Edmunds Bill. The passage of Edmunds was by no means inevitable, despite the Republican majority in both houses. Due to the high number of absences during the votes, unified Democratic voting could have at least altered the legislation. Indeed, unified Democratic senators did succeed in passing one amendment: to make election boards bipartisan. But, for the most part, especially in the final house vote, the Democrats were deeply divided. There is no obvious reason why this division should have been on conspicuously regional lines.

Thus, neither ideological reasons nor strategic ones seem to be able to explain the distinctive pattern of support and opposition, with Northern Democrats mainly voting with the Republican majority and Southern Democrats closely divided. In this chapter I seek a more useful and fine-grained explanation by further exploring both intra-Democratic and intra-Southern differences. I suggest that the division in the Democratic Party reflected a national cleavage around the Republican Party's program of industrial state-building. Mormon rights in the west became part of a much broader struggle over the American political economy.

OPPOSITIONAL SPEECHES ON THE EDMUNDS ACT

The Edmunds Bill was sent to the Senate Committee on the Judiciary in December 1881, and was returned to face votes in both houses in March 1882. Like the Morrill Act before it, the Edmunds Bill made provisions to punish polygamy in the territories, but in order to give these provisions "teeth" the bill also contained a number of hitherto unprecedented restrictions on polygamists' legal and political rights. To make convictions easier to obtain – all-Mormon juries had frequently thwarted attempted prosecutions under the Morrill Act – anyone practicing polygamy was barred from serving on a jury. Sections 8 and 9 of the Edmunds Bill would break down Mormon political hegemony in Utah by preventing any polygamist from voting or holding public office in Utah, and appointing a five-member commission to examine and certify all election returns.

Debate in the house, which took place in March, was mainly technical and procedural. The February debate in the Senate, however, was impassioned and fought over basic matters of democratic principle. It is these debates that provide evidence of the public justifications of Southerners who voted against the Edmunds Bill, as well as the rationales of those who supported it. Though

---

[28] For an account of the politics of statehood admission, see Stewart, Charles, and Barry Weingast (1992). "Stacking the Senate, Changing the Nation: Republican Rotten Boroughs, Statehood Politics, and American Political Development." *Studies in American Political Development*, 6(2): 223–271. For an overview of the American political economy at this time, see Bensel, Richard Franklin (2000). *The Political Economy of American Industrialization, 1877–1900.* Cambridge: Cambridge University Press.

there was no final roll-call vote in the Senate (it was passed with a voice vote accompanied by highly irregular cheering from the galleries), the votes on most of the amendments reveal a pattern very similar to the one in the final house vote, with all Republicans in favor of repressive measures, most Northern Democrats also in favor, and Southern Democrats split. Thus, we can expect that the opinions reflected in Senate debate were similar to those in circulation in the house. The bill was debated in the Senate over the 15 and 16 of February. During this period four Democrats gave substantial speeches against the bill – John Tyler Morgan of Alabama, George Graham Vest of Missouri, Joseph E. Brown of Georgia, and Wilkinson Call of Florida. The language in these speeches is a mix of liberal constitutionalism, defense of due process, and concern about the radical Reconstruction flavor of the Edmunds measure.

Morgan, on February 16, made the argument in terms that would resonate most strongly with contemporary liberals and civil libertarians. He began by pointing out that 300,000 members of Indian tribes had grown up under a system of polygamous marriage within the jurisdiction of the United States, and no attempt had been made to dissuade them from polygamy because "we do not regard them as a Christian people." It is not clear if Morgan was implying that the Mormons should be exempt from Christian moral standards for the same reason, but in both cases, he explained, they would gradually be integrated under civilized law after "a great many years," and a great effort to convince them of the benefits of civilization. Thus, polygamy was not "to be looked at as a question which should invoke our sudden anger, and drive us into legislative excesses." He developed this Madisonian theme in eloquent detail:

> It is one of the highest duties of every government in moments of excitement to stem the current of the tide of fury, of rage, or of wrath, and to appeal to the Constitution; to place the people against whom as assault is made or against whom an accusation is brought upon the ground on which we place all other people in dealing with them, fearing lest we might, in an unguarded moment, do ourselves the wrong of violating the Constitution of the country in our attempt to inflict upon other people harsh and sudden legislation.[29]

Morgan warned the bill was introducing one of the most serious violations of the Constitution imaginable – a bill of attainder, which inflicts punishment on an individual or group without a judicial trial. It may be constitutionally allowable to deprive someone of the vote as punishment for a crime, but this could only be done by proper courts in accordance with the law, not by a five-member electoral commission appointed by the federal government. "That right," Morgan argued, "belonged to American civilization and law long before the Constitution was adopted." For this reason, Morgan was taking the "great risk" of antagonizing the Committee on the Judiciary, because allowing such a bill of attainder would be an unprecedented violation not just of the American Constitution, but of the entire English legal tradition as

[29] Ibid.

well: "Never in the darkest days of the Tudors or the Stuarts, never in any of the darkest days of despotism, I undertake to say here, weighing my words deliberately, was there ever enacted a statute more exactly within the meaning of a bill of attainder than the seventh and eighth sections of this bill."[30]

Joseph E. Brown's speech, delivered the same day, also began with an instructive example of tolerance. Asserting that "three-fourths of the whole population of the globe" practices and supports polygamy, he pointed out that the British have made no attempt to exterminate the practice in India, "indeed they dare not," because they could not possibly enforce such a law. While echoing many of Morgan's themes, Brown also raised the idea that the bill would penalize *belief* in polygamy. A polygamist, according to Webster's Unabridged Dictionary, is "a person who practices polygamy, *or maintains its lawfulness*," and "there is scarcely a man, woman or child in Utah belonging to the Mormon Church who does not maintain the *lawfulness* of polygamy." This led to a fierce exchange with George Edmunds himself, the original sponsor of the bill, who argued that, according to all known laws, a polygamist was someone actually practicing polygamy, and thus this bill would not punish anyone merely for believing in polygamy. However, Brown's prediction that the bill would be "a sweeping disfranchisement of almost the entire people of a territory" was accurate. The officials charged with executing the provisions of the Edmunds Act usually did interpret "polygamist" as meaning anyone who professed a belief in polygamy.[31] Furthermore, the provisions of the successor Edmunds-Tucker Act of 1887 would abolish the distinction between belief and practice altogether.

Brown, a former Confederate governor of Georgia, then laid out concerns about the election commission that went beyond universalistic concerns about rights to the heart of the conjoined material interests of Democrats and Southerners. He remarked that Southerners were more familiar with the practice of returning-boards than Northerners:

> Whenever it is necessary to make a Republican state out of a Democratic state, or a Republican State out of a Democratic Territory, the most convenient machinery for that purpose is a returning board, and it has worked admirably in the south. By fraud, perjury, forgery and villainy, the returning-board system cheated the people of these United States out of a legal election for President. It

---

[30] *Congressional Record*, vol. 11, pp. 1196–1200. We can appreciate more fully the seriousness of the bill of attainder accusation if we consider the competing British and American plans about what to do with Nazi leaders at the close of the Second World War. Notes released from Britain's National Archive show that Churchill was resolutely against any trials for captured German leaders, including Hitler, should he fall into British hands (his specific plan for Hitler was to execute him summarily on an electric chair rented from the Americans, which he saw as a fitting end "for gangsters"). This would be facilitated by an Act of Attainder in parliament. Churchill, however, was forced to abandon these plans when the Americans made it clear that they were intent on trials. ("Churchill: Execute Hitler without trial." *The Sunday Times*, January 1, 2006.)

[31] Arrington (1958).

does not therefore specially commend itself to the American people. It stinks in the nostrils of honest men.

Brown was referring both to the Hayes/Tilden election controversy of 1876, in which the Republican-dominated returning boards of Florida, Louisiana, and South Carolina overturned Tilden victories in those states by disallowing a sufficient number of Democratic votes, and also to the Reconstruction-era practice of returning-boards, which had often disfranchised Democratic voters. Brown accepted that the latter might have been justified, but argued it could not be justified for the Mormons:

> After the end of the war the reconstruction measures were passed. I had then a little taste of the rule that we now propose to apply to Utah. I stood by the polls, disfranchised and not permitted to vote, while my former slaves, emancipated, walked up and deposited their ballots. I made no issue. I accepted it. Why? Because I had no power to do anything; and I held that Georgia had seceded from the Union, and having seceded, and having been conquered, the conquering power had the right to dictate the terms. But the Mormons have not seceded from the Union.

Beyond the normative matter of Mormon rights there was a more immediate material concern, and this was that the Republicans would use the returning boards, as Brown said, "to make a Republican state out of a Democratic territory." Since the Civil War, the Republicans had ensured long-term control of both houses by voting to admit states that would reliably provide Republican congressmen. As will be discussed below, the Republicans had proven far more adept at getting their "rotten boroughs" admitted than the Democrats.[32] The Edmunds Act seemed to be preparing yet another one of these boroughs.

Finally, Brown warned that repressing the Mormons could lead to persecution of other groups: "let us be careful that we do not establish precedents that may lead to the destruction of freedom of opinion and the subversion of constitutional liberty and religious toleration in this country." As Morgan had also warned, the popular feeling against the Mormons today could tomorrow be turned on another group:

> We have passed the period where there is for the present any clamor against any particular sect except as against the Mormons; but it seems there must be some periodical outcry against some denomination. Popular vengeance is now turned against the Mormons. When we are done with them I know not who will next be considered the proper subject of it.

Brown backed this warning with cautionary tales of past religious persecution in America, mainly in New England, such as the persecution of Baptists and Catholics in the New England colonies, the burning of the Ursuline convent in Massachusetts, and New Hampshire's archaic law, only recently

---

[32] Stewart and Weingast (1992).

revoked, that Catholics could not serve in the legislature. Though he insisted he was not trying to be offensive to New England, he did seem to be baiting the north. Referring to Massachusetts, he asked,

> If religious intolerance in this most enlightened and intelligent State was so great forty-eight years ago as to incite men to burn down and desecrate the convents of the Catholic Church, and the riot was permitted with impunity, how can we trust ourselves forty-eight years later to make indiscriminate warfare on any Territory of these United States on account of any opinion of theirs, religious or otherwise?

When he began to tell the story of a school for young colored girls in Connecticut that was burned down by a mob, George Frisbie Hoar of Massachusetts bellowed "How was it in Georgia?"[33]

George Vest of Missouri spoke on both days. On February 16, he delivered a tirade on the bill of attainder theme that is noteworthy because it employs a trope very familiar to twentieth- and twenty-first-century liberals: the idea that in the course of fighting our enemies, we risk becoming worse than our enemies.

> Gentlemen proclaim, and justly proclaim, that the hierarchy which, within the dark chamber inaugurated by Brigham Young and Joe Smith, carry out their ecclesiastical theory to the destruction of both body and soul is monstrous, and so it is; but here we propose to inaugurate another star-chamber of five men, responsible to nobody, governed alone by their own prejudices, or passions, or feelings, or opinions; who can say who shall be elected; who can say who shall vote, and who can pass upon all the laws; who can say to the people of the United States "we order this thing." Never in the days of the inquisition was there any more questionable mode of punishment.[34]

The previous day, Vest had examined the specific constitutional issues involved in this kind of measure. He declared it a priori unconstitutional, because "under the Constitution I say that no man can be deprived of the right to vote or to hold office except after conviction." The Edmunds Bill had been framed largely as a means of reforming a territory, but Vest argued that the bill was not the way to do it because it entailed taking away inalienable individual rights: "If Utah were applying for admission into the Union then we could say to her, 'Accept certain conditions;' and if they were within the limitations of the Constitution those conditions of course must be accepted or rejected. But here these rights have been conferred; they are already given."[35]

Florida's Wilkinson Call, speaking on February 15, made the case in terms most similar to the traditional Southern concern with states' rights. States' rights were not the issue here, as Utah was not a state, and the repressive measures of the Edmunds legislation were unlikely to be directly replicated in any Southern state. Nonetheless, a broader principle of democratic self-determination was at stake. "It seems to me," argued Call,

---

[33] *Congressional Record*, vol. 11, pp. 1202–1205.
[34] Ibid., p. 1201.
[35] Ibid., p. 1157.

that if there is anything in the institutions of this country and in the idea of self-government, that is a proposition [the Edmunds electoral commission] which destroys the whole of it.... For myself, sir, I can never vote for a provision which contains a power of this discretion in defiance of the popular will, based entirely upon five persons selected by the executive power of the country.

Call made the familiar declaration that he would personally like to see polygamy stamped out, but that only the judiciary – not a committee appointed by the executive – was fit to enforce any prescriptions for electoral disqualification. To put this power in the hands of the executive took it away from the realm of justice and into that of politics: "It is a subterfuge of creating an assembly which has been done before and elsewhere – creating an assembly of a particular kind by these five persons to really say who shall be the legislature, or allowing them to pass upon this subject."[36]

What insights can we gain from all this speechmaking? The first is that the overall outcome of the Edmunds Act was not an inevitable product of nineteenth-century illiberalism. That Southern Democrats saw fit to use pleas for tolerance and civil liberties as tools of persuasion shows that they carried substantial rhetorical power and were familiar to nineteenth-century audiences. Appealing to liberal tolerance was clearly an important strategy. Whether they were sincere in their pleas is less important than showing that the language of liberalism and due process was valuable currency in the 1882 Congress. We can look at this in the terms proposed by Schattschneider: the Southern Democrats were trying to expand the scope of the conflict by showing that more was at stake than the individual fates of a few polygamists, using the expansive rhetoric of universal rights.[37] If an executive-appointed committee could disfranchise voters, then the United States was abandoning much of the protection it had traditionally provided for dissident minorities and for individuals generally. Thus, congressmen should not complacently approve the Edmunds measures as a matter of course, thinking they would not affect them personally.

The question, then, is why did these liberal appeals fail? They failed to move any Republicans, a majority of Democrats, and even many Southern Democrats. We may be able to explain away the Republicans by the fact they were obviously voting on strict party lines, but we still need to explain why many Democrats were not swayed. We may get some guidance on this question by looking to debates a few years earlier on the assimilation of Catholic migrants. While anti-Catholic politics in America was usually found in the Republican Party (which had absorbed much of the defunct American Party, or Know-Nothings), Democrats often also acquiesced to anti-Popery, despite the fact their party was the natural political home of

[36] Ibid., p. 1156.
[37] Schattschneider, E.E. (1961). *The Semi-Sovereign People: A Realist's View of Democracy*. New York: Holt, Rhinehart and Winston.

Catholic immigrants. The Blaine Amendment, for example, which would have made it nationally illegal to provide government funds for Catholic schools, while retaining funding for Protestant "common schools," passed the house in 1876 with only seven opposing Democratic votes. Philip Hamburger argues that this nineteenth-century anti-Catholicism was no violation of the American liberal tradition; in fact, the perpetrators of it saw themselves as liberals, and frequently described themselves as such.[38] Anti-Catholicism was part of the nineteenth-century liberal Protestant consensus that had adherents on both political sides, and anti-Catholic citizens, politicians, and clergy believed that breaking down the internal authoritarianism of the Catholic Church was an eminently liberal cause.

It is easy to extend this logic to anti-Mormonism. The perceived authoritarianism of the Mormon Church and family structure was a popular target for crusading liberals. Nineteenth-century liberalism had a decidedly authoritarian tone in America. It was about creating a liberal culture, by force if necessary. Before personal autonomy could be respected, individuals had to be liberated from oppressive influences. This may be why the appeals of the Southern Democrats failed to persuade other Democrats, including some Southern Democrats. They were trumped by the rhetoric of the anti-Mormons, which was made in more muscular liberal terms.

Edmunds, for example, argued that his bill would empower those Mormons who did not support polygamy, whom he had frequently insisted were actually the majority:

> Now if there be in this Mormon Church a body of people, as we believe there are, who have no more faith in this idea of polygamy than any Senator who hears me has, as a fact, and who wish to discourage it and who wish to emancipate themselves from the tyranny of this hierarchy that now has its foot on their necks, there will be a cause for them to assert themselves.[39]

If appeals to crusading Protestant liberalism were inherently more appealing to nineteenth-century American politicians than appeals to constitutionalism and due process, this still does not explain why a majority of Southern Democrats were swayed by the latter rather than the former. To explain this, we must turn to quantitative analysis of the vote itself.

QUANTITATIVE ANALYSIS OF THE EDMUNDS VOTE

From previous scholarship and from the rhetoric of congressional debates, four major hypotheses emerge to explain the regional Democratic split on the Edmunds Bill.

---

[38] Hamburger, Philip (2001). "Illiberal Liberalism: Liberal Theology, Anti-Catholicism, and Church Property." *Journal of Contemporary Legal Issues*, 12: 693–726.

[39] *Congressional Record*, vol. 11, p. 1213.

Hypothesis 1: statehood politics, sectionalism, and party competition

As noted earlier, every congressional Democrat should have had a good reason to vote against Edmunds: if the Mormon population of Utah were disfranchised by the returning board, then the heavily Democratic territory would turn Republican. Charles Stewart and Barry Weingast have extensively documented the role of statehood admission politics in the nineteenth-century Congress. They argue that Republican dominance in Congress, which was vital to the continuation of such policies as the tariff, was maintained by Republican maneuvers around the admission on new states. Republicans, for example took advantage of their overwhelming Civil War majority to admit heavily Republican Nevada in 1862, long before its admission could have been justified on the grounds of population. In 1889, Democrats tried to redress the imbalance with the Omnibus Statehood Admission Bill, which in its original form would have admitted two Democratic and two Republican states. However, Republicans managed to get heavily Democratic (and Catholic) New Mexico excluded from the final act with the help of twenty dissenting Democratic votes. Thus, Brown's warning that the returning board was a vehicle "for making a Republican state out of a Democratic territory" was entirely plausible in the case of Utah.

Stewart and Weingast's analysis does not directly explain variance in Democratic voting on statehood matters, but extending their analysis is simple enough. If the goal of congressional Republican office-holding was to facilitate the enactment and maintenance of particular policies then Democrats who were hurt more by these policies should have been more likely to vote against any legislation that established or increased Republican dominance. Republican economic policies during this period redistributed from South to North. A high tariff barrier protected Northern manufacturing centers at the expense of the cash-crop South, and some rents from the tariff were redistributed to Union Civil War veterans in the form of a pension.[40] Thus, we might expect that Southern Democrats would generally be more hawkish on statehood matters than their Northern counterparts, many of whom were sectionally aligned with manufacturing and may have actually benefited from Republican policies. On the other hand, Northern Democrats, while no more anti-Mormon than their Southern counterparts, would have felt less economically threatened by Republican hegemony in Congress, and thus more free to vote on their anti-Mormon beliefs.

To test this explanation, we need a measure of economic interest that is not reducible to regional effects. For this analysis, I use a logged measure of congressional district-level manufacturing value-added.[41] The most important

---

[40] Bensel, Richard Franklin (1984). *Sectionalism and American Political Development 1880–1980.* Madison: The University of Wisconsin Press.

[41] I obtained the raw measure from Parsons, Stanley B., William W. Beach, and Michael J. Dubin (1986). *United States Congressional Districts and Data 1843–1883.* Westport: Greenwood Books.

caveat about this data is that it does not disaggregate manufacturing activity in urban districts; therefore, I assign to urban districts an average measure obtained by dividing total city value-added by its number of districts. I do not believe this affects the substance of the analysis.[42]

Hypothesis 2: disfranchisement and the legacy of Reconstruction

Scholars who have previously examined the Edmunds vote have emphasized the pain and humiliation of the Reconstruction-era returning boards, and infer that white southerners empathized with the Mormons who were about to be subject to the same "tyranny."[43] This is certainly one of the things Brown's speech implies. We can imagine the victims of a certain technique of repression would be so averse to it that they would oppose the use of it even for individuals and groups they hate. If this explanation is correct, then we should expect to see that congressmen who had closer ties to the Confederacy would be more likely to vote against the Edmunds Act. Congressmen who had served in Confederate armies or governments would be more likely to have personally experienced disfranchisement, and also would be more likely to identify with the plight of the South. To obtain a binary measure of whether the congressman served in the Confederate army or in any Confederate government I searched every congressman's biography using the government's online Biographical Dictionary of the United States Congress, 1774–present.[44]

Hypothesis 3: election boards and racial threat

White Southern Democratic congressmen had good reason to fear any extension of federal authority in state and local elections. Southern Democrats were committed to white supremacy in their states, and were building institutions (such as the White Primary and literacy tests for voting) that would prevent most of the Southern black population from voting until the mid-twentieth century. Edmunds, by allowing federal authorities to decide who could or could not vote, threatened to re-establish a norm of federal intervention which had already been used during Reconstruction to increase black representation at the expense of white Southern Democrats. If this concern was influencing Southern congressmen, then we should expect to see

---

[42] One further problem is that, due to coding error, Colorado's manufacturing score is excluded and thus Colorado's representative James Bedford Burns is excluded. As he was a Republican who voted in favor of Edmunds, his vote has extremely low analytical leverage and the analysis will not suffer by his absence.

[43] Buice (1976); Driggs, Kenneth David, 1988. "The Mormon Church-State Confrontation in Nineteenth-Century America." *Journal of Church and State*, 30(2): 273–289.

[44] Available at http://bioguide.congress.gov/biosearch/biosearch.asp, last accessed February 2, 2013.

significantly more negative votes from congressmen in districts with higher black populations. While Democratic congressmen right across the South might have had strong feelings against federal intervention regardless of their own district's racial make-up, there is good reason to believe that office-seeking politicians would have been particularly wary of electoral reforms that would threaten their own seats. This hypothesis also conforms to the expectations of V.O. Key that whites in areas with higher black populations are more likely to vote to maintain white supremacy.[45]

In this study I use a logged measure of the black population percentage of congressional districts to assess racial threat. The raw data was also obtained from *United States Congressional Districts and Data*, and it contains the same caveats as the manufacturing value-added data.

Hypothesis 4: high marginal product of women

In the only previous systematic quantitative analysis of the Edmunds vote, Anderson and Tollison argue that the most important variable driving the voting pattern was whether congressmen came from states where women possessed a relatively high marginal economic product, as measured by the ratio of female to male manufacturing workers in the state.[46] The political-economic logic is as follows. Polygamy is more attractive to women with a high marginal product, given the greater bargaining power they would enjoy in a polygamous marriage.[47] Polygamy is bad for men with a low marginal product, who tend to lose out in the marriage market as a result. The anti-polygamy movement in Congress reflected male concerns (as only men could vote at the time), among which was the supply of marriageable women. States with a higher ratio of women in manufacturing employment were those in which women generally had the highest marginal product, and so where men had the most reason to be concerned about "leakage" in the marriage market as women left for polygamous communities in Utah or elsewhere (including in-state). Therefore, congressmen from these states should have had the greatest incentive to vote in favor of the Edmunds Bill.

To measure this effect, Anderson and Tollison construct a ratio (FMRATIO) of average number of women employed in manufacturing to average number of men employed in manufacturing in a congressman's state. In earlier quantitative analyses of the vote, this variable proved to be significant and amazingly robust. However, it appears that FMRATIO is a proxy for industrialization in general. FMRATIO correlates with a state-level measure of manufacturing value-added

[45] Key, Valdimer Orlando (1949). *Southern Politics in State and Nation*. New York: Vintage Books.

[46] Anderson, Gary M. and Robert D. Tollison (1998). "Celestial marriage and earthly rents: Interests and the prohibition of polygamy." *Journal of Economic Behavior and Organization*, 37(2): 169–181.

[47] Becker, Gary (1981). *A Treatise on the Family*. Cambridge: Harvard University Press.

at a very high level of 0.82. Given this high degree of collinearity, it seems prudent to drop FMRATIO from the analysis altogether. I am comfortable dismissing Anderson and Tollison's hypothesis as implausible, as the cognitive demands it places on actors are too high. It requires women with high marginal product to be aware of the benefits of polygamy, and congressmen to be aware of the relative threat this poses to their state's marriage market according to female/male manufacturing ratios. Furthermore, urban women who worked in nineteenth-century manufacturing enterprises were more likely to be poor than urban women who did not, which casts doubt on FMRATIO's usefulness as a proxy for high female marginal product.[48]

Analysis

I tested the first three hypotheses using logistic regressions in which the congressman's vote on the Edmunds Act was the binary dependent variable ("yea" = 1, "nea" = 0, non-voters are omitted). I have estimated three models here: the first encompasses the whole sample of voting congressmen; the second is all voting Democrats; and the third is all voting Southern Democrats, including the Border South (congressmen from Kentucky, Maryland, and Missouri).[49] I have included the first model, although no Republicans voted

TABLE 4.2: *Logit analysis of final house vote on Edmunds Bill; binary dependent variable is "yea" vote*

	Whole house	Democrats	Southern Democrats
Logged district manufacturing	.532 (.245)**	.552 (.292)*	.632 (.338)*
Logged district black population	−.585 (.167)***	−.471 (.205)**	−.097 (.362)
Served in Confederate army / government	−.600 (.544)	.405 (.629)	.571 (.670)
Constant	−1.764 (2.262)	−3.305 (2.751)	.447 (6.325)
Pseudo-R^2	0.338	0.178	0.050
N	238	108	64

* Significant at $p < 0.1$;
** Significant at $p < 0.05$;
*** Significant at $p < 0.01$ (Two-tailed)

[48] Thanks to Carrie Miles for pointing this out to me at the annual meeting of the Society for the Scientific Study of Religion, Louisville, KY, October 15, 2008.
[49] I decided to include the latter with the South because they too were subject to some Reconstruction measures, and because previous scholarship on this subject has lumped them together. See Buice (1976).

against the measure, to avoid truncating the sample; it is entirely possible that all Republicans voted sincerely and not out of a sense of party loyalty, in which case we must include them or our estimates for the Democrats could have problems. The results are shown in table 4.2:

The first thing to note here is that only the manufacturing variable retains any significance across all three models. It is positively related to a "yes" on the Edmunds vote in all three samples, suggesting that congressmen from districts with higher levels of manufacturing were more likely to vote in favor of Edmunds. In the Democratic-only and Southern Democratic-only samples, its p-values are 0.059 and 0.062 respectively (in a two-tailed test) – meaning the variable does not quite reach the canonical 0.05 level of significance, but nonetheless allowing for substantial confidence in these results. Thus, it appears that the logistic regression provides support for hypothesis 1, with level of manufacturing explaining intra-Democratic and intra-Southern variance on the Edmunds vote.

The other two variables are insignificant in the Democratic and Southern Democratic models, meaning they probably cannot explain any part of intra-party or intra-regional variance. The black population variable is highly significant in the overall sample, reflecting the joint fact that the overwhelming majority of black Americans lived in Southern Democratic congressional districts and the overwhelming majority of "no" votes against Edmunds came from Southern Democrats. Without significant results in the other two models, however, there is no evidence that the black population measure has any explanatory power over why these congressmen voted as they did. This perhaps suggests Southern congressmen believed the Edmunds provisions could only be applied to territories such as Utah. Post-reconstruction and redemption, the federal government could not impose similar measures on Southern states.

The Confederate disfranchisement variable is not significant at any level. In this case, victims of repressive measures were not deterred from using the same measures against others. Despite the impassioned personal speeches on the Senate floor, formerly disfranchised Southern congressmen were no less adverse to mass disfranchisement than anyone else once we control for more strategic material variables. Overall, then, only the first hypothesis seems capable of explaining the "Southern" character of the "no" vote, and why some Democratic congressmen voted against the long-term strategic interests of their party while others voted against the overwhelming national mood of anti-Mormonism.

Table 4.3, representing the substantive effects of each independent variable, provides further confirming evidence for this picture. Over the whole sample, the difference in probability of voting yes on Edmunds between congressmen from the least and most industrialized districts is about 0.27, while the difference in probability between congressmen from the districts with the lowest and highest black populations is about −0.61. However, the magnitudes

TABLE 4.3: *Change in probability of voting "yea" on Edmunds from minimum to maximum values of independent variables*

	Whole house	Democrats	Southern Democrats
Logged district manufacturing	.265	.535	.632
Logged district black population	−.606	−.514	−.096
Served in Confederate army / government	−.056	.090	.138

of these effects change in opposite directions when we examine more specific sub-samples; the difference in probability between the least and most industrialized jumps to 0.53 within the Democratic sample and 0.63 within the Southern Democratic sample, while the difference between the least and most black districts declines slightly to −0.51 within the Democratic sample and then sharply to −0.09 within the Southern Democratic sample. The difference between having not served and having served in the Confederate army is very small (as well as insignificant) across all three samples.

In summary, the very Southern and Democratic profile of the congressional "no" vote on the Edmunds Act cannot simply be explained by "Southern-ness" or "Democratic-ness" due to substantial variance within these groups. It may be explained by other variables that correlated with Southern and Democratic identity – agrarian economic interests, racial composition of congressional districts, or the presence of men who had experienced disfranchisement as the result of serving in the Confederate army. A careful examination of intra-Democratic and intra-Southern variance, along with variance in the whole house, reveals that long-term strategic considerations based on economic interests are what seem to be the strongest influence on the Southern and Democratic composition of the "no" vote.

One implication of these findings is that while the basis of religious *intolerance* in 1882 was ideological, reflecting the national rise of crusading Protestant liberalism, the basis of religious *tolerance* was material, reflecting the agrarian economic interests of Southern Democrats. Southern Democrats seem to have voted against the Edmunds Bill because the economic interests with whom they most strongly identified had the most to lose from Republican domination of the Congress that could eventuate if Utah became a state with no Mormon voters. Ideational factors such as the trauma of Reconstruction seemed to have little to do with the final vote, though the liberal rhetoric of the floor debates show that they understood the importance of making the argument in ideational terms. This has bleak but important implications for minorities in general. Madison argued that:

> Whilst all authority in it will be derived from and dependent on the society, the society itself will be broken into so many parts, interests, and classes of citizens,

that the rights of individuals, or of the minority, will be in little danger from interested combinations of the majority. In a free government the security for civil rights must be the same as that for religious rights. It consists in the one case in the multiplicity of interests, and in the other in the multiplicity of sects.[50]

Occasionally a repressive movement arises which enjoys a near-consensus; anti-Mormonism in the 1880s was one such movement. Anti-Mormonism could become "an interested combination of the majority" because, like anti-Chinese sentiment, it cut across party lines. An 1870 floor speech by Benjamin Butler, arguing for proposed legislation which would prevent Mormons from serving on juries,[51] provides a stark counterpoint to Madison's vision:

> The feeling of all our people demands this question be settled. I think the sentiments of the people are more enlisted in favor of this measure than of any other that is before the house. Upon this I think there is no party division. There is no division of sentiment among good men on the subject. Upon funding bills, tariff bills and tax bills we disagree and divide into parties and sections of parties. But that something should be done here, I think there is no division of sentiment.[52]

Precisely because polygamy was in some ways such a trivial issue – it affected no one but a small, isolated sect of polygamists – the liberal Protestant crusaders were free to pursue their campaign against Mormons without much fear of treading on anyone else's interests, religious, economic, or otherwise. The only thing that tied Southern Democratic interests to the Mormons was the issue of electoral apportionment, which exposed a sectional cleavage that ran deeper than party competition. Were it not for the fact that the anti-polygamy campaign had the potential to further entrench Republican and industrial interests at the expense of Democrats and especially agrarians, Southern Democrats conceivably would have been as anti-Mormon as anyone else.

THE MORMON REALIGNMENT

The Edmunds Act and its successor, the Edmunds-Tucker Act (1887), constituted the most devastating legislative assault on religious freedom in American history. The Edmunds-Tucker Act abandoned any distinction between polygamy as a practice and the LDS church as an institution. In the words of Sarah Barringer Gordon, "the Edmunds-Tucker Act recognized the connections between faith, marriage and property in Mormon culture; then it set out to destroy them."[53] Concerned the Edmunds Act had failed to

---

[50] Madison, James (1787–1788). *The Federalist Papers*, no. 51. Available at www.ourdocuments .gov/doc.php?flash=true&doc=10&page=transcript, last accessed June 4, 2013.

[51] This legislation, the Cullom Bill, passed the House but died in committee, as did several other pieces of anti-Mormon legislation in the 1870s. Butler's speech reflects the frustration of the vocal anti-Mormons in the House at their failure to enact seemingly popular legislation.

[52] *Congressional Globe*, 41st Congress, Second Session, p. 2145.

[53] Gordon (2003), p. 187.

prevent polygamy by the mid-1880s, Congress passed legislation in 1887 disincorporating the church and allocating its assets to public (i.e., de facto Protestant) schools. Edmunds-Tucker also disfranchised women, replaced local judges with federal appointees, and required polygamous wives to testify against their husbands, abrogating a common-law right. As a religion, the Mormons now faced a serious existential threat. It was this that finally forced the leadership to negotiate a series of bargains that would allow the church to survive and begin the slow process of reintegrating Mormons into mainstream American life.

As federal authorities threatened to seize Mormon temples in the late 1880s, Church President Wilford Woodruff (the successor to Young's charismatic successor, John Taylor) issued a decree, the "First Manifesto," that the Church would abandon plural marriage for the sake of complying with the laws of the land. This restored the vote and representation for Mormons, but they still had yet to achieve full political rights in the form of statehood for Utah, which was still an effective colony of the United States. By 1890 Utah had easily passed the unofficial population threshold required for statehood, but permanent Republican opposition ensured that Utah remained a territory without representation in the Senate.[54]

The Mormon leadership had dissolved the People's Party in 1891, but the necessary Republican support for Utah statehood was unlikely to materialize while Mormons still voted as a bloc for Democratic candidates. From 1892, President Woodruff and his advisers conducted an aggressive campaign to change the affiliation of a large number of Mormons to the Republican Party. It was rumored that national Republicans had offered to quell a national anti-polygamy amendment and to help bail the church out of its financial difficulties in exchange for Mormon support.[55] Three church leaders who had campaigned for the Democratic Party were censured, and despite assurances from the presidency that the church would not dictate how its members should vote, one of the censured leaders noted that other leaders were "interfering with the agency of members of the church by going around trying to get Democrats to become Republicans or getting Democrats to vote for certain Republicans." Thomas Alexander argues "If no ecclesiastical influence had been used to recruit Republicans, it is highly unlikely not only that the old Mormon-Gentile political alignments would have returned in the form of national parties but that the Republicans would have refused to support the movement for Utah statehood."[56]

[54] Stewart, Charles and Barry, Weingast (1992). "Stacking the Senate, Changing the Nation: Republican Rotten Boroughs, Statehood Politics, and American Political Development." *Studies in American Political Development*, 6(2): 223–271.

[55] Arrington and Bitton (1992), p. 247.

[56] Alexander, Thomas G. (1986). *Mormonism in Transition: A History of the Latter-Day Saints, 1890–1930*. Urbana and Chicago: University of Illinois Press, pp. 8–9.

In Mormon folk memory, church authorities traveled to congregations throughout Utah and "divided the people politically according to which side of the meetinghouse they happened to be sitting on at that time." While this is probably apocryphal, one Mormon did swear in an affidavit that a visiting church leader told his congregation in the South of Utah that "the authorities desired us to divide equally on national party lines in order that we could receive favors from whichever party was in power."[57] Thus, the Mormon people were welcomed as full participants in American democracy.

---

[57] Lyman, Edward L. (1986). *Political Deliverance: The Quest for Utah Statehood*. Champaign: University of Illinois Press, pp. 165–166.

5

Jehovah's Witnesses and the flag salute, 1870–1940

INTRODUCTION

When Jehovah's Witnesses suffered mass public violence in the 1940s, observers drew parallels between their ordeal and that of the Mormons. But despite their shared experience of persecution, Jehovah's Witnesses were very different from Mormons and were persecuted in very different ways. While the federal government sometimes targeted Jehovah's Witnesses – most notably after America's entry into each World War, when Witnesses were imprisoned for refusing to be conscripted – the most violent persecutions of Jehovah's Witnesses occurred with passive rather than active state involvement. At the local level, police and sheriffs often allowed assaults and intimidation to take place, sometimes coming to the assistance of Witnesses but other times helping their antagonists. At the federal level, the government condemned the persecution of Jehovah's Witnesses but did almost nothing to stop it.

Jehovah's Witnesses, unlike Mormons, never aspired to create a new polity, and actively avoided political involvement. While the Mormons were a national obsession in the nineteenth century, Jehovah's Witnesses were barely known or understood in the twentieth. As I will show over the next two chapters, the threat they posed to political order was symbolic rather than material. They posed no challenge to state sovereignty, but by refusing to salute the American flag they disrupted a ritual of national unity and consensus. This made them powerful enemies in civil society, especially the American Legion, for whom the flag salute was an important affirmation of the social and political status of war veterans. Local law enforcement agencies, as I will show in the following chapter, had little reason to side with Jehovah's Witnesses over the American Legion in their communities.

In Chapter 6 I explore the patterns of mass violence against Jehovah's Witnesses and explain the state response to it. In this chapter I trace the historical trajectory of Jehovah's Witnesses and the origins of the conflict that led to the spectacular persecution of the 1940s. While the flag salute conflict came to define the experience of Jehovah's Witnesses in the 1940s, it was not the only point of tension between them and broader society. Witnesses were openly hostile to the Catholic Church, and they expected to be persecuted for this reason, but this kind of religious conflict never eventuated. I show why the flag salute in particular became the issue that turned civil society against Jehovah's Witnesses, largely because of the involvement of the American Legion.

ORIGINS OF JEHOVAH'S WITNESSES

Prior to 1919, the sect that came to be known as Jehovah's Witnesses referred to themselves simply as "Bible Students." From their beginnings in 1881 until the death of their founder Charles Taze Russell in 1916, they lacked many features of a traditional religious organization. Russell founded a publishing company rather than a church: the Watch Tower Bible and Tract Society of Pennsylvania. Originally the Bible Students were a loose collection of congregations independently organized around the Watch Tower's scriptural studies. From its earliest days the Watch Tower Society was distinguished by its huge output of printed material, an output that has continued to grow exponentially.[1]

Unlike Joseph Smith, Russell never claimed to be a prophet. Prophecy was at the center of his writings – the Watch Tower's main appeal was the urgency of its message that the end of human existence was near. But Russell's claims were based on his reading and interpretation of the Bible, not divine inspiration. Born in Pittsburgh in 1852, Russell was heavily influenced in the 1870s by Adventist scholars, especially George Storrs and Nelson H. Barbour. From the writings of Storrs he adopted the doctrine of conditionalism – the idea that humans are not born with eternal souls but can only be given them by God through Jesus Christ. For Russell it followed from this that there is no hell; the mortal human soul dies along with the body. From a close association with Barbour, he developed a chronology derived from the Bible that predicted the beginning of the millennial age in the short-term future.

In 1877 Russell and Barbour published *Three Worlds and the Harvest of This World*, which claimed the end times had begun in 1874 and would come to a conclusion with the triumph of Christ's kingdom on Earth in 1914.[2] The rapture of Christ's chosen saints would occur in 1878, according to Barbour's

---

[1] This section on Charles Taze Russell and the early Bible Students draws on two main secondary sources; Penton, M. James (1997). *Apocalypse Delayed: The Story of Jehovah's Witnesses.* Toronto: University of Toronto Press, pp. 13–46 and 184–208; and Beckford, James (1975). *The Trumpet of Prophecy: A Sociological Study of Jehovah's Witnesses.* New York: John Wiley and Sons.

[2] Because the first stage of the end times had already begun, Russell argued that Christ had already returned to earth as an invisible presence. According to Penton, this idea of an invisible return had been circulating in British and American evangelical millenarian circles since the 1820s (1997, p. 18). Russell convinced Barbour and other early associates of the invisible presence of Christ, which resolved apparent problems with their chronology.

calculations. Early Adventist converts to the Russell–Barbour chronology were disillusioned when the rapture did not occur. This non-event, along with Barbour's abandonment of Russell's "ransom price" theory of atonement, caused a bitter split between Russell and Barbour.[3] While Barbour set out to formulate a new chronology, Russell began a new magazine, *Zion's Watch Tower*, and continued to build a following. Not for the last time, he explained that the previously given end date for the transformation of Christ's saints was actually the starting date; he would give the same explanation in 1881 and 1914 when they also failed to transpire as end dates.

Russell broke with both Adventism and mainstream Christianity completely in 1882, when he rejected the doctrine of the Trinity in favor of Arian theology.[4] By this time he was the leader of a distinctive religious movement with a core of followers who had remained loyal despite the eschatological disappointments of 1878 and 1881. He was recognized as "Pastor" by a growing number of congregations organized around his writings, which he would visit for scriptural study sessions. Recognizing that the congregations were becoming too numerous and dispersed for him to reach, he advertised for 1,000 preachers in 1881. That year he also founded the Watch Tower Society in Allegheny, Pennsylvania, and distributed 1.45 million copies of his book *Food for Thinking Christians*. The first Bible Student missionaries went to England and Canada.

The original organization of the Bible Students was democratic and liberal. Congregations elected their own elders, and Russell initially tolerated a wide range of theological beliefs as long as they did not contradict the fundamentals of his teachings. This form of organization reflected Russell's distrust of religious organizations and clergy, which he believed interfered with the message of Christ. The notion that churches and clergy had corrupted scriptural truth, turning the vast majority of nominal Christians away from "true" Christianity, would become an increasingly prominent and aggressive feature of Witness proselytism after Russell's death. While Russell's organization encouraged all students to think of themselves as preachers, they did not engage in the kind of proselytism for which Jehovah's Witnesses would later become famous. Because Christ's truth would become apparent to all as the end times progressed in the lead-up to 1914, when all would be given a

---

[3] In contrast to the Adventist belief that Christ would destroy the earth in the millennium, Russell believed that Christ's death was the "ransom price" paid to Satan to restore the earth and mankind to Edenic perfection. While only a few chosen saints would go to heaven (as in Calvinist theology), for the rest of mankind there was the possibility of eternal life on earth under the rule of Christ.

[4] Arianism was a fourth-century Christian heresy which held that the son of God had not always existed, but had been created by God at a later date and was thus subordinate to him. Jehovah's Witnesses continue to reject Trinitarian theology, arguing also that the Holy Spirit is not a separate person, but the applied force of God's will. See the 2008 Witness publication *What Does the Bible Really Teach?* pp. 201–204. Available at www.jw.org/en/publications/books/bible-teach/

chance to convert, there was little need to preach to outsiders. Students instead concentrated on their own transformation in Christ.

Russell's keenness to avoid the trappings of "religion," however, gradually led him to centralize the Bible Student organization and impose more doctrinal strictness. He warned in *Zion's Watch Tower* against local congregations turning into "social club churches" and encouraged them to hold weekly devotional meetings along with their Bible studies. In 1894 he implemented annual Memorial meetings which brought large numbers of Students together under the supervision of leaders from Watch Tower headquarters, and, in 1899, volunteers assumed responsibility for distributing Watch Tower publications among their own congregations. As Russell further developed his scriptural teachings and became increasingly convinced of the exclusive truth of his version of Christianity, this distribution network enabled him to exercise more doctrinal control over congregations through Watch Tower publishing.[5]

As mentioned earlier, Russell never claimed the mantle of a prophet. His wife, however, encouraged his followers to think of him as the "faithful and wise servant" of the Book of Matthew, the "chief servant of the truth." Russell never openly adopted this title, but he did nothing to discourage it. After his death in 1916, *The Watch Tower* said he had privately admitted that he was indeed the faithful and wise servant.[6] There were schisms in the Bible Student movement in 1894 and 1908–1909, as some followers came to believe Russell was becoming too autocratic and refused to accept his doctrine of the "New Covenant," which he reiterated in 1907.[7] Despite these schisms, Russell's organization continued to flourish. By 1914 Bible

---

[5] Beckford (1975), pp. 7–9; Penton (1997), pp. 29–33. The observation that churches have a central role in American social life has persisted from at least Tocqueville's *Democracy in America* (1835) to Putnam and Campbell's *American Grace* (2010). For just as long and just as persistently, faith leaders demanding more scriptural purity have complained that the social function of churches has surpassed their spiritual function in America. For an extreme but instructive comparison, see Qutb, Sayyid (1951). "The America I Have Seen." Reprinted in Kamal Abdel-Masek, ed. (2000). *America in an Arab Mirror: Images of America in Arabic Travel Literature*. London: Palgrave MacMillan.

[6] Penton (1997), pp. 33–35. Maria Russell originally made the claim in correspondence in the mid-1890s with Bible Students and associates of Russell who were having doubts about his increasing prominence. *The Watch Tower* Memorial Edition of December 1, 1916, stated that "Thousands of readers of Pastor Russell's writings believe that he filled the office of that 'faithful and wise servant,' and that his great work was giving to the household of faith meat in due season. His modesty and humility precluded him from openly claiming this title, but he admitted as much in private" (p. 35).

[7] Russell, and subsequent generations of his followers, believed they were the true church, the "body of Christ," and that 144,000 of them (including "ancient worthies") would ascend to heaven before the millennium, when the rest of mankind would be given the opportunity for salvation. For Russell, this meant that the New Covenant of the scriptures, which replaced the original covenant the Lord made with Moses, was *not* the covenant of the church. Rather, the church, as the body of Christ, was part of the sacrifice and redemption of Christ. Only after the 144,000 had been raptured would the New Covenant then be offered to the whole of mankind (Penton 1997, pp. 40–42 and 187–189).

Students were present in many countries, and Russell was constantly traveling abroad in his role as their Pastor.

For decades, Russell had set 1914 as the firm date by which the rapture of the body of Christ would be complete and the millennium would begin. The outbreak of the First World War averted disappointment; Russell and his followers took it as visible confirmation that the end had at last begun. Russell's death from illness in 1916 presented a far greater crisis of faith, as he had predicted that he and the church would be raptured together at the war's end. With Russell dead but his church and the war both continuing, many followers were at a loss. A predictable succession crisis began, and as the United States entered the war, the Bible Students for the first time came into conflict with the state.[8]

For a founder of an unorthodox, apocalyptic Christian sect who gained thousands of followers, Russell generated relatively little controversy outside of his own church. Later polemicists who wanted to discredit Russell had to rely on the only contemporary denunciation of him – a 1916 obituary by the *Brooklyn Eagle*, a paper against which he had litigated for seven years. The obituary stated that "Although he styled himself a 'pastor' and was so addressed by millions of followers around the world, he had never been ordained and had no ministerial standing in any religious sect other than his own." It also suggested that Russell had moved from Pennsylvania to Brooklyn to escape adverse publicity over alimony litigation, and that the Bible Students were primarily a money-making operation for Russell.[9]

While the *Eagle's* obituary denied Russell's clerical credentials and accused him of fraud, it was probably only written because of Russell's close proximity to the newspaper and his personal battles with it. Despite being a national (and indeed international) religious figure by this point, Russell's death attracted no other media attention. In the century since his death there has been little effort to expand knowledge of his life. In his study of American religious outsiders, R. Laurence Moore notes that relatively little is known about the life of Russell, despite his founding of a publishing empire, his establishment of an international missionary network, and his own copious output of prophetic writing:[10] "Unlike many other religious innovators in the nineteenth century, Joseph Smith, Ellen White, Mary Baker Eddy, we do not have any adequate

---

[8] Penton (1997), pp. 45–46. Russell urged conscientious objection to the war effort, which brought an irate official reaction in Canada. This stance, according to Penton, was a manifestation of "apolitical Apocalypticism."

[9] "'Pastor' C.T. Russell dies; burial here." *Brooklyn Eagle*, November 1, 1916. For "anti-cult" tracts that attack the Witnesses and make use of this obituary, see Hoekema, Anthony A. (1963). *The Four Major Cults: Christian Science, Jehovah's Witnesses, Mormonism, Seventh-day Adventism*. Grand Rapids: William B. Eerdmans Publishing Company; and Martin, Walter (1996). *The Kingdom of the Cults*. Minneapolis: Bethany House Publishers.

[10] Russell's written works total around 50,000 pages, and during his lifetime nearly 20 million copies of his books were distributed (Penton 1997, p. 26).

biography of Russell. That is too bad, because he is one of the most interesting."[11]

The contrast with Joseph Smith is particularly stark. As shown in Chapter 3, Smith received prodigious media attention in his own lifetime. Numerous biographies have been published since his death that continue to revisit the controversies of his life.[12] Russell's name, however, is hardly known at all. Part of the disparity in interest between the two leaders – whose religions are today roughly equal in size – must lie in the nature of their prophecies. Russell's teachings were diffused over tens of thousands of pages of Bible studies. While radical, his theology was grounded in earlier Adventist and other heterodox Christian thought, and many would have found it difficult to distinguish his teaching from that of other evangelical millenarians who gained followings in the nineteenth century. Smith, on the other hand, presented a text of supposedly divine origin for which he claimed equal authority with the Bible. Russell's work, while it also had a compelling message, was much easier to ignore for those who were unconvinced by it.

Russell, additionally, was not a political leader. He attracted followers by his writings, whose exposure he maximized though an impressive distribution network. His authority lay in his interpretation of the scriptures, and was limited to the spiritual lives of his students. Smith built a religion that was also a polity. Mormons made not just religious, but also social, economic, and political commitments to Smith, to the extent of living in communities under his rule. The extent of Smith's power created far more tension and conflict with broader society than Russell ever did, and hence attracted far more public interest.

Russell's successor, however, was different. Joseph Franklin Rutherford was a much more ambitious, antagonistic leader who demanded and received far greater loyalty from his followers. Rutherford was the leader who redefined the Bible Students as Jehovah's Witnesses, a totalistic sect defined by their hostility to the outside world and their mission to redeem it.

Rutherford and the transformation of Jehovah's Witnesses

"Judge" Joseph Rutherford was a Missouri-born lawyer, trained through the traditional apprenticeship system, who had been baptized as a Bible Student in 1906. He had served important legal and administrative roles in Russell's organization, and because the organization was a publishing company rather than a church, his administrative skills made him a good candidate to take over the presidency of the company after Russell's death. He was unanimously elected as president in 1917, but this did not make him Russell's spiritual heir; in

[11] Moore (1986), pp. 136–137.
[12] Fawn Brodie rekindled debates about whether Smith was a fraud with *No Man Knows My History*, published in 1945. The controversy has not gone away, and Brodie's work continues to be widely read and cited.

this respect Russell had left no successor. Rutherford refused to take Russell's title of "Pastor." [13]

Rutherford immediately asserted his authority. He expelled four opponents from the Watch Tower Society board, against Russell's apparent wishes that board directors would hold life appointments. Rutherford consolidated his power at the 1918 Annual General Meeting, where he was re-elected along with his personal nominees for board directors. Many prominent Bible Students left the organization in protest, which only served to strengthen Rutherford's authority. By 1923, internal opposition to Rutherford was virtually extinguished. The external threats he faced in his early years as president were more serious.

In the summer of 1917, Rutherford escalated the Bible Students' campaign denouncing militarism and clerical support for the war, particularly through the pamphlet *The Finished Mystery*. Bible Students who refused military service in Canada were imprisoned in camps where they were subject to brutal treatment.[14] Possession of Bible Student literature became a crime in Canada in 1918, punishable by up to five years in prison. In the United States, eight Watch Tower directors, including Rutherford, were arrested for sedition under the new American Espionage Act. Judge H.B. Howe of the US District Court in Brooklyn sentenced seven of the eight to twenty years' imprisonment for "conspiracy to cause insubordination, disloyalty, and refusal of duty in the military forces of the United States." Howe's blistering opinion left no doubt about the state's priority of national consensus over religious freedom in wartime:

> In the opinion of the court, the religious propaganda which these defendants have vigorously advocated and spread throughout the nation, as well as among our allies, is a greater danger than a division of the German Army. If they had taken guns and swords and joined the German army the harm they could have done would have been insignificant compared with the results of their propaganda. A person preaching religion usually has much influence, and if he is sincere, he is all the more effective. This aggravates rather than mitigates the wrong they have done.[15]

After the proceedings, Howe reaffirmed his contention that religion was an aggravating rather than a mitigating factor in wartime treason, telling another judge "They are worse than traitors. You can catch a traitor and know what he

---

[13] Penton (1997), pp. 47–48. Russell had nominated no successor at all; Beckford says this "suggests that he understood the peculiar nature and locus of the paternalistic authority that he had exercised for nearly forty years" (1975, p. 22). Russell had instead intended that the editorial functions of the magazine be taken over by a committee of five, completely separating the administration of publishing from his role as spiritual leader.

[14] Penton, James M. (1976). *Jehovah's Witnesses in Canada: Champions of Freedom of Speech and Worship*. Toronto: MacMillan of Canada, pp. 69–70.

[15] *New York Times* (1918). "20 Years in Prison for Seven Russellites: Judge Howe Scores Men Who Give Aid to the Enemy under the Guise of Religion." June 22, 1918, p. 18.

is about. But you cannot catch a man who does what they did under the guise of religion." The other judge reportedly nodded in agreement.

This mass incarceration incapacitated the movement as Bible Students suffered violent harassment in the streets, foreshadowing the treatment they would receive during the Second World War.[16] However, Rutherford and the other directors were only held for nine months. Supreme Court Justice Louis Brandeis ordered their release on bail in March 1919. In April, the US Circuit Court of Appeals reversed their convictions, ruling that the defendants had not received a fair trial. Judge Henry G. Ward found that the government had intimidated witnesses during the trial and prejudiced the jury.[17] A year later the Federal District Court in Brooklyn dismissed all charges against them, though Judge Chatfield "expressed the opinion that the result of the first trial was beneficial, both to the defendants and the country."[18] As difficult as this period was, shared persecution probably strengthened the bonds of solidarity between Rutherford and the Bible Students, who re-elected him and his directors in absentia in January 1919.

On his release, Russell began to organize the proselytizing effort that became, and remains, central to the identity of Jehovah's Witnesses. Bible Students began house-to-house distribution of a new magazine, *The Golden Age*, and from 1920 all congregants had responsibility for evangelism. Whereas Russell had proudly told other religious leaders that his organization kept no membership rolls, Rutherford instituted a system, still in use, in which all individual Bible Students had to report on their proselytizing activity.[19] By making evangelism

---

[16] While this episode of persecution certainly deserves more attention in this book, there is unfortunately very little information about it. The mobbing of Bible Students and the arrests of their leaders receive little more than passing mentions in the major historical works on Jehovah's Witnesses in the United States. There were only about a dozen brief articles in major newspapers about the convictions of Watch Tower directors, and none about violence against Bible Students. The Canadian case is covered more thoroughly in Penton (1976).

[17] *New York Times* (1919). "High Court Annuls Russellite Verdict: U.S. Circuit Court Judges Find Men Convicted of Obstructing Draft Did Not Have Fair Trial." May 16, 1919, p. 24.

[18] *New York Times* (1920). "Nine Russellites Go Free: Eight Had Served Part of 20–Year Espionage Sentences." May 6, 1920, p. 6.

[19] For contemporary Jehovah's Witnesses, around sixteen hours of service per month are required for a Witness to be considered a "publisher," the minimal tier of full membership (the designation in Rutherford's era was "class worker"). Pioneers must commit to ninety hours of proselytism per month, and auxiliary pioneers to sixty. All must report their hours of service, and the organization makes aggregate data on service available every year in the *Year Book of Jehovah's Witnesses*. In 2004, the global peak number of publishers was about 6.5 million, and they collectively performed about 1.3 billion hours of service. Many individuals who identify as Jehovah's Witnesses but do not qualify as publishers attend the annual Memorial Service, originally instituted by Russell, for which attendance is also kept. Global 2004 attendance was around 16.8 million. Jehovah's Witnesses are perhaps the only large religious group in the world who regularly track exits of their members; as such, their data is far more accurate and reliable than most. See Stark, Rodney, and Laurence R. Iannaccone (1997). "Why the Jehovah's Witnesses Grow *so* Rapidly: A Theoretical Application." *Journal of Contemporary Religion*, 12(2): 133–157.

the central responsibility of religious life, Rutherford had implemented a doctrinal shift away from Russell's emphasis on "character development," the Students' own transformation in Christ. This alienated many older Bible Students who could not be swayed from Russell's very clear views on the subject. Rutherford, to make the changes he saw as necessary, needed to break the identification of the Watch Tower with Russell. To this end, he published articles in 1927 discrediting the idea of Russell as "the faithful and wise servant," instead arguing the "servant" was the remnant of the elect of God on Earth, the 144,000 saints.[20]

The change of name to "Jehovah's Witnesses" from "Bible Students" reflected that by the end of the 1920s, many Bible Students had turned away from Rutherford and formed independent congregations remaining (they believed) faithful to Russell's teachings. Several Russellite organizations still exist, and some sociologists of religion argue that Jehovah's Witnesses should be seen as the largest offshoot of the Russell organization rather than a continuation of it.[21] From 1931, Rutherford used the term "Jehovah's Witnesses," derived from the Book of Isaiah, to distinguish his followers from the "evil servants" who had formed independent Bible Student groups.[22]

Rutherford took a much darker view of the millennium than Russell. He believed humanity would be divided into saved and unsaved classes, which were already visible in the world. Satan's corruption permeated every organization apart from Rutherford's own, and those with allegiances to other organizations would not be saved. The most corrupt institutions of all were the state and religions – the Witnesses did not regard themselves as a religion, which is an instrument of Satan. Their hostility toward religion and state would become a defining theme of their literature and their interactions with the world.

WITNESS ANTI-CATHOLICISM: UNRECIPROCATED HOSTILITY

Previous historical accounts have agreed that the confrontational style of proselytism the Witnesses adopted during the Rutherford era contributed to their persecution at the hands of civic groups.[23] Not all confrontations, however, elicited the same response. While Witnesses' refusal to salute the American flag was the greatest provocation for violence against them, Witnesses were not trying to be provocative over the flag salute issue. Where the Witnesses actually looked for and expected confrontations was in the arena of religious rivalry – and in particular their campaign against the Catholic Church. Here, they believed they were in direct conflict with Satan, and they expected to bring persecution upon themselves. Yet, for the most part, the

---

[20] Penton (1997), pp. 59–60.
[21] Stark and Iannaccone (1997), p. 134.
[22] Penton (1997), p. 62.
[23] Manwaring (1960), pp. 163–165.

Catholic Church did not play its part as persecutor. It is worth examining Witness anti-Catholicism in some depth, because it is a good example of how religious antagonism alone has not been enough to cause religious conflict in the United States.

Jehovah's Witnesses had one of the most "exclusivist" theologies imaginable during the Rutherford era, as opposed to the inclusiveness of the Russell period.[24] Russell had believed all of mankind would be given the opportunity for salvation, but in Rutherford's understanding only Christians who recognized the great truths revealed by Jehovah's Witnesses had any chance of being saved. Rutherford put it in stark terms in "Angels," a 1934 pamphlet: "The two classes are clearly and distinctly marked out by the Scriptures, one doomed to absolute and complete destruction, the other having a possibility of recovery."[25]

The Witnesses distinguished themselves, true Christian people, from "religions," instruments of Satan. Religions, including other Christian churches, were actively obstructing salvation. In 1937 Rutherford coined a slogan that would become central to their proselytism, "Religion is a racket."[26] When they defended their constitutional rights during the persecutions of the 1940s, Jehovah's Witnesses almost never referred to "freedom of religion," but to their freedom of speech, assembly, and their right to worship Jehovah God as they saw fit. In legal documents individual Witnesses would refer to themselves as "a Christian" or "one of Jehovah's Witnesses," never as "a Jehovah's Witness," which would have reified the name to refer to them as members of a man-made group.

Though all religions were corrupted and doomed in Witness thinking, the Catholic Church always held a privileged position in Witness demonology. Rutherford and other leaders spilled far more ink denouncing the Catholic hierarchy than any other religious group. Witness critiques of Catholicism, especially the accusation that Catholics were intent on destroying American democracy and religious freedom, reflected century-old American Protestant fears about the foreign, authoritarian religious monolith. The Witnesses may have had a distinctive theological justification for loathing the Catholic Church, but their anti-Catholicism also followed established patterns in the rhetoric of American religious conflict.

For Jehovah's Witnesses, Catholicism represented the original corruption of Christianity. Rutherford's introduction to the 1927 Yearbook of the International Bible Students' Association tells a lengthy story that illustrates the way that Jehovah's Witnesses defined themselves in opposition to Catholics. Rutherford's account is intended to refute "[t]he enemy," who has "attempted

[24] Glock, Charles Y. and Stark, Rodney (1966). *Christian Beliefs and Anti-Semitism*. New York: Harper and Row.
[25] Stroup, Herbert Hewitt (1945). *The Jehovah's Witnesses*. New York: Columbia University Press, p. 150.
[26] Ibid., p. 152.

to induce the people to believe that the International Bible Students' Association is another religious sect operated for selfish purposes." Rutherford identifies the Witnesses as contemporary performers of the divine commission of evangelism described in the Book of Isaiah,[27] a commission that Jesus and his disciples had begun to perform.

Jesus's disciples planted the "noble vine" of God's church, but soon after "Satan planted the false seed among the true"; selfish men entered the church and used it for their own aggrandizement. They posed as representatives of the Lord, but were "the representatives of the world, which is the Devil's organization." The selfish men – the clergy – sought worldly rank and distinction and allied themselves with the state. They relied on state revenues rather than voluntary contributions and the church became an enormous source of wealth, while the clergy became lazy and indifferent to the wants of the people. Magistrates enforced dogmas. An imposing hierarchy was formed, culminating in the Bishop of Rome, and men rose through its ranks not by their piety but by their influence with the powerful. "The Catholic system," writes Rutherford, "organized in the name of the Lord, soon became a mighty component of the Devil's organization. The true worship of God was forgotten, and there was substituted formalism instead, and the Devil's organization paraded in the name of the Lord."[28]

Rutherford's charges against Catholicism bound together secular and religious complaints; that the Catholic Church was inherently oppressive because of its alliance with the state was a long-standing accusation by American Protestants who juxtaposed their own traditions of state non-involvement with the specter of Catholic allegiance to foreign princes.[29] He relied heavily on nineteenth-century American historians whose work reflected this anti-Catholic sentiment, especially John Lord's book *The Old Roman World*.[30] Rutherford's own innovation was to argue that the church–state alliance was the means by which Satan had brought the religious organization under his control.

<hr>

[27] "The Spirit of the Lord God is upon me; because the Lord hath anointed me to preach good tidings unto the meek: he hath sent me to bind the broken-hearted, to proclaim liberty to the captives, and the opening of the prison to them that are bound; to proclaim the acceptable year of the Lord, and the day of vengeance of our God; to comfort all that mourn." Isaiah 61: 1, 2.

[28] Rutherford, Joseph F. (1926). "Introduction" in *Year Book of the International Bible Students Association*. Brooklyn: International Bible Students Association.

[29] See Chapter 6; see also Higham, John (1965). *Strangers in the Land: Patterns of American Nativism 1860–1925*. New York: Atheneum, pp. 77–87.

[30] Rutherford quotes Lord extensively. Lord, who was very popular in the late nineteenth century, argues that the church–state alliance fatally weakened the Roman Empire. Some of his arguments – that state revenues made the clergy lazy, unresponsive, and obsessed with political power – echo Adam Smith's arguments about the sclerosis of established churches that depend on the state, a line of thought that has been revived in recent decades by "supply side" scholars of religion in economics, political science and sociology. See Iannaccone, Laurence R. (1998). "Introduction to the Economics of Religion." *Journal of Economic Literature*, XXXVI: 1465–1496.

Rutherford believed the Protestant churches were also part of "Satan's organization," but he at least credits their founders (such as Luther and Calvin) with making "bold strokes for religious freedom" and "turning the minds of the people back to the true worship of God," and he notes there were many good and honest Christians in the Protestant churches before they were captured by the enemy. The means by which they were captured was association with worldly power: "All of these so-called church organizations combined and affiliated with the political part of Satan's organization, and there properly applies to them the name of Babylon."

Jehovah's Witnesses defined themselves as the group that would save Christianity from Satan's various earthly fronts. For 1,500 years, Rutherford explains, "true Christians" had been captives of the religious organizations, and all they could do was pray for the second coming of Christ to deliver them completely. Charles Taze Russell was one of those who was hoping for the second coming, and while studying the Lord's word God "opened his mind to a clearer understanding," revealing to him some of the "great truths" that had been suppressed by the self-interested leaders of religious organizations. The great truths Rutherford describes form the core of doctrine that distinguish Jehovah's Witness theology from mainstream Christianity: that hell is a condition of oblivion rather than eternal torment, that the judgment of men will be based on their actions after the resurrection when they are given the chance to know the Lord, and the Lord's kingdom will be established on Earth. Russell began to preach these revelations, and thus the Lord began to gather the "true saints," truly consecrated Christians who had been in captivity to the false church systems. When they saw the truths proclaimed by Russell they "broke away from Babylon....The Lord turned their captivity into freedom, and they rejoiced in the knowledge that he had given them and delighted to spread this good news to others."

This account, which the prolific Rutherford repeated in many publications, is the constitutive story of the Jehovah's Witnesses during the period of his leadership. It is a story that implies the necessity of antagonistic proselytism among other Christian denominations, so that other "true Christians" might hear and recognize the great truths that have been suppressed by their religious leaders. As the agents of Satan had for centuries been suppressing true Christianity while using Christianity as protective coloration, Witnesses could expect organized resistance to their efforts – this was how they explained the various persecutions they encountered across America and around the world. Whatever the evidence, in the 1930s and early 1940s Jehovah's Witnesses nearly always saw the Catholic Church at the root of these persecutions. They may have objected to all other churches, but, like other American Protestants a century earlier, the Witnesses saw the Catholic Church as "the enemy," the prime antithetical force against which they defined themselves.[31]

---

[31] For a discussion of constitutive stories of peoplehood, see Smith, Rogers (2003). *Stories of Peoplehood: The Politics and Morals of Political Membership.* New York: Cambridge University Press.

For Rutherford the ultimate culminations of the satanic church–state alliance were Nazism and Fascism, which he believed were directed by the Vatican. Jehovah's Witnesses were particularly concerned with Nazism because Bible Students in Germany were being imprisoned and killed by the regime; the first conscientious objector executed in Germany was August Dickmann, a Bible Student, shot for "refusing to fulfill his duties as a soldier" in September of 1939.[32] By the end of the war 10,000 German Bible Students had been put in concentration camps and 2,500 had been killed.[33]

In 1940 the *New York Post* interviewed Rutherford about the persecution of Jehovah's Witnesses, and the Watch Tower Society published an expanded version as *Judge Rutherford Uncovers Fifth Column*, one of the most useful documents available for understanding the Rutherford-era worldview of the Jehovah's Witnesses and one to which individual Witnesses repeatedly referred in legal documents.[34] When asked why there has been "a sudden recent outburst of violence against Jehovah's Witnesses in widely separated parts of the country," Rutherford replies "The Roman Catholic Hierarchy, operating what they call 'Catholic Action,' are carrying out a well-laid scheme to destroy everything in this world that publishes the truth, and this the Hierarchy are doing to camouflage their own wicked action in attempting to grab control of the nations of the earth."

The Hierarchy, Rutherford claims, is working in worldwide concert with the Nazis, Fascists, and Communists. In the United States various public officials have acted in conjunction with Catholic priests to attack Jehovah's Witnesses because they have written and published more than anyone else against Nazism, Fascism, and Communism. The oft-repeated charge that Jehovah's Witnesses are "fifth columnists" serves to disguise the efforts of the Catholic Church to bring about a totalitarian seizure of the United States: "When the time comes, and that seems to be in the near future, it will be found that there are at least ten million 'fifth columnists' in America, and that ninety percent of these are under the absolute control of the Roman Catholic Hierarchy."[35]

Against a bleak picture of global Catholic and Satanic domination, Rutherford identifies the United States as an historic bastion of righteousness and Christianity. He does not hold the United States responsible for persecution of Jehovah's Witnesses, nor even its military or "martial spirit." The United States was "founded as a Christian nation, not a religious nation," by men who

[32] "Germans Execute Objector to War." *New York Times*, September 17, 1939.

[33] Hesse, Hans (ed.) (2001). *Persecution and Resistance of Jehovah's Witnesses during the Nazi Regime 1933–1945*. Chicago: Edition Temmen.

[34] One of the reasons this pamphlet is useful is that Rutherford uses it to summarize the arguments he makes in many of his other voluminous writings, which he accuses the press of ignoring. Among his other writings and lectures he cites in this pamphlet are: *Vindication, vol.* 2 (1932), *Enemies* (1937), *Face the Facts* (1938), *Fascism or Freedom* (1938), and *Government and Peace* (1939).

[35] Rutherford, Joseph F. (1940). *Judge Rutherford Uncovers Fifth Column*. Brooklyn: Watchtower Bible and Tract Association, Inc., pp. 6–8.

"loved God and His Kingdom" and who "prayed and worked for righteousness." American case law and the fundamental laws state "this is a Christian nation." But the United States is under siege from the Catholic hierarchy, who have installed agents in every newspaper and government. "Nazi-Catholic Action" does not only operate by institutional subterfuge; Rutherford stresses that "they are a military organization," and in one passage he suggests using the House Un-American Activities Committee to unmask it:

> Why not let the public press demand of Congress an investigation of the cellars and crypts of the Catholic cathedrals in the United States and prove to the public whether or not they have stored away a great amount of arms and ammunition to use against the government? Why does not the Dies Committee go after the Hierarchy and the Nazis? If the Hierarchy deny that they have a large amount of guns and ammunition stored, then they should not object to being investigated. If they do vigorously deny it, that is the best reason why an investigation should be had. There are many people in the United States who have worked in building these crypts or cellars, and others who have helped unload what appeared to be piano boxes, which were filled with rifles and are stored in these crypts.[36]

Rutherford was suggesting the existence of a full-blown treasonous conspiracy of the Catholic hierarchy against the free and Christian United States, complete with military plans to aid a Nazi takeover. It was understandable, given these kinds of pronouncements, that Witnesses fought bitterly against state attempts to make laws against inciting religious hatred. In the 1941 Illinois court case of *Bevins v. Prindable*, Jehovah's Witnesses sued state and county officials for arresting Witnesses under the Revised Statutes of Illinois, which stated it was illegal to sell or offer literature that exposed any "race, color, creed or religion to contempt, derision or obloquy or which is productive of breach of the peace or riots." The defendants quoted the above passage as an example of the kinds of statements that had led to the arrests of Witnesses distributing literature in Belleville and Harrisburg, Illinois. The Witness plaintiffs claimed predictably that the defendants "have conspired among themselves and with priests and representatives of the Roman Catholic Hierarchy and its allies to shield and protect said Roman organization from exposure in its nefarious work of destroying democracy."[37]

If Witness anti-Catholic rhetoric seems extreme in the context of the 1940s, it would not have been out of place in nativist circles during the nineteenth century. Despite the restraints of temporal power under which the Catholic Church operated in the United States, mid-nineteenth-century Protestant intellectuals repeatedly referred to Catholic power in the old world from which dissident Protestant sects had fled, and claimed there was an open

---

[36] Ibid., p. 22.
[37] *Bevins v. Prindable*, 39 F. Supp. 708 (E.D. Ill. 1941). The Eastern District of Illinois found the statute was valid.

Catholic plot to subsume the United States under the power of the Vatican. When Irish and German Catholic voting blocs became electoral majorities in major cities, nativists claimed this was the beginning of the fulfillment of the Popish plot for domination.[38]

Rutherford's accusation that Catholic Action was acting as the beachhead for Papal–Nazi domination of the United States fits this basic narrative well. Though the American version of Catholic Action was small, poorly organized, and politically ineffective compared to its European counterparts, it nonetheless aroused xenophobic suspicions about Catholic and immigrant power in the cities, and in the lead-up to the Second World War anti-Catholic groups (some of them left-wing Italian organizations) successfully smeared it as a pro-Mussolini organization.[39] Although Rutherford and the Witnesses had a more elaborate theological story for explaining Catholic evil, their rhetoric accorded with the well-established elements of a scheming Catholic hierarchy tied to a despotic foreign power, attempting to use local political organizations to overthrow religious freedom in the last truly Christian country on Earth. Rutherford was prepared to advocate the use of a particularly repressive state apparatus (the Dies Committee) to free America from the Catholic plot.

Despite the vast and widespread dissemination of anti-Catholic literature by Jehovah's Witnesses, there were few responses from the Catholic Church or Catholic laity. Even those Catholics who did respond seemed to care little about the Witnesses' anti-Catholicism and much more about their supposed anti-Americanism. One example was *Judge "For Four Days" Rutherford*, written in 1940 by the well-known anti-Communist radio campaigner Rev. Edward Lodge Curran. Described by *Time* in 1939 as the "florid, bald, hammer-handed president of the International Catholic Truth Society ... a specialist in picturesque 'and' invective," Curran was beyond the bounds of mainstream clerical or political respectability.[40] Despite being published under the auspices of the International Catholic Truth Society, the 32-pamphlet devotes relatively little space to tackling Rutherford's accusations against the Catholic Church, and gives equal space to his attacks on Protestants and Jews.

Though he describes Rutherford as "a greater enemy in our midst than Adolf Hitler" and "a Fifth Column all by himself," Curran says nothing in response to Rutherford's charges that the Catholic Church is seeking a Nazi takeover of the United States and the World. The main emphasis of *Rutherford* is that he is personally fraudulent (he is not entitled to be known as "judge") and willfully misinterprets the scriptures, including on the flag issue – Curran implores

---

[38] Hamburger, Philip (2002). *Separation of Church and State*. Cambridge: Harvard University Press, pp. 201–219; Davis (1960).

[39] Issel, William (2009). *For Both Cross and Flag: Catholic Action, Anti-Catholicism, and National Security Politics in World War II San Francisco*. Philadelphia: Temple University Press.

[40] "Religion: Shatterer," *Time*, May 29, 1939.

Witnesses to "return to true Americanism and salute the flag."[41] Curran also accuses Rutherford of promoting hatred of the United States. His tract hardly seems to be a specifically Catholic response to Rutherford and his anti-Catholicism.

There also appears to have been little Catholic involvement in later mob violence. Though Jehovah's Witnesses remained convinced that the Catholic hierarchy must be behind the persecution, they did not produce any evidence of organized Catholic involvement, and the numbers of Catholics they identified in mobs were disproportionately low compared to the overall population.[42] Nor was there much reporting of violence against Jehovah's Witnesses in heavily Catholic areas of the country, despite the notoriously confrontational tactics Witnesses often used in these areas. In April 1940 two Witnesses faced charges of breaching the peace in Connecticut for touring a neighborhood that was 90 percent Catholic and playing phonographs of Rutherford's lecture "Enemies." In that lecture Rutherford claims "a great religious system, operating out of Rome, has by means of fraud and deception brought untold sorrow and suffering on the people."[43] While the state's Supreme Court was very concerned about the effect that such provocations would have in the religiously divided state of Connecticut, there is no evidence that aggressive Witnessing in specifically Catholic neighborhoods ever led to violence or even police harassment.

This lack of a Catholic response to Witness provocations suggests that the Witness penchant for confrontation is of limited value in explaining how and why they were persecuted in the early 1940s. Jehovah's Witnesses made extremely serious allegations against Catholics. While the claim that the Catholic Church was an instrument of Satan could have been dismissed as absurd, the claim that it was in alliance with the Nazis was genuinely inflammatory. These and other anti-Catholic claims appear far more in Witness literature than writings about the flag salute. Nonetheless, it would be their alleged lack of patriotism and not their hostility to other religious groups that generated public violence against them.

JEHOVAH'S WITNESSES AND THE FLAG SALUTE

Rutherford first publicized opposition to flag saluting at the Witness convention of 1935. While the refusal to salute the flag followed naturally from the Witnesses' expansive prohibitions against idolatry, it was persecutions in Nazi Germany that gave Rutherford reason to press the issue that year. He urged American Witnesses to follow the courage of German Bible Students and reject the public school flag salute ritual as Bible Students had rejected the Hitler

[41] Curran, Edward (1940). *Judge "For Four Days" Rutherford*. Brooklyn: International Catholic Truth Society.
[42] Manwaring (1960), p. 170.
[43] "Religion: Freedom of Faith," *Time*, April 8, 1940.

salute, to their great cost. As Rutherford and others pointed out, the flag salute practiced in American schools at that time distinctly resembled the Hitler salute (both were derived from Roman salutes).[44]

In September of that year, ten-year-old Witness Carlton Nicholls attracted national attention when he refused to salute the flag at his school in Lynn, Massachusetts.[45] The *Chicago Tribune* reported "Nichols [*sic*] is a member of Jehovah's Witnesses, a religious sect, and maintained the flag was a symbol of man-made government. All things, he contended, that were man-made were controlled by the Devil."[46] Nicholls inaugurated more than a decade of legal confrontations between Witnesses and state authorities, which would culminate in nearly forty Supreme Court cases. When the Lynn school board expelled Nicholls, his family accepted the help of the American Civil Liberties Union, which had long fought against forced demonstrations of "loyalty" imposed on dissidents of all kinds in American educational institutions.[47] The ACLU would remain the staunchest ally of Jehovah's Witnesses, despite their disparate worldviews. The Nicholls case ended in a crushing defeat – the Supreme Court of Massachusetts found in 1937 that the state's flag salute laws were justified and constitutional – but the example of Nicholls emboldened Witnesses around the country.[48]

Other children and their families followed Nicholls, urged on by Rutherford. By 1939, the number of expulsions nationwide had climbed into the hundreds, spread across sixteen states. State laws and local regulations around the flag salute varied across the country (see Figure 5.1). Some states had no laws compelling Witnesses to salute, and in other jurisdictions authorities quietly accepted their right to refuse the salute. Massachusetts and Pennsylvania led the way in punitive actions against Witnesses.[49] In many cases, the punishment of Witnesses and their families did not end with expulsion; authorities would subsequently charge Witnesses with delinquency.[50] Even attempts to make

---

[44] Peters (2000), p. 25.
[45] Shawn Peters interviewed some of the Witness children who had refused to salute the flag when conducting research for his book nearly fifty years later. He observes that some children were reluctant participants in the refusal, urged to do so by their parents and dreading the prospect of ostracism and expulsion. Nicholls, however, was reportedly a "firebrand" who acted on his own initiative and eloquently defended his actions. Ibid., p. 27.
[46] *Chicago Daily Tribune* (1935). "Child Refuses to Salute Flag; School to Act." September 24, 1935, p. 1.
[47] The ACLU began life as a radical left-wing organization, and many of its early struggles in the 1920s were in defense of schoolteachers and professors who were hounded from their posts because of their real or perceived communist sympathies. By the 1930s the organization had shifted toward liberalism and was adopting a strategy of court challenges rather than direct action. See Kutulas, Judy (2006). *The American Civil Liberties Union and the Making of Modern Liberalism, 1930–1960.* Chapel Hill: University of North Carolina Press.
[48] Peters (2000), pp. 166–167.
[49] Manwaring (1960), pp. 56–57.
[50] Peters (2000), pp. 168–177.

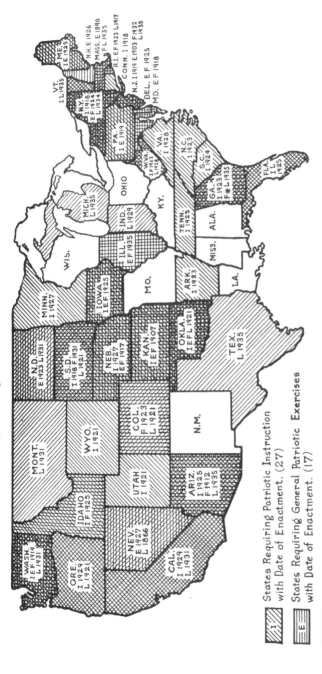

Compulsory Patriotism in the Schools

States Requiring Patriotic Instruction with Date of Enactment. (27)

States Requiring General Patriotic Exercises with Date of Enactment. (17)

States Requiring Flag Exercises with Date of Enactment. (18) **F.**

States Requiring Special Oaths of Loyalty from Teachers with Date of Enactment. (21)

* In Georgia a pledge of allegiance is required to state flag only.

NOTE: Of the 18 states requiring flag exercises, only 13 make salute compulsory.

FIGURE 1: Map of statewide flag salute laws in 1936. Copyright 1936, American Civil Liberties Union. Originally appeared in "How Goes the Bill of Rights: The Story of the Fight for Civil Liberty, 1935–1936." New York: American Civil Liberties Union.

alternative educational arrangements for Witness children could lead to conflict with the state.

In April 1936, the Mayor of Monessen, Pennsylvania, shut down a tiny private school in his city that catered to nineteen Witness children who could not attend Pennsylvania public schools. He ordered the school to be raided and its single teacher arrested because it was "teaching Communism" to children by refusing to salute the flag or recite the Pledge of Allegiance. The following month, 148 Witnesses descended on Monessen to protest. The city police arrested them and kept them in jail for a night, releasing them with $5 fines. Before they were released, Mayor James C. Gold personally lectured them, accusing them of coming to Monessen to stir up public opinion against him. "We have to maintain the peace here," he declared "and your actions in trying to stampede the residents of Monessen caused them to complain to the police."[51] This incident was a precursor to the widespread disturbances of the 1940s, when local authorities objected to large numbers of Witnesses arriving in their towns, which they saw as a threat to public order.

In Massachusetts, Georgia, New Jersey, California, New York, and Florida, the states' highest courts upheld flag salute laws between 1937 and 1940. In similar language, all of them elevated the rights of the state to inculcate patriotism over the religious objections of Jehovah's Witnesses, which some courts plainly did not take seriously.[52] But by far the most influential case was *Minersville School District v. Gobitis*, which was heard by a Pennsylvania district court in 1938 and by the United States Supreme Court in 1940. The plaintiff was Walter Gobitas (consistently misspelled as "Gobitis" in court), whose children William and Lillian were expelled from Minersville Public Schools in October 1935. Minersville, an overwhelmingly Catholic town, had informally implemented the flag salute ritual as early as 1914, five years before even Pennsylvania's flag salute law, which was one of the earliest in the country. The family found it exceedingly difficult to find alternative sources of education for the children. Gobitas, like many Witnesses, believed the Catholic Church was at the heart of his ordeal.

---

[51] Ward, Henry (1936). "Many Pittsburghers in Group Fined $5 after Being in Jail All Night." *Pittsburgh Sun-Telegraph*, May 25, 1936.

[52] Manwaring (1960), pp. 56–80. The opinion of Florida's Supreme Court, cited by Manwaring, is a good example of the low regard in which judges held Witness objections to the flag salute: "Like all law, this command … [Exodus 20:4–6, prohibiting graven images] grew out of the exigencies of the times and we cannot see that it has any relation whatsoever to the present situation. It would be as pertinent to rely on some requirement of the Assyrian, the Hittite, or the Hammurabi Code.… To symbolize the flag as a graven image and to ascribe to the act of saluting it a species of idolatry is too vague and far-fetched to be even tinctured with the flavor of reason.… If an objection as remote from religious grounds as the one involved here may be successfully interposed … then there is no limit to the reasons that conscientious objectors may advance as grounds for avoiding patriotic duties. Individual judgment in matters of religion no less than in civic controversies must give way to the instrumentality set up by the State to direct it." *State ex rel. Bleich v. Board of Public Instruction*, quoted in Manwaring (1960), p. 73.

Judge Albert B. Maris of the Philadelphia District Court was one of the first in the country to make the argument that the flag salute requirement violated the constitution's religious freedom provisions, rejecting the widespread doctrine that religious objections had no bearing on secular rituals.[53] The Minersville School District quickly appealed the ruling, which was upheld by the Third Circuit of the US Court of Appeals. The case went to the US Supreme Court in March 1940; the court found in favor of the School District in an 8–1 decision, upholding the flag salute as a secular activity that did not place an undue burden on religion. Felix Frankfurter, who wrote the majority decision, echoed earlier judgments about the right of the state to impose patriotic rituals, declaring "national unity is the basis of national security."[54] Frankfurter's opinion seems to have been shaped by his personal fears about national security, shared by much of the American public, as the Nazis made a shocking series of advances through Europe.[55]

Jehovah's Witnesses would fight ferociously in court over the next three years for their right to refuse the flag salute. These legal struggles have been well documented by David Manwaring in *Render Unto Caesar* and Shawn Peters in *Judging Jehovah's Witnesses*. In June 1943, the Supreme Court handed down a decision in *West Virginia State Board of Education v. Barnette* that decisively refuted *Gobitis*. The majority opinion, authored by Robert Jackson, cast doubt on the efficacy of the flag salute as a tool of building national unity, and on national unity itself as a goal that had to be placed above all others. Most importantly, Jackson argued that the Bill of Rights existed to "withdraw certain subjects from the vicissitudes of political controversy, to place them beyond the reach of majorities and officials and to establish them as legal principles to be applied by the courts."[56] Legal scholars regard *Barnette* as a watershed in expanding legal protection of religious freedom and free speech.

Given the importance of the flag salute struggle, it is easy to overstate the extent to which Witnesses rejected patriotism and national allegiance. In fact, the Witnesses did not want to be known as unpatriotic and did not seek out confrontations over the flag – this conflict was largely foisted on them by their antagonists. By 1942 the Witnesses had devised an alternative flag salute for Witness schoolchildren, emphasizing allegiance to everything for which the flag stands, just not the flag itself, which they hoped would allow their expelled children to be reinstated in public schools.[57] The Witnesses, in other words,

---

[53] Ibid., pp. 91–92.

[54] *Minersville School District v. Gobitis*, 310 U.S. 597 (1940).

[55] Danzig, Richard (1977). "How Questions Begot Answers in Felix Frankfurter's First Flag Salute Opinion." *Supreme Court Review*, 1977: 257–274; Danzig, Richard (1984). "Justice Frankfurter's Opinions in the Flag Salute Cases: Blending Logic and Psychologic in Constitutional Decisionmaking." *Stanford Law Review* 36(3): 675–273.

[56] *West Virginia Bd. of Ed. v. Barnette*, 319 U.S. 624 (1943).

[57] The ACLU archives contain many examples of petitions for reinstatement that Jehovah's Witnesses presented to school boards in early 1942 suggesting an alternative ceremony for Witness children. The petition would ask:

tried to reduce rather than increase this area of tension between themselves and broader society. One of the most provocative things they did was to label their opponents "unpatriotic" and "un-American," indicating that they normatively embraced patriotism. As mentioned in the previous section, Rutherford actually idealized the United States as the last bastion of resistance to the encroachment of Catholic power, which Witnesses saw as the real enemy.

It is also easy to overstate the extent to which *Gobitis* turned the American public against Jehovah's Witnesses. The case attracted, as Manwaring notes "a complete absence of comment in the general circulation magazines."[58] The rumor that Jehovah's Witnesses were a Nazi "fifth column" attracted some media attention, but state authorities monitoring the circulation of wartime rumors did not detect this rumor in the population at large.[59] Newspaper coverage of Jehovah's Witnesses was scant even at the height of the flag salute controversy. Reporters included general information about the Witnesses in nearly every article they wrote involving them, indicating they believed their readers would probably not know who they were. The reporting was rarely very deep or detailed, and often reflected condescending amusement rather than serious concern; the *Chicago Daily Tribune* carried a story in September 1940 titled "44,000 Americans Join Freak Cult That Hates Everything!"[60]

Public antagonism toward Witnesses over the flag salute came largely from a single, identifiable source: the American Legion, and the Great War veterans it represented. In the next chapter I explore how this antagonism translated into state-sanctioned violence; I devote the remainder of this chapter to the nature, ideology, and imperatives of the American Legion.

"Since the highest court of the land has shifted the burden of deciding this matter from the courts to the boards of education, we come to you and respectfully ask to be permitted to substitute for the prescribed pledge and ceremony the following, which we can and gladly will subscribe to and publicly declare, to wit:

'I have pledged my unqualified allegiance and devotion to Jehovah, the almighty God, and to his Kingdom, for Jesus commands all Christians to pray.

'I respect the flag of the United States and acknowledge it as a symbol of freedom and justice to all.

'I pledge allegiance and obedience to all the laws of the United States that are consistent with God's law, as set forth in the Bible.'" (From petition to the school board of Adair County, Missouri, April 11, 1942, ACLUP vol. 2414.)

[58] Manwaring (1960), p. 160.

[59] In September 1942 the Massachusetts Committee on Public Safety collected more than 1,000 war-related rumors circulating in all parts of the country which the assistance of *Reader's Digest*, which urged its readers to send rumors they had heard to the Committee. Of these rumors, 9.3% were anti-Semitic, compared to 6.9% which were about the Fifth Column. There were more rumors about Jews than about any other group, including Negroes (3.1%) and Russians (0.6%). There were no rumors at all recorded about Jehovah's Witnesses, according to James Sparrow, who has examined the rumor file (personal correspondence, 2009). Knapp, Robert H. (1944). "A Psychology of Rumor." *Public Opinion Quarterly*, 8(1): 22–37; Allport, Gordon W., and Leo Postman (1965). *The Psychology of Rumor*. New York: Russell and Russell.

[60] *Chicago Daily Tribune*, September 11, 1940.

THE AMERICAN LEGION AND ITS MOTIVES

> One thing it did. It gave expression to the purpose of the victorious American soldier to be a little more than an average routine citizen. It said in clear and ringing tones that we wanted the United States for which we fought to achieve our highest hopes as the United States where we would live.
> – Richard Seelye Jones (1946), *A History of the American Legion*, p. 34

From its birth in 1918, the American Legion was a civic association that blurred the boundaries between state and non-state and political and non-political. While it was formed independently of any government organization (including the military), its sole criterion for membership was service in the largest federal bureaucracy: the armed forces. For those who had served, moreover, the Legion's stated goal was to *continue* to serve outside the formal structure of the military in peacetime. As the preamble to the Legion's constitution puts it:

> **We Associate Ourselves Together For The Following Purposes**
> To uphold and defend the Constitution of the United States of America; to maintain law and order; to foster and perpetuate a one hundred percent Americanism; to preserve the memories and incidents of our associations in the Great Wars; to inculcate a sense of individual obligation to the community, state and nation; to combat the autocracy of both the classes and the masses; to make right the master of might; to promote peace and good will on earth; to safeguard and transmit to posterity the principles of justice, freedom and democracy, to consecrate and sanctify our comradeship by our devotion to mutual helpfulness.[61]

The text is thick with verbs: uphold, defend, maintain, foster, perpetuate, preserve, inculcate, combat, make, promote, safeguard, transmit, consecrate, sanctify. It was not enough to desire that America be just, free, and harmonious; members of the American Legion expected the task would be theirs to fulfill. The preamble contains both vague and specific elements of a program of action that Legionnaires would follow faithfully, and some of those elements (such as "maintaining law and order") suggested the need to take part in functions of the state.

"One hundred percent Americanism" would serve as the Legion's slogan from 1919 and became the official abbreviation of its aims.[62] The term had arisen in the First World War to denote private and government campaigns to promote patriotism and cultural unanimity, and to suppress "foreign cultural and political traditions that seemed to nurture antiwar or anti-American sentiments."[63] For the post-war Legion, "one hundred percent Americanism"

---

[61] "For God and Country," preamble to the Constitution of the American Legion, quoted in Rumer, Thomas A. (1990). *The American Legion: An Official History.* New York: M. Evans & Company Inc., p. vii.

[62] Rumer (1990), p. 89.

[63] Gerstle, Gary (1997). "Liberty, Coercion and the Making of Americans." *Journal of American History*, 84(2): 524–558; see also Tischler, Barbara L. (1986). "One Hundred Percent Americanism and Music in Boston during World War I." *American Music*, 4(2): 164–176.

referred to constructive as well as repressive efforts. While Legion branches ("posts") would sometimes challenge the credentials of schoolteachers in their districts suspected of harboring anti-American tendencies, their better known and longer lasting contribution to patriotism in American schools was the widespread implementation of the flag salute.

From the early 1920s the Legion's Americanism Commission lobbied across states and school districts for the adoption of various patriotic exercises in schools, most notably the flag salute, along with compulsory citizenship classes for children and night courses that would offer the same to immigrants. The Legion-organized National Flag Conferences of 1923 and 1924, which involved other patriotic organizations along with government officials, were watershed moments in spreading the adoption of flag rituals.[64] This campaign brought both material success and organizational prestige. In 1924, as states and cities began making patriotic exercises mandatory and adopting Legion regulations for the care and use of the flag, the Americanism Commission reported to the Legion's Sixth Annual Convention that "nothing ever undertaken by the Legion has done more good than the Flag Conference and the flag campaigns inaugurated by us.... (they) placed Legion squarely before the people as standing for those principles and ideals (for which they were willing) to sacrifice."[65] By 1935 fifteen states had made the flag salute compulsory, along with countless school districts.[66]

It is an oversight in previous scholarship on Jehovah's Witnesses that while all agree on the important role that refusal to salute played in their persecution, most previous work overlooks that the flag salute was so widely institutionalized largely because of the efforts of the American Legion.[67] Marc Leepson's history of the flag in America discusses the great symbolic importance of the flag to the Legion's self-image and public standing. He describes a pro-Legion cartoon titled "The New National Figure," which "depicts a giant of a man attired in a World War I army hat and britches, his face resolute, his well-muscled arms crossed at his chest, and the words 'American Legion' on his shirt. Behind him a large American flag is unfurled. At his feet are small, shiftless figures labeled 'Anarchy,' 'Lawlessness,' 'Class Autocracy,' and 'Petty Politics.'"[68]

[64] Ellis, Richard J. (2005). *To the Flag: An Unlikely History of the Pledge of Allegiance*. Lawrence: University Press of Kansas, pp. 50–68.

[65] Pierce, Bessie Louise (1933). *Citizens' Organizations and the Civic Training of Youth*. New York: Charles Scribner's Sons, pp. 33–45.

[66] Fennell, William G. and Edward J. Friedlander (1936). *Compulsory Flag Salute in Schools: A Survey of the Statutes and Examination of their Constitutionality*. New York: American Civil Liberties Union.

[67] Even Marvin and Ingle's insightful account of the role of the flag in the American psyche does not address the political question of how the flag salute became such a widespread institution, changing the everyday relationship that citizens had with the flag. Marvin, Carolyn, and David W. Ingle (1999). *Blood Sacrifice and the Nation: Totem Rituals and the American Flag*. New York: Cambridge University Press. An exception is Ellis (2005).

[68] Leepson, Marc (2005). *Flag: An American Biography*. New York: St. Martin's Press, p. 195.

The American Legion's vow to "combat the autocracy of both the classes and the masses" was another expression of its drive for national harmony and unity over radicalism and division. This could be seen as a cover for conservative anti-labor belligerence, especially since state and city governments had previously used the "one hundred percent Americanism" battle-cry while intervening forcefully in labor disputes on behalf of industrialists.[69] One Marxist critic charged that the Legion "clearly represents an interest group in American society, an interest group which has a very definite stake in the preservation of the status quo and wishes to see its interest protected against those forces which recognition of class conflict might release.... Its middle class membership pretty largely identifies its interests with the interests of those who are in control of American society."[70]

Legionnaires did violently skirmish with strikers where they suspected Communist involvement, and the killing of four Legionnaires by Wobblies in Centralia, Washington, in 1919 became a "baptism in the blood of martyrs" with powerful symbolic importance.[71] However, while the Legion was certainly anti-Communist and anti-radical, it was not on the whole anti-labor or even anti-union. The national Legion leadership saw union men as naturally patriotic and an important source of recruitment, and worked hard to maintain relations with the AFL, with whose leadership it shared concerns about Bolshevik attempts to infiltrate American labor. The Legion issued statements supporting labor's right to organize, and Walter Pencak notes that by the early 1920s "The Legion's cooperation with the AFL reached the point where anti-union Legionnaires in fact wondered whether the Legion was becoming a tool of organized labor."[72] The Legion was definitely "pro-establishment," but it was not identifiably on one side of any major cleavage in American politics.

Indeed, both the campaign for patriotism in schools and the attempt to broker peaceful labor relations represented an urge to transcend "politics." In a hagiographic but revealing 1946 account of the Legion's interwar years, Richard Jones triumphantly describes the success of the Legion's non-"political" politics:

> From the outset the American Legion kept out of politics. As a result it rapidly acquired great political power. It supported no political party, endorsed no candidate for office. All parties and officeholders sought its approval. By adhering to principles and avoiding partisanship it became so powerful that books were

[69] Barrett, James R. (1992). "Americanization from the Bottom Up: Immigration and the Remaking of the Working Class in the United States, 1880–1930." *Journal of American History*, 79(3): 996–1020.

[70] Gellerman, William (1938). *The American Legion as Educator*. New York: Bureau of Publications, Teachers College, Columbia University.

[71] Jones, Richard Seelye (1946). *A History of the American Legion*. Indianapolis: Bobbs-Merrill, p. 41.

[72] Pencak, William (1989). *For God and Country: The American Legion, 1919–1941*. Boston: Northeastern University Press, p. 217 and see ch. 8.

written about it as a "political pressure group," and about its national legislative committee as the "Legion Lobby." Advertised by its opponents, its influence upon the Congress became in time a tradition, steeped in mystery and magic, a thing to conjure with. There was in fact some basis for this illusion, but a good deal of it was mythical.[73]

A clause in the Legion's 1919 constitution prohibited any part of the organization from promoting a candidate for office, thwarting Legionnaires who wanted to use the numerical power of the Legion's membership to install candidates friendly to their aims. In this way, the organization secured its "absolutely non-political" image. However, the Legion intended to influence government through its National Committee on Legislation, a permanent bureau in Washington that it resolved to establish the same year. The office would lobby Congress directly but also keep all members and posts informed of forthcoming congressional activity so that they could lobby their own Representatives and Senators.[74] At the 1920 convention when some members demanded the Legion get involved in elections, the "non-political" clause was reaffirmed with the clarification that Legionnaires could "publicize disagreements" between the Legion and hostile legislators, but could not openly support their opponents "as Legionnaires" (though they were free to do so "as individuals").[75]

"Staying out of politics," then, meant avoiding parties and elections, the venues of conflict that required participants to take one side or the other of a social divide. The Legion had much loftier aims than that, as an organization devoted to national unity and consensus. This was reflected in its direct, friends-in-high-places style of lobbying, which Jones notes it never referred to as lobbying because "lobbying was used as a term of shame or infamy."[76] Individual Legionnaires were not prohibited from holding political office (though political office-holders were prohibited from holding Legion offices) and Legionnaires in the Federal and State legislatures became valuable allies. In 1924 Legionnaires accounted for 14 of the 21 members of the House Veterans' Affairs Committee and 1 of the 5 members of the Senate's Veterans' Sub-committee; by 1941 at least 9 state Governors were Legionnaires, along with 24 U.S. Senators and 145 Congressmen.[77] The large number of legislators with ties to the American Legion doubtless simplified lobbying greatly, and the Legion's presence in both parties enhanced the reputation for nonpartisanship which Jones claims was a major source of its political power.[78]

The Legion's self-image repudiated existing divisions in American society based on class, ethnicity, and party. Its membership, after all, was composed of

---

[73] Jones (1946), p. 45.
[74] Ibid., pp. 45–50.
[75] Pencak (1989), p. 110.
[76] Jones (1946), p. 45.
[77] Pencak (1989), p. 112.
[78] Jones (1946), p. 45.

veterans who had been drawn from nearly every social niche. A major part of the Legion's mission was to ensure that veteran status trumped other social identities, both in the lives of its members and in the eyes of the public. This meant the Legion organized veterans as a political interest group of their own; the most impressive use of its legislative influence was to secure increased benefits and bonuses for Great War veterans. Initially, the Legion's efforts in this area appeared simply to represent social consensus. In 1920 the Legion mobilized friendly senators to support the Sweet Bill, raising the total disability pension from $30 to $80 per month. This legislation was relatively uncontroversial and had already passed the House, but the Legion's achievement was getting it before the consideration of the Senate while it faced a daunting backlog of matters related to the Treaty of Versailles. Richard Jones, the chronicler of Legion accomplishments, describes how this happened:

> On December 16 the Legion conference recessed at noon. Each Department Commander agreed to call that afternoon on the senators from his state. National Commander D'Olier would call on the majority leader and on Senator Reed Smoot, of Utah, Chairman of the Finance Committee. The calls were made and the talk was of the immediate needs of the disabled. That evening a congressional group dined with the Legion leaders. They heard again about the Sweet Bill. Twenty-four hours later the Finance Committee favorably reported the bill to the Senate. The next day it was passed under suspension of the rules.
>
>   The Legion lobby could carve the first notch in its gun. The war disabled were living on a compensation basis.[79]

This passage describes Legion power at its most idealized, with Legionnaires quietly and persuasively working with all sides to ensure agreeable legislation escaped congressional red tape. By the 1930s, however, after a string of Legion-inspired increases in the veterans' bonus, many of which involved Congress overriding presidential vetoes, some commentators were describing the Legion as a "pressure group," whose interests were at odds with those of the American people more broadly.

Marcus Duffield of *Harper's* and *The Nation* made this point in 1931 with a book-length denunciation, *King Legion*. Duffield estimates that, courtesy of Legion lobbying, veterans were by this time costing $900 million a year in taxes, and the bonus they were then demanding would cost an extra $3.5 billion. Chapter VII of his book, titled "Mutual Helpfulness Extended" (referring to the last line of the Legion's constitutional preamble) begins with the observation that

> Once ex-soldiers, in the process of obtaining legislation for disabled comrades, realize their power and learn how to use it, a strong temptation arises to employ their combined voting strength and skill to obtain financial benefits for themselves. For a veterans' organization the temptation is doubly strong because such

---

[79] Ibid., p. 48.

a policy helps build up the organization by making evident to non-members to tangible results of uniting.[80]

While Duffield accurately perceived the organizational imperatives of the American Legion, he was wrong about the means by which they were able to act on them. The Legion could not bring much electoral pressure to bear on legislators. In a 1943 article, V.O. Key describes the Legion's impressive track record of mobilizing congressmen to override presidential vetoes of bonus bills and tests whether the source of its influence was an ability to discipline congressmen at elections. Comparing the electoral fortunes between 1922 and 1936 of congressmen who supported the Legion position on the bonus with those who did not, Key finds almost no evidence for this. The differences between the likelihoods of getting re-elected for each group were so slight that "the claims of mighty veteran influence in elections become ridiculous." The electoral threat posed by veterans could only sway congressional votes if Representatives had a completely exaggerated idea of it, and Key posits that Legion influence instead came through the kind of lobbying process Jones describes: "The simple fact that a group is represented before Congress by skilled and aggressive legislative strategists may bring it influence. The aggressive personalities in the person-to-person Legion-Congressional relationships are apt to get what they ask for in the absence of counter-balancing demands."[81]

The Legion, then, did faithfully "stay out of politics" to the extent that Legionnaires did not even constitute an electoral bloc. The Legion disavowed the electoral mechanism of democracy – the ability to punish at the polls – in favor of inside lobbying that depended on its strong personal relationships and its broader prestige. On the one hand, Legion power rested on the skill and long tenure of its Washington and Statehouse operatives, especially National Legislative Committee chief John Thomas Taylor, whom one Senator described as "the greatest lobbyist the world has ever known."[82] On the other hand, the Legion was fittingly obsessed with its symbolic capital. The Legion's self-appointed role as guardian of the flag, its nationwide organization of youth baseball leagues, and its occasional violence against subversives all helped to enhance its standing as a patriotic organization that worked tirelessly for the whole American community, even as it labored to elevate the status and well-being of one particular group – the veterans of the Great War.

When discussing the Legion's maintenance of its symbolic capital we can depart from referring to "The Legion" as a unitary actor and examine more closely the actions of individual Legionnaires. The cultivation of the Legion's

[80] Duffield, Marcus (1931). *King Legion*. New York: Jonathan Cape and Harrison Smith, p. 70.
[81] Key, V.O. (1943). "The Veterans and the House of Representatives: A Study of a Pressure Group and Electoral Mortality." *Journal of Politics*, 5(1): 27–40. Key's findings were replicated with later data in Somit, Albert, and Joseph Tannenhaus (1957). "The Veteran in the Electoral Process." *Journal of Politics*, 19(2): 184–201.
[82] Pencak (1989), p. 120.

prestige depended on thousands of uncoordinated local activities every day. Local Legion posts and individual Legionnaires were the communicators of the Legion's principles, the organizers of its picnics, and its vigilantes against un-American schemes. Due to the Legion's federal structure, nearly all its activity depended on the initiative of these local units. The Legionnaires' relationship with local power structures in many ways resembled the Legion's relationship to national power. Legionnaires developed strong relationships with and wielded great influence over elected and unelected officials alike. They were frequently able to enlist them, in the name of quelling subversion, in their fights to preserve the status of symbols of veteran privilege, most importantly the American flag.

As noted earlier, the campaign to implement the flag salute in schools was instigated by a centralized national body of the American Legion (the Americanism Committee) but was executed at the local level. State-level Legion lobbying resulted in some states making the flag salute compulsory, and this was preceded by campaigns at the school district level to persuade individual school boards to adopt various flag salute rituals. When individual Jehovah's Witnesses first began challenging the flag salute in schools in Massachusetts in 1935, American Legion branches led the fight to preserve the flag ritual's sacrosanct status.[83] An AP article from October 1935 notes the state's tough flag salute legislation was "sponsored by the American Legion and fathered by Representative Thomas Dorgan, Boston world war veteran," and that it was "pushed through over the practically unanimous opposition of heads of Massachusetts institutions of higher learning."[84] The Principal responsible for expelling the first child who had refused to salute the flag was a Great War Veteran, who had shouted "I will stand for no such insult to the American flag" when the child, Carleton Nicholls, refused to stand during the salute ceremony at the school's assembly.[85]

A *Washington Post* article from 1936 describes typically direct local lobbying by Legionnaires on the flag salute issue. When four children refused to salute the flag in Oxon Hill, Maryland, the local Command Post met to discuss the issue. Post Commander Paul Smith refused to say whether his organization took a position on the issue until the post meeting, highlighting the local and democratic nature of American Legion activism.[86] A few days later the *Post* reported that the Prince Georges County School Board had voted to expel the children and that officials "had been visited during the day by members of the Marlboro American Legion Post who urged that respect of the flag be made a paramount factor."[87]

[83] Manwaring (1960), p. 175.
[84] "Flag Dispute Now Involves Religious Sect." *Chicago Daily Tribune*, October 13, 1935.
[85] "'Jehovah Witness' and Kin of Henry James Are Arrested for Flag 'Insult' at Lynn." *New York Times*, October 1, 1935.
[86] "Legion to Act Tonight in Flag Salute Incident." *Washington Post*, May 25, 1936.
[87] "Prince Georges School Expels Four Who Refused to Salute Flag." *Washington Post*, June 10, 1936.

Grass-roots activism on the flag issue reflected Legionnaires' concerns about the local as well as the national prestige of the American Legion. Because states and local districts were responsible for implementing and maintaining flag rituals and because local Legion Command Posts shouldered the burden of lobbying for them, the failure of a district to enforce the salute would have reflected poorly on the status and influence of Legionnaires in that area compared to other areas. Local Legionnaires would have faced a similar problem when Jehovah's Witness proselytizers began appearing in their towns. Legionnaires knew that Jehovah's Witnesses defied the flag salute, so the sight of them distributing literature on local streets would have appeared to be an affront to the local Command Post.

Legionnaires had a history of physically attacking those they considered "subversives" in the name of maintaining law and order and Americanism. In the mid-1930s the militant leader of the Legion's Americanism Office, Homer Chaillaux, had a "general demeanor" that encouraged local posts to "go beyond the law," according to Walter Pencak. After a series of "spectacular" public brawls with Communists and Socialists in Manhattan and Jersey City in 1937 and 1938, newspapers condemned the American Legion's excessive zeal and its continuing role in leading public disruptions. National Commander Daniel Doherty, realizing that these disruptions were hurting the Legion's image, issued a public statement condemning the tactics and a private warning to New Jersey's State Commander. When New York Legionnaires broke the windows of Bund leader Fritz Kuhn's home and engaged Bundists in fights in 1938, Chaillaux himself stepped in, warning that "the publicity was not good."[88] There were no further Legion attacks on Communists or Bundists after mid-1938.

These incidents showed that, despite the autonomy of local Legionnaires and Command Posts, the national offices had both the desire and the capacity to rein in local branches when they posed a threat to the Legion's image, especially on widely publicized law and order issues. Crucially, however, no national Legion officials ever responded publicly to reports of Legionnaires engaged in violence against Jehovah's Witnesses. When the ACLU asked National Commander Lynn Upshaw Stambaugh to prevent further Legion violence against Witnesses in 1941, Stambaugh replied that the National Command had no control over the actions of local posts.[89] This suggests that for local Legionnaires, there was no prohibition on attacking Jehovah's Witnesses as there was on attacking more high-profile enemies such as Communists and Bundists.

American Legionnaires, then, had multiple incentives for attacking Jehovah's Witnesses that were far more concrete than suspicions that they might be enemy agents or sympathizers. They wanted to defend the honored status of the flag,

[88] Pencak (1989), pp. 239–247.
[89] Letter of Lynn Upshaw Stambaugh to Roger N. Baldwin, December 31, 1941. ACLUP vol. 2386.

which for them was a symbol not just of patriotism, but also of the national prestige of veterans and their organization. They wanted to demonstrate the strength and status of the Legion in their own jurisdictions, which reflected personally on the esteem of Legionnaires both in their communities and within the broader organization. And because the attacks on Witnesses brought little or no national publicity, Legionnaires were free to use attacks on Witnesses to play the role of protective vigilantes, defending their communities against spies and subversives.

6

Mass violence against Jehovah's Witnesses, 1940–1942

INTRODUCTION

Between 1940 and 1942 there were hundreds of violent attacks on Jehovah's Witnesses in the United States, with estimates of the exact number as high as 2,500. These attacks nearly always took place in public spaces, and frequently with the acquiescence of local law enforcement officials. In the words of Witness attorney Marley Cole, "In 44 states they were beaten, kidnapped, tarred and feathered, forced to drink castor oil, tied together and chased through the streets, maimed, shot, and otherwise consigned to mayhem."[1] In Litchfield, Illinois, and Kennebunk, Maine, anti-Witness riots involved entire towns, gaining national attention. In thousands of other instances Jehovah's Witnesses were subject to threats, intimidation, arbitrary arrest, and detention. By the Witnesses' own count there were 18,866 arrests of Witnesses between 1933 and 1951, and these arrests peaked during the early 1940s in conjunction with the violence in the streets.[2] This violence and harassment, while it resulted in no recorded deaths, was nonetheless an extraordinary episode in American history. It is one of very few times when Americans have been persecuted in the course of fulfilling a religious duty – in this case, proselytism.

Beginning with the earliest contemporary accounts, observers characterized this episode of violence as the work of spontaneous mobs, outraged by the Witnesses' refusal to salute the flag and inflamed by rumors that the Witnesses were a "fifth column" for the Nazis. The 1941 ACLU pamphlet *The Persecution of Jehovah's Witnesses* gives the following account of the persecution of Jehovah's Witnesses, a "record of violence against a religious organization unparalleled in America since the attacks on the Mormons":

---

[1] Cole, Marley, "Jehovah's Witnesses." *The Crisis*, April 1953.
[2] Zygmunt, Joseph F. (1977). "Jehovah's Witnesses in the U.S.A., 1942–1977." *Social Compass* XXIV, 1977/1, p. 48.

The cause of this extraordinary outbreak was the "patriotic" fear aroused by the success of the Nazi armies in Europe and the panic which seized the country at the imagined invasion of the United States. From California to Maine this emotion expressed itself in searching out "Fifth Columnists" and "Trojan Horses" – phrases which sprang into almost immediate popularity to characterize those thought to be opposed to national defense.

Jehovah's Witnesses were the object of immediate and widespread attack, chiefly because of their position on flag saluting, well advertised by their wide-spread distribution of the May 29, 1940 issue of *Consolation* giving the details of the hearing before the U.S. Supreme Court of the Gobitis flag salute case. Following the decision of June 3, 1940, in which school boards were upheld in their right to expel children of this sect who refused to salute the flag, this propaganda was taken by some as seditious.[3]

To this day anti-Witness violence tends to be remembered – when it is remembered at all – as aberrant and irrational, an unfortunate result of wartime panic. Along with the "fifth column" rumors, the sparse literature on the violence emphasizes the public's misreading of the *Gobitis* case.[4] Beulah Amidon, a journalist for *Survey Graphic*, supplied one of the most famous anecdotes about anti-Witness hysteria. He reported a conversation with a sheriff in an unnamed Deep South village who had passively observed a jeering mob running a disheveled group of men and women out of town under a under a hail of brick fragments and other missiles. When Amidon asked the sheriff what this was all about, he replied "Jehovah's Witnesses, they're running 'em out of here. They're traitors – the Supreme Court says so, ain't you heard?"[5]

While the *Gobitis* decision, wartime tensions, and fifth column rumors all contributed to the persecution of Witnesses, they do not explain the basic patterns of public violence and state acquiescence. Ordinary citizens, on the whole, knew little about Witnesses and less about their legal battles. There were rumors about them, but, as noted in the previous chapter, these paled in comparison to rumors about Jewish and Negro sedition. Most puzzlingly, violence against Witnesses actually subsided after the United States entered the war in 1941, and had all but disappeared by 1943. This contradicts previously established patterns of wartime mob violence; in the First World War, it was America's entry in 1917 that triggered mob violence, some of it lethal, against suspected traitors.

Above all, the standard story does not explain why so many state officials either let the persecution happen or actively joined in. Hundreds of sworn affidavits testify that local police, sheriffs, and peace officers across the

---

[3] American Civil Liberties Union (1941), p. 3.
[4] See Manwaring (1960), ch. 8; Peters (2000), chs. 2 and 3.
[5] Amidon, Beulah (1940). "Can We Afford Martyrs?" *Survey Graphic*, September 1, 1940, pp. 457–460. This story, preserved by the ACLU in the Religious Freedom section of its archive, is a major and striking piece of evidence in Peters' account of the effect of *Gobitis* on the public.

country refused to intervene in violent incidents or used their authority to help the aggressors. This is despite the fact that police forces were notably effective in the late 1930s at protecting other hated groups, such as Communists and Nazis, from violence. Why did law enforcement officers compromise their own authority by allowing mob rule when it came to Jehovah's Witnesses? While the federal government did not condone anti-Witness violence, its reaction to it was slow, quiet, and ineffective, despite the frantic efforts of Witnesses and the ACLU to draw attention to this mass violation of the First Amendment. Why did the federal government – whose powers of surveillance and coercion were expanding dramatically – mostly ignore a swell of violence that threatened the basic rights of citizens?

In this chapter, I show that the anti-Witness wave of 1940–1942 should be understood as "establishment violence," a form of extra-legal collective violence the American state has historically tolerated more than other forms. This kind of violence is usually sanctioned or organized by local elites and is carefully targeted and controlled, sometimes with quasi-judicial procedures. Most importantly it supports rather than subverts existing political order, and local state officials have often welcomed it as a means of maintaining social control where their own capacity to do so is weak. The most important "establishment" characteristic of anti-Witness violence was the heavy involvement of the American Legion. As noted in the last chapter, the Legion was a high-status civic group that operated on the permeable boundary of state authority in mid-twentieth century America.

What has been called "mob" violence throughout history is usually both purposive and legitimate in the minds of its perpetrators, not an automatic mass response to external changes.[6] Collective violence against Jehovah's Witnesses was not simply a manifestation of wartime "hysteria" or an inevitable result of Fifth Column rumors. The term "mob," frequently used by observers in the 1940s to describe the violence, is itself misleading, implying a lack of organization and purpose. Anti-Witness violence, I will argue, displayed the signs of having been well organized and rationally executed, in ways that often earned tacit approval from state officials. To show this, I turn to a unique dataset composed of hundreds of descriptions of the violence by Witnesses who suffered through it. By recovering these accounts of both major and minor acts of intimidation, I hope to make a historiographic as well as a theoretical contribution to our understanding of this episode. The

---

[6] E.P. Thompson warns against the use of the terms "mob" and "riot" in describing mass disturbances. These terms, according to Thompson, convey the "spasmodic view of popular history," wherein "common people can scarcely be taken as historical agents" but simply as predictable, violent respondents to negative stimuli such as economic downturns. Thompson argues in contrast that every contentious crowd action has "some legitimizing notion," that its members believed they were defending traditional rights or customs and enjoyed widespread social consensus and sometimes tacit official approval. Thompson, E.P. (1971). "The Moral Economy of the English Crowd in the Eighteenth Century." *Past and Present* 50: 76–136.

perpetrators of violence did not usually commit their intentions to paper, but detailed affidavits describing their actions, however biased, reveal consistent patterns in their words and actions.

My findings are similar to those of Christopher Capozzola, who surveys the responses of government agencies, newspapers, and prominent intellectuals to mob violence during the First World War. Capozzola concludes that their preoccupation with the category of the "mob" obscured the role of organized groups and local elites, and helped legitimize "the more systematic, organized and passionless coercions."[7] This, I argue, was equally true of violence during the Second World War. I will spend the first part of this chapter further elaborating the theory of establishment violence and showing how it has operated in other American contexts. This is necessary for developing a coherent account of why state actors would allow mass violence to take place within the geographic boundaries of their authority. In the second part of this chapter I show how this theory applies to the experience of Jehovah's Witnesses, using data from Witness affidavits in the ACLU archives to show the fundamentally establishment character of anti-Witness violence.

THE THEORY OF ESTABLISHMENT VIOLENCE

Establishment violence in America

When does the state – the monopolist of legitimate violence – cede part of that monopoly to other actors? In the context of American history, this question makes more sense if we do not think of the state as a unitary actor. As discussed in Chapter 2, the American state for most of its history has been a chaotic assortment of institutions and agencies with shifting, contentious roles and permeable boundaries of authority. When have those state actors and agencies with responsibility for the use of violence tolerated the use of it by those without the authority of the state? The United States has a long record of extra-legal violence, much of which has been tolerated by state actors, which may supply answers and provide insights into why so many state actors in the 1940s allowed violence against Jehovah's Witnesses.

H. Jon Rosenbaum and Peter Sederberg coined the term "establishment violence" to describe vigilante activity in the United States.[8] They define establishment violence as "the use of violence by established groups to preserve the status quo at times when the formal system of rule enforcement is viewed as ineffective or irrelevant." Robert Ingalls, building on this analysis, argues that collective violence in the United States has been "distinguished by its

---

[7] Capozzola, Christopher (2002). "The Only Badge Needed Is Your Patriotic Fervor: Vigilance, Coercion and the Law in World War I America." *The Journal of American History*, 88(4): 1354–1382.

[8] Rosenbaum, H. Jon and Peter C. Sederberg (1974). "Vigilantism: An Analysis of Establishment Violence." *Comparative Politics*, 6(4): 541–570.

conservatism," as opposed to the historically anti-systemic nature of non-state collective violence in Europe. The status quo conservatism to which Ingalls refers is not just the enforcement of the law. It also refers to maintaining the established position of privileged groups within the political order.[9]

Richard Brown's landmark historical study of American vigilantism identifies 326 organized vigilante movements, which between 1767 and 1910 executed 729 individuals and inflicted corporal punishment on thousands more. Brown distinguishes these groups from impromptu lynch mobs, which between 1882 and 1951 put 4,730 people to death.[10] Vigilante organizations were not simply mobs that came together for the purpose of committing a murder and then disbanded. They were civic groups that saw themselves as having a permanent or quasi-permanent role in law enforcement, and they had a corporate identity. While vigilante movements and impromptu lynch mobs often shared similar politics – maintaining established social hierarchies, including racial hierarchies – vigilantes enjoyed much higher status. Lynch leaders often escaped prosecution, but vigilante leaders acted as an alternative source of law.

Establishment violence and boundary control of conflict

A natural home of vigilante establishment violence was on the frontier, where state capacity was at its weakest and struggles over newfound resource wealth were fierce. The most dramatic example of a frontier vigilante movement was the San Francisco Vigilance Committee, which first appeared in 1851 and then again in 1856. Claiming to act for "the people," free of all other political, class, or sectarian attachments, the Vigilance Committee's mission was to ensure that "no thief, burglar, incendiary or assassin shall escape punishment either by quibbles of the law, the insecurity of prisons, the carelessness or corruption of police, or a laxity of those who pretend to administer justice."[11] While the stated reason for the establishment of the Vigilance Committee was the mayhem and impunity of mainly Australian criminals who controlled parts of the city,[12] another clear motive for the predominantly middle-class and Anglo-Saxon

[9] In the words of Richard Maxwell Brown, "Much of our nineteenth- and twentieth-century violence has represented the attempt to established Americans to preserve their favored position in the social, economic and political order." Brown, R. (1975). *Strain of Violence: Historical Studies of American Violence and Vigilantism*. New York: Oxford University Press, p. 5. Quoted in Ingalls (1987), p. 614.
[10] Brown, Richard Maxwell (1976). "The History of Vigilantism in America." In H. Jon Rosenbaum and Peter C. Sederberg (eds.), *Vigilante Politics*. Philadelphia: University of Pennsylvania Press, pp. 80–81.
[11] Kirkpatrick, Jennet (2008). *Uncivil Disobedience: Studies in Violence and Democratic Politics*. Princeton: Princeton University Press, pp. 42 and 48–49.
[12] Asbury, Herbert (1933). *The Barbary Coast: An Informal History of the San Francisco Underworld*. New York: Alfred A. Knopf, ch. 3.

Committee was to wrest political control from the Irish-Catholic Democratic municipal machine.

The Vigilance Committee enjoyed the height of its power as a parallel law enforcement structure in the summer of 1856, when it publicly hanged four criminals. A few well-publicized acts of extrajudicial justice were all that was required for the Vigilance Committee to effectively assume control of the city; after that it was able to leave routine law enforcement to the regular police and judges whose corruption and ineffectiveness it had scorned.[13] However, there were limits to the Vigilance Committee's power and capacity for violence. A respectable opposition emerged (the Law and Order Committee), and while it was not strong enough to challenge the Vigilance Committee's power in San Francisco, it had the potential to summon outside authorities. The Vigilance Committee was forced to refrain from executing a Law and Order Committee judge who had stabbed one of them during a botched arrest because this would have brought federal intervention.[14] However helpful local authorities may find vigilantes, or however much vigilantes may intimidate them into sharing power, the central state is likely to be far less tolerant of actors who engage in routinized violence without state authority. Even if a vigilante organization establishes local supremacy, it stands to lose control if its actions alert outside authorities to the need for intervention or if it causes local opposition to raise the alarm in the broader polity.

This situation conforms to Schattschneider's model of boundary control: the winners of political conflicts are those who can control who joins them.[15] Vigilante groups walk a fine line, as their local dominance is based on the perception of their capacity for violent retribution, which can both intimidate enemies and induce local authorities to cooperate if they believe it will maintain order. However, violence that crosses some threshold of quantity, brutality, or publicity will cause the central state to reassert its authority as the sole purveyor of legitimate violence, in accordance with Weber's model of state function. For vigilantes to enjoy continued status as suppliers of establishment violence, that violence must both serve the political aims of the state and be controlled in such a way that it does not threaten state authority.

The greater the level of organization in a vigilante association – that is, the extent to which it has a decision-making hierarchy and a corporate identity – the more likely it is to restrain the use of violence in order to deter outside intervention. There are four reasons for this. First, organized groups have a permanent or semi-permanent status and are involved in repeated interactions rather than one-shot events. They must take into account the reactions of others (the authorities, their enemies) when they decide on a course of action. Restraint becomes a necessary strategy for a vigilante group if it is interested in continuing

---

[13] Brown (1976), p. 94.
[14] Brown (1976), pp. 97–98.
[15] Schattschneider, E.E. (1960). *The Semisovereign People: A Realist's View of Democracy in America*. New York: Holt, Rhinehart and Winston.

as a vigilante group without state interference that would force it to cease its activities.

Second, the leaders of vigilante groups are concerned with social and political status, and they will opt for restraint to protect that status even if it means compromising the effectiveness of their violence. The consequences of outside intervention by state authorities typically involve not just termination of vigilante activity but also a reversal of status from protector to criminal. Vigilante groups are fundamentally concerned with protecting established patterns of social power, and as such are often composed of local elites, especially in the leadership ranks, as documented by Brown. These elites have much to lose from either a personal loss of respectability or from their locale gaining a reputation for disorder. Maintaining the appearance of decency in the eyes of other local and national elites weighs heavily in their decision calculus, leading them to curtail violent spectacles that attract undue attention or provoke feelings of disgust.

Third, individuals may join vigilante organizations because of the status it confers on them, while organizations that exist for other purposes may begin vigilante activities because of the status it will confer on the organization. In these cases, actual effectiveness in controlling crime or maintaining social order is a secondary concern to fulfilling a high-status social role, and the rank and file will be just as committed as the leadership to maintaining the respectability of the organization while putting on a show of protecting the community. Many quite harmless vigilance organizations during the First World War fit this description, such as local Committees on Public Safety, and the government made public distinctions between them and the lawless "mobs" that engaged in lynchings.[16]

Fourth, vigilante organizations can discipline the often-volatile specialists in violence they attract to their ranks, while unorganized groups are more likely to follow the lead of their most extreme members. Simone Chambers and Jeffrey Kopstein illustrate this "containment" argument with a quote from Minuteman leader Robert DePugh, who argues that society is better off with "kooks and nuts" inside rather than outside organizations such as his: "If they decide to blow somebody up, okay they go blow somebody up. But if they are part of a group … well then there's a good chance that someone in the organization will know about it and they're going to take steps to bring this person under control."[17]

In summary, while hierarchical organization and corporate identity can certainly increase the capacity of a group of vigilantes to do violent damage, it also imposes restraints that reflect the interests of the organization and its leaders.[18] They seek an optimal level of violence that maximizes local control

[16] See Capozzola (2002).
[17] Chambers, Simone and Jeffrey Kopstein (2001). "Bad Civil Society." *Political Theory*, 29(6): 837–865; the Robert DePugh quote is originally in Rosenblum, Nancy (1998). *Membership and Morals: The Personal Uses of Pluralism in America*. Princeton: Princeton University Press.
[18] In this sense vigilante groups conform to Michels' "iron law of oligarchy" in organizations.

while minimizing the probability of outside interference and broader negative publicity. The optimal level will depend on historical and geographical circumstances. A key variable is the capacity of the central state. For the San Francisco vigilantes of the 1850s, the federal government was sufficiently weak and remote that they could kill a few criminals without the risk of intervention, though they had to stop short of killing a judge. By the 1950s the federal government was taking steps to ensure its judicial and police capacity to investigate and prosecute in lynching cases where local and state governments were unwilling or unable to act; killings of any kind became risky enterprises for vigilante organizations that wanted to avoid federal intervention.[19]

Threats and branding of establishment violence

While warding off outside intervention and bad publicity, vigilante organizations must remain locally credible. They must be seen as willing to do violence to those who transgress their order without fear of retribution from any higher authority. This poses a difficult problem: how does an organization maintain a local reputation for violence and terror while seeming innocuous to state and federal authorities?[20] The key to this problem lies in the effectiveness of threats. Vigilantes take advantage of the difference between the way the state views threats to public order and the way individuals view threats to themselves.

The state is obliged to investigate and counteract dangers to public order. However, its agents are bound by legal norms – they must follow often costly and time-consuming procedures to protect the rights of those they investigate – and limited resources. They cannot investigate every possible problem and must make choices between them. In the course of their jobs, law enforcement officials are likely to see, or hear of, thousands of individuals making physical threats to other individuals. The vast majority of these threats never amount to anything and for an experienced official most threats can safely be dismissed as "cheap talk," not worthy of investigation. Individuals, however, are usually much less accustomed to hearing violent threats and are less able to judge the low probability that they will be carried out. Their judgment of the importance of threats is also naturally clouded by their psychological reactions to personal danger.

---

[19] Belknap (1987), pp. 20–21.
[20] Mafia bosses may face similar dilemmas. Roberto Saviano, an Italian journalist who has reported on the Neapolitan Camorra, describes the threat of public exposure for organized crime figures: "As one penitent former boss has said, the *camorristi* want to be VIPLs: very important persons at a local level; they want to be famous in their own territory, feared for their military power, but on a national or international level, they want to be anonymous. Having their exploits told to a wider audience than the local press was a major blow because it drew public attention to their illegal affairs. I am often asked why the Camorra, this great, powerful criminal organisation, is afraid of me. I always try to make it clear: they're not afraid of me, they're afraid of my readers." Saviano, Roberto (2015). "My Life under Armed Guard." *The Guardian*, January 14, 2015.

The effectiveness of a threat of physical violence, then, is not proportionate to the likelihood that the state will respond to it. A violent threat that is highly effective in controlling an individual's behavior may not provoke any response from a state official, if the official even hears of it – part of the effectiveness of a threat might be that it persuades its target not to go to the authorities. Vigilantes will often prefer threats that leave no material evidence. Written or recorded threats make state intervention more likely because they provide tangible evidence that the threat actually occurred, making it harder for authorities to ignore or dismiss. Vigilante threats will be most effective when they are circulated by word of mouth and rarely publicized in any kind of media.

The effectiveness of threats is also magnified by reputation. Vigilante organizations will be most successful when they can intimidate by their violent reputations alone. The vigilante association must become a "brand" linked with violence. This requires a strong associational identity – it must be widely recognized, and its members must be widely recognizable as members. Various symbols such as uniforms, rituals, and distinctive language can propagate the brand and its violent identity. The association also needs stories and rumors to circulate about the vigilantes' violence or potential for violence. Actual or apocryphal violent events should enjoy a long shelf-life in local memory.

An example of a group that consciously tried to maintain a threatening local reputation and a respectable national reputation was the reconstituted Ku Klux Klan of the 1920s. The new Klan was inaugurated in the shadow of one of the highest-profile lynchings in American history, the killing of Leo Frank in Marietta, Georgia, in August of 1915 (see Chapter 8). Two months after the lynching the Klansmen burned a cross on Stone Mountain, ten miles from Atlanta. The Populist newspaper editor who had helped instigate the Frank killing, Tom Watson, had urged the re-formation of the Klan ("to restore HOME RULE") in response to vehement Northern condemnation of the lynching.[21] *Birth of a Nation*, which celebrated Reconstruction-era Klan violence at its peak, had premiered in Los Angeles earlier in the year and was set to open in Atlanta in December. The new Klan, under William J. Simmons, consciously associated its inception with the violent past of its predecessor organization, as well as the most high-profile lynching of that period.

After a slow initial start – it had fewer than 2,000 members by 1920 – the Klan enjoyed rapid growth throughout the early 1920s. A major reason for the sudden growth was a newly organized, highly incentivized recruiting scheme in which recruiters/salesmen ("Kleagles") would sell costly subscriptions and robes on commission.[22] It had also expanded its targets of prejudice from its

---

[21] Woodward, C. Vann (1938). *Tom Watson, Agrarian Rebel*. New York: Oxford University Press, pp. 446 and 448–489.

[22] Moseley, Charles (1972). "Latent Klanism in Georgia, 1890–1915." *Georgia Historical Quarterly*, 56(3): 365–386; Fryer, Roland G. and Steven D. Levitt (2012). "Hatred and Profits: Under the Hood of the Ku Klux Klan." *Quarterly Journal of Economics*, 127(4):

traditional obsession with blacks to fears about Jews, Catholics, immigrants, and various social deviants such as bootleggers. This allowed for recruitment drives beyond the South, especially in the West and Midwest. Importantly, Simmons marketed the Klan as a fraternal order with connotations of exclusivity, respectability, and lawfulness. He told a congressional hearing that:

> If the Knights of the Ku Klux Klan has been a lawless organization, as has been charged, it would not have shown the remarkable growth it has, for in the Klan is as fine a representative body of citizens as there is in the United States. In each community where there is a Klan will be found members from the leading citizens, men who stand at the forefront in their cities. These men would not stand for lawlessness.[23]

Simmons wanted the Klan to be seen as a status-improving organization for its members, and the high price of joining probably ensured that its membership was disproportionately composed of social elites. In their analysis of Klan membership in Indiana and Pennsylvania, Fryer and Levitt find Klan members were better educated and more likely to be professionals than the average American.

The mid-1920s was the height of the Klan's membership and respectability and also the nadir of its violence. The involvement of the second Klan in acts of violence is often difficult to establish,[24] but the level of violence the Klan inflicted in the 1920s was minute compared to that of the guerilla-style Klan of Reconstruction or the covert terrorist Klan of the 1950s and 1960s. National Klan leaders, seeking to expand their political influence, condemned violence in their publications and claimed the Klan had a positive record of preventing it. Hiram Evans, who wrested control of the national organization from Simmons in 1922, threatened in 1923 to discipline Klansmen who participated in illegal vigilante activity. He attributed the large numerical decline in Southern lynchings to the presence of the Klan.[25] The far less violent nature of the second Klan is a likely reason why the federal government did not seek to stamp it out, unlike Reconstruction and Civil Rights-era Klans. The politics of the second Klan was also far more supportive of established political order; it did not seek to resist federal authority.

The second Klan's anti-violence rhetoric was aimed at building its image in the national media. Rory McVeigh writes that Klan leaders were interested in curtailing the "unorganized and non-selective use of violence," but promoted selective and institutionalized violence as a means of achieving Klan ends. The Klan actively recruited police officers and Klansmen would offer their assistance

---

1883–1925; and McVeigh, Rory (2009b). *The Rise of the Ku Klux Klan: Right-Wing Movements and National Politics*. Minneapolis: University of Minnesota Press, p. 21.

[23] McVeigh (2009b), p. 22.

[24] Newton, Michael (2001). *The Invisible Empire: The Ku Klux Klan in Florida*. Gainesville: University of Florida Press, pp. 49–53.

[25] Horowitz, David A. (1999). *Inside the Klavern: The Secret History of a Ku Klux Klan of the 1920s*. Carbondale and Edwardsville: University of Southern Illinois Press, pp. 3–4.

to local law enforcement agencies, where it was often welcome. The Klan was careful about where it actually applied violence, avoiding trouble in places where there was organized opposition or where law enforcement was unfriendly – recovered Klan documents from Indiana include notes on the relative supportiveness of various local law enforcers and politicians.[26] Experience taught the Klan what thresholds it could not cross without attracting outside intervention, and those thresholds were usually well short of murder. In 1923, for example, Oklahoma Governor Jack Walton declared martial law after a series of Klan floggings.[27]

At the same time, Klans across the country cultivated local reputations for terror. The two signature displays of Klan force – cross-burnings and parades in white robes – communicated the Klan's presence and its potential for violence, and were used around occasions such as elections to warn their enemies against challenging the social order.[28] Shows of intimidation were designed to frighten the Klan's targets, even if others did not take them seriously.[29] The Klan's effectiveness as agents of terror in this period is debatable; Fryer and Levitt argue that their impact on politics and social order was negligible. But it certainly tried to bolster white Protestant dominance by invoking symbols of violence, while curtailing its actual violence to meet organizational aims of respectability and good relations with the state.

Vigilante activity is not a uniquely American phenomenon. But compared to other countries, vigilantism in the United States has been more widely practiced, more persistent over time, and more culturally accepted as a permanent (if undesirable) feature of social organization.[30] One of the main reasons for this is the strength and density of civil society organizations in the United States. Acts of collective violence require planning and coordination, and high levels of trust among the individuals involved. These same factors are necessary for any

---

[26] McVeigh (2009b), pp. 160–163.

[27] Horowitz (1999), p. 4.

[28] Newton (2001), p. 49.

[29] Gerlach, Larry R. (1982). *Blazing Crosses in Zion: The Ku Klux Klan in Utah*. Logan: University of Utah Press, p. 79.

[30] Ray Abrahams notes that the overwhelming majority of scholarship on the subject has concentrated on the American context and there are very few comparative studies. For some exceptions, see Rosenbaum and Sederberg (1974 and 1976) for comparative theory building; in Rosenbaum and Sederberg's 1976 edited volume, see Lebow, Richard Ned, "Vigilantism in Northern Ireland"; Mazrui, Ali A., "Black Vigilantism in Cultural Transition: Violence and Viability in Tropical Africa"; and Potholm, Christian P., "Comparative Vigilantism: The United States and South Africa"; see also Kowalewski, David (1991). "Counterinsurgent Vigilantism and Public Response: A Philippine Case Study." *Sociological Perspectives*, 34(2): 127–144; Abrahams, Ray (1998). *Vigilant Citizens: Vigilantism and the State*. Cambridge: Polity Press; Fleisher, Michael L. (2000). "*Sungusungu*: State-Sponsored Village Vigilante Groups Among the Kuria of Tanzania." *Africa*, 70(2): 209–228; and Godoy, Angelina Snodgrass (2006). *Popular Injustice: Violence, Community and Law in Latin America*. Palo Alto: Stanford University Press. I make my claim for the uniqueness of the form that vigilantism takes in the United States based on the observations in these studies.

civic activity. A celebrated body of literature from De Tocqueville's *Democracy In America* to Putnam's *Bowling Alone* suggests that Americans have been uniquely adept joiners and organizers, reflected in their historically high membership of organizations that both promote fellowship and also work for specific political goals.[31]

The richness of civic participation in the United States has provided the habits of community participation necessary for vigilante activity,[32] and in some cases it provided the organizational framework for vigilantism itself. Many vigilante organizations in American history were specifically constituted as such, but other vigilante organizations served multiple roles as civic associations, and turned to vigilante activity after establishing or while establishing reputations as fraternal organizations or community associations. The original Ku Klux Klan began as a social club for Confederate veterans in 1865 (the term "Ku Klux" was derived from the Greek *kyklos*, meaning "circle") and adopted violent tactics in response to Reconstruction measures.[33] The second Klan, as noted, emphasized its role as an elite fraternity. The American Legion began in 1918 as an advocacy and social organization for veterans of the Great War, and turned to vigilantism during the "Red Scare" of the early 1920s.

In the same way individuals join organizations in order to develop their social capital, and organizations undertake public tasks and activities for the same reason, so we should expect both individual and group participation in vigilantism to be performed as a status-enhancing exercise. This does not preclude other altruistic (and self-interested) motives for vigilantism, but I argue that patterns of vigilante activity will reflect the status-seeking nature of it, especially for vigilante groups with dual identities as civic associations. As well as protecting their communities, vigilantes try to act in ways that enhance community recognition of their protective role. For this reason, the acquiescence of the local state is one of the most important aims of vigilante associations. Their status as protectors will also grow if they magnify community perceptions of the threats they face.

Establishment violence and its limits in the Second World War

In the lead-up to America's entry into the Second World War the federal government encouraged public vigilance, though not violence. In the First World War, a large network of government-sanctioned and semi-sanctioned

---

[31] See Skocpol, Theda, Marshall Ganz, and Ziad Munson (2000). "A Nation of Organizers: The Institutional Origins of Civic Voluntarism in the United States." *The American Political Science Review*, 94(3): 527–545.

[32] Capozzola (2002) shows that the government fostered vigilantism during the First World War by "appealing to habits of voluntary association" to create organizations such as committees of safety, women's vigilance leagues, and home guards.

[33] Wade, Wyn Craig (1987). *The Fiery Cross: The Ku Klux Klan in America*. New York: Simon and Schuster, p. 33 Foner, Eric (1988). *Reconstruction: America's Unfinished Revolution, 1863–1877*. New York: Harper Collins. pp. 425–426.

vigilante organizations such as the American Protective League had targeted perceived dissidents of all kinds: German nationals, socialists, religious pacifists, and sympathizers with any of these groups. There were multiple lynchings of individuals accused of being spies, often on the basis of little or no evidence.[34] In the most famous case – the murder of Robert Prager by a Southern Illinois mob – historians cannot agree whether the victim was targeted because he was German or because he had known socialist sympathies.[35] The violent excesses of these groups haunted the historical memory of the federal government, and with the approach of the Second World War the government refrained from commissioning any more vigilante organizations.

It did, however, encourage citizens to be vigilant in the face of encroaching threats. The federal government openly nurtured fears of a "Fifth Column." As Francis MacDonnell's definitive account of the Fifth Column scare shows, the Roosevelt Cabinet, the House Un-American Affairs Committee, and the FBI all publicly warned of the need for vigilance against an enemy within.[36] Each of them had their own uses for the Fifth Column rumor. For the Roosevelt Administration it was a pretext to attack anti-war opponents on the Right who, they could insinuate, were doing Hitler's work by removing the threat of American intervention. For HUAC, the Fifth Column rumor was a chance to attack the Roosevelt Administration and the Communists who supposedly held many high-ranking positions in it. For the FBI, the scare showed the necessity of its own work, and was a reason for greatly increased funding and power.[37]

In 1940 Martin Dies, the chair of the House Un-American Affairs Committee, published *The Trojan Horse in America*, a compendium of the threats posed by domestic organizations working for foreign powers. The chapter titles give a good idea of the tenor of the book: "The Whole World Becomes a Modern Troy," "Stalin Bids for American Youth," "A Trojan Horse for Negroes," "An Australian Communist Controls American Shipping," "The Communist Party is Run from Moscow," "Treason is a Communist Virtue," "Kuhn Rides a Trojan Horse for Hitler," "A Trojan Horse of German War Veterans," "Mussolini's Trojan Horse in America." The contents would have been familiar to any American who had followed the news of HUAC's hearings since 1938, which had found that hostile foreign powers (particularly the Soviet Union) had installed a network of agents in the U.S. government. Some were consciously working for the nation's enemies, while others were unknowingly helping them.

[34] Capozzola, Christopher (2002). "The Only Badge Needed Is Your Patriotic Fervor: Vigilance, Coercion and the Law in World War I America." *The Journal of American History*, 88:4.

[35] Schwartz, E.A. (2002). "The Lynching of Robert Prager, the United Mine Workers, and the Problems of Patriotism in 1918." *Journal of the Illinois State Historical Society*, 95(4): 414–437.

[36] MacDonnell, Francis (1995). *Insidious Foes: The Axis Fifth Column and the American Home Front*. New York: Oxford University Press.

[37] MacDonnell (1995), ch. 4 (esp. pp. 78–81), chs. 8 and 9; for a summary, see pp. 6–7.

Dies was a professional anti-communist who considered far-right figures such as Gerald K. Smith reliable authorities on the subject of Communist infiltration. This made the Roosevelt Administration wary of him, and he believed his work was always under threat. His strategic inclusion of fascist groups in hearings of HUAC earned him much-needed publicity and credibility by furthering the "Brown Scare" – the Roosevelt Administration's campaign from 1939 onward to smear isolationists as fascist sympathizers.[38] This campaign was direct and public. In May 1940, Roosevelt called the America First Committee "unwitting agents for Hitler" in one of his radio addresses. Gary Fine argues that while the use of judicial or legislative sanctions against right-wingers during the "Brown Scare" was less frequent than the use of comparable sanctions against left-wingers during either "Red Scare," the use of government propaganda and rhetoric affected many more individuals in the "Brown Scare."[39]

Despite the unpopularity of various "subversive" groups, vigilantism against them had largely disappeared by the Second World War. The government had decommissioned vigilante organizations such as the American Protective League, and others such as the Ku Klux Klan had lost public esteem. With the decline of the Klan in the late 1920s, the American Legion was left as the only large supplier of organized, establishment political violence. The American Legion not only remained organizationally strong, but also had covert approval for "vigilant" activity from one of the highest levels of government. Athan Theoharis's archival work shows that in late 1940 J. Edgar Hoover initiated a secret program to commission thousands of Legionnaires as "Confidential National Defense Informants." The Legionnaires would perform surveillance in their communities and workplaces of individuals they considered suspicious. Legionnaires lobbied Hoover for this program after they were rebuffed by Attorney General Robert Jackson when they offered him their services in mid-1940. Hoover notes in his memos that Legionnaires were upset by the treatment they received from Jackson, and he argues that if the federal government did not take advantage of their offer they would take their intelligence services to state and local governments, which would welcome them. While Hoover's contact program did not amount to an endorsement of vigilante violence, it shows that Legionnaires saw themselves as auxiliary law enforcers and they expected governments to see them in the same way. Theoharis argues that Hoover in particular was prepared to delegate quasi-state powers to them because he saw them as conservative allies.[40]

---

[38] Ribuffo, Leo P. *The old Christian Right: The Protestant Far Right from the Great Depression to the Cold War*. Philadelphia: Temple University press, ch. 5.

[39] Fine, Gary A. (2007). "The Construction of Historical Equivalence: Weighing the Red and Brown Scares." *Symbolic Interaction*, 30(1): 27–39; see also Fine, Gary A. and Terence McDonnell (2007). "Erasing the Brown Scare: Referential Afterlife and the Power of Memory Templates." *Social Problems*, 54(2): 170–187.

[40] Theoharis, Athan (1985). "The FBI and the American Legion Contact Program, 1940–1966." *Political Science Quarterly*, 100(2): 271–286.

As the only remaining vigilante organization in America by the Second World War, it is not surprising that patterns of vigilante violence at this time would reflect the American Legion's organizational aims. Jehovah's Witnesses were particularly offensive to Legionnaires, for reasons described in the previous chapter, and were also the only group with which they could violently engage without endangering their status as a pro-law and order organization. I posit this is why Bundists, Communists, Socialists, and other pacifists had little to fear from public violence in the lead-up to the Second World War while Jehovah's Witnesses experienced large-scale persecution. I also posit that anti-Witness violence declined as the United States entered the Second World War because the symbolic threat Witnesses posed to the Legion declined. The Legion would not have been involved in every act of violence against Jehovah's Witnesses, and much of it was probably initiated by individuals who simply disliked the strangers distributing suspicious literature in their towns. Nonetheless, Legion involvement would have been great enough to affect the overall pattern of violence, and especially the pattern of state acquiescence. In the next section, I test these propositions using a unique source of data: the words of those who experienced the violence.

PERSECUTION OF JEHOVAH'S WITNESSES AS ESTABLISHMENT VIOLENCE

Theoretical expectations

Before evaluating data on the nature of anti-Witness violence, it is important to identify what my theory of establishment violence would expect from it, and what alternative hypotheses would explain other findings. First and foremost, I expect to find high levels of American Legion involvement in the violence. The highest estimate of Legion involvement in anti-Witness violence to date is involvement in just fewer than 20 percent of violent incidents; I expect it to be substantially higher. I expect this involvement to be particularly high in conjunction with incidents involving Witnesses' refusal to salute the American flag. Furthermore, I expect involvement of the American Legion to be more likely when more people were involved in violent acts, reflecting its organizational capacities.

The main alternative hypothesis would be that the likely culprits of most violence were the same people largely responsible for illegal collective violence everywhere: young and often socially marginal men, acting impulsively.[41] If this is the case, then an alternative explanation for why violence declined when the United States entered the war would be that the draft largely removed the

---

[41] See, e.g., Courtwright, David (1999). "The Cowboy Subculture." In Jan E. Dizard, Robert M. Muth and Stephen P. Andrews (eds.), *Guns In America: A Reader*. New York: NYU Press.

population of young risk-takers from the streets.[42] It is important to note that Legionnaires themselves, at least by 1940, were not young men, as service in the First World War was a prerequisite for membership. My explanation for the decline of violence – that it reflected the declining concerns of the American Legion with the need to defend their symbolic capital from Jehovah's Witnesses – suggests we should see American Legion involvement in violence drop more steeply and rapidly than violence as a whole.

I also expect local boundary maintenance to be a major theme of the violence, especially where the American Legion was involved, in accordance with the idea that Legionnaires were concerned with keeping "their" jurisdictions free of people who insulted the flag. The focus of the violence should be on running Jehovah's Witnesses out of town rather than trying to incapacitate them through death, wounding, or imprisonment. An alternative hypothesis is that attackers should have been concerned with the larger subversive threat that Witnesses posed, and so would have tried to report or turn them over to the FBI or some other authority. Finally, I expect to see acts of cooperation between the Legion and law enforcement officials during violent incidents. I argue that law enforcement officers failed to intervene in the violence because they saw it as maintaining local political order. This non-intervention would have been more likely where the perpetrators of the violence were members of a respected local civic group.

Data

I use a unique dataset to explore the 1940s persecution of Jehovah's Witnesses, drawing on the papers of the American Civil Liberties Union. From 1940 onwards the ACLU encouraged Jehovah's Witnesses to write affidavits recording incidents of violence and police harassment and send them to the Solicitor General, Francis Biddle. Witnesses would often send copies of these affidavits to the ACLU, which it kept in its State Correspondence archive. The total number of affidavits and other legal documents regarding persecution of Jehovah's Witnesses in this archive amounts to 3,677 pages, which I read and scanned from the microfilm version of the ACLU archives contained in the University of Michigan library.

While other authors including Shawn Peters and David Manwaring have examined and used documents from this archive before, I am the first to use it to construct a complete, systematic dataset. Taking each "incident" as an observation,[43] I coded all of them on multiple dimensions, including the dates

---

[42] Thanks to Paul Poast for suggesting this alternative hypothesis.

[43] An "incident" here can refer to more than one event, if the events were mentioned in the same document. For example, many affidavits describing arrests in detail also mention previous arrests or harassment. I did not record these other events as separate "incidents" because of the great disparity in information between the main event described and these secondary mentions. This means that my overall counts of incidents are undercounts.

and locations of incidents, whether an assault took place, what threats were made, whether arrests or detentions took place, whether members of the American Legion were identified among the assailants or referred to, whether law enforcement officers refused to protect Witnesses, and whether the flag salute problem was mentioned. I therefore have a large quantitative as well as a rich qualitative dataset, and I use both aspects of it.

This dataset has notable limitations. It is almost certainly not a representative sample of all the actual violence that took place. Witnesses were probably far more likely to write affidavits about incidents where law enforcement officials were involved or were acquiescent, as these were the incidents in which the Civil Rights Section was interested. It is also not the complete sample of affidavits that Witnesses wrote; in the 1950s Manwaring briefly had access to the affidavits housed in the Department of Justice archives; from the description in his book this archive was larger.[44] Manwaring compiled some basic data from these affidavits, which no longer appear to exist. In terms of temporal and spatial distribution our data follow roughly the same patterns, which gives me confidence that my dataset is fairly representative of the affidavits as a whole if not the violence as a whole.

There are three overlapping categories of incidents in my dataset: violence, threats of violence, and police harassment, including arbitrary arrest and imprisonment. Of the 538 total incidents in my dataset, 254 involved physical assaults and 253 involved threats of violence that went beyond any violence actually committed; 245 incidents involved arrests, 168 involved detentions, and in 232 cases the affiant mentions that law enforcement authorities explicitly refused to protect Witnesses or failed to intervene when asked to do so. There is substantial geographic concentration. Although affidavits came from nearly every state, five states between them had 53 percent of incidents: Texas, 110 incidents (20 percent); Oklahoma, 59 incidents (11 percent); Illinois, 54 incidents (10 percent); Mississippi, 35 incidents (7 percent); Indiana, 26 incidents (5 percent).

Findings

Overall involvement of Legion and socially marginally young men
Quantitatively, my data provides partial if not complete support for my theory. The American Legion is specifically mentioned in 199 of 538 incidents in the ACLU affidavits, while "war veterans" were mentioned in another 4 affidavits and Veterans of Foreign Wars are mentioned in a further 6 affidavits. In my sample, therefore, the American Legion features in 37 percent of incidents, while all veterans and veterans groups appear in 39 percent of incidents. These numbers include mostly incidents where affiants identified their persecutors as Legionnaires, but also a few cases where law enforcement

---

[44] Manwaring (1960), pp. 167–173.

officials made explicit threats to turn Witnesses over to the American Legion when the Legion itself was not visible. For example, one affidavit describes how a city patrolman and deputy sheriff in Winslow, Arizona, interrogated and detained three Witness women and one man after hearing that they had been distributing "Fifth Column stuff." After calling the Chief of Police to ask what to do with the Witnesses in custody, the patrolman informed them they would have to leave town within an hour or the police would bring charges against them, and "next time they returned to Winslow they would be turned over to the American Legion."[45]

In cases where actual assaults took place, the Legion or veterans were mentioned in 107 out of 253 incidents, or about 42 percent. They were mentioned in 82 out of 242 arrest cases, or 34 percent. In cases where affiants claimed that law enforcement officers had refused to protect them from possible violence, the American Legion was mentioned 111 out of 235 times, or approximately 47 percent. In 56 cases, the affiant identified a law enforcement agent as a Legionnaire. These are all almost certainly underestimates of actual Legion involvement. Given that affiants only mentioned the American Legion where they were specifically able to identify Legionnaires or when other assailants mentioned them, the number of false negatives where Legionnaires were not identified is likely to be much higher than the number of false positives in which they were incorrectly identified. In any case, the amount of Legion involvement in persecution and harassment of Witnesses was certainly much higher, probably more than twice as high, as has previously been recognized. Legionnaires may have been involved in at least half of all violent incidents.

There is little evidence for the commonsense alternative hypothesis that assailants were disproportionately young or marginal men, the group we would normally expect to be responsible for most assaults and harassment in public.[46] While assailants were nearly always male, there are very few occasions when affidavits describe them as young. Most of the affidavits in which young men are specifically mentioned refer to events in a single location: a series of assaults in South Bend in the summer of 1941. Between July and October of 1941 Witnesses described being assaulted by a gang of "hoodlums" aged between 16 and 20. However, they appear to have been under the control of a local Legion Commander, John DeGrove, who regularly appeared at the scenes of assaults and warned Witnesses to leave. Occasionally DeGrove participated in assaults himself. One of the young assailants, Harry Stanfield, told police in an interview that he was nineteen and that John DeGrove had told him and others to carry out the assaults, adding "they say that the American Flag is a rag

---

[45] Affidavit of Roy Crabb, January 9, 1941, ACLUP vol. 2317.
[46] The State Department's *International Religious Freedom* reports, for example, indicate that in Eastern Europe, adolescent males are responsible for the vast majority of assaults of Jews and vandalism of Jewish cemeteries and memorials.

and I don't like that. He won't go in the draft and I will."[47] DeGrove was brought to the police station for questioning several times but was never charged. On one occasion a detective admitted to one of the affiants that "the police force was ninety percent American Legion, that the Legion ran the town and that the police had no control over the Legion."[48]

In two statements Witnesses describe being attacked by children; in one of those incidents the American Legion again played the organizing role. A letter from a Witness to the ACLU in October 1940 describes how "an angry mob dragged and beat two men" in Connersville, Indiana, while others "threw stones and decayed fruit." Members of the American Legion were present, "directing and advising the men how to go about beating the two men," and "the riot was premeditated by the aforementioned [American Legion] because the small children near the age of twelve gathered decayed fruit in the afternoon that it might be used that night."[49] In another statement, a Witness describes a series of attacks by "a mob of boys ranging from ten years old upwards" in Corning, California. The Witness describes how the boys had "the backing of the town" and they were specifically urged to act by prominent local businessmen. In one case: "The boys were encouraged by a Corning business man, Mr. A.B. Steelman, who is manager and proprietor of the Hotel Corning. The boys obtained a large flag on a staff and tried forcing some of the Witnesses to salute the flag. Because the Witnesses would not salute the flag the boys tormented the Witnesses with paper bags filled with water and clumps of dirt. Another Witness was struck many times."[50] Prior to the attacks, an American Legion member had ordered the Witnesses to leave town.

Apart from the South Bend cases, Witnesses rarely described their attackers in terms suggesting criminality or social deviance. While they sometimes claimed their assailants were drunk, this was nearly always in reference to Legionnaires, who had a reputation for drunkenness.[51] Rather than marginality, Witness affidavits often emphasized the high social status of their persecutors. When Witnesses recognized their attackers they would sometimes provide their occupations along with their names, and businessmen and professionals are disproportionately represented in these accounts.

---

[47] Statement of Allan D. Weaver, July 5, 1941. See also letters of A.M. Mellander to Department of Justice Civil Liberties Unit, July 3, 1941 and July 11, 1941; statements of Anton Kadjzik, David Nalepinski, Ray Rose, and Mae Armstrong, June 28, 1941; statements of A.M. Mellander, Mike Mesarik, Lane Hare, William Baumgartner, Eugenia Buzalski, and Robert Barwig, October 3, 1941. All contained in ACLUP vol. 2328.

[48] Statement of Harry Barwig, October 16, 1941. ACLUP vol. 2328.

[49] Letter to ACLU (author name not visible), October 22, 1940. ACLUP vol. 2230.

[50] Letter of Payne Creek Company of Jehovah's Witnesses to Department of Justice Civil Liberties Unit, January 14, 1942. ACLUP vol. 2319.

[51] Drinking was such an important part of the Legion's social activities that in 1923 one Legion leader identified the Women's Christian Temperance Union as an "Un-American" organization (Pencak 1989, p. 9).

In Sandpoint, Idaho, in December 1941 the Chief of Police told a group of Witnesses who had been working there for a year that they would have to leave because they were about to be mobbed. There was nothing he could do to prevent this because "the largest percent of the businessmen were against (them)" and they would be "hurt and killed" if they did not leave. A month later the president of the Bonner County National Bank, along with three other bank employees, attacked one of the Witnesses as he worked in the street, kicking him and striking him in the face as he passed by an American flag hanging in front of the Elks Building. The affidavit mentions that all four were members of the Elks Lodge.[52] This story indicates that higher-status rather than lower-status individuals may have been primarily responsible for anti-Witness violence, partly because they were able to intimidate law enforcement officers and partly because, as posited by my theory, they were more defensive of their towns' symbolic capital.

Levels of Legion involvement declined as time went on. Legionnaires are recorded as having been involved in 47 percent of incidents in 1940, 36 percent of cases in 1941, and 24 percent of cases in 1942. This conforms to the theoretical expectation that Witness involvement would decline faster than overall violence because of the rapidly increasing status they enjoyed as the United States prepared for and entered the war.

Crowd numbers

As predicted, American Legion involvement in incidents increased as the crowd numbers mentioned by affiants rose. Jehovah's Witness affiants identified specific numbers of assailants in 154 incidents, and in a further 97 incidents identified a "mob." The American Legion was present in 30 of the 55 incidents where a group of more than 20 was involved, in 14 out of 23 incidents where a group of more than 100 was involved, and in all 10 incidents where a group of more than 300 was involved. In these very large incidents Legionnaires nearly always played leading and instigating roles. Large crowd incidents required not only organization but also some sense of legitimacy, which the American Legion was able to provide. Two incidents demonstrate the extent to which the Legion could both mobilize crowds and authorize them to commit violence.

In Holyoke, Colorado, on June 24, 1940, Emil Koch and his family were distributing petitions protesting the Ohio State Fair Association's cancellation of the annual Jehovah's Witness convention at the Columbus fairgrounds.[53]

---

[52] Letter of Read A. Wilkinson to Department of Justice Civil Liberties Unit, January 17, 1942. ACLUP vol. 2408.

[53] Witnesses distributed this petition, addressed to the Governor of Ohio, nationally. It read as follows:

"We, the citizens of the United States, are unalterably in favor of freedom of speech and worship, as guaranteed by the fundamental law of the land.

Jehovah's Witnesses, a body of Christian people, have been invited to hold their annual convention at the Ohio State Fair Grounds, Columbus, July 24–29, 1940. The Ohio State Fair

A bystander, John Zeiler, ordered them to stop their work and leave town, then forcibly took a petition and destroyed it. When Koch asked him by what authority he gave these orders, he answered "By the authority of the American Legion!" In the meantime, a crowd had gathered under Zeiler's leadership and stopped the Witnesses from doing any further work. The Chief of Police appeared, and Koch asked him if he had violated any ordinance that would warrant arrest. The Police Chief replied "I've got this bunch behind me. Leave town and don't come back." According to Koch, "we were pushed, approximately a block, back to our car. While we were being escorted, we were threatened by the mob."[54]

In Guymon, Oklahoma, in August 1940, a crowd of 1,000 gathered outside a courthouse where six Jehovah's Witnesses entered pleas on charges of violating an anti-peddling ordinance that had been passed a few weeks earlier at the instigation of a local Legion and VFW member. After all six pleaded not guilty a local man, not a court official, rose to make a speech. According to an affidavit, he declared before the court that

> Jehovah's Witnesses were un-American, that they did not believe in laws made by man, that they said the flag was the same as an old shirt on a fence post, and that they distributed literature that was un-American. He stated that until the laws were enacted which would stop the spread of such literature that the people would stop it, and the organizations of the Veterans of Foreign Wars, the American Legion, and others were behind them in this. The court house rang with applause.

Outside the courthouse, members of the crowd subsequently beat the affiant "so badly about the face and head that [he was] hardly recognizable."[55]

The flag salute

The American Legion appears in 71 out of 143 affidavits in which refusal to salute the flag was mentioned as a specific source of antagonism, indicating that they were even more disproportionately represented in these incidents than in

---

Association has previously contracted with and agreed with Jehovah's Witnesses for the holding of that convention.

Acting under pressure of selfish interests, the Association has canceled the contract and refuse Jehovah's Witnesses the use of the Fair Grounds. This affects more than thirty simultaneous conventions to be tied in with the key assembly at the Fair Grounds.

We vigorously protest against efforts of selfish religious organizations and others to induce the cancellation of said contract. We demand that the officials of the Fair Association carry out the contract that the convention of Jehovah's Witnesses may be held and that the fair name of Ohio may not be besmirched by selfish opponents of freedom of speech, worship and assembly."

Incidents involving this petition appear in dozens of affidavits from around the country in June and July of 1940. It is difficult to tell whether the act of distributing petitions was itself particularly antagonistic, or whether the petition is highly represented in the early affidavits because this was one of the major activities of the Witnesses at the time that other factors converged to begin the initial wave of persecution.

[54] Affidavit of Emil Koch, July 3, 1940, ACLUP vol. 2220.

[55] Affidavit of Ernest Miller, Jerome Fain, and Otto Bauer, August 14, 1940. ACLUP vol. 2242.

others. Among the ACLU's documents is a copy of a Syracuse, Nebraska, newspaper from July 1940 which contains one of the few written statements in existence about the American Legion's position on Jehovah's Witnesses. The document is a letter by a local Legionnaire in response to an article a week earlier that had alleged Legion involvement in "mob rule and violence" against Jehovah's Witnesses. The Legionnaire, W.K. Kathly, writes as follows:

> What happened is this. A certain organization, whose principles are against saluting the American flag and against other primary ideals which we all hold dear, and which has led to disturbances in other communities of this nation, appeared soliciting at the various doors of Syracuse householders on Sunday morning.
>
> The Syracuse American Legion, which is not a law enforcing body, appealed to the Marshal to request to these people to refrain from disturbing the peace and leave town.... Because we felt the peace of a Sunday morning shouldn't be disturbed by the happenings which have marred other towns, when requests were made to salute the flag, caused outbursts of patriotism, and led to harm to those disloyal to our principles.
>
> The Sheriff without any officiousness, but with calm, merely told these people that they were not wanted in this town, and they left. He himself can testify that there were no threats of violence, but an orderly assembled gathering with pride of the town's good name in their hearts, and patriotism, that led them to resent in their minds the intrusion of a non-patriotic organization in their midst.
>
> This is not an apology, we are patriotic Americans, we believe that all who are sheltered under our glorious American Flag should be proud of its protection, and we of the American Legion affirm our allegiance, that we will always be on guard against anything subversive, but always, like Sunday, through properly constituted authority.[56]

This is an important document because it shows how the American Legion wanted its vigilance to be seen on the public record – as an orderly aid to properly constituted authority. Furthermore it shows the pre-eminence of the flag in the Legion's self-image and how it wanted to be seen. The final paragraph equates the flag, the Legion, and the protection of nation and community. As discussed in the previous chapter, this made the ejection of Jehovah's Witnesses an especially important symbolic activity for the American Legion.

American Legion "authority" to defend the flag was not always so properly constituted. In St. Clairsville, Ohio, in March 1941, vigilantes apprehended thirty-five Jehovah's Witnesses from nearby Wheeling and took them to the American Legion Hall where a Legion spokesman told them to leave, and said "the only thing we have against you people is that you don't salute the flag." As the Witnesses protested that they respected the flag as a symbol of freedom of speech and religion, around 60 people gathered in the hall, turning the proceeding into a pseudo-judicial hearing. The Witnesses were "not allowed

[56] W.K. Kathly, "What Happened Sunday in Syracuse?" *The Syracuse Journal-Democrat* (Otoe County), July 5, 1940.

to say much," but one townsperson spoke up for them, declaring they had a constitutional right to distribute their literature because they were living in a democracy. The Legion spokesman retorted "Are you one of them? Why don't you go over with them?" They were eventually escorted out of town.[57]

Concerns with local boundary maintenance

There is overwhelming evidence in the affidavits that the primary concern of all assailants, not just Legionnaires, was removing Jehovah's Witnesses from their towns and cities. The vast majority of arrests, assaults and threats involved some form of the utterance "get out of town." Witnesses were always well-armed with the legal citations and copies of various government documents stating that their work was not subversive and was allowed under the constitution. They would display these to city officials or others who were harassing them, and frequently – in 97 of the affidavits – they met with the reply that the law or constitution didn't apply here, because "we are the law in this town," or "I am running this town," or some other similar statement. The American Legion was involved in 94 of these 97 incidents, and in several cases the statement took the form of "The American Legion is running this town."

A series of incidents in Snohomish, Washington, in June and July 1940 illustrate the influence the American Legion had in some towns and the extent to which their crusading caused the wave of anti-Witness activity. On June 18 a Snohomish insurance agent approached Edmond Perrenoud, a Witness and resident of nearby Everett, and told him that "We have taken up the matter of you people at our last Legion meeting and we are going to stop you." Four days later, Chief of Police O.D. Morse warned Perrenoud and other Witnesses to stop their work or they would be mobbed. He told them that he was not interrupting their work at the behest of city officials, but because of an "outside source." When "ardent" Legionnaire Noble Des Press began harassing the Witnesses while they worked on July 6, the Police Chief arrested them. Mayor Chas Banworth was present at the police station and when the Witnesses asked him why they had been arrested he answered "because you people don't salute the American flag."

The mayor then told the Witnesses he was letting them go but warned them "Don't come back with your propaganda anymore." They asked Banworth who turned in the complaint against them and he replied "the American Legion," which was immediately confirmed by two Legionnaires present at the station – Noble Des Press and John Bird. The Witnesses, as was customary, began trying to explain their work, but the mayor waved his arms and shouted over them "we won't listen to you. All we want is for you to get out of town and stay out. The American Legion says your literature is subversive propaganda and they will lynch you fellows if you don't get out of town." The Witnesses tried to explain that *Lovell v. Griffin* had established that they were

---

[57] Affidavit of R.L. Drummond, June 4, 1941. ACLUP vol. 2339.

within their rights to distribute literature but the mayor refused to listen, threatening them again with mob action.[58]

This incident demonstrates three important characteristics common in small-town police harassment of Jehovah's Witnesses. First, the American Legion often exercised considerable influence over law enforcement and city officials. Second, the American Legion in this case seems to have been the main channel of information through which the "subversive" rumor was spreading. Third, the Legion's aim was to get the Witnesses out of town, and to accomplish this they threatened a lynching in order to force city officials to take action.

An affidavit by an Oklahoma attorney entitled "Is this Germany or is it America?" tells a similar story of law enforcers acting according to Legion instructions. On July 7 the attorney (whose name is illegible) traveled to Guthrie in Logan County to represent two Jehovah's Witnesses charged with peddling without a license. The Witnesses had told him that no attorney in Guthrie would defend them because of the "public sentiment." The attorney agreed to represent them "though not believing as do Jehovah's Witnesses, and though their literature condemns certain of my ideas." He traveled to Guthrie motivated by the belief that everyone has the right to a fair trial and a defense, and "believing as Voltaire said 'I despise the thing you say but will defend to the death your right to say it.'"

The attorney defended the two Witnesses, Mr. Nichols and Mrs. Sprague, before a police judge. When he gave notice of appeal, two other Witnesses stepped forward to provide bond, at which point they were immediately arrested and thrown in jail. Then "a number of officers and legionnaires" rushed the attorney and demanded that he salute the flag. The attorney replied that he had no objection to saluting the flag but would like to make a statement. They shouted "No! Any lawyer that would represent the sons of bitches is just as bad as they are!" The crowd pushed and shoved the attorney, took his wallet, watch, and keys, and then scattered his papers and put him in jail. A number of officers later took him to be fingerprinted, and they told him the Legion was planning to tear down the jail that night. Sometime between midnight and 1:00 a.m., Police Chief Fred Streeter took him from the jail to another room and told him that he was allowed to go, but there were Legionnaires in the city hall and the police could not guarantee his safety. The police could put him on a bus, said Streeter, but he could not promise that the Legionnaires would not take him off. They might then take him to the city limits and leave him there. When the attorney asked to call friends to come and get him the Police Chief refused, saying that would be dangerous. He said, "I want you to know that I will not give you protection for if the Legionnaires get hold of you, there will be bloodshed and I will not shed any of their blood to protect you

---

[58] Edmond M. Perrenoud affidavit, July 8, 1940, ACLUP vol. 2249.

because this is my home and I have to protect it." Eventually the attorney persuaded the Police Chief to take him to the nearby town of Coyle.[59]

Again, the major theme here is local boundary maintenance. The Legion was determined to eject the attorney because he defended individuals who refused to salute the flag. The way they accomplished this was by threatening violence that forced law enforcement officials to remove the "offender." And though there was a definite element of "lawlessness" in the Legionnaires' actions, they were allowed to take a very active role in legal proceedings. This is a recurrent pattern in the affidavits: the appearance of cooperation between Legionnaires and law enforcement officials who claim to be scared of them. An Orlando, Florida, Witness reported in June 1940 that the city's Police Chief had expressed his view that anyone who refused to salute the American flag ought to be investigated, and remarked that they "had better be careful, or some of those patriotic Legionnaires will get after them." The following day, the Witnesses had been apprehended by a carload of Legionnaires who took them by force to the Legion Hall, questioned them, and threatened them. The Legionnaires claimed they had been deputized by the police. While the police chief later denied this, other Orlando Witnesses reported that police had picked them up and turned them over to the Legion at their hall.[60]

In only one incident that I could find did the American Legion – or any other assailant – discuss the need to keep Jehovah's Witnesses out of *other* towns, or anywhere else. J.W. Jones, a Witness and resident of Pascagoula, Mississippi, had been distributing the *Watchtower* there without incident on street corners for most of 1942, but at the beginning of April he was approached by the Chief of Police who told him that "I don't know anything about your work, and don't want to know, but I do know that we are not going to have it here in Pascagoula." Five weeks later the Chief personally arrested Jones on a charge of peddling without a license. Jones's explanation of events follows the usual Witness theory that all persecution was masterminded by the Catholic hierarchy: "My observation of Chief Ewell is that he would not willfully persecute Christians, but there is considerable cumulative evidence that his unfortunate part in the persecution of Jehovah's witnesses was apparently due to pressure from the American Legion, which does the bidding of the Roman Catholic Hierarchy at Vatican City, Rome."

In the meantime, the American Legion had been conducting its own "investigation" of Jones and his activities. On April 14 the local Legion Commander and a deputy sheriff had interrupted Jones's work in the street, claiming that they "represent the law here in Pascagoula" and requesting Jones appear before the American Legion post the following evening so the Legion could thoroughly investigate his work. The deputy, Lee Byrd, instructed Jones to "bring all you got, don't hold back anything," while the Legion Commander,

[59] "Is This Germany Or Is This America?" Affidavit, July 19, 1940, ACLUP vol. 2220.
[60] Affidavit of John R. Barnes, July 15, 1940, ACLUP vol. 2220.

L.L. Stigler, warned him "if your work is not on the square it is going to be bad for you." Jones appeared before the Legion post the next evening ("at considerable inconvenience") where the scene resembled a "kangaroo court." Before thirty to thirty-five Legionnaires and with Stigler acting as a kind of presiding judge, Harold Gautier (a "Catholic Legionnaire") conducted a "very harsh and severe cross-examination" for nearly two hours, despite Jones suffering an attack of angina.

Jones says he was interrupted too frequently to be able to him explain himself and Witness doctrine, which he was eager to do despite the uncomfortable circumstances. Legionnaires, however (some of them drunk), were permitted to make speeches. Some Legionnaires urged that Jones be arrested because of the subversive threat he posed, rather than allowed to go free. "Why dump our garbage on some other town?" asked one Legionnaire. "If we don't arrest him tonight, he will sneak off to some other town and continue his detestable propaganda, and that would not be fair to the other town." Jones describes the pseudo-judicial conclusion to the ordeal:

> After a considerable display of "parliamentary law" involving motions and a substitute motion, and considerable speech making and strict admonition from Stigler that "the will of the people is the law," and strict instructions that whatever they voted to do with me WOULD BE DONE, and after the final vote, I was "politely" dismissed for the stated reason that they "invited" me there, but that I and all other persons of like "ilk" must DESIST at once within the "jurisdiction" of Post #160, and the boundaries of the post were carefully defined. Otherwise, failure to desist immediately would result in my arrest as American Legion Post #160 would see that I was arrested.

A few days later an article by Stigler appeared in the *Chronicle Star*, the leading newspaper of Jackson County, urging anyone who was subjected to "Jehovah witness propaganda" to call the police or the American Legion and to detain the Witness until somebody arrived to arrest him. After the Chief of Police arrested Jones on May 9 he was visited by a group of Legionnaires in the county jail. They warned him that "we gave you a chance to get out of town and you didn't go … we will keep on fighting you. The Constitution says everyone must salute the flag.… Those who refuse will be put in concentration camps."

Jones continued to distribute literature after his arrest and was harassed by multiple law enforcement authorities. On May 30 a county highway patrolman alerted the sheriff to Jones's activities, and the sheriff physically menaced him. When Jones requested protection from the patrolman he walked away. The sheriff called Jones a "dirty cur" and said he couldn't afford to beat him up in front of all the people in the street, but that if he ever caught him alone "I am going to beat the living hell out of you." Jones replied that the sheriff was there to protect him instead of persecuting him, to which the sheriff sneered "You're not worthy of protection. You won't salute the flag." He added that he had been elected twice as sheriff and enjoyed the full esteem and support of the people.

On another occasion a county patrolman apprehended Jones and called the sheriff to see what he should do. The sheriff's department referred him to the Legion Commander, L.L. Stigler, who in turn referred him to the Legion's "investigator," Harold Gautier. Gautier advised the patrolman not to arrest Jones but to keep an eye on him, as he was "studying the law on my case" before making an arrest. This patrolman, unusually, indicated he was sympathetic to Jones, and was also a Catholic.

Matters came to a head on June 3, when three Jehovah's Witnesses went to the mayor's and sheriff's offices to present a written notice that Jehovah's Witnesses would hold the county and city answerable for any damage to their persons or property if the county and city refused them protection. Three hours later a small group of drunken Legionnaires threatened and assaulted Jones on a lonely country roadside. While restraining Jones "with the strength of a madman," their leader told him that "This war has got to come first with everybody, you're no better than anyone else; who is Jehovah? Damn Jehovah!" Jones's account continues:

> He became wildly hysterical and shouted "You have tried to make a fool out of the officers here. They have had their chance to handle you and your God damn propaganda. They have failed. Now we, the American Legion Post #160, are going to handle you. If you are not out in 24 hours, and have all your belongings out, we are not going to kill you, but we are going to put you across a log and give you a damn good beating. We had figured on the penitentiary for you, but if you are not already cleared out in 24 hours, you won't be able to get to a penitentiary or a concentration camp either."

Just before the Legionnaires forced Jones and his wife into their car, threatening to "break every bone in your God damn body," Jones asked their leader where the American Legion got its authority. "From 130 red-blooded Americans, members of post 160," he replied. On returning to town, Jones visited the sheriff's office, requesting urgent protection. A receptionist told him that the sheriff and his deputies were gone for the day, their resources urgently needed to attend to another emergency. Jones concludes his affidavit that "if I were going to be killed, I wanted to make this statement before that happened."[61]

This incident shows that, ultimately, Legionnaires cared most of all about keeping Jehovah's Witnesses out of their own Command Posts. Even though they discussed the "unfairness" of passing the Witness along to another town with his "detestable propaganda," they would only take action to keep him out of their city. When the law failed to do so, local Legionnaires became infuriated and asserted their authority to keep Jones out of their town. In no other affidavit was there ever even a discussion of turning Witnesses over to a higher authority – anti-Witness action was almost exclusively about local boundary maintenance, and Legionnaires, local officials, and other citizens did not want to involve the outside state.

---

[61] J.W. Jones affidavit, June 8, 1942, ACLUP vol. 2414.

THE FEDERAL GOVERNMENT AND THE END
OF THE VIOLENCE

Franklin Roosevelt talked consistently about a Fifth Column threat through to the fall of 1942, while J. Edgar Hoover frequently mentioned it until early 1943. The prominent capture of a few German saboteurs in the summer of 1942 was a major publicity coup for Hoover, and, in Francis MacDonnell's telling, by 1944 "whenever Hoover discussed the Axis Fifth Column, he did so with the pride of a man who feels he has done his job well." He told newspapers of how he had "erased" the Fifth Column threat.[62] The Fifth Column threat remained a prominent part of American discourse throughout 1941 and 1942. In 1942 alone, Hollywood made more than seventy films dealing with the subject.[63]

The federal government never intended Fifth Column rumors to target Jehovah's Witnesses. News of attacks on Witnesses apparently motivated by these rumors led to attempts by Roosevelt Administration liberals to redirect anti-Fifth Column vigor. Solicitor General and civil libertarian Francis Biddle, who was often at odds with other Justice Department officials obsessed with national security and enemy propaganda,[64] warned in a June 1940 radio address that mob outrages against Jehovah's Witnesses "who had committed no crime" would be investigated, and that "we shall not defeat the Nazi evil by emulating its methods."[65] Writing in her syndicated "My Day" newspaper column of June 21, 1940, Eleanor Roosevelt described brutal mob violence against Witnesses in Wyoming and asked, "Are we going to be swept away from our traditional attitude toward civil liberties by hysteria about 'Fifth Columnists,' or are we going to keep our heads and rid ourselves of 'Fifth Columnists' through the use of properly constituted government officials?"[66]

David Manwaring attributes the decline of violence in 1942 to the actions of the Civil Rights Section of the Justice Department that year. 1942 had seen the first (and only) successful prosecution of a law enforcement official who had participated in anti-Witness violence: Deputy Sheriff William Catlette of Richwood, West Virginia. This was one of the first prosecutions under Section 20 of the criminal code,[67] giving credibility to future threats by U.S. attorneys to prosecute local officials who oversaw violence against Jehovah's Witnesses. The Civil Rights Section sent a memo to US attorneys in May 1942 instructing them how to deal with local authorities that consistently

---

[62] MacDonnell (2005), p. 186.
[63] Ibid., p. 136.
[64] See Gary, Brett (1999). *The Nervous Liberals: Propaganda Anxieties from World War I to the Cold War*. New York: Columbia University Press, ch. 5 (esp. pp. 182–183) for an account of this tension.
[65] Reprinted in American Civil Liberties Union (1941), *The Persecution of Jehovah's Witnesses*. New York: American Civil Liberties Union.
[66] Eleanor Roosevelt, "My Day." June 21, 1940. United Feature Syndicate.
[67] Section 20 made it a misdemeanor offense for anyone "under any color of law" to subject any inhabitant to the deprivation of any constitutionally guaranteed rights, privileges or immunities.

presided over harassment of Jehovah's Witnesses. The memo emphasized mediation and education about Witnesses while mentioning the possibility of prosecution. Manwaring writes that this resulted in a "wave of admonitions" from US attorneys to local officials that "served to make the Jehovah's Witnesses a little more respectable." This extended earlier mediation efforts when Civil Rights Section officials had traveled to trouble spots such as West Texas and given speeches about the harmlessness of Jehovah's Witnesses and the nature of their constitutional rights. Thus, "the Civil Rights Section of the Department of Justice must receive almost all of the credit for finally putting an end to the rash of anti-Witness activity."[68] He further notes that after the memo arbitrary arrests declined at a much faster rate than private violence, thus indicating that the message got through to local law enforcement officials.

While the memo may have had an effect, particularly on the incidence of formal arrests, it came when persecution was already in a second phase of steep decline, down from rates in 1941 that were lower than rates in 1940. *Catlette*, which was a remarkably brutal and grotesque case in which a deputy sheriff openly led a mob attack in front of thousands of eyewitnesses, would not have inspired much fear of prosecution in local officials who often abetted violence by simply not turning up. The federal government had been threatening mob leaders and those officials who assisted them with prosecution since mid-1940, and the ACLU had publicly offered rewards for people who provided evidence that could lead to prosecutions. These never seemed to have any deterrent effect.

Furthermore, the Civil Rights Section had a reputation for ineffectiveness and had its hands full with racist violence in the South. In 1941 the unit had changed its name from the Civil Liberties Unit to the Civil Rights Section to reflect its shift in priorities away from labor and free speech issues and toward protection for African Americans. The chief of the unit, Victor Rotnem, also wanted to break any linguistic association with the "radical" American Civil Liberties Union.[69] The Civil Rights Section was tiny even at its peak in the 1940s, employing just twelve attorneys and a handful of assistants.[70] This lack of staff meant the unit had to rely on US attorneys to carry out any legal action; even if these attorneys sent "admonitions" to local officials on the instructions of the Civil Rights Section it is doubtful whether anyone would have expected them to lead to prosecutions. On issues of race the US attorneys had been deliberately ineffective at actually prosecuting violations because they came from the areas where violations took place and often sympathized with those they were supposed to prosecute.[71]

---

[68] Manwaring (1960), pp. 180–181 and 186.
[69] Goluboff, Risa (2007). *The Lost Promise of Civil Rights*. Cambridge: Harvard University Press, p. 112.
[70] McMahon, Kevin J. (2004). *Reconsidering Roosevelt on Race*. Chicago: University of Chicago Press, p. 145.
[71] Belknap, Michal R. (1987). *Federal Law and Southern Order: Racial Violence and Constitutional Conflict in the Post-Brown South*. Athens: University of Georgia Press, p. 35.

The progress of the war is a much better explanation for why violence declined. Counter-intuitively, American entry into the war reduced enthusiasm for hunting traitors. The onset of the war brought huge organizational benefits to the American Legion, including the prospect of a vastly increased membership and the generally increased esteem for veterans, the natural consequence of involvement in a new war. These factors probably meant that for Legionnaires, any sense of urgency about the need to protect their honor from Jehovah's Witnesses would have sharply declined in relative importance. More importantly, the onset of the war meant a new draft, which resulted in the federal government detaining Witnesses who refused to serve. By November 1942 more than 450 Witnesses had been imprisoned for refusing to respond to induction notices. By the end of the war, 3,992 Witnesses had been convicted for violations of the Selective Service and Training Act.[72] This coercive action probably convinced Legionnaires that the federal government had now taken responsibility for dealing with the Witnesses, just as it previously had taken responsibility for dealing with Communists and Bundists, and so further vigilante action would be unwelcome and maybe bring federal intervention. Persecution was halted not by the Justice Department "making Witnesses more respectable," but by the Draft Board making them less respectable.

In 1945 Nathan T. Elliff, a Justice Department official who headed the Internal Security Section, wrote a painstaking analysis of the government's treatment of Witnesses in the *Virginia Law Review*. He was concerned that "the wholly unprecedented situation of approximately 4,000 members of a religious sect convicted during the past five years" appeared inconsistent with the individual rights Americans expected. Elliff noted an unexpected decline in repressive violence against Witnesses from its peak in 1940 to almost nothing in 1945, despite the "tension and stress" of the war years, which might have been expected to heighten repression. He argued that this "seems to be in keeping with the general restraint shown towards nonconformists during the war," and that the federal government's own actions toward Witnesses reflected a similar restraint. No unfairness, he claimed, had been shown to the many Witnesses who were denied ministerial exemptions from service. All cases had been judged on their individual merits, and Witnesses who had not been engaged in "full-time" Witnessing could not be considered ministers (the average Witness spent only 14.7 hours per week proselytising, while holding a full-time secular job).

Elliff emphasized the near-impossibility of governmental accommodation of Witness beliefs. Witnesses refused alternative forms of non-military service because any compliance with wartime service would make Witnessing impossible, and would be contributing to the state's war effort and violating Witness neutrality in the struggles between nations. Furthermore, they did not

---

[72] Elliff, Nathan (1945). "Jehovah's Witnesses and the Selective Service Act." *Virginia Law Review*, 31(4): 811–834.

want to be called conscientious objectors to war – the traditionally accepted grounds of religious refusal – because of their professed willingness to fight in defense of God's kingdom. This exceptional set of claims, according to Elliff, meant the United States could not be said to have departed from its cherished principles of religious freedom by refusing to recognize them. Instead, Witnesses were locked up in such large numbers because of their own misguided tactics. By insisting they were all ministers, and attempting to challenge their legal classification by refusing to comply with induction orders, they courted conviction. Congress and legal precedent had established citizens could only seek judicial review of their status under the Selective Service Act after induction; there was simply "no suitable alternative method of selecting the personnel of a large army." It was unfortunate, Elliff concluded, that this rule could cause hardship to Witnesses, but (citing a judgment in a previous Witness case) "scruple, however tender we may be towards it, must have a limit, when it stands in the path of a vital national purpose."

Elliff's article is a revealing document about the perceptions of state actors and the predicament of Jehovah's Witnesses. He did not consider the beliefs or the behaviors of Witnesses dangerous, but he could not tolerate their refusal to comply with laws to ensure the army could operate at full capacity during wartime. The United States was not acting illiberally; rather, the Witnesses had turned down every option the government had given them. The imprisonment of Witnesses was a sound administrative response to chaotic transgressions of the law, not anything to do with religious persecution or wartime "hysteria." Elliff was sincere in his concern that Witnesses would not fall victim to such hysteria, which he opposed in all forms.[73] His arguments were a far cry from those of the fire-breathing federal judge who in 1918 declared the "religious propaganda" of Bible Students a "greater danger than a division of the German Army." Nonetheless, Witnesses were a threat to political order. By continually challenging the system that sorted citizens into combatants and non-combatants, they had stretched the state's tolerance of difference to its limits.[74]

As much as it seemed to outsiders that Jehovah's Witnesses courted trouble with the state, this was not the case. As Chapter 5 shows, the Witnesses did have a deliberately provocative agenda, but these provocations were directed against their perceived religious enemies, not the state. Their insistence that they

---

[73] A year later he would recommend against a treason prosecution for Iva Toguri, aka "Tokyo Rose," on the grounds that her broadcasts from Japan had been innocuous. He determined that "Tokyo Rose" was not a single real person but a moniker applied by Allied soldiers to numerous female English-speaking Japanese radio announcers. Kutler, Stanley I. (1980). "Forging a Legend: The Treason of Tokyo Rose." *Wisconsin Law Review* 6 (1980): 1341–1382.

[74] Joseph Zygmunt in a 1977 article states that Witnesses convicted of selective service violations received penalties "significantly harsher than those suffered by any other category of religious objectors," citing a 1947 U.S. Department of Justice report titled *Federal Prisons, 1946*. I have not been able to track down the original report, but if true, this may suggest Witnesses did face consistent discrimination in the federal legal system, contrary to Elliff's belief that there was no problem of unfairness because the law was applied to them neutrally (Zygmunt 1977, pp. 45–57).

could not salute the flag or assist any wartime activity of the state arose from specific, consistent theological convictions Witnesses follow to this day. They did not break the law for the sake of being dissidents or martyrs, which many Witnesses found a huge burden. Nor was their law-breaking an attempt to warn the United States of the impending apocalypse; that was reserved for their literature and proselytism. Witnesses tried, however unfeasibly, to devise compromise solutions, such as their own pledge of allegiance to "all the laws of the United States that are consistent with God's law," and their self-categorization as ministers to avoid alternative service and the "conscientious objector" label. Most state actors did not genuinely suspect Witnesses of treason, but in these actions they saw implacable stubbornness and hostility to properly constituted authority. They did not appreciate the baffling semantics of Witness theology, dismissing as "scruples" things that for Witnesses marked the boundary between the Kingdom of God and the world of Satan. The tireless Witness legal challenges to laws they considered incompatible with their duties showed that Witnesses had faith in the common law and the constitution, both of which they regarded as God-given and which ultimately would have to vindicate them.

CONCLUSION

In this chapter I have argued against the "spasmodic view" of mass violence, to adapt a term of E.P. Thompson's. The vigilantes and law enforcement officers who beat and harassed Jehovah's Witnesses did so in defense of a symbolic order rather than material rights, but they were no less rational and strategic because of that. Even as they inflicted damage on those they considered unpatriotic, made lurid threats, and repeatedly violated the law, they carefully chose their targets and acted within boundaries to ensure that their violence was a status-enhancing rather than a status-diminishing activity.

The ACLU data suggests to some extent that anti-Witness violence was an organized phenomenon that conformed to the strategic aims of a particular group: the American Legion. The fact that the Witnesses' refusal to salute the flag was the proximate cause of the violence has misled previous accounts, which have emphasized the importance of the flag as a national symbol rather than the importance of the flag as a status symbol of the Legion. The decentralized structure of the flag salute regime combined with the federal structure of the Legion gave individual Legionnaires at the local level the responsibility for maintaining this symbolic capital, which they sometimes did with violence and the help of acquiescent officials. Anti-Witness violence was an outgrowth of American civil society, made possible by habits of interpersonal trust and community participation, and serving the aims of a prominent civic association. It flourished for two years because Legionnaires and others understood the limits of the state. They knew how much the state was prepared to tolerate non-state violence, and what kind of violence was acceptable.

7

The Catholic experience in America

INTRODUCTION

Catholics were historically a large but marginal minority in American civic life. At the time the United States was founded, several states denied Catholics access to political office. These prohibitions dissolved within a few decades, but anti-Catholic prejudice did not. The election of John F. Kennedy in 1960 marked only the second time in history a Roman Catholic had secured the presidential nomination of a major party. Even Kennedy's election did not represent the transcendence of the sectarian divide. According to the American National Election Study, Kennedy won the support of 81.7 percent of Catholics but just 37.6 percent of Protestants, a religious gap of 45 percentage points that has never come close to being repeated.[1] In 1959, 25 percent of Americans said they would not vote for a Catholic presidential candidate of their own party; the figure had been 30 percent when Gallup first asked the question in 1937.[2]

Despite Protestant distrust of Catholics, Catholics were not subject to the same kind of persecution in the United States as Mormons or Jehovah's Witnesses. This is not to say that Catholics never suffered violence, or that their political rights were never threatened. In the 1830s, arson against Catholic properties in New England was so widespread that insurance companies refused to places policies on Catholic buildings made of noninflammable materials.[3] The 1850s saw several lethal election riots between Catholics and Protestants. However, Catholics ultimately enjoyed the protection of the state. Governors and federal authorities acted quickly to put an end to anti-Catholic violence,

---

[1] Kinder, Donald R. and Allison Dale-Riddle (2012). *The End of Race? Obama, 2008, and Racial Politics in America*. New Haven: Yale University Press, pp. 68–79.

[2] Saad, Lydia (2011). "In U.S., 22% are hesitant to support a Mormon in 2012." Gallup polling, available at www.gallup.com/poll/148100/hesitant-support-mormon-012.aspx, last accessed May 20, 2013.

[3] Dohen, Dorothy (1967). *Nationalism and American Catholicism*. New York: Sheed and Ward, p. 65.

which was spasmodic rather than sustained. In the mid-nineteenth century, Nativists took political power in several states and cities with ambitious schemes for the exclusion of Catholics from the polity. They managed to enact symbolic and often insulting anti-Catholic measures such as instituting state inspections of convents, but failed to achieve their most prized legislation of extending the waiting period for naturalization to twenty-one years. Catholics continued their slow but steady process of incorporation into the United States.

The relative peace that has prevailed between the Catholic minority and Protestant majority despite high levels of tension, especially since the 1850s, is surprising for a number of reasons. Unlike the Mormon presence in the United States, the Catholic presence has been large and widespread. Unlike Jehovah's Witnesses, Catholics have always been well known. And unlike either religion, Catholicism originates outside the United States, and throughout much of the nineteenth and twentieth centuries it was legitimately associated with foreignness and ethnic difference. But despite some ferocious and popular anti-Catholic rhetoric, the lives and rights of American Catholics remained relatively safe from the mid-nineteenth century onwards, even if they could not hope to elect one of their own as president.

Within the theoretical framework of this book, there are three reasons why Catholics did not suffer sustained persecution, despite their unpopularity, political salience, and the perception that they posed an alien threat. First, it was impossible to delegitimize Catholics as a religion. Centuries of religious conflict and mutual oppression may have made Catholics enemies to Protestants, but there was no escaping that they were religious enemies. All but the most vehement anti-Catholics recognized that religious tolerance meant nothing if it did not include Catholics. Second, it was impossible for anti-Catholic forces to contain the boundaries of Catholic-Protestant conflict. Catholics were numerous and widespread enough that local conflicts had national implications, and state and local authorities did not want to embark on economic suicide by driving away immigrants to more friendly locales.

In addition to these factors, there was a third important political contingency. By the late 1850s the Republican Party had decisively triumphed over both the Whigs and the Know-Nothings for supremacy on the non-Democratic side of American politics. The Republicans had little patience for anti-Catholicism, which they considered a distraction from the far more important cause of anti-slavery. As we have seen in previous chapters, the Republicans explicitly linked anti-Mormonism to the abolitionist agenda, but there was no room for anti-Catholicism, which could alienate large blocs of potential supporters. As the Republicans rapidly incorporated the remnants of the old American Party, Nativists shelved their anti-Catholicism to join the abolitionist cause. Anti-Catholicism thus lost its political sponsorship and disappeared to the fringes of respectable politics, despite its continuing prevalence in the Protestant population at large.

THE RISE OF CATHOLIC AMERICA

The colonial period was fertile for anti-Catholicism. Many early colonists carried ancestral memories of persecution at the hands of the Catholic Church in Europe. The Huguenots and various Anabaptists had fled directly from violent persecution in Catholic states. Catholic rule was long extinct in England, but fear of Catholic power remained strong among the English puritans, whose many complaints against the Church of England included that it was too similar to the "Whore of Rome." Colonial competition with France and Spain added an element of existential threat to late-seventeenth-century anti-Catholicism, especially given the role of the Catholic Church in drawing Indians to the French side of colonial wars.[4] In this environment, anti-Catholicism flourished. The sixteenth- and seventeenth-century fears and hatreds of European Protestants regarding Catholicism fossilized in America and were preserved well beyond the point where they disappeared throughout most of Europe.

Despite the virulence of colonial anti-Catholicism, by the time of the revolution Catholics were beginning to benefit from the increasing climate of religious pluralism that had first allowed quarreling Protestant sects to make peace with each other. The revolutionary war itself was important, as it gave Catholics the opportunity to prove their patriotism (in contrast to many Anglicans who remained loyal to the Crown) and because the Continental Congress was forced to seek out Catholic France as an ally. Catholics were no longer an external or internal threat; they only numbered around 40,000 in 1790 – less than 1 percent of the total population.[5] During Washington's presidency "even the most devout Protestants were now sometimes forced to concede that Catholicism represented a species of Christianity."[6] Institutional arrangements for religious tolerance in the colonial period had often excluded Catholics, but from the foundation of the Republic, Catholics were recognized nationally as a legitimate religious presence.

Catholicism, however, was more than a religion. Gordon Allport observed "the chief reason why religion becomes the focus of prejudice is that it usually stands for more than faith – it is the pivot of the cultural tradition of the group."[7] As Irish and German immigrants became the face of Catholic America in the nineteenth century, Catholicism became enmeshed in a complex web of ethnic, linguistic, and cultural associations. As the second party system consolidated, religion became increasingly important to political

---

[4] Preston, Andrew (2012). *Sword of the Spirit, Shield of Faith: Religion in American War and Diplomacy*. New York: Knopf, pp. 24 and 50.

[5] Gillis, Chester L. (2012). "American Catholics, 1800–1950." In Stein, Stephen J. (ed.), *The Cambridge History of Religions in America: Volume II, 1790 to 1945*. New York: Cambridge University Press, p. 251.

[6] Beneke, Chris (2006). *Beyond Toleration: The Religious Origins of American Pluralism*. Oxford: Oxford University Press, pp. 180–186.

[7] Allport, Gordon W. (1958). *The Nature of Prejudice* (abridged). New York: Doubleday, p. 414.

identity. Ethno-cultural historians of American politics such as Philip Kleppner, Richard Jensen, and Robert Swierenga have described the interplay of theology, culture, and party politics during this period. They identify a continuum of ethno-religious groups with hierarchical "liturgical" groups such as Catholics, Lutherans, and Episcopalians at one end, and "pietistic" Protestant groups stressing Biblical faith and the imminent return of Christ at the other. Pietists used the Whig Party as a vehicle to pursue a social reform agenda aimed at eradicating deviant behavior associated with immigrants, such as drinking on the Sabbath.[8] Liturgicals were attracted to the Democratic Party, which viewed religion as a private matter and believed the state had no role in legislating social behavior.[9]

From this new political cleavage emerged two very different views of religious freedom, which would resurface in similar form in debates over Mormon polygamy half a century later (see Chapter 4). Catholics and other liturgicals defended their communal rights to religious practices that were hierarchical, separatist, and foreign. They maintained separate parochial schools for their children, said mass in foreign languages, and their bishops exercised considerable social and political influence over adherents. To them, religious freedom was government non-interference in religious life. For pietist Protestants, however, the authoritarian structure of Catholicism denied freedom of conscience to its own flock and threatened the freedom of all other Americans.

The abuse of clerical power featured heavily in anti-Catholic propaganda in the early nineteenth century. Anti-Catholicism, in the words of Richard Hofstadter, was "the pornography of the Puritan," and anti-Catholic stories would depict libertine priests running amok in convents where nuns were helpless captives. The best-known work in this genre was *The Awful Disclosures of Maria Monk*, published in 1836, which described the strangling of babies born from trysts between priests and nuns.[10] As outlandish as this might have seemed, two years earlier similar stories had motivated a mob in Charlestown, Massachusetts, to burn down the Ursuline Convent on the suspicion that a woman was being held there against her will. Captivity narratives about Catholic women in the first half of the century

---

[8] Ray Allen Billington ([1938] 1952). *The Protestant Crusade, 1800–1860*. New York: Rinehart & Co., Inc. According to Billington, "The lack of respect on the part of foreigners for such an American institution as the Puritan Sabbath was a source of never-ending regret to New Englanders both in New England and the west. Equally annoying to many was the Irish devotion to whiskey and the German to beer, which aroused the antagonism of temperance advocates everywhere. In many of the larger cities, they complained, most the grog shops were kept by Irish with the open connivance of their priests" (p. 195).

[9] Swierenga, Robert P. (2007). "Ethnoreligious Political Behavior in the Mid-Nineteenth Century: Voting, Values, Cultures." In Noll, Mark A. and Luke E. Harlow (eds.). *Religion and American Politics: From the Colonial Period to the Present*. Oxford: Oxford University Press, p. 150.

[10] Hofstadter, Richard ([1964] 1996). *The Paranoid Style in American Politics and Other Essays*. Cambridge: Harvard University Press, p. 22.

created a template for similar narratives about Mormon women in the second half of the century (see Chapter 4).

Thomas Whitney, a nativist editor and politician, argued Catholics were unfit to vote because by submitting to priestly authority, an individual "divests himself of all individuality" and becomes a "mere instrument."[11] Reverend W.C. Brownlee, another nativist editor in New York, wrote "the pope considers all Roman Catholics his subjects, bound by his commands," and made the familiar claim that Catholic monarchs were conspiring to destroy the United States by filling it with their excess populations.[12] Samuel Morse warned that the Pope himself was a puppet of the Habsburg Emperor. Both Catholicism and imperial despotism operated through the same system of servitude, which was being imported to the United States by increasingly politicized Catholic immigrants:

> These conspirators against our liberties who have been admitted from abroad through the liberality of our institutions, are now *organized* in every part of the country; they are all subordinates, standing in the regular steps of slave and master, from the most abject dolt that obeys the commands of his priest, up to the great master-slave Metternich ... They report from one another, like the sub-officers of an army, up to the commander-in-chief at Vienna (not the Pope, for he is but a subordinate of Austria.)[13]

Tyler Anbinder has shown that Morse's explicit connections between immigration and Catholic-monarchical plots had a major and negative effect on opinions about immigration, which Americans had previously seen as beneficial.[14]

David Brion Davis draws important parallels between the literatures of anti-Catholicism, anti-Mormonism, and anti-Masonry. What distinguished them all was a preoccupation with "a secrecy that cloaked the members' unconditional loyalty to an autonomous body."[15] Members of these groups could not be free people, because they surrendered their very consciences to the shadowy hierarchies of their organizations. They could not be trusted, because their group allegiance overrode any loyalty to common institutions or principles. They were inherently subversive. Despite the similarities between anti-Catholic

---

[11] Hamburger, Philip (2002). "Illiberal Liberalism: Liberal Theology, Anti-Catholicism, and Church Property." *Journal of Contemporary Legal Issues*, 693: 704–705.

[12] Brownlee, William Craig (1836). *American Protestant Vindicator and Defender of Civil and Religious Liberty against Inroads of Popery*. Quoted in Bennett, David H. (1995). *The Party of Fear: The American Far Right from Nativism to the Militia Movement*. New York: Vintage, p. 38.

[13] "Brutus" (Samuel Morse), (1835). *Foreign Conspiracy against the Liberties of the United States*. New York: Leavitt, Lord and Co., p. 54.

[14] Anbinder, Tyler (1992). *Nativism and Slavery: The Northern Know Nothings and the Politics of the 1850s*. New York: Oxford University Press, p. 9.

[15] Davis, David Brion (1960). "Some Themes of Counter-Subversion: An Analysis of Anti-Masonic, Anti-Catholic, and Anti-Mormon Literature." *The Mississippi Valley Historical Review*, 47(2): 205–224.

and anti-Mormon propaganda, by the 1880s there was bipartisan federal legislation to counter Mormon subversion, while anti-Catholicism had been confined to the margins of politics and proposed legislation to thwart the Catholic menace had consistently failed. To understand why, we need to examine the trajectory of anti-Catholicism in the context of partisan competition.

THE FIRST WAVE OF POLITICAL ANTI-CATHOLICISM

No-Popery emerged as an organized political movement around 1840. By this point, the Democrats had "apparently bartered their birthright for foreign votes," while the Whigs had flirted with nativist ideas but refused to translate them into political action.[16] The 1841 New York elections were instructive for Democrats, who had tried to stay silent on the contentious issue of whether Catholic schools should receive public money. This attempt to avoid alienating both nativist and Catholic constituencies failed; the Democrats lost the election by 290 votes, but would have won if they had retained the support of 2,220 voters who opted for a specifically Catholic ticket.[17] From the 1840s onwards, the Democrats would identify openly with Catholic and immigrant interests, generally to their electoral advantage. Alarmed by the apparent favoritism toward immigrants shown by Democratic governments in cities like New York and Philadelphia, local nativist associations formed in several major cities, and were enjoying electoral success by the mid-1840s.

The overwhelming policy concern that united these local parties when they consolidated into the American Republican Party was reform of naturalization laws. Though they could implement some marginal restrictions on immigration through control of city governments, the nativists needed Congress to get the reform they really wanted, which was extending the naturalization period for twenty-one years before immigrants could vote. Through its representatives in the House and sympathetic senators, the American Republican Party and the upstart Native American Party managed to get this measure to the judiciary committee stage, but there it repeatedly stalled in both houses. Ray Allen Billington characterizes the American Republicans as "unable to foster a successful program in Congress or in the States, nevertheless ... an important factor in creating antagonism against aliens and Catholics."[18] Anti-Catholicism in the 1840s had a political voice, and had political representatives, but it lacked the allies it needed to implement a political program. The unwillingness of the more established parties to back anti-immigrant measures heightened nativist resentment, and increased the volume and virulence of anti-Catholic rhetoric in nativist publications as the decade went on.

---

[16] Billington ([1938] 1952), p. 200.
[17] Ibid., pp. 151–154.
[18] Ibid., p. 209.

Early political nativists had been relatively careful to minimize overt anti-Catholicism and avoid charges of religious intolerance that could be used to kill off nativist legislation. The congressional nativist parties, however, attracted aggressive rabble-rousers who made no attempt to hide the religious prejudice that was an important component of their mass appeal. Lewis C. Levin, the Native American Party leader in the House, made long, incendiary speeches that antagonized other members of Congress. His speeches in support of naturalization legislation in 1845 were openly anti-Catholic, but contained a note of outrage that the nativists were being accused of bigotry and sectarianism. "So far from interfering with freedom of conscience," claimed Levin, "we will resist any sect that shall ever attempt to invade its sanctity – we will resist any sect that attempts to combine, as such, to accomplish a political project, whether that sect be Baptist, Methodist, Presbyterian, Episcopalian, or Roman Catholic."[19] Despite the neutral rhetoric of this litany, Levin's audience would have been well aware of the old, persistent accusation that Catholics in particular pursued political ends through their church.

The political limits of nativist anti-Catholicism were clear: the more intense it got, the more it repelled people with real power. The nativist parties and their proliferating newspapers developed a strong following in the major cities, especially among native-born workers who were competing with immigrants for jobs. This support base raised the ever-present fear of mob action and made it difficult to find allies in the propertied classes. These fears appeared to be realized in the Philadelphia riots of 1844, in which working-class nativists inflicted serious damage on the city's Irish community, including several deaths and the burning of churches. The riots, which were quelled by the military and were denounced in newspapers across the country as a national disgrace, reversed the political momentum of the nativist parties, which were deserted by voters outside of the urban cores of sectarian conflict.[20]

As support for the first iteration of political anti-Catholicism declined, Catholic immigration grew. A total of 2.9 million immigrants arrived between 1845 and 1854, and the immigrant proportion of the population reached 14.5 percent, which has never been equalled since.[21] Propelled by the potato blight, the 1.5 million Irish who migrated to the United States were overwhelmingly Catholic, and far poorer and less skilled than previous generations of Irish immigrants. German migration was also much higher, poorer, and more Catholic than in preceding decades. Nativist sentiment

---

[19] *Congressional Globe*, House of Representatives, 29th Congress, 1st session. Appendix, p. 49.
[20] Billington ([1938] 1952), p. 234. In his account: "The Philadelphia riots, with their bloodshed, property destruction, and church burning deeply shocked the majority of Americans whose natural conservatism led them to view any attack on private property with suspicion. Particularly alarmed were the sober, church-going citizens who had been attracted to the anti-Catholic cause by the New York school controversy and who now shrank from a continued alliance with such a lawless group as the nativists had demonstrated themselves to be."
[21] Anbinder (1992), p. 3.

again escalated, and various fraternal orders maintained an organizational network for a political nativism that would be ready to take opportunities when they arose.

THE KNOW-NOTHING MOVEMENT

The demise of the Whigs in the mid-1850s opened up new space for nativists in the party landscape. The Whigs had been fatally divided over the expansion of slavery, but they had also been torn on immigration and public money for Catholic schools. The parochial school funding issue re-emerged in the 1850s, along with heated controversy over whether Catholic churches should be allowed to consolidate property in the hands of their bishops, which to some Protestants was a license for clerical tyranny.[22] President Franklin Pierce's appointment of a Catholic Postmaster General convinced many Americans that "politicians would stoop to any level to capture immigrant votes," enraging Democratic as well as Whig nativists.[23]

In the first years of the 1850s, the anti-Catholic backlash was incubated outside the party system in secret societies such as the Order of the Star-Spangled Banner and the Order of United Americans. Even as anti-Catholic writers railed against the secrecy of the Catholic hierarchy, anti-Catholic political organizers understood the appeal of secretive fraternal organizations, which conferred on members an illusion of status and exclusivity that helped break the mob stigma of the Philadelphia riots.[24] The secret orders also heightened nativist paranoia: Catholic plots were so sinister and wide-reaching that patriotic Americans could only fight them by adopting the enemy's methods. Inductees into the Order of the Star-Spangled Banner had to be able to prove they were American-born, with Protestant parents, and not married to a Catholic. They were sworn not to vote for Catholics or foreigners and, if they were elected to political office, to devote themselves to a program of removing Catholics and aliens from government.[25]

---

[22] See Hamburger (2002). The issue was greatly aggravated by the prolonged visit of Papal Nuncio Gaetano Bedini to the United States to settle disputes between schismatic parishes in Buffalo and Philadelphia. His trip attracted much attention and suspicion about the Vatican's designs on America. See Anbinder (1992), pp. 27–28.

[23] Ibid, p. 30.

[24] David Brion Davis captures the complex relationship between the loathing of conspiratorial societies and the desire to emulate them: "What distinguished the stereotypes of Mason, Catholic and Mormon was the way in which they were seen to embody those traits that were precise antitheses of American ideals. The subversive group was essentially an inverted image of Jacksonian democracy and the cult of the common man; as such it not only challenged the dominant values but stimulated those suppressed needs and yearnings that are unfulfilled in a mobile, rootless and individualistic society. It was therefore both frightening and fascinating." Davis (1960), p. 208.

[25] A section of the Order's constitution dealing with its political objectives proclaimed that: "The object of this organization shall be to protect every American citizen in the legal and proper exercise of his civil and religious rights and privileges; to resist the insidious policy of the Church

The Know-Nothings emerged from these fraternal lodges as a separate political party in 1854. They enjoyed surprising success in the spring elections, massive membership growth in the summer, and then stunning victories in the fall elections, including sweeping the state of Massachusetts. Historians disagree over exactly what prompted more than a million Americans to desert the traditional parties in favor of the Know-Nothings that year. Billington claims the only thing uniting the diverse organization was hatred of Catholics, which took precedence over more generalized concerns about aliens. They were completely incoherent on other issues. "Campaign pamphlets issued in the south and north," writes Billington, "read like those of entirely different parties." The party leaders deliberately ignored the problem of slavery, which Billington says would have exposed a Whig–Democrat divide within the party.[26] Anbinder, however, argues sympathy for nativism was a secondary factor, and the Know-Nothings owed their rapid success to the failure of the major parties to provide a pro-temperance and anti-slavery alternative. The Southern Whigs' acquiescence to the Kansas–Nebraska Act sealed the fate of their party. This is not to downplay the importance of anti-Catholicism, which was intimately associated with anti-slavery at that time. The only thing that actually linked the Know-Nothings to anti-slavery was that most Northerners believed the Catholic Church condoned slavery and that Irish immigrants in particular favored it.[27]

Electoral success did not translate into legislative success for the Know-Nothings. After the 1854 congressional elections, Know-Nothings (organized under the name "American Party") held the balance of power in both houses of Congress. While the major parties needed Know-Nothing support to pass legislation, they made it clear that they would not support anti-Catholic or nativist legislation in return. Schemes to exclude Catholics from office were impossible from the outset because of the constitutional prohibition on religious tests for office, as opponents of the Know-Nothings were quick to remind the nativist newcomers. While Know-Nothings concentrated their efforts on the naturalization laws, insisting they posed no threat to religious freedom, their opponents referred back to the literature of the anti-Catholic orders from which they had sprung as evidence that their real agenda was religious proscription. Mississippi Democrat William Barry, in a heated encounter with Massachusetts Know-Nothing Nathan Banks in December 1854, produced the oath of the Order of the Star-Spangled Banner that required of members that "if it may be done legally, you will, when elected to any office, remove all foreigners, aliens or Roman Catholics from office." Barry went on to assault the secrecy of the

---

of Rome, and all other foreign influence against our republican institutions, in all lawful ways; to place in all offices of honor, trust or profit, in the gift of the people, or by appointment, none but native-born Protestant citizens, and to protect, preserve and uphold the Union of these states and the Constitution of the same." Reproduced in Billington ([1938] 1952), p. 386.

[26] Ibid., pp. 386–387.
[27] Anbinder (1992), pp. 43–48.

Know-Nothing organizations and assert the mainstream position on religious tolerance in Congress:

> The Boston Investigator has for years avowed and advocated principles utterly at war with Christianity; yet, no body of men that I know of, has leagued together, by solemn oaths, to disfranchise the editor or his readers of their civil rights. The Unitarianism prevalent in and about Boston is as little acceptable to the great body of Christians in this country as Catholicism; but the truly noble tolerance of the people has not thought it just or politic to attempt the extinction of heresy or infidelity by imposing civil disabilities. The best, the only proper remedy for erroneous opinion, is argument and truth, offered in the spirit of respect and kindness; and a party in which, in a free country, attempts to drive men by secret or open proscription, and to punish freedom of thought by covert assaults of intolerance, can achieve only a temporary success, and escape for but a little while the condemnation which enlightened men visit upon every form of persecution.[28]

While anti-Catholic secret societies had been vital for building the nativist movement in the early 1850s, once that movement was in Congress its shadowy origins became a handicap and it was open to the same accusations of subversion it leveled against the Catholic Church. Even when they framed their naturalization proposals in terms that minimized anti-Catholicism, the congressional Know-Nothings attracted little support for immigration reform.

The Know-Nothings also failed to pass legislation advancing their agenda in states where they had gained legislative majorities – Massachusetts, Maryland, Connecticut, Indiana, and California. State assemblies could do relatively little about immigration and suffrage, the Know-Nothings' main preoccupations. Their modest attempts to legislate in these areas were usually stifled by their own incompetence – the Know-Nothings were nearly all novices in politics, and had no idea how to effectively advance legislation even in chambers that they dominated. In Massachusetts and Maryland, the Know-Nothings' signature innovations were state inspections of convents and Catholic schools, which turned into embarrassing farces when evidence of libertinism and captivity failed to materialize. For Billington, this ineptitude is what doomed nativism as a political movement: "The almost complete failure of the Know-Nothings to carry into effect the doctrines of anti-Catholic and antiforeign propagandists contributed to the rapid decline of this nativistic party."[29]

The spectacle of rioting also returned in 1854 and 1855, marring elections in cities across the country and further damaging the respectability of the Know-Nothings. This violence was of a different quality from the 1844 Philadelphia riot or the 1835 Ursuline Convent burning, which had overtly religious targets and relatively clear distinctions between Catholic victims and anti-Catholic perpetrators. The election riots of the mid-1850s were more like gang

---

[28] *Congressional Globe*, House of Representatives, 33rd Congress, 2nd session. Appendix, pp. 49–53.
[29] Billington ([1938] 1952), pp. 407 and 412–417.

warfare. In David Grimsted's authoritative account, anti-Catholicism "was perhaps (the) least important" component of the volatile mix of tribal politics, juvenile delinquency, and sensationalist media that generated the riots, though he acknowledges that arrests of anti-Catholic street preachers for vagrancy helped to arouse the anger of Know-Nothing mobs. There were twenty-two riots between Democratic and Know-Nothing groups in the 1850s, the largest and bloodiest coming in Baltimore, Louisville, and Cincinnati between 1854 and 1856. Two-thirds of the riots are believed to have been started by Democrats while one-third were begun by the Know-Nothings, but ethnic groups supporting the Democrats suffered the heaviest losses.[30]

Opponents of the Know-Nothings increasingly painted them as the party of violent urban disorder, and pro-slavery forces exploited this reputation to crush opposition in contentious cities such as Washington. In June 1857, President James Buchanan dispatched 110 marines to Washington to protect the polls, in response to reports that nativist gangs from Baltimore were intimidating voters. Mayor William D. Magruder ordered the troops to fire on a polling crowd in unclear circumstances late in the afternoon of the election, resulting in the deaths of more than ten people. While the local Democratic press initially hailed this action as a triumph of law and order, it later emerged that most of the dead were innocent Washington citizens, and the only Baltimore gang members among the casualties were both Democrats. In Grimsted's words,

> this, the strongest action to repress Know-Nothing electoral violence, occurred where no violence was going on and took the lives of at least two Germans, two blacks, two teenage boys and only some other local citizens, only one of them a known American Party supporter. It was a slaughter of Americans voting peaceably by marines ordered out by a proslavery president under a drunk proslavery mayor.[31]

Slavery was another political factor that had benefited the Know-Nothings early in the 1850s but led to their demise later in the decade as it grew to subsume all other issues. Even more than legislative failure and the stigma of violence, the awkwardness of the Know-Nothing position on slavery condemned the party to ultimate irrelevance. In July 1854, the Republican Party was founded as a single-minded anti-slavery party. In the meantime, the Know-Nothings persisted in their attempts to ignore the issue and avoid dividing the American Party on sectional lines. In 1855, the party's national convention adopted a resolution "disparaging any agitation" over the Kansas–Nebraska Act, effectively approving it. With state Republican Parties now available as a clear alternative, fifty-three Northern delegates defected from the Know-Nothings, believing the party had no chance in the North without an anti-slavery platform.[32]

[30] Grimsted, David (2003). *American Mobbing, 1826–1861: Toward Civil War*. New York: Oxford University Press, p. 226.

[31] Grimsted (2003), pp. 241–242.

[32] Foner, Eric (1970). *Free Soil, Free Labor, Free Men: The Ideology of the Republican Party before the Civil War*. New York: Oxford University Press, p. 240.

The new Republican Party had a distinctive cultural politics: traditional Yankee pietist inclinations toward evangelical Protestantism, temperance, and sabbatarianism. As such, it was a natural home for nativists who opposed slavery and were finished with the Know-Nothings. However, the Republican leadership showed a marked impatience with any issue that might distract them from the central problem of slavery. Radicals within the party actively fought nativism, suspecting that the whole Know-Nothing movement was a Southern plot to cripple abolitionism. Another element of the party, associated with William H. Seward, was ideologically opposed to nativism, instead favoring an assimilationist approach that emphasized the potential of all immigrants to become good citizens. For other Republicans, electoral mathematics was the overriding concern. After 1855, Republican leaders refused even to adopt temperance platforms, believing it could cost them votes that would be vital to the anti-slavery cause.[33]

By 1856, when the Republican Party was nationally organized, it was winning the battle for ascendancy on the non-Democratic side of American politics. Republicans co-opted Know-Nothing Nathan Banks in the bitter contest over the House speakership in 1856, eventually winning the contest and creating a (briefly) victorious Congressional Republican Party while destroying the congressional Know-Nothings. The party platform of 1856 disavowed the nativist proscription of foreigners (to satisfy the party's German bloc) and Republicans nominated the radical John C. Frémont for President in the face of unfounded accusations that he was a Catholic. Frémont probably lost the election because of the loyalty of a number of Know-Nothings to Millard Fillmore, which handed the election to James Buchanan. Nonetheless, the 1856 election showed that nativist votes were overwhelmingly going to the Republicans despite their antipathy to the nativist cause. By 1860, the Republicans had curbed nativist influence within their party in the former nativist strongholds of Massachusetts, Pennsylvania, New York, and Connecticut, and the increasingly powerful German leaders in the party secured an even stronger anti-nativist plank.[34] There was no nativist candidate in the 1860 election, and the Know-Nothings ceased to exist as a political force.

ANTI-CATHOLIC POLITICS AFTER THE KNOW-NOTHINGS

The fall of nativism as an electoral power did not eradicate anti-Catholicism from public opinion. Some of the best-known artifacts of American anti-Catholicism, such as Thomas Nast's famous "American River Ganges" cartoon, appeared in the decade after the Civil War.[35] State aid to Catholic

[33] Ibid., pp. 234–241.
[34] Ibid., pp. 247–260.
[35] www.harpweek.com/Images/SourceImages/CartoonOfTheDay/May/050875m.jpg, last accessed June 18, 2013.

education yet again surfaced as a political issue in the 1870s. Dozens of states passed "Blaine Amendments" to their constitutions prohibiting the use of state funds for religious schools.[36] Despite the generic language of these amendments, they were aimed at Catholic education. Protestant enculturation continued unimpeded in the common schools, where readings from the King James Bible were a normal feature of the curriculum. The Supreme Court has noted that the prevalent condemnation of "sectarian" education was a coded term for "Catholic."[37] In 1875, federal Republicans took up the cause of a federal Blaine Amendment. John Higham argues they "desperately needed a new issue to replace their now discredited Reconstruction policies and to distract the public from the scandals of the Grant regime."[38] The proposed amendment, which Grant supported, passed the House easily but failed in the Senate.

Anti-Catholic prejudice persisted, and was occasionally exploited by Republicans in the late nineteenth century when they tried to smear Democrats with Catholicism by association. It was not always a successful tactic. In 1884, Republican presidential nominee James G. Blaine (author of the federal Blaine Amendment) lost a close election in which a prominent evangelical supporter had labeled Democrats the party of "Rum, Romanism and Rebellion." This slur is believed to have cost Blaine the heavily Irish vote in New York, and thus the entire election.[39] For the most part, anti-Catholicism

---

[36] The bulk of these amendments were passed in the second half of the nineteenth century, but some came earlier, and several states passed them in the twentieth century. In chronological order, the states that passed Blaine Amendments were Indiana (1816), Virginia (1830), Florida (1845), New York (1846), Wisconsin (1848), Michigan (1850), Ohio (1851), Minnesota (1857), Oregon (1857), Kansas (1859), Illinois (1870), Pennsylvania (1874), Missouri (1875), Nebraska (1875), Colorado (1876), Texas (1876), Georgia (1877), New Hampshire (1877), California (1879), Nevada (1880), Washington (1880), Montana (1889), North Dakota (1889), South Carolina (1889), Wyoming (1889), Idaho (1890), Mississippi (1890), Kentucky (1891), Utah (1895), Delaware (1897), Alabama (1901), Arizona (1910), Oklahoma (1910), New Mexico (1911), Massachusetts (1919), Alaska (1956), Hawaii (1959).

[37] DeForrest, Mark Edward (2003). "An Overview and Evaluation of State Blaine Amendments: Origins, Scope, and First Amendment Concerns." *Harvard Journal of Law and Public Policy*, 26: 55–626. Today, these amendments have far more neutral connotations, and are part of the general legal framework of the "wall of separation" between church and state in America. Some Catholic scholars argue that Blaine Amendments are persecutory because they impose barriers to public benefits based on religious preferences (see Duncan, Kyle (2003). "Secularism's Laws: State Blaine Amendments and Religious Persecution." *Fordham Law Review*, 72: 493–592.) The Catholic Church has taken the position that the right of parents to choose religious education on equal terms with other forms of education is a basic human right, derivable from the Universal Declaration of Human Rights and the Declaration of the Rights of the Child (see Morris, Andrew B. (1998). "By their fruits you will know them: Distinctive features of Catholic education." *Research Papers in Education*, 13(1): 93–95).

[38] Higham, John ([1955] 1971). *Strangers in the Land: Patterns of American Nativism 1860–1925*. New York: Atheneum, pp. 28–29.

[39] Hoffmann, Karen S. (2000). "Presidential Character in the Nineteenth Century." *Rhetoric and Public Affairs*, 3(4): 653–664: 661.

gradually faded from mainstream political life, though it lived on in numerous secret societies and periodicals. Higham notes that in the late nineteenth century, increasing urban secularism effectively banished anti-Catholicism from its traditional home in the major cities, but it gained a new following in the rural South and Midwest. He claims that it "often lacked genuine religious feeling," but was "connected with an unsatisfied progressivism" that channelled rural suspicions that farmers were constantly being thwarted by forces operating in the cities. This form of No-Popery was "strong in propaganda outlets" during the early twentieth century, but "suffered particularly from inadequate organization."[40]

The last major spasm of organized anti-Catholicism came with the re-organization of the Ku Klux Klan in the 1920s. Outside of the South, the Klan's major preoccupations were Catholicism, Jews, immigrants, and bootleggers. The Klan shared many features in common with the secret societies of the nineteenth century. It cleverly sold prospective members on the appearance of exclusivity and respectability, though in reality it was a massive multilevel marketing scheme, with two million members in the Midwest alone, that played on the status anxieties of rural Protestants. Despite its claims to be an "invisible empire," it was famously ineffective politically, and remained on the political fringe despite its huge numbers. In rural towns Klan members would sometimes organize boycotts of Catholic merchants, but these tended to occur in locales where there were very few Catholics. The second Klan collapsed under the weight of multiple leadership scandals in the late 1920s.[41]

Protestant distrust of Catholics continued throughout the twentieth century, particularly among Southern evangelicals. Rapprochement came in the early 1970s, when the Southern Baptist Convention abandoned its liberal stance on abortion to join Catholic activists in opposing Roe v. Wade.[42] This laid the groundwork for a new religious realignment in the United States that saw religious conservatives of all kinds unite against a coalition of religious liberals and secularists over issues such as abortion, gay marriage, and religion in public space.[43] The "culture war" brought large numbers of conservative Catholics into the Republican coalition, weakening (though not destroying) the 150-year-old link between Catholics and the Democratic Party. By 2012, evangelical conservative Republicans were looking to Catholic figures such as Rick Santorum and Paul Ryan for electoral leadership, and the most vehement criticism of Catholicism arguably came from left-liberal quarters.[44]

[40] Higham ([1955] 1971), pp. 181–182.
[41] McVeigh, Rory (2009). *The Rise of the Ku Klux Klan: Right-Wing Movements and National Politics.* Minneapolis: University of Minnesota Press; Fryer, Roland G. and Steven D. Levitt (2012). "Hatred and Profit: Under the Hood of the Ku Klux Klan." *The Quarterly Journal of Economics,* 127(4): pp. 1883–1925. See also Chapter 5.
[42] See Dochuk, Darren (2011). *From Bible Belt to Sun Belt: Plain-Folk Religion, Grassroots Politics, and the Rise of Evangelical Conservatism.* New York: Norton, pp. 346–353.
[43] See Putnam and Campbell (2010).
[44] Jenkins, Philip (2003). *The New Anti-Catholicism: The Last Acceptable Prejudice.* New York: Oxford University Press.

CONCLUSION

Anti-Catholicism has been remarkably ineffective in the United States, given how widespread, persistent, and intense it has been. Since the early nineteenth century, Catholics have usually been better organized politically than anti-Catholics. They have been able to trust state and local governments to intervene during outbreaks of violence, and have nearly always been able to rely on the Democratic Party to thwart discriminatory legislation at the national level. Anti-Catholic forces have been able to stir up popular fears of foreign and Papal subversion, but have often been organized in forms that themselves seem subversive and have alienated potential allies among ruling elites. When they did briefly achieve political success, they continued to be outsiders, unable to take advantage of their numerical power, and they were quickly subsumed by a more disciplined party carrying the full weight of the Protestant establishment.

8

The Jewish experience in America

INTRODUCTION

The treatment of Jews has long played an important part in discussions of religious freedom in the United States. Legal scholars have considered Jews the "hard test" of religious tolerance, the benchmark for whether the protection of religious belief and practice truly extends beyond the Christian mainstream.[1] In eighteenth-, nineteenth-, and even twentieth-century descriptions of American religious diversity, Jews would usually be the only non-Christians mentioned. Part of the significance of Washington's famous letter to the Newport Synagogue (see Chapter 2) was the implication that if even Jews were safe in the United States, then all religious groups would be safe.

The background to America's self-congratulatory tolerance of its Jewish minority was the catastrophic violence that at some point befell Jews in nearly every European country.[2] A large body of scholarship has been devoted to explaining the global longevity, universality, and lethality of anti-Semitism.[3] During the Christian period of the Roman Empire, state authorities transferred

[1] Miller, William Lee (1986). *The First Liberty: Religion and the American Republic*. New York: Knopf, p. 196; Feldman (2003), p. 227.
[2] In chapter 2 of James Joyce's *Ulysses*, an anti-Semitic school headmaster explains to a young teacher that Ireland "has the honour of being the only country that never persecuted the jews.... Because she never let them in." Joyce, James (1922). *Ulysses*. Paris: Shakespeare and Company.
[3] A comprehensive survey of this literature is impossible here, but some landmark works include: Cohn, Norman ([1967] 1996). *Warrant for Genocide: The Myth of the Jewish World Conspiracy and the Protocols of the Elders of Zion*. London: Serif; Wilson, Stephen (1982). *Ideology and Experience: Antisemitism in France at the Time of the Dreyfus Affair*. Rutherford: Fairleigh Dickinson University Press; Katz, Jacob (1980). *From Prejudice to Destruction: Anti-Semitism, 1700–1933*. Cambridge, MA: Harvard University Press; Pulzer, Peter G.J. (1964). *The Rise of Political Anti-Semitism in Germany and Austria*. New York: Wiley; Pauley, Bruce F. (1992). *From Prejudice to Persecution: A History of Austrian Anti-Semitism*. Chapel Hill: University of North Carolina Press; Michlic, Joanna Beatta (2006). *Poland's Threatening Other: The Image of the Jew from 1880 to the Present*. Lincoln, NE: University of Nebraska Press; Sartre, Jean-Paul

culpability for Christ's death almost entirely to the Jews, and a series of hostile measures culminated in the Justinian Code that consigned Jews to a separate existence from gentile society. State-enforced separatism and the stigma of being Christ-killers continued to define Jews throughout the Middle Ages, and during the Crusades this developed into a full-blown demonology of Jews as the children of Satan. During the Enlightenment, distrust of Jews became overlain with anxiety about modernity. As political entrepreneurs forged new national identities in fragmented societies, ghetto-dwelling Jews became a useful scapegoat for everything that was inorganic, alien and threatening in the disorienting new world of urbanization and commerce. Across much of Europe, Jews came to represent the antithesis of the nation, a threat to national sovereignty by their very presence, and this perception easily developed into conspiracy theories about international cabals of Jews controlling the governments and economies of Christian countries.[4]

The United States was never immune from anti-Semitic prejudice. Being a predominantly Christian country, traditional Christian complaints about Jews have had considerable traction in America. As late as 1966, Charles Glock and Rodney Stark found that a third of Protestants in a survey of Northern California churchgoers definitively believed that Jews remained unforgiven by God for "what they did to Christ," while up to 60 percent acknowledged that this might be true. Glock and Stark professed surprise at their findings of how strongly this religious belief was causally associated with modern, secular stereotypes of Jews as avaricious, egocentric, and unpatriotic.[5] We can safely assume that earlier generations of Americans were even less liberal-minded than this. Why did this prejudice fail to develop into sustained campaigns of violent persecution, as it had done in nearly every country from which Americans were descended?

One possibility is that Americans simply did not have a strong enough kind of prejudice. In another important study of anti-Semitism, Daniel Levinson noted that at mid-century, anti-Semitic prejudice in the United States tended to be "pseudodemocratic" rather than "openly antidemocratic," with the latter defined as "active hatred, or ... violence that has the aim of wiping out a minority group or putting it in a permanently subordinate position." Instead, Americans voiced their prejudices in qualified terms such as "Jews have their rights, but ..."[6] This study, however, took place at a time (1950) of dramatically improving relations between religious groups in the United

([1948] 1995). *Anti-Semite and Jew: An Exploration of the Etiology of Hate.* New York: Schocken Books.

[4] Cohn ([1967] 1996) argues that the global Jewish conspiracy theories typified by *The Protocols of the Elders of Zion* are a continuation of Christian demonologies about Jews dating back to the Roman Empire (pp. 24–26).

[5] Glock and Stark (1966). *Christian Beliefs and Anti-Semitism.* New York: Harper Torchbooks, pp. 60–80, 130–138, and 207.

[6] Adorno, T.W., Else Frenkel-Brunswik, Daniel J. Levinson, and R. Nevitt Sanford (1950). *The Authoritarian Personality.* New York: Harper and Row, p. 60.

States. The experience of shared sacrifice during the Second World War, and the government's vigorous promotion of Godly ecumenicism during the early Cold War, had raised the esteem of Jews in America to new heights by the early 1950s.[7] Still-fresh revelations about the horrors of Nazi death camps may also have muted more vicious anti-Semitic sentiments.

As I will show below, there is ample evidence of "active hatred" toward Jews in America in the preceding century. It never engulfed the whole population, or even the majority of it, but in a country the size of the United States even a minority of hard-core anti-Semites might be expected to make life dangerous for Jews, especially if anti-Semitism was concentrated in particular regions. This chapter explores why an often strong prejudice against Jews was never politically mobilized in an effective way in the United States. I argue that, because of the broader social movements with which it was associated, anti-Semitism was even more toxic to state authorities and the political establishment than anti-Catholicism. As much as anti-Semites complained about Jewish subversion in America, and found a popular audience for those complaints, in the eyes of the state it was anti-Semites themselves who posed the subversive threat.

MASS JEWISH MIGRATION AND THE CIVIL WAR

Like Catholics, Jews in colonial America faced an array of discriminatory measures which some states maintained into the early days of the republic. Beneke explains that Jews in the eighteenth century were actually more highly regarded than Catholics, "[p]artly because they possessed no official ties to foreign powers, refrained from proselytizing, and confined themselves to small, respectable communities, America's Jews never attracted the same kind of animus that Catholics and some evangelical groups encountered in eighteenth-century America."[8] Laws restricting public office to believers in the New Testament vanished shortly after the Constitution was adopted, and other forms of official discrimination had melted away by the early nineteenth century. The United States developed a non-persecuting reputation among Jews around the world. In 1861, Philadelphia publisher Isaac Leeser wrote that "the stars of the American flag have appeared to Jews in Europe and Asia as a grand distant constellation of liberty and hope."[9]

Mass migration from Germany in the 1840s and 1850s brought Jews as well as Catholics, and the Jewish population of the United States increased from

---

[7] See Moore, Deborah Dash (2004). *GI Jews: How World War II Changed a Generation.* Cambridge: Harvard University Press; Herzog, Jonathan P. (2011). *The Spiritual-Industrial Complex: America's Religious Battle against Communism in the Early Cold War.* New York: Oxford University Press.

[8] Beneke (2006), p. 186.

[9] Quoted in Adams, Peter (2014). *Politics, Faith, and the Making of American Judaism.* Ann Arbor: University of Michigan Press, p. 7.

about 15,000 in 1840 to 150,000 by the eve of the Civil War. The Civil War, like the Revolutionary War before it and the Second World War after, would have the effect of cementing the place of religious minorities in American life, including that of Jews. In the words of Bertram Korn, "Enduring the hardship of battle, burying sons and husbands and friends, participating in the multifarious welfare activities of the home front, taking part in political arguments – these and a thousand other aspects of life in a nation at war with itself Americanized the large immigrant population at a much more rapid rate than that of more peaceful times."[10] However, the war also precipitated the most notorious incident of official anti-Semitism in American history – a mass expulsion that had echoes of the hostile treatment of Jews in European states.

In Union-controlled border areas, trade embargoes against the Confederacy put economic pressure on communities and opened up lucrative opportunities for smugglers and speculators. In the midst of rising corruption and declining public trust, Jews in the border areas came under widespread suspicion of profiteering from the war; traditional Christian distrust of Jews was compounded by the fact that Jews were known to be active on both the Union and Confederate sides.[11] Rumors of Jewish smuggling were prevalent throughout the army as well as the civilian populace, and in 1862 General Ulysses S. Grant, future president and commander of the Department of the Tennessee, ordered the removal of Jews from his territory. The notorious "General Orders No. 11" read as follows:

> The Jews, as a class violating every regulation of trade established by the Treasure Department and also department orders, are hereby expelled from the department within twenty-four hours from the receipt of this order.
>
> Post commanders will see that all of this class of people be furnished passes and required to leave, and any one returning after such notification will be arrested and held in confinement until an opportunity occurs of sending them out as prisoners, unless furnished with permit from headquarters.
>
> No passes will be given these people to visit headquarters for the purpose of making personal application for trade permits.
>
> By order of Maj. Gen. U.S. Grant:[12]

By designating Jews as a "class," Grant seemed to be going beyond the usual American anti-Semitism of stereotypes and generalizations, and reviving the medieval doctrine of collective guilt for the sins of Jews.[13] Jewish leaders understandably saw this as a moment of great danger for their people, and Jews in and nearby the affected territory acted quickly to try to stop the order. Cesar Kaskel, a Prussian-born merchant in Paducah, Kentucky, sent a telegram

[10] Korn, Bertram W. (1961). *American Jewry and the Civil War*. Cleveland and New York: Meridian Books, pp. 217–218.
[11] Sarna, Jonathan D. (2012). *When General Grant Expelled the Jews*. New York: Schocken, pp. 5–6 and 30.
[12] Reproduced in Sarna (2012), p. 7.
[13] Ibid., p. 32.

to President Lincoln describing the order as "the grossest violation of the Constitution," which threatened to stigmatize Jews "as outlaws before the whole world." When there was no response from Lincoln, Kaskel went directly to Washington to visit him, assisted by Cincinnati congressman Addison John Gurley and other Jewish leaders across the Midwest. During his journey, Jewish organizations around the country began to mount delegations and petitions to Washington as news of the order slowly spread, partly thanks to Kaskel's efforts. Sarna describes this strategy thus:

> Following the time-tested traditions of Jewish politics, Kaskel began by appealing to the highest governmental power available. Long experience with persecution had persuaded Jews that "their ultimate safety and welfare could be entrusted neither to the erratic benevolence of their gentile neighbors nor to the caprice of local authorities." Kaskel appealed instead to the President of the United States.[14]

The actions of Kaskel and other Jewish leaders are a paradigmatic example of the strategy of expanding the scope of conflict. They knew that Lincoln, who at that time was preparing the Emancipation Proclamation, would be much more susceptible than local military officials to the claim that Grant's order was unconscionable because it violated religious freedom. When Kaskel finally met Lincoln, accounts of their meeting (which are probably apocryphal) describe them talking in Biblical terms that linked the people of ancient Israel to America's self-conception as the Promised Land.[15] The appeal was successful; Lincoln revoked the order about three weeks after it had originally been issued. Because of slow wartime communications, only about a hundred Jews out of the thousands in the Tennessee Department had actually been subject to removal.[16]

In Washington, Grant was condemned in Congress and in newspapers for "this most atrocious, illegal, inhuman and monstrous order," in the words of Kentucky Senator Lazarus Whitehead Powell.[17] Grant ultimately emerged unscathed, but would spend the rest of his political career rebuilding his relations with the Jewish community. In 1869 Grant, now president, appealed to Tsar Alexander II to revoke an order expelling Jews from the borderlands of the Russian empire. His appeal earned the gratitude of American Jewish organizations, though it had little effect on the worsening condition of Jews in Eastern Europe.[18]

SOUTHERN POPULISM AND THE LYNCHING OF LEO FRANK

Pogroms in the Russian empire during the 1880s spurred a wave of Jewish immigration that dwarfed all previous flows. By 1924 more than two million

---

[14] Ibid., p. 9.
[15] Ibid., p. 21.
[16] Ibid., p. 17.
[17] Adams (2014), p. 61.
[18] Ibid., pp. 123–127.

Jews had migrated from Eastern Europe to the United States. Massively increased immigration created new image problems for American Jews, as it had for Catholics before them. The new immigrants from Eastern Europe were poor, crammed into unsanitary urban neighborhoods, and seemed to have much less hope of assimilation than the previous wave of German Jewish immigrants. The economic stresses of the 1890s raised old fears about Jews in new forms. Some populists connected Jews with gold, and believed that the government's determination to maintain the gold standard masked a Jewish bid for control of the economy. Many Americans of different political leanings associated the Jews with large, international economic forces that were devastating their lives, and questioned whether Jews could possess any national loyalty. While anti-Semitic action at this point was mostly limited to taunting and stone-throwing in Northern cities, there were two arson incidents in the South aimed at driving out Jewish landlords, probably perpetrated by indebted farmers.[19]

By the early decades of the twentieth century, the presence of Jewish-owned factories in the South was causing tension. Southern elites from outside the traditional plantation aristocracy welcomed industrial capitalism in cities such as Atlanta. To them, factories funded by Northern capital represented the future of the New South, no longer dependent on cotton and ready to reconcile with the rest of the country. To others, factories represented an alien and degrading presence. Under the influence of industrialists, the Georgia state legislature allowed factories to employ children as young as ten, which caused local and national outrage. As declining cotton prices forced many rural Southern families into the city, they often had no better choice than to send their children to work in these dangerous, dirty environments. Some Christian populists laid blame for the crimes of the whole industrialist class at the feet of Jews, who owned some of the factories.[20]

In 1913 the murder of teenage Atlanta factory worker Mary Phagan detonated an explosive mix of Christian anti-Semitism and Southern populism in Georgia. The suspect was Leo Frank, a Jew born in Texas but raised in New York. He ran the National Pencil Company factory where Mary Phagan had worked, and the prosecution alleged he had killed her to keep her from talking after making advances on her. He was never likely to get a fair trial. In C. Vann Woodward's account:

> The trial lasted thirty days, attended throughout by manifestations of mob spirit. On the final day the howl of the mob, packed for many blocks about the courthouse, was continually in the ears of the jurors. The crowd in the courtroom repeatedly jeered, laughed, and applauded. Editors of city papers joined in a petition to the presiding judge to adjourn the case for the day, because an acquittal

---

[19] Higham ([1955] 1971), pp. 66–67 and 92–93.
[20] Oney, Steve (2003). *And the Dead Shall Rise: The Murder of Mary Phagan and the Lynching of Leo Frank*. New York: Random House, pp. 6–7.

would "cause such a riot as would shock the country and cause Atlanta's streets to run with innocent blood. Threatening messages were received by court officials: "Hang the Jew or we will hang you."[21]

Frank was found guilty and sentenced to die, but his execution date was repeatedly postponed, and national disgust mounted over the circumstances of the trial. It seemed Frank was considered innocent everywhere outside of Georgia, even in other southern states such as Tennessee and Texas, whose legislatures passed resolutions asking for Frank's life to be spared.

The backlash against "outside interference" in Georgia was ferocious. Tom Watson, a former leader of the Populist Party and an editor of several publications, described a Jewish conspiracy that was trying to force the state into submission. He wrote in 1914 that "Frank belonged to the Jewish aristocracy, and it was determined by the rich Jews that no aristocrat of their race should die for the death of a working-class gentile." Frank was "the typical young libertine Jew who is dreaded and detested by the city authorities of the North for the very reason that Jews of this type have an utter contempt for the law, and a ravenous appetite for the forbidden fruit – a lustful eagerness enhanced by the racial novelty of the girl of the uncircumcised." Furthermore, Frank was a "Sodomite," a "lascivious pervert, guilty of the crime that caused the Almighty to blast the cities of the plain."[22]

Watson's editorials show how closely class grievances and Christian morality could be bound up with anti-Semitism during this period. The Frank case seemed to confirm the worst fears of rural Georgians about encroaching industrial capitalism: not only would it exploit their children economically, it would also crush their bodies and corrupt their souls. It was all too easy to identify Jews as the chief engineers and beneficiaries of the monstrous new system that was destroying what was left of their world, and the Frank case appeared to display the true nature of the Jewish intrusion. When outgoing Governor John Slaton commuted Frank's sentence to life imprisonment, Slaton was placed under military protection and Frank was lynched soon afterwards by a well-organized mob of prominent citizens.

The lynching of Frank gave birth to two new civic organizations that would play major roles in the struggle between anti-Semites and Jews in the United States. As noted in Chapter 6, the newly reconstituted Ku Klux Klan was formed in Georgia a few months after Frank's death, possibly in response to Watson's call to "defend home rule" from outsiders. In the 1920s, the Klan became strongly associated with anti-Semitism. This temporarily increased the prominence of anti-Semitism, but also limited its political potential. The Klan excelled at appearing ferocious and enriching its leaders, but was politically useless outside of the South, where it was redundant, and ultimately helped

---

[21] Woodward, C. Vann ([1938] 1963). *Tom Watson, Agrarian Rebel*. New York: Oxford University Press, pp. 435–436.
[22] Ibid., pp. 436–438.

discredit every political cause with which it was associated. On the other side, the B'nai B'rith organization founded the Anti-Defamation League in direct response to the Frank trial in 1913. The ADL monitored anti-Semitic speech and activity in the United States, and continues to publish regular reports on anti-Semitism. The ADL has consistently linked its own mission with the fight against other forms of bigotry, and has been instrumental in drafting and lobbying for hate crime legislation that covers all forms of violence motivated by prejudice.[23] While the ADL has often been controversial,[24] especially in recent decades, it has also been undeniably successful in drawing attention to and stigmatizing anti-Semitism.

INTERWAR ANTI-SEMITISM

While the Frank case may have increased the long-term organizational strength of the Jewish community, in the immediate term it signaled the beginning of the most dangerous period in history for American Jews. Anti-Semitism took on an explicitly racial tone. With American involvement in the Great War, all things German became objects of suspicion, including the most established segments of the Jewish community. The Russian Revolution sparked fears that the Jewish immigrant community harbored millions of radicals who were ready to take the side of the Bolsheviks.[25] Sometimes the racist and anti-Communist elements of anti-Semitism were conflated; a 1919 editorial in the *Chicago Tribune* warned that under the guise of Bolshevism, "Jewish radicals" were plotting "the establishment of a new racial domination of the world" that was "necessarily anti-Anglo-Saxon."[26] *The Protocols of the Elders of Zion*, a Tsarist forgery purporting to be a blueprint for global Jewish domination, was disseminated throughout the world by right-wing Russian forces after the revolution. It appeared in the United States in 1920, and received great publicity from Henry Ford's *Dearborn Independent*. A collection of articles from the *Independent* was published as *The International Jew: the World's Foremost Problem*, and sold half a million copies in the United States.[27]

Higham describes the 1920s as a period of national excitement about and "*sotto voce* approval" of anti-Semitic conspiracy theories. Already, however, the political limitations of anti-Semitism were becoming clear. Woodrow Wilson and William Howard Taft joined hundreds of other distinguished Americans in denouncing the *Independent*, and no respectable newspaper

---

[23] Freeman, Steven M. (1992). "Hate Crime Laws: Punishment Which Fits the Crime." *Annual Survey of American Law*, 1992/1993: 581–586.

[24] See, e.g., Chomsky, Noam (1989). *Necessary Illusions: Thought Control in Democratic Societies.* Appendix V. http://home.nvg.org/~skars/ni/ni-c10–s20.html.

[25] Higham ([1955] 1971), pp. 278–281.

[26] Cohn ([1967] 1996), pp. 172–173.

[27] Ibid., pp. 174–178. The most significant impact of *The International Jew* may have been in Germany, where it sold many copies in translation and was later cited as an influence by prominent Nazis including Hitler, who kept a photo of Henry Ford in his office.

would back up or air its claims. This determined political opposition may have induced Ford to back away from *The International Jew* in the early 1920s. The most organized anti-Semitic force was the Klan, for which anti-Semitism was a secondary concern. Direct action was limited to occasional boycotts and violence was very rare.[28] The disdain of political elites for anti-Semitism did not mean they were free of prejudice. Exclusion of Jews from private clubs and resorts was a widely accepted fact of elite social life in the early twentieth century. Some Ivy League universities, worried about the rapidly growing influx of Jewish students, designed new admissions requirements to limit their numbers.[29] It is possible this elaborate system of social discrimination diminished the appeal of political anti-Semitism among more privileged Anglo-Saxon Americans, who felt secure in their position at the top of the ethnic hierarchy.

Anti-Semitic public opinion peaked in the United States in the 1930s and early 1940s.[30] At this time Father Charles Coughlin, a Catholic priest and popular broadcaster from suburban Detroit, could be heard telling millions of listeners about connections between Jews, international finance, and the coming European war into which President Roosevelt (some believed his real name was "Rosenfeld") seemed intent on dragging the United States. Coughlin's weekly publication *Social Justice* extensively excerpted the *Protocols of the Elders of Zion* in 1938. Protestant anti-Semites who found Coughlin's Catholicism unpalatable had their own prophet in Gerald B. Winrod, a Kansas evangelist who alerted readers that "Modern Communism and old Jewish Illuminism are one and the same thing."[31] Charles Lindbergh told a Des Moines crowd in 1941 about the pernicious effects of Jews' "large ownership and influence in our motion pictures, our press, our radio and our government." Although he felt the Nazis had handled their Jewish problem "unreasonably," Lindbergh nonetheless warned that Jewish leaders should cease "agitating for war," because America's tolerance for them was unlikely to endure a prolonged armed conflict.[32] This comment reflected public sentiment uncovered in a 1938 Gallup poll, in which 54 percent of respondents said that Jews were partly responsible for their own persecution in Europe, while 11 percent said they were entirely responsible; 12 percent said they would support "a widespread campaign against Jews in this country."[33]

---

[28] Higham ([1955] 1971), pp. 285–286.
[29] See Karabel, Jerome (2006). *The Chosen: The Hidden History of Admission and Exclusion at Harvard, Yale and Princeton*. New York: Houghton Mifflin.
[30] Dinnerstein, Leonard (1995). *Antisemitism in America*. New York: Oxford University Press.
[31] Lipset, Seymour Martin and Earl Raab (1970). *The Politics of Unreason: Right Wing Extremism in America, 1790–1970*. New York: Harper and Row, p. 161.
[32] Wallace, Max (2005). *The American Axis: Henry Ford, Charles Lindbergh, and the Rise of the Third Reich*. New York: MacMillan.
[33] The Gallup results are reproduced at www.volokh.com/posts/1226283758.shtml, last accessed January 31, 2013.

As the United States greatly increased its intake of Jewish refugees from 1938, rumors spread that they were taking American jobs, assisted by the government and major capitalist enterprises. The 1939–1940 *American Jewish Yearbook* reported:

> The persecutions abroad, the recurring emergencies attracting refugees, and the widespread discussion in this country of refugee problems, gave rise to rumors and whispering campaigns, zealously spread by false propaganda, to the effect that this country was being swamped by refugees who were displacing Americans from jobs, and that large department stores were deliberately discharging their American employees to make room for refugees.[34]

After the United States entered the war, anti-Semitic rumors tended to follow the theme that Jews were not doing their part for the war effort or were undermining it for their own profit. Gentiles often suspected their Jewish neighbors of war profiteering or getting their sons out of the draft. The profiteering rumors – that Jews had monopolized the government's drives to collect rubber and other important war materials and were making money from shortages that made life difficult for Americans – became an open part of wartime popular culture, appearing in songs and jokes that were anthologized in books. Many rumors emphasized that Jews were President Roosevelt's "intimate advisors" and they "ran" Washington.[35]

These rumors echoed old and dangerous accusations against Jews: that they controlled governments and capitalism, that they started wars for their own profit, that they undermined national and religious solidarity among Christians, and that Christians always bore the brunt of suffering caused by Jewish schemes.[36] Despite the seriousness of the anti-Semitic rumors that raged between 1938 and 1945, however, incidents of violence and vandalism against Jews or Jewish businesses were relatively isolated and likely to be stigmatized as acts of juvenile hooliganism rather than dangerous expressions of community sentiment. While Morris Fine stated in the 1939–1940 *American Jewish Year Book* that "the activities of Jew-baiting groups and persons not only increased, but were brought out into the open more than ever before,"[37] his detailed report contained no accounts of violence or vandalism as a result of organized anti-Semitic campaigns.

The political impotence of anti-Semitism during this period almost certainly had something to do with the taint of Hitler and Mussolini. Anti-Semitism was now strongly associated with national disloyalty, a perception the Roosevelt

[34] Fine, Morris (1940). "Review of the Year 5699, Part 1: The United States." In *American Jewish Year Book 1939–1940*. Philadelphia: American Jewish Committee.

[35] Sparrow, James T. (2011). *Warfare State: World War II Americans and the Era of Big Government*. New York: Oxford University Press, pp. 89–94.

[36] These were all common themes of the *Protocols of the Elders of Zion*; see Bronner, Stephen Eric (2000). *A Rumor about the Jews: Reflections on Antisemitism and the Protocols of the Learned Elders of Zion*. New York: St. Martin's Press; and also Cohn ([1967] 1996).

[37] Fine (1940), p. 209.

administration used to tarnish opponents of American involvement in the war. Ever since the Frank case, anti-Semitism had contained a populist critique of industrial capitalism and finance, even despite the sponsorship of Henry Ford.[38] The depression intensified the anti-capitalist elements of anti-Semitic literature and broadcasts, which did not detract from their typically vehement anti-communism. Charles Coughlin's broadcasts in the early 1930s had initially been supportive of Roosevelt and the New Deal, calling for the nationalization of banks to guarantee full employment. As the decade progressed, however, his denunciations of "international bankers" became more explicitly anti-Semitic, and he accused the Roosevelt administration of being in their thrall. By 1938, he declared that democracy needed to be thrown out along with capitalism and replaced with a corporatist system that bore a close resemblance to fascism.[39] The right-wing anti-capitalism of anti-Semites such as Coughlin and Winrod ensured anti-Semitism would never find allies in either major party.[40]

By the outbreak of the Second World War, anti-Semitism in America was not just marginal; it was under surveillance. The FBI, despite its conservative proclivities, was eager to curry favor with the Roosevelt administration by compiling files on its right-wing opponents. In the mid-1930s it had files on

---

[38] Higham observes that the arch-industrialist's immense personal popularity in the American heartland was related to his loyalty to his rural background: "Ford carried over into the industrial field not only the personal traits but also the social ideas typical of his rustic background. The son of Michigan tenant farmers, he looked upon big cities as cesspools of iniquity, soulless and artificial. He hated monopoly and special privilege. He jealously guarded his enterprises from banker influence and was regarded, in the words of the *Detroit News*, as 'the recognized crusader against the money changers of Wall Street.' In short, Ford, for all his wealth, typified some of the key attitudes for which (Tom) Watson had once stood. It is hardly surprising that in Ford and in many others with an agrarian background, nativism took a violently anti-Semitic turn at a time of depression, isolation and disillusion." Higham ([1955] 1971), p. 283.

[39] Lipset and Raab (1970), pp. 168–171.

[40] Philip Roth's 2004 novel *The Plot Against America* supplies an interesting counterfactual scenario. In Roth's story, Charles Lindbergh decides to run for President, and gains the Republican nomination by acclaim at a chaotic party convention. He wins the election on a platform that is anti-war and openly anti-Semitic, blaming Jews for wanting to send Americans to their deaths in Europe. After signing a non-aggression pact with Hitler, the Lindbergh administration embarks on a policy of Americanizing Jews by forcibly relocating Jewish children to the Christian heartland. In an increasingly anti-Semitic atmosphere, pogroms break out across Midwestern cities, beginning in Detroit. The idea that anti-Semitism could have been imported into mainstream politics via isolationism is one worth considering, but ultimately there was very little likelihood that it ever could have happened. The Republican Party was not clamoring for an anti-war candidate – 62% of Republican voters, along with 74% of Democrats, supported Roosevelt's Lend-Lease measures at the time that Lindbergh was railing against them. The America First committee was a marginal presence in American politics, shunned by Republicans who were repelled by Lindbergh's anti-Semitism and his tendency to draw a moral equivalence between the British and German governments. See Dueck, Colin (2010). *Hard Line: The Republican Party and U.S. Foreign Policy since World War II*. Princeton: Princeton University Press, pp. 51–55; Roth, Philip (2004). *The Plot against America*. New York: Random House.

Coughlin, and by 1939 it was also maintaining files on Lindbergh.[41] As noted in Chapter 6, the late 1930s saw a "Brown Scare" in which the administration accused right-wing critics of belonging to a fascist "fifth column." The presence of anti-Semitism in the files of right-wing organizations and individuals helped the administration to build its case. As part of this effort, the FBI also helped to suppress the organizations with the most violent anti-Semitic potential. The most dangerous of these was the Black Legion, a Michigan-based offshoot of the Ku Klux Klan dedicated to taking "the Jew out of business and the Catholic out of politics." Unlike the Midwestern Klan, the Black Legion was prepared to murder. In 1934 Legionnaires killed an African American laborer, allegedly for "entertainment," and in 1935 they murdered a Catholic worker who was accused of beating his Protestant wife.[42] Other murders were threatened and planned, but in 1936 the FBI and state authorities dismantled the organization, whose leaders were discussing an insurrection against the government.[43]

There is an historical irony in the FBI's suppression of anti-Semitic violence and politics. The FBI itself, as James Morone has explained, originated with the Mann Act, a response to a 1910s panic about "white slavery" in which Jews and other immigrants were believed to be luring naïve rural girls into captivity in urban brothels. In Morone's words, "Nothing launches political programs quite like rumors of Jews stealing (never mind selling) country girls."[44] The Mann Act, which effectively made prostitution a federal crime, empowered a reform movement that also took aim at obscenity, contraception, abortion, and ultimately alcohol. The FBI, with its sweeping new police powers, emerged as the arm of the government responsible for enforcing the new moral order. The Brown Scare changed the FBI's role in the mid-1930s, expanding its scope and power beyond anything imagined even by the architects of the Mann Act. Whatever other damage the Brown Scare did to the American polity, it probably made it safer for Jews.

CONCLUSION

Anti-Catholicism and anti-Semitism have been notable and much-studied features of American history, far more so than hostility toward Mormons and Jehovah's Witnesses. There has been much less attention to why these hatreds failed, usually, to translate into sustained state-sponsored violence or

[41] O'Reilly, Kenneth (1982). "A New Deal for the FBI: The Roosevelt Administration, Crime Control, and National Security." *The Journal of American History*, 69(3): 638–658. The Lindbergh files are archived at www.charleslindbergh.com/fbi/, last accessed January 7, 2013.
[42] The latter case of Charles Poole became the basis of the 1937 Humphrey Bogart film *Black Legion*.
[43] Churchill, Robert H. (2009). *To Shake Their Guns in the Tyrant's Face: Libertarian Political Violence and the Origins of the Militia Movement*. Ann Arbor: University of Michigan Press. pp. 153–173.
[44] Morone (2003), p. 278. See, in general, Chapter 9.

discrimination. Part of the answer is the tolerant legal, and normative framework of the United States, but this is not the whole answer as it did not protect other hated minorities. Anti-Catholicism and anti-Semitism succeeded as prejudice but failed as politics. For persecution to succeed, it needs to be embedded in a broader political agenda that has allies and influence in the heart of the political mainstream. Anti-Catholicism once came close to that kind of success, when the Know-Nothings were briefly the most credible anti-slavery party. Anti-Semitism, despite its sponsorship by such popular figures as Henry Ford and Charles Lindbergh, was destined to remain on the margins because of its anti-establishment politics.

9

The Islamic experience in America

INTRODUCTION

The experience of Islam in the United States makes for a complicated mixed case in this book. Islam is a broader and more diverse religious category than any of the others examined here. Like Judaism and Catholicism, Islam in America is made up of many different communities with distinctive ties of ethnicity and nationality as well as religion. Unlike these other religions, however, there has historically been a lack of mutual recognition between Islamic communities and relatively little sense of a shared Islamic American identity. This has been exacerbated by the presence of groups of Americans who regard themselves as Muslims but whom other Muslims view as unacceptably unorthodox.

These differences within American Islam have been closely related to how the American state has seen and responded to Islam. Throughout most of the twentieth century, state actors regarded immigrant Muslims as a worthy part of the American ethno-religious mosaic. Even when immigration from predominantly Muslim countries was cut off between the 1920s and 1960s, the state saw Muslims as part of a broad coalition of the American faithful who would sustain the country during the protracted fight against Communism. This attitude toward Islam was reflected in a foreign policy that frequently tried to enlist Islam against Communism in the proxy struggles of the Cold War. However, the state was deeply suspicious of any version of Islam that was associated with African Americans. From the beginning, African American Islam in all its varieties was associated with threatening politics. In particular, the heterodox Nation of Islam was subject to extensive surveillance, harassment, and disruption by the FBI and other government agencies who regarded it as a dangerous political movement rather than a legitimate religion.

The criteria constituting threatening and non-threatening Islam began to shift following the Iranian revolution. There was an increased consciousness of "fundamentalist" Islam as something antithetical to American identity, even as the United States continued to nurture fundamentalist Muslim combatants in the Middle East and central Asia. The Ayatollah, a recognizably religious figure, became a popular villain in the American media and public. With the end of the Cold War, the 1993 World Trade Center bombing, and the 1996 bombing of the *USS Cole*, Islamic fundamentalism became an increasingly prominent domestic and international enemy of the United States. With the 9/11 attacks, Islamic terrorism became the sole pre-eminent enemy, shaping domestic and foreign policy for a decade.

After 9/11, official and public discourse about Islam in America saw an uncompromising distinction between "peaceful" Islam and Islam that would "do us harm." Terms such as "Jihadist" and "Islamofascist" appeared in the media to distinguish the threatening version of Islam – anti-American, anti-Western, inherently violent, and terroristic – from the peaceful version of Islam, understood as something assimilated and apolitical. George W. Bush went so far as to suggest the former is a "perversion of Islam," rather than the real thing, which is a "religion of peace." The underlying message, which at first glance looked like an appeal for tolerance, was that there could be no overlap between the two, and religious tolerance would be reserved only for Muslims who unreservedly renounced hostility toward the United States.

Post-9/11 state policy toward Islam at all levels was two-pronged. On the one hand state actors saw domestic Islamic institutions as potential sources of support for terrorism, and implemented an extensive surveillance regime to monitor Muslim individuals, communities, and institutions. This surveillance regime has imposed restrictions on individual rights that other Americans would find intolerable if it were applied either to themselves or to another minority group. On the other hand, the state has also acted decisively to counteract popular Islamophobia. From the president down, state officials have condemned prejudice against American Muslims. Law enforcement agencies at all levels have devoted considerable energy and resources to prevent and prosecute hate crimes targeting Muslims. Anti-Islamic politics has generally been marginal, confined to quixotic campaigns against Sharia law in state legislatures and local protests against mosque construction. While there is a popular Islamophobia industry that has attracted some prominent adherents, most national politicians on both sides have avoided associating with it, instead hewing to the rigid distinction between the "peaceful" religion of Islam and the "perverted" ideology of terrorism.

The state, then, has seen both Islam and the persecution of Islam as a political threat in the wake of 9/11. Rather than joining anti-Muslim campaigns emanating from civil society, the state has aggressively sought to stamp them out. But it has maintained its own repressive apparatus, largely out of public sight, to identify Islamic individuals and groups it sees as a threat, while using its protective apparatus to shield "innocent" Muslims from populist persecution. This decidedly mixed response reflects the depth of the distinctions state actors have made between peaceful Islam and threatening Islam, which makes the

Islamic case very different from the experiences of the other religious groups in this book. Nonetheless, both the pre- and post-9/11 experiences of Muslims fit the theoretical framework of this book. The state response to Islam has been shaped by state actors' perceptions of the relative political threats posed by Muslims and the persecution of Muslims.

Another unusual feature of this case is the predominance of foreign policy in the calculus of state actors. In both the Cold War and the War on Terror, the domestic response to Islam has been conditioned by foreign policy imperatives. The protective response to Islam has resulted at least partly from the need to maintain strategic alliances with Muslim countries, while the persecutory response to it has been motivated by perceptions of transnational security threats to the United States (this was true even of the Nation of Islam, which the FBI suspected of pro-Japanese sympathies in the Second World War, and of afterwards undermining the loyalty of black Americans to the United States). Foreign policy has been close to the surface of all the cases in this book. The conflict between Mormons and the U.S. government was bound up with the politics of westward territorial expansion; anti-Catholic politics and its failure hinged on immigration policy and the changing political priorities leading up to the Civil War; debates over the role of the United States in the Second World War formed the backdrop to both the persecution of Jehovah's Witnesses and the federal response to anti-Semitism. It is in the case of Islam, however, that the state response to a religion has reflected dimensions of global struggles. This is why the federal government, particularly the executive, plays such a prominent role in this case.

This chapter proceeds in four parts. First, I briefly explore the experience of "immigrant" Islam (as opposed to African American Islam) in the mid-twentieth century, noting the perception of Muslims as a "white ethnic" group whose faith fitted comfortably in the mosaic of American religion during the early Cold War. Second, I examine the trajectory of the Nation of Islam, a particularistic black American version of Islam that was in near-constant conflict with the state until the 1970s, when its leader Wallace D. Muhammad implemented reforms, encouraged by various state agencies, that reduced state perceptions of it as a political threat. Third, I show how the Iranian revolution and a new awareness of terrorism began to change American perceptions of Islam and Muslims, even as the United States began backing fundamentalist Muslim insurgents as part of its Cold War strategy. Finally, I examine the state response to Islam after 9/11, a response that has been shaped by state perceptions of a twin threat from both Islamic extremism and popular Islamophobia.

IMMIGRANT ISLAM IN THE TWENTIETH CENTURY

In this study I use the term "immigrant Islam" to denote varieties of American Islam practiced by immigrants and their descendants from the Middle East,

South Asia, and the Balkans. More recently, immigrant Islam also includes Muslims of West African, Central Asian, and South-East Asian descent. Although practitioners of "immigrant Islam" include native-born Americans of several generations, the term refers to the fact that the state and public tend to see Islam as foreign-originated, as opposed to home-grown, syncretic versions practiced by African Americans. This foreignness and connection to a recognized world religion has been a source of religious legitimacy for these communities, but also a source of out-group status.

Between 1820 and 1920 around 300,000 people migrated to the United States from various parts of the Ottoman Empire, with the largest number arriving in the early twentieth century.[1] In the first half of the twentieth century, Syrian immigrants successfully petitioned courts for citizenship on the grounds they were white. The classification of Syrians as white, which occurred gradually over numerous court cases, depended on a number of factors. Along with satisfying various "scientific" racial requirements for whiteness, Syrians were found to meet the criterion that the "average man" would recognize them as white, which could not be said of Chinese or Indians. Part of this recognition was socioeconomic – Syrians were successful entrepreneurs – and part of it was religious, as the bulk of the prewar Syrian community (which in turn was the majority of the American Arab population) was Christian.[2]

Courts initially did not bestow citizenship on Arab Muslims, whom they regarded as racially different from Syrians and not sufficiently proximate to Europeans. In 1943, however, the INS ruled that citizenship should be available to all Arabs, including Muslims. The reasoning was that the Arabian peninsula was outside the Asiatic zone of exclusion defined by the Immigration Act of 1924, and that Arabs were related to Syrians and Jews, whose right to citizenship was unquestioned. A history of "European contact," according to the INS, had rendered Arabs, Syrians, and Armenians "white." Sarah Gualtieri argues that this redefinition of whiteness in cultural terms reflected the height of unease over racial exclusion brought about by fighting the Nazis.[3]

By the 1950s, then, most immigrant Muslims were seen as "white ethnics." This legitimized their religion, in contrast to African American versions of Islam. In the words of Edward Curtis:

> It was fine for foreign religionists to retain their religious practices as long as they assimilated to other American values; in fact, it was laudable for them to retain their religious traditions, since this act demonstrated the Cold War claim that

[1] Kaya, Ilhan (2004). "Turkish-American Immigration History and Identity Formations." *Journal of Muslim Minority Affairs*, 24(2): 295–308, 297.

[2] Gualtieri, Sarah M.A. (2009). *Between Arab and White: Race and Ethnicity in the Early Syrian American Diaspora*. Berkeley: University of California Press, pp. 1–5. See also López, Ian Haney (2006). *White By Law: The Legal Construction of Race*. New York: NYU Press, ch. 3.

[3] Gualtieri, Sarah M.A. (2001). "Becoming 'White': Race, Religion, and the Foundations of Syrian/ Lebanese Ethnicity in the United States." *Journal of American Ethnic History*, 20(4): 29–58.

America was uniquely free – you could practice whatever religion you liked. But the flip side of that argument was that those indigenous Americans who chose freely to associate with a foreign religion – a religion that was not perceived to be part of their a priori culture – were denying their true ethnic roots as Americans. Mainstream media echoed these claims, framing black Muslims as persons who adopted a false sense of ethnic identity.[4]

State actors had come to see "real" Islam as a welcome part of the American religious landscape, worthy of respect. Powerful symbolic confirmation of this came with Dwight Eisenhower's inauguration in 1952. Eisenhower saw an urgent need to foster religiosity in America, believing like Harry Truman that religion was the only force that could defeat the quasi-spiritual appeal of Communist ideology. Leading by example, Eisenhower was publicly baptized into the Presbyterian Church a few days after his inauguration. His inaugural parade had featured "God's float," embossed with the words "In God We Trust" and depicting places of worship from across America. A mosque was pictured alongside Catholic and Protestant churches and a synagogue.[5]

Eisenhower's famous comment that "our form of government has no sense unless it is founded in a deeply felt religious faith, and I don't care what it is" reflected an official mindset that served immigrant Muslims well during the first decades of the Cold War.[6] Nativism was in retreat from its interwar heights, and in 1965 Congress overwhelmingly passed the Immigration and Nationality Act that abolished the almost exclusive preference for European immigrants instituted in 1924. Like the Civil Rights Act and Voting Rights Act, this was undertaken with at least one eye on the Cold War. The 1965 act allowed the United States to project itself as an antiracist and internationalist power, and to build diasporic links between American society and the emerging Third World. It introduced (or reintroduced) Islamic groups from Asia that today make up substantial parts of the American Muslim population, including Indian, Pakistani, Bangladeshi, and Iranian communities.

Asian communities, including their Muslim members, often came to be seen as "model minorities" in the United States. This term refers to groups characterized in public discourse by stereotypes that conform to classic American values such as hard work, educational achievement, entrepreneurialism, and economic success.[7] This did not mean these groups were free from negative stereotypes or racial

---

[4] "The Black Muslim Scare of the Twentieth Century: The History of State Islamophobia and Its Post-9/11 Variations." In Carl W. Ernst (ed.) *Islamophobia in America: The Anatomy of Intolerance*. New York: Palgrave MacMillan, pp. 75–106 and 96.

[5] Herzog, Jonathan P. (2011). *The Spiritual-Industrial Complex: America's Religious Battle against Communism in the Early Cold War*. New York: Oxford University Press.

[6] Henry, Patrick (1981). "'And I Don't Care What It Is': The Tradition-History of a Civil Religion Proof-Text." *Journal of the American Academy of Religion*, 49(1): 35–49.

[7] Junn, Jane (2007). "From Coolie to Model Minority: U.S. Immigration Policy and the Construction of Racial Identity." *Du Bois Review: Social Science and Research on Race*, 4(2): 355–373; Puar, Jasbir K. and Rai, Amit S. (2004). "The Remaking of a Model Minority: Perverse Projectiles under the Specter of (Counter)Terrorism." *Social Text*, 22(3): 75–104.

prejudice, but neither were they victimized by the state. Some have argued that model minority discourse is primarily used in white power structures as a weapon against African Americans, whose continuing disadvantage is attributed to their failure to conform to these values.[8] The trajectory of moral minorities is supposedly apolitical: these groups do not agitate or organize for better conditions; rather, they improve themselves through the opportunities available in a system of free enterprise. The immigrant Muslim, unlike the black Muslim, was imagined as having a religious life that buttressed rather than attacked American values.

THE NATION OF ISLAM

The Nation of Islam, an African American religion founded in 1930 by Wallace D. Fard and led until recently by Louis Farrakhan, has little in common theologically with most other variants of Islam. It recognizes Fard as divine and his successor Elijah Muhammad as a prophet; it contains beliefs, such as the myth of Yakub, found nowhere in the Quran. It appears directly at odds with the universalism of orthodox Islam. For these reasons, it is tempting to classify the Nation of Islam as something completely separate from "real" Islam. In this study I resist making such an absolute distinction. Throughout the history of Islam, as Edward Curtis documents, there have been political struggles between particularistic variants of the Islamic tradition and the "universalizing" dominant tendencies.[9] It is impossible to draw historically consistent boundaries around a "real" Islam.

Importantly, in the context of this study, the American state itself drew hard distinctions between authentic, universal Islam and the "black supremacist" Nation of Islam, which it regarded as a political cult. While state authorities were correct that there were vast differences between the Nation of Islam and most variants of orthodox Islam, they drew attention to these differences specifically to delegitimize the Nation as a religion and to justify targeting them for surveillance and disruption. Rather than simply reproducing the state's distinction between an essentialized real Islam and the Nation of Islam, I instead examine how state actors and others, including the Nation itself, constructed this distinction politically, and how it changed over time. While the Nation's founders had far more knowledge of the Bible than of Islamic texts, over time later generations introduced more orthodox and Quranic content, culminating in Wallace Muhammad's reinvention of the group as an internationally recognized branch of Sunni Islam and a subsequent schism with Farrakhan, who has maintained a following emphasizing the

---

[8] Kim, Carrie Jean (2003). *Bitter Fruit: The Politics of Black-Korean Conflict in New York City.* New Haven: Yale University Press; Prashad, Vijay (2000). *The Karma of Brown Folk.* Minneapolis: University of Minnesota Press.

[9] Curtis IV, Edward E. (2002). *Islam in Black America: Identity, Liberation and Difference in African-American Islamic Thought.* Albany: State University of New York Press, pp. 7–12.

particularistic elements of Elijah Muhammad's teachings. The responses of various state actors to the Nation of Islam also changed over time.

Origins of the Nation of Islam

The Nation of Islam emerged from interwar black nationalist movements that were seeking to redefine African American identity.[10] The largest and best known of these movements was Marcus Garvey's Universal Negro Improvement Association (UNIA). Several future leaders in the Nation of Islam, including Elijah Muhammad and Malcolm X, came from Garveyite backgrounds. Garvey built a huge transnational organization, originally based in his home country of Jamaica, dedicated to pan-African unity. He moved to the United States in 1916, and by 1919 had incorporated the Black Star Line of Delaware, a shipping company aimed to facilitate mass migration from the new world to Africa. Garvey's program of political and economic self-determination for people of African descent was a resonant alternative to the continuing, often futile struggle for better conditions in white-dominated societies, though it alienated him from black leaders such as W.E.B. Du Bois who were dedicated to that struggle.[11]

Garvey inspired numerous other black nationalist groups, including Islamic versions, but he also served as a bleak example of how the state would treat black nationalists. In 1919 J. Edgar Hoover, then a rising star in the Bureau of Investigation, launched investigations into numerous black political organizations, believing that the race riots of that summer were a product of left-wing agitation among blacks. Garvey was one of the main targets in the campaign that inaugurated Hoover's lifelong obsession with black disloyalty. The Bureau regarded Garvey as a socialist revolutionary alien, a view that was confirmed by a black Methodist bishop who wrote to the Bureau in 1918 that he was "in every respect a 'Red,' an adventurer and a grafter, bent on exploiting his people to the utmost limit." Hoover searched in vain for a reason to deport Garvey, complaining in 1919 that he "has not yet violated any federal law whereby he could be proceeded against on the grounds of being an undesirable alien." In 1923, however, he successfully prosecuted Garvey for mail fraud related to the Black Star Line, and he was deported to Jamaica after serving a prison sentence.[12]

---

[10] In the first three decades of the twentieth century, numerous black artists and intellectuals sought to re-establish a connection with Africa to enhance black American prestige. Their depictions of Africa as a source of civilization and culture reversed centuries of stereotyping of Africa as primitive chaos, a source of black inferiority. The term "African American," which implied membership of a global diaspora, originated from this milieu. See Corbould, Clare (2009). *Becoming African Americans: Black Public Life in Harlem, 1919–1939.* Cambridge: Harvard University Press.

[11] See Grant, Colin (2008). *Negro with a Hat: The Rise and Fall of Marcus Garvey and His Dream of Mother Africa.* London: Jonathan Cape.

[12] Ellis, Mark (1994). "J. Edgar Hoover and the 'Red Summer' of 1919." *Journal of American Studies,* 28(1): 39–59, 48–49.

The 1920s saw the establishment of a number of Muslim organizations that targeted African Americans for conversion. These included Muhammad Sadiq's Ahamdiyya mission and Dusé Mohamed Ali's Universal Islamic Society, both of which were based in Detroit and had links to UNIA. Satti Majid founded a successful multinational Sunni mosque in New York City and the African Moslem Welfare Society in Pittsburgh. But these immigrant-founded groups faced home-grown competition from North Carolina-born Noble Drew Ali, founder of the Moorish Science Temple of America (MSTA) in Chicago. The MSTA had few connections to other Muslim groups, but had a black nationalist philosophy overlain with Islamic and Masonic symbolism.[13] Noble Drew Ali taught that African Americans were part of a Moroccan nation ("Moors") that was Asiatic and Islamic. He advocated creating a new religious identity for African Americans because this would free them from persecution: "the legal right to oppose citizens, individuals and organizations alike for their religious beliefs does not exist in the United States. The door of religious freedom made by the American constitution swings open to all, and people may enter through it and worship as they desire." This turned out to be a naïve hope for any group associated with black nationalism.[14]

The Moorish Science Temple was a precursor to the Nation of Islam, which was founded in Detroit in 1930 and soon eclipsed the MSTA. Relatively little is known about the earliest days of the Nation of Islam or its founder, Wallace D. Fard. Many accounts of this period rely heavily on Erdmann Doane Benyon's 1938 article, "The Voodoo Cult Among Negro Migrants in Detroit." Fard was a peddler whose ethnic and national background was impossible to discern, which added to his mysterious appeal. While initially using the Bible as his central text, he denounced Christianity as a tool of Caucasian oppression. Like Noble Drew Ali, he taught black Americans that they were alienated from their Asiatic origins and Islamic faith. He described himself as a prophet who had come to America from the Middle East to restore to the people their language, faith, and culture. Fard had little knowledge of the Islamic tradition, and primarily relied on the Bible in his teachings because that is what both he and his followers understood. The following passage from Benyon gives an idea of the electicism of Fard's teaching:

> The prophet's message was characterized by his ability to utilize to the fullest measure the environment of his followers. Their physical and economic difficulties alike were used to illustrate the new teaching. Similarly, Biblical prophecies and the teachings of Noble Drew Ali were cited as foretelling the coming of the new prophet. As additional proofs of his message, the prophet referred his followers to the writings of Judge Rutherford, of Jehovah's Witnesses, to a miscellaneous

---

[13] Curtis (2013), pp. 85–89.
[14] GhaneaBassiri, Kambiz (2013). "Islamophobia and American History: Religious Stereotyping and Out-grouping of Muslims in the United States." In Carl W. Ernst (ed.) *Islamophobia in America: The Anatomy of Intolerance*. New York: Palgrave MacMillan, p. 67.

collection of books on Freemasonry and its symbolism, and to some well-known works, such as Breasted's *Conquest of Civilization* and Hendrik van Loon's *Story of Mankind.*[15]

The title of Benyon's article refers to the name Detroit police used for the Nation of Islam, and the article makes it clear that the Nation was in conflict with city authorities from its inception. Fard quickly accumulated a substantial following. According to Benyon, in 1932 "the people of Detroit became conscious of the presence of the cult through its first widely publicized human sacrifice." For a brief period in the 1930s, Fard apparently taught his followers that it was necessary for "every Muslim to sacrifice four Caucasian devils in order that he might return to his home in Mecca." The exact meaning of this teaching is disputed and unclear, but in Benyon's account it inspired at least one sacrificial murder, for which the victim volunteered. Police reportedly prevented another man from sacrificing his wife and daughter in 1937.

There is no independent corroboration for these incidents other than Benyon's article, which is the source for all subsequent accounts of the alleged sacrifices, including the FBI's. However, the teaching certainly seems to have been widely known, even if the practice was extremely rare, and it provoked schisms within the movement, isolation from the black community, and police surveillance. All these consequences were causally related; as noted in Chapter 3, religious apostates are often responsible for bringing the alleged misdeeds of their former brethren to the attention of the public and the state. In Benyon's words, "Attacks made on the cult by the Police Department have been instigated usually by the leaders of Negro organizations."[16]

It is hardly surprising that Detroit police considered Wallace Fard a threat to civic order, and they appear to have forced him out of the city at some point in 1933. His fate after leaving Detroit is unknown. Fard's departure left a power vacuum in the Nation of Islam, which by then numbered around 8,000 according to the group and 5,000 according to police – in either case, a large number for a new religion specific to Detroit.[17] Benyon describes numerous attempts by outside groups to infiltrate and exploit the Nation, including the Communist Party, the Japanese and Ethiopian governments, and "anti-union interests," none of which had any lasting success. By 1934 Elijah Muhammad, one of Fard's earliest followers and apparently the man who convinced Fard of

---

[15] Benyon, Erdmann Doane (1938). "The Voodoo Cult Among Negro Migrants in Detroit." *The American Journal of Sociology*, 43(6): 894–907, 900.

[16] Benyon (1938), p. 904. Martha Lee cites Elijah Muhammad's statement that "W.D. Fard did teach us that if everyone kills four devils at the proper time he will have free transportation to Mecca. This teaching had stirred the police department in Detroit against him. Ever since they began to persecute us and charge us." She also notes Essien-Udom's observation that some followers apparently interpreted the teaching as a symbolic allusion to the overcoming of the "Four Beasts" of the Book of Revelation. Lee, Martha (1996). *The Nation of Islam: An American Millenarian Movement.* Syracuse: Syracuse University Press.

[17] Benyon (1938), p. 897.

his own divinity, attempted to establish himself as Fard's successor.[18] However, the Nation of Islam was disintegrating violently in Detroit, and Muhammad left the city in 1935 under threat from authorities and rivals within the organization, including his younger brother.

The leadership of Elijah Muhammad and conflict with the FBI

Elijah Muhammad re-established the Nation of Islam in Chicago. Muhammad had much more familiarity with the Islamic tradition than Wallace Fard, having been exposed to numerous immigrant Islamic communities in the Detroit area. While Muhammad enshrined the divinity of Fard in Nation of Islam teaching, he also may have drawn from sources other than Fard to create his own particularistic black Islam.[19] Elijah Muhammad's teachings, along with Quranic and Biblical content, contained his own dispensationalist myth of Yakub, which expanded Fard's and Noble Drew Ali's theories that black Americans had been separated from Islamic civilization.

According to Elijah Muhammad, the single great black tribe of Shabazz had inhabited the earth for 66 trillion years, speaking Arabic and practicing Islam. A mad scientist named Yakub created the white race 6,600 years ago, over the course of 600 years, and it was prophesied that this devil race would exist for another 6,000 years.[20] For most of their existence, whites had lived in barbarous conditions in Europe, cut off from Islamic civilization. Allah sent the prophets Jesus and Muhammad to try to spread Islam among the white race, but to no avail. Slavery, initiated in the sixteenth century, had allowed the white devils to rule over the earth, but had also fulfilled a prophesy that would guarantee their own destruction at the hands of Allah in the soon-to-be end times.[21] Muhammad used passages from both the Quran and the Bible as evidence for the Yakub story.

Elijah Muhammad was constantly watching for signs of upheaval that might herald the end of white civilization and the deliverance of black people. He believed the appearance of Wallace Fard signaled the beginning of a revelatory period for black Americans and the apocalypse would soon follow. In the early 1940s, the Second World War was full of millenarian promise for the end of the Christian West – like Jehovah's Witnesses in this period, Muhammad believed the process had begun in 1914.[22] Also like Jehovah's Witnesses,

---

[18] Lee (1996), p. 25.

[19] Curtis (2002), p. 71. In particular, Curtis suggests Ahmadiyya Islam may have helped shape Muhammad's thinking. Ernest Allen also detects Ahmadiyya influences on Elijah Muhammad, reflected in use of the pseudonym "Gulam Bogans" in the 1930s and 1940s. Allen, Jr., Ernest (1996). "Religious Heterodoxy and Nationalist Tradition: The Continuing Evolution of the Nation of Islam." *The Black Scholar*, 26(3/4): 2–34, 7.

[20] Curtis (2002), pp. 74–75. These repetitive numbers also show the influence of numerology on Elijah Muhammad's thought.

[21] Ibid., pp. 75–76.

[22] Ibid., p. 76.

Elijah Muhammad and his followers would have no part in a war on behalf of a power that they saw as hostile to them. They refused to register for the draft, claiming to be citizens of the Nation of Islam.

Globally, many non-white nationalists had seen the Japanese empire as a potentially liberating force since Japan's victory over Russia in 1906.[23] Aware of possible pro-Japanese sympathies in various black nationalist organizations, the FBI investigated several such groups in the early 1940s. The Bureau found pro-Japanese sentiments expressed openly at Nation of Islam meetings, and in 1942 it arrested sixty-five Muslims along with twenty members of two other black nationalist groups. Fifty-six of the Nation of Islam defendants received three-year prison sentences for violation the Selective Service Act, and Elijah Muhammad was put on trial for sedition.[24] He was not convicted, and served out a draft evasion charge in federal prison in Michigan until 1946.

The Nation of Islam grew rapidly after the war and was subject to intense FBI scrutiny at every step. In the late 1940s the Nation, under Elijah Muhammad's leadership, began to take on the forms that became so well known in the 1950s and 1960s. In Curtis's words, it became "the organization known for disciplined corps of bow-tied men hawking bean pies, salvation, and copies of his (Muhammad's) books; the 'supportive' white-robed women who attended 'Muslim Girls Training'; and most important of all, an articulate, good-looking young minister named Malcolm X."[25] The FBI's Security Index from 1939 to 1971 contained 673 members of the Nation of Islam, the largest group represented in the index (there were 476 Communists). In 1956, J. Edgar Hoover requested authority from the Attorney General to install technical surveillance in Elijah Muhammad's house. He explained that members of the Nation of Islam "fanatically follow the teachings of Allah, as interpreted by Mohammed [*sic*]; they disavow allegiance to the United States; and they are taught they need not obey the laws of the United States. Allegations have been received that its members may resort to acts of violence in carrying out its avowed purpose of destroying non-Muslims and Christianity."[26]

Mattias Gardell argues that the agency targeted the Nation of Islam because of the threat it posed to America's self-image. He sees the FBI as "a reflection of American society and culture," populated with "carefully recruited agents from conservative, mainstream, white, male culture." As such, the Nation's anti-white and anti-American message was intolerable to it, even if the Nation posed no material threat:

---

[23] See Lake, Marilyn and Henry Reynolds (2008). *Drawing the Global Colour Line: White Men's Countries and the International Challenge of Racial Equality*. Cambridge and New York: Cambridge University Press, ch. 11.

[24] Gardell, Mattias (1996). *In the Name of Elijah Muhammad: Louis Farrakhan and the Nation of Islam*. Durham: Duke University Press, pp. 70–71.

[25] Curtis (2002), p. 72.

[26] Gardell (1996), p. 72.

In practice the members of the Nation were denied their constitutional rights, which guarantee all Americans the freedom of speech, freedom of assembly, and the freedom of belief. The rationale for disregarding the very Constitution the agents were employed to protect, I believe, can be explained by the apparent NOI transgression the unwritten code of Americanity. By publicly reversing the fundamental values of American civil religion and desecrating its prime symbols, the Nation of Islam became "un-American" and thus was targeted for counter-intelligence actions.[27]

While the FBI's conservatism was undoubtedly a factor in the selection of its targets, the Bureau's documents reveal a rationale that was more concerned with preserving state authority than the social status quo. The Nation of Islam's radical critique of the United States was not enough to justify targeting it; the FBI justified its "investigative concern" with the Nation by depicting it as a fundamentally political organization that had nothing to do with the authentic religion of Islam.

In 1955 the FBI internally circulated a monograph titled *The Muslim Cult of Islam*, which was distributed to every major urban field office and was required reading for every agent assigned to investigate the Nation of Islam. It is a rare example of a state agency explaining to its own operatives why it is necessary to repress a religious group.[28] One of the main purposes of the document is to show FBI agents the distinctions between orthodox Islam and the Nation of Islam, and it contains a remedial introduction to Islam "inasmuch as a knowledge of the orthodox religion of Islam is considered essential to an understanding of one of its most deformed branches." Referred to throughout as the "Muslim Cult of Islam" (or MCI), the document described the Nation as an "especially anti-American and violent Cult" with an "absolute lack of a doctrinal core." The FBI's conclusions about the MCI's threat were as follows:

1. The MCI is a fanatic Negro organization purporting to be motivated by the religious principles of Islam, but actually dedicated to the propagation of hatred against the white race. The services conducted throughout the temples are bereft of any semblance to religious exercises.
2. Organizationally, the MCI is a collection of autonomous temples bound by a tremulous personal relationship between the heads of the temples and the headquarters of the Cult in Chicago, Illinois.
3. The MCI, although an extremely anti-American organization, is not at the present time either large or powerful enough to inflict any serious damage to this country; however, its members are capable of committing individual acts of violence.

[27] Gardell (1996), p. 96.
[28] This document is one of many FBI documents pertaining to the Nation of Islam that Gardell initially obtained through FOIA requests. It is available at: http://vault.fbi.gov/Nation%20of%20Islam/Nation%20of%20Islam%20Part%201%20of%203/view, last accessed June 19, 2015.

4. The aims and purposes of the MCI are directed at the overthrow of our constitutional government, inasmuch as the Cult members regard it as an instrument of the white race; therefore, it is obvious that this group, as long as it retains the ideas now motivating it, will remain an investigative problem to the FBI.[29]

Like most of the anti-systemic groups the FBI monitored, the Nation of Islam had no realistic chance of achieving its more radical goals. It was enough to constitute a threat that a group with an anti-government and anti-white ideology had members who might be prepared to commit individual acts of violence in the service of that agenda. The report noted the group's numerous run-ins with local and federal authorities, its wartime Selective Service violations and its continuing defiance of the draft, its apparent sympathy with Japan during the Second World War, and its violent and apocalyptic pronouncements throughout the 1950s. While the report concluded that there was no indication the MCI is "under any direct influence of the Communist Party of the United States, or any other subversive group," it nonetheless labeled the group as a "Potential Threat to the Internal Security." In a one-sentence section under this heading, the authors reported that:

> Based upon an analysis of the rabid teachings of this group, it is definitely considered that these people represent a threat to the internal security of the United States, and would, with the right number of followers and the opportunity, be more than willing to perform any acts which would subvert American principles and endanger the existence of the American nation as such.[30]

This analysis of the Nation of Islam was followed by a detailed comparison with orthodox Islam. Whereas "the orthodox Muslim sincerely believes in Allah as the divine being who created the universe," for the MCI "Allah, together with unexplained digits and pseudo-scientific data, has become merely a name to be memorized." Racial prejudice is "the very foundation of all the teachings of the cult," but it appears "nowhere in the tenets of the orthodox religion of Islam." Orthodox Muslims are "forbidden to provoke war," and "personal violence, such as murder and revenge, are punishable under Moslem law." For the MCI, however, "the element of desire for violence seems to be an emotional stimulant for every practicing member."[31]

The FBI denied not only the Nation's claims to be Islamic, but to be religious at all. If the group's aims were primarily political, driven by violent anti-white animus, and its members had no sincere belief in a divine being, then the group lacked religious legitimacy and could instead be targeted as a dangerous political organization. The existence of the quasi-military Fruit of Islam organization further suggested the group's nature was revolutionary rather

---

[29] Federal Bureau of Investigation (1955). *The Muslim Cult of Islam.* Washington, DC: captioned monograph, pp. i–iii.

[30] FBI (1955), pp. 37–47.

[31] Ibid., pp. 52–56.

than religious. The FBI's distinctions between the authentic religion of Islam – peaceful, universalistic, and motivated by sincere spirituality – and the deformed cult – political, motivated by hate, and primed for violence – predated by fifty years a similar taxonomy that various western governments would impose on Islam after 9/11. Robert Bosco shows in *Securing the Sacred* that the British, French, and U.S. governments have all sought to frame "real" Islam as something that embodies similar core principles to other world religions, and which "coincides with a variety of liberal values such as the embrace of secularity, toleration, freedom, citizenship and democracy."[32] The terrorist threat, on the other hand, comes from "pseudo-religion," which "perverts" and "hijacks" true Islam.

Tensions with orthodox Islam and Malcolm X

The FBI's monograph also suggested that other American Muslims did not accept the Nation of Islam as genuinely Islamic. The source of this claim was an unnamed individual who was president of the Philadelphia branch of a Sunni organization headquartered in Newark. After attending several of the group's meetings in 1954, this person "classified the MCI as the most unorthodox and least acceptable Moslem group in the country." His report seemed to accord with the FBI's own distinctions between true and false Islam: "He stated there were no evidences in the Koran to support the MCI's teaching of civil disobedience and nonconformity to the laws of the country, their adherence to principles of racial prejudice, or the militaristic approach to their religion."[33]

Directly or indirectly, the FBI's assessment of the Nation of Islam shaped the way the group subsequently interacted with the rest of civil society. It is certainly true that the Nation, with its belief in contemporary prophets and

---

[32] Bosco, Robert M. (2014). *Securing the Sacred: Religion, National Security, and the Western State*. Ann Arbor, MI: University of Michigan Press, p. 28.

[33] FBI (1955), p. 67. According to the report, the unnamed informant also listed as "not acceptable to orthodox Muslims" the Moorish Science Temple and "Ahmadyyia, which group recognizes a living prophet in India called Ahmad." The latter group, which would have been virtually unknown in the United States in 1954, struggles for acceptance throughout the Muslim world, and the U.S. government today denounces the persecution of Ahmadi Muslims at the hands of other Muslims. While the group is officially recognized as Islamic in India, in Pakistan Ahmadis are banned from referring themselves to Muslims because they do not accept Mohammad as the final prophet of Islam. Under the auspices of the 1998 International Religious Freedom Act, the US State Department extensively documents and expresses concern about the harassment and discrimination suffered by the Ahmadiyya at the hands of the Pakistani state, as well as persecution by non-state actors in other countries such as Bangladesh and Indonesia. The contemporary US government's advocacy of the global Ahmadiyya cause demonstrates that a state's criteria for what qualifies a sect as a "genuine" part of a world religion may change over time, as well as varying between states, and scholars should resist essentialist distinctions between "true" and "false" variants. See US Department of State (2013). "Pakistan 2012 International Religious Freedom Report." Available at www.state.gov/documents/organization/208650.pdf.

the myth of Yakub, would have been unacceptably unorthodox to most Muslims. But in 1955 the Nation was so small and little-known that hardly any other Muslims are likely to have had an opinion about it. Muslim organizations only began distancing themselves publicly from the NOI in 1959. In the mid-1950s one Sunni Muslim newspaper, *The Moslem World and the USA*, gave the Nation extensive and relatively positive coverage. In 1959, however, the TV documentary *The Hate that Hate Produced*, presented by Mike Wallace of CBS News, created such a public backlash against the Nation that Muslim groups across the country rushed to distinguish themselves from it. In African American newspapers, black and immigrant leaders of Sunni Muslim groups joined the widespread denunciation of the Nation as a "black supremacist" group, as opposed to real Islam which "does not preach hate."[34] Gardell claims the outcry was part of a large-scale FBI campaign to discredit the Nation through the media; the Bureau "briefed selected journalists who willingly channelled the view of the Bureau to the American public."[35]

In 1963 it became apparent that the Nation of Islam had converted Cassius Clay, later known as Muhammad Ali, a contender for the world heavyweight boxing title. Clay, a close friend of Malcolm X, initially kept his public distance from the Nation, knowing a public backlash could jeopardize his planned title fight with Sonny Liston. But the association became impossible to ignore when Clay invited Malcolm X to his training camp in January 1964. The fight's promoter, Bill MacDonald, feared he would be unable to sell seats to the match in Miami when Clay's religious affiliation became public knowledge, especially as Liston was also deeply unpopular with the white public.[36] Nonetheless, the fight went ahead with Malcolm X in attendance, and Clay upset Liston to win the world heavyweight championship at the age of twenty-two.

The win elevated Clay to tremendous celebrity and influence. At that time, the title of world heavyweight boxing champion was the most prestigious in sports. Already popular with the black public, he became one of the most recognizable figures in the country and, ultimately, the world. This made him the Nation of Islam's most formidable publicist. Shortly after the title bout he changed his name to Muhammad Ali under the direction of Elijah Muhammad. Ali defended his title twice in 1965. In 1966, the US Army draft board reclassified him as eligible for active service (it had previously declared his IQ too low). Shortly thereafter Ali became the Vietnam War's most high-profile domestic opponent when he told a reporter "I ain't got no quarrel with them

---

[34] Curtis (2002), pp. 79–81.
[35] Gardell (1996), p. 73.
[36] In the words of David Remnick: "The David-versus-Goliath fight he thought he was getting was fast losing its balance of moral forces, especially among white Floridians,who were not inclined to see a brash young black man, much less a Black Muslim, in the role of David." Remnick, David (1998). *King of the World: Muhammad Ali and the Rise of an American Hero*. New York: Vintage, ch. 9.

Vietcong." At that moment he reportedly knew little about the war or its politics, but over the next few months Ali became a ferocious and well-educated dissident. He linked his anti-war stance to both his religion and his skin color: as a Muslim he would not take any part unless it was declared by Allah, he refused to kill for a country that so violently mistreated his own people, and he claimed an exemption from the draft as a minister of Islam. The government did not recognize his rights as a conscientious objector, and this stance earned him a five-year prison sentence and a $10,000 fine (the maximum penalty for refusing the draft). He did not serve the sentence, which the Supreme Court unanimously overturned in 1971, but his boxing license was suspended and he would be unable to fight for three years.

The inner life, organization, and politics of the Nation of Islam in the 1950s and 1960s are well known thanks to *The Autobiography of Malcolm X*, published in 1965, and the subsequent Spike Lee film produced in 1992. Importantly, neither of these works downplays the sincere spirituality of the Nation of Islam. The FBI's portrayal of the Nation as a primarily political organization was mirrored, albeit in far more sophisticated and sympathetic terms, by the first and most influential scholarly study of the group, C. Eric Lincoln's *The Black Muslims in America* (1959). Lincoln, a justly renowned sociologist of religion, interpreted the Nation as first and foremost a black nationalist group: "The fundamental attraction of the Black Muslim movement is its passion for group solidarity, its exaggerated sense of consciousness-of-kind. What matters above all is that individuals acknowledge themselves as black or white and that all blacks work together to accomplish their group aims." Lincoln consigns religion to "secondary importance" in the movement: "Although the Black Muslims call their movement a religion, religious values have secondary importance. They are not part of the movement's basic appeal, except to the extent that they foster and strengthen the sense of group solidarity."[37]

Later generations of scholars such as Martha Lee, Mattias Gardell, and Edward Curtis have shown that this functionalist interpretation of the Nation's religiosity is grossly inadequate.[38] *The Autobiography of Malcolm X* provides perhaps the most vivid refutation of the view that religion had nothing to do with the movement's appeal. Malcolm describes recruiting converts exiting black churches, who on Sunday afternoons were keen to go anywhere

---

[37] Lincoln, C. Eric ([1959] 1994). *The Black Muslims in America* (third Edition). Grand Rapids: William B. Eerdmans Publishing Company, p. 26.

[38] See especially Curtis (2002), p. 2: "he [Lincoln] seemed to distinguish 'politics' from 'religion' as if the two were diametrically opposed, as if politics were this-worldly and religion were other-worldly. Lincoln's definition of religion seemed to assume that 'true' religion dealt mainly with issues of theology, salvation, and meaning, a definition seemingly shaped by Lincoln's own Protestant Christianity. His use of religion and politics as analytical categories ultimately obscured more than they revealed since he underemphasized the legitimately religious aspects of the movement's nationalistic activity."

they could hear "good preaching."[39] Black nationalist politics certainly contributed to the movement's appeal and convinced many that Islam rather than Christianity was the "true" religion of the black American. But these converts were nonetheless choosing between religions, and the Nation of Islam would have been unable to compete with Christianity if adherents had not seen it as a religion.

The crisis that led Malcolm X away from the Nation of Islam was, famously, a spiritual one, albeit one entangled with the internal politics of the movement. When he discovered that Elijah Muhammad had fathered children with three different women in the Nation, he began to question whether Muhammad, who had so egregiously violated the Nation's own moral code, could really be a prophet of Allah. At the same time, Muhammad was growing wary of Malcolm's growing charismatic influence in the movement, and he silenced him in 1963 after his public comment that the Kennedy assassination represented "chickens coming home to roost." Malcolm found himself increasingly on the outside of the Nation and drawn to more orthodox interpretations of Islam. Elijah Muhammad's youngest son, Wallace Muhammad, joined Malcolm X in exile from the movement. Having undertaken the Hajj, Malcolm describes his encounters with Muslims of many races in his *Autobiography*, and proclaims the universalism of true Islam.[40]

Malcolm X was himself in constant conflict with the state and in many ways is the anti-establishment figure par excellence in American political history. His late drift away from black particularism in no way detracts from the fact that his autobiography is the most influential articulation of American black nationalism ever penned, and most of the book is a sympathetic portrait of particularist black Islam. But ultimately *The Autobiography of Malcolm X*, a work of the Nation's most famous apostate, contributed to the state's preferred narrative that the Nation of Islam was not real Islam.

Succession of Wallace Muhammad and schism with Farrakhan

Malcolm X was assassinated at a public function in Harlem in 1965. Three men served extensive prison sentences for his murder, but the exact nature of their connection to the Nation of Islam has never been established. The prevalent theory ever since 1965 has been that the Nation of Islam ordered the murder, which is consistent with the frequent threats Malcolm received and an earlier attempt on his life. But there have always been alternative theories that the FBI or CIA was at least partly responsible (in Lee's film, the FBI knew what was about to occur). At the very least, the FBI fostered the growing conflict between Malcolm X and Elijah Muhammad through informants and agents provocateurs. FBI informants supplied Malcolm with the information about

[39] X, Malcolm (1965). *The Autobiography of Malcolm X, As Told to Alex Haley*. New York: Random House, p. 223.
[40] Ibid., pp. 325–348.

Muhammad's womanizing, and suggested to Muhammad that Malcolm was building a personal power base.[41]

The FBI's techniques of infiltration and disruption were used frequently, and often to great effect, against various black power movements in the 1960s and 1970s.[42] In the counterintelligence program (COINTELPRO) of the late 1960s, the Nation of Islam was subsumed under the heading of "Black Nationalist Hate Groups." The threat any of these groups posed may have been negligible on their own, but the FBI was determined to "prevent the coalition of militant black nationalist groups" that "might be the first step toward a real 'Mau Mau' in America, a true black revolution."[43] Numerous FBI field offices actually recommended against including the Nation of Islam in COINTELPRO efforts, seeing it as a nonviolent religious organization. Centrally, however, the Bureau remained convinced that the Nation was a dangerous element in the black nationalist mix, and it escalated its campaign to cause internal strife within the organization.[44]

A number of violent incidents shook the Nation of Islam in the early 1970s. In 1971, unknown assailants shot and injured Elijah Muhammad's son-in-law and chief bodyguard, Raymond Sharrieff. Shortly afterwards (in "apparent retribution"), two members of a small dissident faction of the Nation were murdered. In 1972 four people died in a bloody street battle with Baton Rouge police; Elijah Muhammad initially denied that any of the dead or arrested were Muslims, but then conceded he was unsure. The minister of the Newark temple was murdered in 1972, and the *Chicago Tribune* reported that three more dissidents had been killed in likely retaliation.[45]

In the last few years of his life, possibly as a result of the pressure his organization was experiencing, Elijah Muhammad began moving toward a more conciliatory position with both the United States and global Islam. These moves foreshadowed the wholesale changes his son Wallace, now back within the Nation's fold, would make when he assumed the leadership upon Elijah's death. By 1971, in Lee's words, Muhammad was "de-eschatologizing" his teaching. Rather than prophesying the destruction of the white race, Muhammad now claimed they could be saved through Islam during the Millennium. Muhammad, who had previously kept non-black Muslims at arm's length, began to establish links with the governments of Libya, Abu Dhabi, and Qatar, who donated millions to the Nation for the purpose of "promoting Islam" in the United States.[46] Muhammad's solicitation of these

---

[41] Gardell (1996), pp. 76–81.
[42] See Davenport, Christian (2014). *How Social Movements Die: Repression and Demobilization of the Republic of New Africa*. New York: Cambridge University Press.
[43] Gardell (1996), p. 86.
[44] Gardell (1996), pp. 87–92.
[45] Lee (1996), pp. 51–54.
[46] Ibid.

funds reflected that the Nation was in a state of financial crisis and was desperate for new sources of income.[47]

Gardell's FBI documents suggest the Bureau had been planning for Elijah Muhammad's death since the late 1960s. According to a 1969 document, "When he dies a power struggle can be expected and the NOI could change direction. We should be prepared for this eventuality. We should plan how to change the philosophy of the NOI." It cannot be determined whether the FBI actually played any role in the succession struggle leading up to Elijah's death in February 1975, but it is clear that Wallace D. Muhammad, who succeeded, was the FBI's candidate of choice. In one report, Wallace was mentioned as "the only son of Elijah Muhammad who would have the necessary qualities to guide the NOI in such a manner as would eliminate racist teachings."[48]

One of Elijah Muhammad's final editorials in *Muhammad Speaks*, which appeared after his death, stated "I say that the Black Man in North America has no one to blame but himself. If he respects himself and will do for himself, his once slavemaster will come and respect him and help him do something for self."[49] The previous year, Muhammad had shared the stage with whites at the organization's annual Savior's Day in Chicago. As well as this rapprochement with whites, the Nation had been making ecumenical gestures toward black Christian denominations. Some city authorities were beginning to embrace the softening Nation of Islam. In January 1975, with Elijah Muhammad's health rapidly failing, Mayor Richard Daley declared the following Savior's Day, February 26, to be Nation of Islam Day in Chicago. Similar honors followed from the mayors of Oakland, Berkeley, Los Angeles, Gary, Newark, and Atlanta.[50]

Within a few years Wallace Muhammad had changed the Nation of Islam beyond recognition on almost every dimension. Theologically, followers were no longer to regard Wallace Fard as divine or Elijah Muhammad as a prophet. The myth of Yakub was shelved. The tenets of orthodox Sunni Islam became the sole basis of religious belief and practice in the Nation. In 1976, the name of the organization changed to the World Council of Islam in the West (WCIW). Wallace renounced all traces of black particularism and opened membership to non-black members. Where Malcolm X had come to see Islamic universalism as the solution to racial oppression in the United States, Wallace downplayed the problem of racial oppression considerably. In a 1978 interview he argued that "the problem is we don't identify with America ... We haven't been raised to believe that citizens have a voice and power." As well as establishing and deepening links with global Sunni organizations, Wallace encouraged a new

---

[47] Allen, Jr., Ernest (1996). "Religious Heterodoxy and Nationalist Tradition: The Continuing Evolution of the Nation of Islam." *The Black Scholar*, 26(3/4): 2–34, 15.

[48] Gardell (1996), p. 101.

[49] Lee (1996), p. 55.

[50] Ibid.

American patriotism among adherents, and displays of the American flag became prominent in WCIW literature and rallies. Wallace was personally politically conservative, and supported Republican candidates throughout the 1980s and 1990s. These politics were to some degree consistent with the increasing emphasis on self-reliance and economic development in the post-Malcolm X Nation of Islam.[51]

Some of Wallace's earliest reforms dealt with the aspects that had caused the most tension between the Nation of Islam and the state. He abolished the Fruit of Islam, the paramilitary organization founded by Wallace Fard in the 1930s. He also ceased the practice whereby the Nation paid the legal fees of any member in trouble with the law. Wallace dismantled most of Elijah Muhammad's murky financial empire, which had attracted claims by the FBI and others that the Nation of Islam existed for his personal enrichment – one of the most frequent and damaging claims leveled against the leaders of all new religions. In its place, Wallace created new (and far more transparent) business enterprises to fulfill his vision of black entrepreneurial renewal. One of these, a food service business called Salaam International, received a $22 million contract from the Department of Defense in 1979.[52]

Wallace's reforms did not please everyone within the Nation of Islam. The most vocal dissident was Louis Farrakhan, a former calypso singer who had been close to Elijah Muhammad and was the most hard-line defender of his particularistic doctrines. From the 1950s Farrakhan had enjoyed a similarly charismatic (if smaller) profile to Malcolm X's within the Nation, and he was the author of what became the most famous piece of Nation literature, *The Trial*, which featured at the beginning of Mike Wallace's *The Hate That Hate Produced* and C. Eric Lincoln's *The Black Muslims in America*.[53] Farrakhan had a following of his own within the Nation of Islam, and had been one of Wallace's obvious rivals for the leadership as Elijah Muhammad's death grew near.

In January 1978, Farrakhan told an interviewer that he was "not welcomed in the World Community of Al-Islam in the West and I know it." In March, he severed all ties with Wallace's organization and announced plans to rebuild the Nation of Islam. Wallace offered Farrakhan the Harlem Mosque (his power

---

[51] Allen (1996), pp. 16–17.
[52] Lee (1996), pp. 69–70.
[53] In the famous climax of the play, a white man is sentenced to death before a black courtroom for his crimes against the black race. The litany of charges, heard in full at the beginning of *The Hate that Hate Produced* and transcribed by Lincoln, is as follows: "I charge the white man with being the greatest liar on earth! I charge the white man with being the greatest drunkard on earth … I charge the white man with being the greatest gambler on earth. I charge the white man, ladies and gentlemen, with being the greatest peace-breaker on earth. I charge the white man with being the greatest adulterer on earth. I charge the white man with being the greatest robber on earth. I charge the white man with being the greatest deceiver on earth. I charge the white man with being the greatest trouble-maker on earth. So therefore, ladies and gentlemen of the jury, I ask you, bring back a verdict of guilty as charged!" Lincoln ([1959] 1994), p. 1.

base) and urged his followers not to picket or disrupt Farrakhan's movement, but stated that Farrakhan could "not change the world of the racists or the separatists."[54] Farrakhan refused any help from Wallace and slowly began to reconstruct the Nation of Islam in a way that remained faithful to his interpretation of the teachings of Elijah Muhammad. The new NOI organization was barely visible until 1984, when Farrakhan played an unexpectedly prominent role in Rev. Jesse Jackson's presidential campaign. From that point on it grew quickly into an organization that, despite its fidelity to Elijah Muhammad, was quite different from the entity he had created.

Farrakhan's support for Jackson – which ultimately became a liability for Jackson – showcased his political engagement and openness to working with black allies of other faiths. He also became closely associated with anti-Semitism during this period, and this more than anything else has contributed to his unpopularity outside urban African American communities. After a black reporter, Milton Coleman, publicized Jackson's description of New York as "Hymie Town," Farrakhan went on the offensive, calling Coleman a Judas and a "no good filthy traitor." In later interviews he characterized Zionism as a "gutter religion." Jackson eventually disassociated himself from Farrakhan. Farrakhan came to see Jackson's failure at the 1984 Democratic convention as evidence that white America was incapable of saving itself, but he saw the barrage of negative publicity he received as helpful in building his support "with the masses of black people."[55]

Despite his marginal (indeed poisonous) status in mainstream politics, Farrakhan's Nation of Islam did not attract the same hostile attention from the state as it had in the days of Elijah Muhammad. Perhaps the most important reason for this was the overall decline of black militant organizations; the post-Hoover FBI no longer saw black militancy as a threat that needed constant monitoring. In his own way, Farrakhan was also a more accommodationist leader than Elijah Muhammad had been. Farrakhan may have reintroduced some of Elijah Muhammad's apocalyptic rhetoric, but like Wallace Muhammad he also courted public money. The only lingering association between the Nation and violence was a positive one – the Nation developed a (perhaps overblown) reputation for ridding urban black communities of drug dealers.[56] At the height of the "crack epidemic" in the 1980s various government agencies were accepting whatever help they could get in the war

---

[54] Lee (1996), p. 70.

[55] Ibid., pp. 80–83.

[56] In a 1997 study of Muslims in Los Angeles, Kambiz GhaneaBassiri found that African American Muslims did not experience the same kinds of prejudice as Muslims from other ethnic backgrounds. According to GhaneaBassiri, "Given the success of African-American Muslim organizations, such as the Nation of Islam, in countering the negative impact of drugs, alcoholism, gang activities and prostitution in the ghettos, most non-Muslims have a sense of respect for African-American Muslims." GhaneaBassiri, Kambiz (1997). *Competing Visions of Islam in the United States*. Westport: Greenwood Press, pp. 75–76.

on drugs, and Farrakhan's security firms received federal and local grants in numerous cities.[57] Unlike in previous decades, intra-Muslim schisms were no longer a source of violence. After an initial period of mutual coldness, the Nation of Islam enjoyed cordial relations with Wallace Muhammad's organization, which by the end of the 1980s had ceased to exist as a distinctive entity.

ISLAM AS FOREIGN POLICY ALLY AND ENEMY

Prior to the 1979 Iranian revolution, the United States saw Islam as a near-universal ally in its global struggle with Communism. It consistently backed Islamic political movements against Third World nationalism, which it saw as a tool of Soviet interests. US intelligence agencies supported Islamists in Indonesia, Pakistan, and Egypt, as well as conservative governments throughout the Arab world. The Iranian revolution, which was Islamist, nationalist, anti-Communist and explicitly anti-American, complicated the relationship between the United States and political Islam. Mahmood Mamdani argues that the revolution taught the United States to distinguish between two faces of political Islam: the "revolutionary," which encouraged mass participation, and the "elitist," which contained it.[58]

The Iranian revolution and subsequent seizure of American hostages at the US embassy dramatically changed both popular and official discourse around Islam within the United States. Americans experienced the 444-day televised hostage saga as a humiliating, nationally traumatic event. The crisis sealed the fate of the Carter Administration, and its resolution, simultaneous with Ronald Reagan's inauguration, signaled a new era of thinking about an Islamic threat. The day the hostages were released, Reagan announced terrorism would replace human rights as the country's most important foreign policy concern. For the first time, "terrorism" referred to something that directly imperiled the United States, and anti-terrorism became the prism through which the Reagan Administration justified increasing military involvement in the Middle East in the 1980s. At the same time, Islam became the dominant signifier of the Middle East for Americans.[59]

Elizabeth Shakman Hurd recalls how, as an elementary school student, the Iran hostage crisis shaped her sense of identity as an American:

> The red marks on the calendar in my classroom (marking the days of the crisis) sparked a sense of curiosity about whose actions warranted the symbolic oblitera-tion of an entire day, day after day, month after month. We were told that the Iranians were angry at the United States and that they had taken innocent Americans hostage. They were religious fanatics, very distant, and completely

---

[57] Allen (1996), p. 19.

[58] Mamdani, Mahmood (2004). *Good Muslim, Bad Muslim: America, the Cold War, and the Roots of Terror*. New York: Pantheon Books, ch. 3.

[59] McAlister, Melani (2001). *Epic Encounters: Culture, Media and U.S. Interests in the Middle East, 1945–2000*. Berkeley: University of California Press, pp. 198–201.

different from us. Americans, as I interpreted the situation, were not Iranian, not fanatical, and not particularly religious. Americans were rational, secular and democratic. It was the first time I had ever heard of Iran.[60]

The revolution and hostage crisis created a new anti-American religious "other" alongside the godless Soviet other. Melani McAlister notes the American media tended to explain all Iranian actions in terms of Islam (rather than the specific history of US–Iranian relations), and also that it increasingly identified the United States as a Christian country.[61] It was not just that the two countries followed different faiths; the Iranian version of Islam was fanatical, implacable, and inseparable from anti-American politics. Americans' faith, in contrast, was privately held and properly separated from the state, allowing for religious and other freedoms. As Hurd explains, for Americans this kind of democratic secularism was intimately linked to the Judeo-Christian tradition and could not be achieved in a country such as Iran, which was dominated by Islam.[62]

As anti-Khomeini novelty items became popular throughout the United States, some state-linked scholars developed a theory of Islamic theocracy as a form of totalitarianism. The historian Bernard Lewis advanced the idea that Islam is an inherently "political religion," and Jeanne Kirkpatrick and Daniel Patrick Moynihan argued that terrorism was linked to a conceptual absence of political boundaries that allowed no private sphere in which the innocent could be protected.[63] But even as high political discourse emphasized the irreconcilability of militant Islam with the United States, foreign policy actors continued to invest their hopes of winning the Cold War in a collection of Islamic holy warriors in central Asia. As well as uniting Muslims worldwide against Communism, the CIA believed that jihad in Afghanistan could create a political divide between Sunni and Shiite Islam, further marginalizing Iran.[64]

Over the course of the Reagan and Bush administrations the United States became embroiled in a succession of wars and other engagements across the Middle East. These included the Iran–Iraq war, the Afghanistan war, civil war in Lebanon, the Iran-Contra scandal, the bombing of Libya, the Palestinian intifada, and the Persian Gulf War of 1991. It is difficult to say what effect these near-continuous engagements, along with American deaths from bombings in Lebanon and Lockerbie, had on relations between American Muslims and broader American society. Yvonne Yazbeck Haddad wrote in

---

[60] Hurd, Elizabeth Shakman (2008). *The Politics of Secularism in International Relations.* Princeton: Princeton University Press, p. 102.

[61] McAlister (2001), pp. 210–212.

[62] Hurd (2008), pp. 110–111.

[63] McAlister, pp. 219–220. McAlister notes that throughout the hostage crisis, the media focused on the hostages as private individuals who wished to return home to their families, rather than as diplomatic personnel being used as pawns in negotiations between two governments.

[64] Mamdani (2004), ch. 3. As Mamdani writes, "The Islamic world had not seen an armed jihad for nearly a century. But now the CIA was determined to create one in service of a contemporary political objective."

1991 that "American foreign policy has had a profound influence on Muslim identity and on the ways in which Muslims choose to participate in the American process. U.S. dealings in the Middle East over the last forty years appear to have alienated a majority of its Muslim citizens."[65] She described how some Muslims had adopted an increasingly militant identity in response to "American distaste for Islam, to rampant prejudice, and to the perception of being ruled out of the system when national leaders call America a Judeo-Christian country."[66]

While American Muslims certainly felt the effects of ubiquitously negative media portrayals of the Islamic world and felt alienated from a state that repeatedly took sides against Muslims in the Middle East, they did not have to contend with persecution. All immigrant groups faced incidents of racist violence in the 1970s and 1980s, but these were relatively rare, and not usually motivated by religious identity. Most importantly, the state did not regard American Muslims as a domestic enemy. Even after the World Trade Center bombing in 1993, which was carried out by six Muslims, investigations correctly focused on foreign terrorist networks. Prior to the apprehension of Timothy McVeigh many people erroneously assumed that Muslims had been responsible for the 1995 Oklahoma City bombing, and Muslims reported incidents of verbal abuse and vandalism. They did not, however, report victimization by the state.[67]

MUSLIMS AND THE STATE AFTER 9/11

"Peaceful" and "perverted" Islam

On September 20, 2001, President George W. Bush addressed both houses of Congress to explain how his Administration would respond to the terrorist attacks of 9/11.[68] Identifying the organization responsible as al Qaeda, Bush

---

[65] Haddad, Yvonne Yazbeck (1991). "American Foreign Policy in the Middle East and Its Impact on the Identity of Arab Muslims in the United States." In Yvonne Yazbeck Haddad (ed.), *The Muslims of America*. New York: Oxford University Press, pp. 217–235 and 227.

[66] Ibid., p. 229.

[67] GhaneaBassiri's study of Los Angeles Muslims does not mention any complaints of police harassment or government discrimination. The respondents in this study were most concerned about media depictions of Muslims and Islam, which they held responsible for the prejudice they experienced (about half of his sample reported experiencing some kind of prejudice). GhaneaBassiri does, however, argue that the government's handling of the Oklahoma City bombing reflected more sensitivity to right-wing militias than Muslims could ever hope to receive: "When it was discovered that the bombing was a 'domestic' problem, various militia leaders were summoned to Capitol Hill to tell their stories in order for the government to discover the roots of such a tragedy; various documentaries and media reports also emerged for the same purpose. Few, however, have attempted to give voice to Muslim concerns in any conflicts." GhaneaBassiri (1997), p. 71.

[68] The transcript is available at www.washingtonpost.com/wp-srv/nation/specials/attacked/tran-scripts/bushaddress_092001.html

described the group in the terms that would come to characterize all official discourse about the relationship between terrorism and Islam.

> Al Qaeda is to terror what the Mafia is to crime. But its goal is not making money, its goal is remaking the world and imposing its radical beliefs on people everywhere. The terrorists practice a fringe form of extremist Islam that has been rejected by Muslim scholars and the vast majority of Muslim clerics; a fringe movement that perverts the peaceful teachings of Islam.

Later in the speech Bush acknowledged the fears of many citizens, and appealed for calm in the face of the continuing terrorist threat. Without mentioning Muslims directly, he asked Americans to be tolerant:

> I ask you to uphold the values of America and remember why so many have come here. We're in a fight for our principles, and our first responsibility is to live by them. No one should be singled out for unfair treatment or unkind words because of their ethnic background or religious faith.

Actors at all levels of the state understandably feared a violent backlash against people who appeared Arab or Muslim. The backlash was ultimately smaller than expected, thanks in part to the efforts of law enforcement officials. But as the "global war on terror" progressed, the importance of suppressing Islamophobia took on new dimensions. Increasingly dependent on Muslim allies in its fight against al Qaeda, the US government feared alienating the Muslim world when Islamophobic sentiments appeared in the US media or military. Moreover, the consequences of highly publicized western Islamophobia could include violent repercussions against US personnel in Muslim countries, as well as the loss of innocent life in riots triggered by antiwestern protests. Bush and his successor, Barack Obama, have repeatedly stated that the United States is "not at war with Islam." While they have had limited success in convincing the Muslim world of this,[69] the U.S. government has tried to appear consistently on the side of American Muslims against popular Islamophobia.

Post-9/11 hate crime and state response

Since 1990, criminal acts motivated by a victim's religious identity have come under the official rubric of "hate crimes," along with attacks motivated by race, ethnicity, national origin, disability, and sexual orientation. The federal Hate Crimes Statistics Act requires law enforcement agencies to collect specific data on these crimes, and many states have laws penalizing hate crimes more heavily than other crimes. This legal framework allows state actors to isolate, publicize, and wage campaigns against prejudicial violence. It also gives

---

[69] See Kull, Steven (2011). *Feeling Betrayed: The Roots of Muslim Anger at America*. Washington: Brookings Institution Press; and Telhami, Shibley (2013). *The World Through Arab Eyes: Arab Public Opinion and the Reshaping of the Middle East*. New York: Basic Books.

victimized groups the means to identify their struggles with those of other victimized groups and to demand a response from the state. After 9/11, law enforcement agencies, Muslim groups, the media, and other civil society groups all reacted to attacks on Muslims as hate crimes, deserving of the highest condemnation and harshest response.

According to the FBI there were 481 hate crimes against Muslims in the months following 9/11, a 1600 percent increase from the previous reporting period. These incidents included intimidation and vandalism, which were much more common events than assaults. However, the extent of retaliatory hate crime against Muslims after 9/11 has been blurred by the fact that victims also included Arab Americans of any religion and Asian Americans of other faiths who were apparently mistaken for Muslims.[70] The first and highest-profile victim was Balbir Singh Sodhi, a Sikh gas station owner murdered in Arizona by a man who had declared his intention on 9/11 to "go out and shoot some towel-heads."[71] The 2004 documentary *Mistaken Identity: Sikhs in America* claims there were 295 attacks on Sikhs in the weeks following 9/11. By 2012, the New York-based Sikh Coalition estimated there had been 700 attacks on Sikhs. As hate crimes against Muslims spiked again between 2010 and 2012, so too did crimes against Sikhs, but with deadlier consequences. Police believed two elderly Sikhs shot dead in Elk Grove, California, in 2011 had been mistaken for Muslims. In August 2012 a neo-Nazi gunman shot six Sikhs dead in their temple in Oak Creek, Wisconsin, a particularly shocking violation of Washington's promise that "every one shall sit in safety under his own vine and figtree, and there shall be none to make him afraid."[72]

After the Oak Creek massacre, there was again speculation that Sikhs had been proxy victims for Muslims. One Sikh explained to the *New York Times* that he had been called "Osama bin Laden" because of his turban, which in the popular imagination is associated with bin Laden and al Qaeda, though the vast majority of Americans who wear turbans are Sikhs.[73] Others, including Sikh activists, resisted the "mistaken identity" narrative, which seemed to suggest anti-Muslim violence would be more legitimate than anti-Sikh violence.[74] Prior

---

[70] In their detailed analysis of the FBI data, Disha, Cavendish and King (2011) note that in addition to hate crimes specifically reported as anti-Muslim, there was a large spike in crimes against persons of "other" ethnicity, which they posit referred mainly to Arab Americans, the largest ethnic group that does not constitute a separate category in the FBI's data. Disha, Ilir, James C. Cavendish, and Ryan D. King (2011). "Historical Events and Spaces of Hate: Hate Crimes Against Arabs and Muslims in Post-9/11 America." *Social Problems*, 58(1): 21–46.

[71] Biggers, Jeff (2012). *State Out of the Union: Arizona and the Final Showdown over the American Dream.* New York: Nation Books, p. 65.

[72] See http://edition.cnn.com/2012/08/06/us/sikhs-bias-crimes/index.html and www.splcenter .org/get-informed/intelligence-report/browse-all-issues/2011/summer/two-sikhs-murdered-in -california-were

[73] Bronner, Ethan (2012). "Mourning Victims, Sikhs Lament Being Mistaken for Radicals or Militants." *New York Times*, August 7, 2012, p. A14.

[74] Freedman, Samuel G. (2012). "If the Sikh Temple Had Been a Mosque." *New York Times*, August 11, 2012, p. A12.

to Oak Creek, the FBI had made no religious or ethnic distinctions between victims of Middle Eastern or South Asian origin. This may be an accurate reflection of the motives of attackers, who themselves fail to make such distinctions. Despite the additional hostility to Muslims generated by 9/11, Islamophobia can be understood as part of a broader phenomenon of "outgrouping" of those not seen as authentically American.[75] This puts Sikhs in a similar predicament to Muslims. Naunihal Singh observed that after Oak Creek, President Obama referred to Sikhs as "members of the *'broader American family,'* like some distant relatives."[76]

Islamophobic politics and its limits

Unlike Sikhs or other religious minorities, however, Muslims have also had to contend with political discourse and occasionally legislation that specifically targets their religion. During the Bush Administration almost no politician or state official would openly associate with domestic Islamophobia. Republican legislators who may have been sympathetic to anti-Islamic politics were effectively disciplined by the Administration's rhetorical frame that the United States was not at war with Islam and American Muslims were valuable citizens.[77] Islamophobic discourse was instead propagated through right-wing media, blogs, and dedicated anti-Islamic think tanks, headed by conservative activists who disagreed vehemently with Bush's insistence that terrorism had nothing to do with "real Islam."[78]

One of the few Republican congressmen to break ranks during the Bush years was New York representative Peter King, who said in a 2007 interview "there are too many mosques in this country" and "too many people sympathetic to radical Islam. We should be looking at them more carefully and finding out how

---

[75] Kalkan, Kerem Ozan, Geoffrey C. Layman, and Eric M. Uslaner (2009). "'Bands of Others'? Attitudes Towards Muslims in Contemporary American Society." *Journal of Politics*, 71(3): 847–862.

[76] Singh, Naunihal (2012). "An American Tragedy." *The New Yorker*, August 13, 2012.

[77] Sidney Milkis and Jesse Rhodes argue that Bush inaugurated a "new synthesis" between the presidential leadership and the party at the congressional, organizational and grassroots levels. One result was unusually high party discipline in the service of the president's aims. Milkis, Sidney M., and Jesse H. Rhodes (2007). "George W. Bush, the Republican Party, and the 'New' American Party System." *Perspectives on Politics*, 5(3): 461–488.

[78] The Centre for American Progress argues that the "Islamophobia Network" of the Bush years was small – consisting most importantly of five think tanks and seven donors – but highly influential. The CAP's 2011 report on Islamophobia notes the influence of this network outside the United States. Anders Breivik, the Norwegian gunman responsible for 76 deaths in a 2011 rampage, had published an online manifesto against the "Muslimization" of the west which cited a handful of American anti-Islam pundits and their websites hundreds of times. Ali, Wajahat, Eli Clifton, Matthew Duss, Lee Fang, Scott Keyes, and Faiz Shakir (2011). "Fear, Inc. The Roots of the Islamophobia Network in America." Center for American Progress, August 26, 2011. www.americanprogress.org/issues/religion/report/2011/08/26/10165/fear-inc/, last accessed June 19, 2015.

we can infiltrate them."[79] King, the ranking Republican on the House Homeland Security Committee, was articulating a view prevalent in some parts of the law enforcement and intelligence communities that was rarely expressed publicly.[80] This was the other face of the state's relationship with the Muslim population during the Bush years (as I will discuss further below), which was usually kept out of political discourse. After 2008, as more Republicans adopted anti-Islam stances, King would become an increasingly prominent leader in political Islamophobia.

Three phenomena contributed to a surge in Islamophobic discourse in politics beginning in 2009. The first was the election of Barack Obama, whom a large number of conservatives considered a Muslim or Muslim sympathizer, and which threw Republican Party discipline into chaos. The second was a rash of protests against the construction of mosques, precipitated by the Park 51 project near the Ground Zero site in New York. The third was a series of campaigns in state legislatures to ban Sharia law from their legal systems.

As early as 2007, rumors had circulated that Democratic presidential candidate Barack Hussein Obama was a closeted Muslim. Obama's name and Kenyan background seemed to hint at Islam, as did the portion of his childhood spent in Indonesia.[81] During the 2008 Democratic primaries, chain emails from anonymous sources spread claims, amplified in conservative media, that Obama had spent time in a "radical madrassa" in Indonesia and that he had been sworn into the Senate on a Koran.[82] By the 2008 election around a quarter of survey respondents were consistently answering "Muslim" in response to questions about Obama's religious affiliation, a number that has never subsided.[83]

While no political figure of any prominence would endorse these misconceptions about Obama – in 2008, Republican candidate John McCain explicitly refuted them – numerous politicians, especially Republican

---

[79] Reilly, Daniel W. (2007). "Rep. Peter King: There are too many mosques in this country." *Politico Live*, September 19, 2007. www.politico.com/blogs/thecrypt/0907/Rep_King_There_are_too_many_mosques_in_this_country__Page4.html, last accessed June 19, 2015.

[80] King later claimed he did not mean there were too many mosques *per se*, but too many individuals within mosques who were not cooperating with law enforcement and counter-terrorism efforts. (Ibid.)

[81] Marable, Manning (2009). "Racializing Obama: The Enigma of Post-Black Politics and Leadership." *Souls: A Critical Journal of Black Politics, Culture and Society*, 11(1).

[82] The latter claim took advantage of confusion between Obama and Representative Keith Ellison, an African American from Minnesota who was the first Muslim elected to Congress in 2006, the same year Obama was elected to the senate. Ellison was sworn in on the Koran that had belonged to Thomas Jefferson.

[83] See Smith, David T. (2010). "The First Muslim President? Causes and Consequences of the Belief that Barack Obama is a Muslim." Paper presented at the annual meeting of the Midwest Political Science Association, Chicago, 2010; and Smith, David T. (2014). "The Mormon or the Muslim? Perceptions of Presidential Candidates as Religious Outsiders." Paper presented at the annual meeting of the Midwest Political Science Association, Chicago, 2014.

presidential candidates, burnished their conservative credentials by suggesting that Obama is sympathetic to radical Islam or that the United States under his leadership is "submitting" to Islam.[84] Obama's conciliatory Cairo speech in 2009 – later framed by GOP presidential contenders as an "apology tour" – and footage of him bowing while shaking hands with Saudi Arabia's King Abdullah have often been taken as evidence of his supposedly defeatist and sympathetic posture toward Islamism.[85] Candidates seeking conservative (and particularly Tea Party) support did not need to make explicit the connection between the "submission" trope and the rumor that Obama is himself a Muslim.

The claim that America was allowing Islam to triumph was one source of the fury that greeted the planned construction of an Islamic center two blocks from the former World Trade Center. Imam Feisal Abdul Rauf's proposal for the multistory Cordoba House Islamic community center, including a prayer space, attracted little controversy or attention of any kind when his group first announced it in December 2009. Conservative commentator Laura Ingraham praised the project, in vague terms, in a little-noticed interview on Fox News.[86] The atmosphere changed five months later when the New York City community board unanimously approved the project. Pamela Geller, an influential anti-Muslim blogger who referred to the project as the "WTC Mosque," began the soon-widespread assertion that Muslims were erecting the "mosque" on the site of the 9/11 attacks as a symbol of their victory over the United States and the west.[87] Andrea Peyser of the *New York Post* and Sean Hannity of Fox News gave Geller extensive and sympathetic coverage on the issue, and soon both outlets were running frequent stories expressing outrage over the "Ground Zero Mosque." There were several protests near the site.

In a careful analysis of public opposition to the Park 51 project (as it was renamed), Jeane Halgren Kilde shows that much of the opposition came from outside this Islamophobic and adversarial frame.[88] Ground Zero was widely seen as sacred ground, and the sensitivity around it had previously led to conflict over other construction projects, including the rebuilding of the site itself by

---

[84] Chris Parker and Matt Barreto point out that Michele Bachmann, at one point the standard-bearer of the Tea Party in the lead-up to the 2012 Republican primaries, refused in an interview to deny the claims, popular among her supporters, that Obama was a Muslim or was not born in the United States. Parker, Christopher S. and Barreto, Matt A. (2013). *Change They Can't Believe In: The Tea Party and Reactionary Politics in America*. Princeton: Princeton University Press, p. 8.

[85] See Gans, John A. (2011). "America 2012: Duelling Exceptionalisms." *Survival: Global Politics and Strategy*, 53(3): 169–186.

[86] Elliott, Justin (2010). "How the 'Ground Zero Mosque' Fear-Mongering Began." Salon.com, August 16, 2010. www.salon.com/2010/08/16/ground_zero_mosque_origins/, last accessed June 19, 2015.

[87] According to Geller's original post, "This is Islamic domination and expansionism. The location is no accident. Just as Al-Aqsa was built on top of the Temple in Jerusalem." (Ibid.).

[88] Kilde, Jeane Halgren (2011). "The Park 51/Ground Zero Controversy and Sacred Sites as Contested Space." *Religions*, 2: 297–311.

its owners. But the Islamic element made Park 51 particularly contentious, and raised the possibility of civic disorder. Various New York power-brokers including Governor David Paterson, Archbishop Timothy Dolan, and former Mayor Rudolph Giuliani, suggested a "compromise" solution whereby the state would find land for the center much further away from the site. President Obama and Mayor Michael Bloomberg supported the right of Park 51 to proceed, but other Democrats were equivocal, including Senate leader Harry Reid, who expressed the widespread view that the state must respect freedom of religion but the mosque should be built elsewhere.[89]

The Republican Party was also divided on the issue. New Jersey Governor Chris Christie, perhaps the party's most prominent anti-Islamophobe, warned Republicans not to "paint all of Islam with the brush of terrorism," a position reminiscent of Bush-era rhetoric.[90] But former Vice Presidential candidate Sarah Palin labeled Park 51 an "unnecessary provocation" that "stabs hearts," while future GOP presidential candidate Newt Gingrich likened it to "the Japanese putting up a site next to Pearl Harbor" or Nazis putting up "a sign next to the Holocaust Museum in Washington."[91] Gingrich, who would later position himself as the most anti-Muslim candidate in the 2012 GOP primary, won praise in conservative media outlets for repeating the claim that the Cordoba House project was intended as a symbol of Islamic victory.[92]

---

[89] Rogan, Tom (2010). "Park 51 Dividing Lines." *The Guardian*, August 21, 2010. www.theguardian .com/commentisfree/cifamerica/2010/aug/21/ground-zero-mosque, last accessed June 19, 2015. At the time, Reid was facing a tough re-election battle in Nevada.

[90] Haberman, Maggie (2010). "Chris Christie warns GOP on mosque." *Politico*, August 16, 2010. www.politico.com/news/stories/0810/41141.html, last accessed June 19, 2015. In 2011 Christie vigorously defended his appointment of a Muslim judge, Sohail Mohammed, labeling as "crazy" right-wing claims that he may try to introduce Sharia law. Lennard, Natasha (2011). "Chris Christie calls fears over Muslim judge 'crap.'" Salon.com, August 4, 2011. www.salon.com/ 2011/08/04/christie_defends_muslim_judge/, last accessed June 19, 2015.

[91] Rogan (2010).

[92] In Gingrich's words: "There should be no mosque near Ground Zero in New York so long as there are no churches or synagogues in Saudi Arabia. The time for double standards that allow Islamists to behave aggressively towards us while they demand our weakness and submission is over. The proposed 'Cordoba House' overlooking the World Trade Center site – where a group of jihadists killed over 3,000 Americans and destroyed one of our most famous landmarks – is a test of the timidity, passivity and historic ignorance of American elites. For example, most of them don't understand that 'Cordoba House' is a deliberately insulting term. It refers to Cordoba, Spain – the capital of Muslim conquerors who symbolized their victory over Christian Spaniards by transforming a church there into the world's third-largest mosque complex. Today, some of the Mosque's backers insist this term is being used to 'symbolize interfaith cooperation' when, in fact, every Islamist in the world recognizes Cordoba as a symbol of Islamic conquest." Quoted in Pinkerton, James M. (2010). "America Needs Willpower – And the Right Leaders." FoxNews.com, July 29, 2010. www.foxnews.com/opinion/2010/07/29/ james-pinkerton-world-trade-centre-arizona-alqaeda-wikileaks-ground-zero-mosque/, last accessed June 19, 2015.

The controversy ultimately died down, and a scaled-down version of the center opened in late September 2011.[93] In the meantime, conflicts around Islamic building projects had developed in Temecula, California, Sheboygan, Wisconsin, and Murfreesboro, Tennessee. An organizer of opposition to the Temecula Islamic center, Diana Serafin, told a reporter she had learned about Islam at Tea Party rallies and from books by former Muslims now critical of Islam. Serafin worried that

> in 20 years with the rate of the birth population, we will be overtaken by Islam, and their goal is to get people in Congress and the Supreme Court to see that Shariah is implemented.... I do believe everyone has a right to freedom of religion, but Islam is not about a religion. It's about a political government, and it's 100 percent against our constitution.[94]

Tennessee's lieutenant governor Ron Ramsey, preparing for a Republican gubernatorial primary, made similar arguments in relation to the Murfreesboro Islamic center. In response to a constituent's question about the Muslim "threat," Ramsay affirmed he is "all about freedom of religion," but cast doubt on whether Islam qualifies as a religion. "You could even argue whether being a Muslim is actually a religion or is it a nationality, way of life, cult or whatever you want to call it." Ramsey later elaborated in an email to a reporter that "My concern is that far too much of Islam has come to resemble a violent political philosophy more than a peace-loving religion."[95] Despite local opposition groups who organized protests and legal injunctions to stop the Islamic Centers, both the Temecula and Murfreesboro projects were approved by city authorities and courts, and were ultimately built.

The one area in which civic opponents of Islam successfully mobilized legislators was a series of campaigns against Sharia law. The charge that Islam is foremost a system of political control, often heard in the anti-mosque campaigns, echoes centuries of attempts to delegitimize minority religions in America. Catholics and Mormons had faced similar accusations, portrayed as something antithetical to America's Protestant tradition of liberation from clerical tyranny. The Nation of Islam had also been characterized as a "political cult," in contrast to pious orthodox Islam that supposedly exemplified American values. In the twenty-first century opponents of Islam successfully revived theories, prevalent in the 1980s, that Islam has failed to

---

[93] Zraick, Karen and Vera Dobnik (2011). "Ground zero mosque opened to public Wednesday." *Christian Science Monitor*, September 22, 2011.

[94] Goodstein, Laurie (2010). "Across Nation, Mosque Projects Meet Opposition." *New York Times*, August 7, 2010.

[95] Mackey, Robert (2010). "Tennessee Official Says Islam May Be a Cult." *New York Times*, The Lede, July 27, 2010. http://thelede.blogs.nytimes.com/2010/07/27/tennessee-official-says-islam-may-be-a-cult/?_php= true&_type=blogs&_php=true&_type=blogs&_r=2, last accessed June 19, 2015.

achieve a proper separation between religion and politics.[96] State bans on Sharia law represent the peak of efforts so far to cast Islam as an un-American system of political control that poses an imminent threat to be resisted.

In 2010 and 2011, according to one report, "more than two dozen states considered measures to restrict judges from consulting Sharia, or foreign and religious laws more generally." These measures originated with two anti-Muslim activists, David Yerushalmi and Frank Gaffney. Yerushalmi, a New York-based lawyer, claimed Islamic militants "had not 'perverted' Islamic law, but were following an authoritative doctrine that sought global hegemony." Gaffney, president of the anti-Muslim Center for Security Policy, suggested after President Obama's Cairo speech that Obama might be a Muslim. Gaffney's network provided the organizational and financial means to find support for Yerushalmi's model legislation that would prevent state judges from considering foreign laws or rulings in their decisions. Yerushalmi had originally proposed a law making the observance of Sharia law a felony akin to sedition, but this gained little traction. By framing the model legislation in more broadly nationalist terms he and Gaffney successfully appealed to a new wave of state Tea Party activists and legislators.[97]

The first state to pass anti-Sharia legislation was Oklahoma. In the 2010 elections, the state's voters passed by 70 percent the "Save Our State" constitutional amendment, which specifically prohibited judges from considering Sharia law. The author of the amendment, state representative Rex Duncan, had described it as part of a "war for the survival of America."[98] In 2013 a US District Judge found the Oklahoma law was unconstitutional because it discriminated between religions without justification. As of 2015 six other states have passed similar legislation, in most cases following Yerushalmi's broader proscription of foreign laws and rulings.[99] It is likely that other states will adopt similar measures in the future (they are under consideration in thirty states), but also that these measures will face legal challenges.

Many critics of the anti-Sharia laws have pointed out that the United States constitution and every state constitution already prohibit Sharia law (or any other religious law) from becoming the law of the United States. The main effect of the anti-Sharia laws is symbolic, painting Islamic law as a threat to the state and the nation. However, the laws can seriously inconvenience Muslims. The initial challenge to the Oklahoma law came from Muneer Awad, who protested that in addition to stigmatizing Muslims, the Save Our State amendment

---

[96] See, e.g., Pipes, Daniel (1983). *In the Path of God: Islam and Political Power*. New York: Basic Books.

[97] Elliott, Andrea (2011). "The Man Behind the Anti-Shariah Movement." *New York Times*, July 30, 2011, p. A1.

[98] Nelson, Leah (2011). "Oklahoma's Shariah Law Ban Creates Controversy." Southern Poverty Law Center *Intelligence Report*, Spring 2011, 141.

[99] Brown, Matthew (2013). "North Carolina Becomes 7th State to Ban Muslim Sharia Law." *Deseret News*, August 28, 2013. The other states are Arizona, Kansas, Louisiana, North Carolina, South Dakota, and Tennessee.

violated his First Amendment rights because it would invalidate his last will and testament, which made reference to Islamic law.[100] Currently courts can consider Sharia law, like other religious sources of law, where it does not conflict with U.S. law. Some state lawmakers have refused to pass anti-Sharia laws because of their potential interference with banking, family law, and adoption procedures, all of which may involve elements of Sharia for Muslims.[101]

While some presidential aspirants, most notably Newt Gingrich, took up the anti-Sharia cause, the national Republican Party showed little interest in it.[102] Peter King's much anticipated Homeland Security Committee hearings on Islamist radicalization attracted hardly any mention of threats from Sharia law.[103] The surviving anti-Sharia laws in some ways resemble the state-level Blaine Amendments of the nineteenth century, which prohibited the use of government funds for schools with religious affiliations. Aimed at defunding Catholic education, these laws were couched in religiously neutral language that avoided violating the First Amendment. Like the anti-Sharia laws they had no chance of succeeding at the federal level, though in the 1880s congressional Republicans actually attempted to pass a federal Blaine Amendment.

Like the anti-polygamy campaigns of the nineteenth century, a discourse about women in captivity has also been central to anti-Sharia campaigns. Lawmakers in Kansas, for example, framed their ban on foreign laws in terms of a women's rights issue, making sure "women know the rights they have in America."[104] The horrors of honor killings, domestic violence, and enforced wearing of Islamic garb feature heavily in anti-Muslim literature, making every Muslim woman a likely victim of her own husband or father. Juliane Hammer has shown that the discourse of oppressed women is at the heart of the

[100] Huus, Kari (2012). "Federal court deals blow to anti-Shariah efforts." NBC News, January 10, 2012. http://usnews.nbcnews.com/_news/2012/01/10/10097954–federal-court-deals-blow-to -anti-shariah-efforts?lite, last accessed June 19, 2015.

[101] See, e.g., Missouri Governor Jay Nixon's veto of his state's anti-Sharia laws. Among other things, Nixon said the laws "could jeopardize a family's ability to adopt children from other countries." McDermott, Kevin (2013). "Nixon vetoes 'Sharia Law' bill, saying it would endanger foreign adoptions." *St. Louis Post-Dispatch*, June 3, 2013.

[102] The threat posed by Sharia law was a prominent theme of Gingrich's 2010 film, *America at Risk*. In a July 2010 speech at the American Enterprise Institute, Gingrich called Sharia "a mortal threat to the survival of freedom in the United States and in the world as we know it." Shane, Scott (2011). "In Islamic Law, Gingrich Sees a Mortal Threat to U.S." *New York Times*, December 21, 2011, p. A22.

[103] The transcript is available at: http://www.gpo.gov/fdsys/pkg/CHRG-12hhrg72541/pdf/ CHRG-12hhrg72541.pdf.
Most mentions of Sharia law refer to the anti-Sharia campaign, to convicted terrorist Kevin James, who advocated Sharia law in Southern California prisons, and to Anwar al-Awlaki, a Yemeni American imam with ties to numerous terrorists whose targeted assassination in 2010 was authorized by Barack Obama.

[104] Representative Peggy Mast, quoted in Hammer, Juliane (2013). "Center Stage: Gendered Islamophobia and Muslim Women." In Carl W. Ernst (ed.) *Islamophobia in America: The Anatomy of Intolerance*. New York: Palgrave MacMillan, p. 124.

construction of the Islamic threat. In this discourse "the assumed gender inequality and oppression of women by Islam is juxtaposed with a quintessentially American gender-egalitarianism and respect for women's rights," making the oppression of women a foreign threat that needs to be counteracted.[105] This in some ways echoes anti-Mormon rhetoric of the late nineteenth century, which depicted Mormon polygamy as akin to the hated and defeated institution of slavery, and hence incompatible with the nation's burgeoning liberal culture.

The anti-Sharia campaigns, however, have not enjoyed the same widespread popularity and national success of the anti-polygamy campaigns. A likely reason for this can be found in the different composition of the political coalitions that formed around each cause. The anti-polygamy campaign of the 1880s had the backing of mainstream feminism, which at that time had a political voice in the radical wing of the Republican Party. Prominent feminists such as Harriet Beecher Stowe were among those calling for a federal effort to liberate Mormon women, who supposedly could not liberate themselves. Here feminists found common cause with Protestant conservatives and nativists, who saw Mormonism as antithetical to American culture.

The anti-Sharia movement is not as broad as the anti-polygamy coalition. While it uses an approximation of feminist rhetoric, has attracted few feminists, progressives, or liberals. Its appeal is confined to conservative Republicans, and its prospects for success appear limited to states dominated by conservative legislators (which have relatively low Muslim populations).[106] Many feminists from within and outside the Muslim world have critiqued gender relations in Islam; feminist social movements fight for reform of oppressive institutions and structures in Muslim-majority countries, often at considerable risk and often with support from American organizations.[107] Hardly any feminists, however, have aligned themselves with the American anti-Sharia movement.[108] Unlike

---

[105] Ibid., p. 121.

[106] The states that have passed Sharia or "foreign law" bans have the following levels of Muslim adherence per 100,000 residents: North Carolina, 273 (20th nationally), Kansas, 271 (21st nationally), Tennessee, 242 (24th nationally), Louisiana, 216 (26th nationally), Oklahoma, 197 (30th nationally), South Dakota, 164 (34th nationally), Arizona, 134 (36th nationally). The national rate of Islamic adherence per 100,000 is approximately 600. Data from the US Religion Census: Religious Congregations and Membership Study, available at http://rcms2010.org/index.php

[107] See, e.g., Segran, Elizabeth (2013). "The Rise of the Islamic Feminists." *The Nation*, December 23/30; Reed, Betsy (ed.) (2002). *Nothing Sacred: Women Respond to Religious Fundamentalism and Terror*. New York: Thunder's Mouth Press; Moghadam, Valentine M. (2002). "Islamic Feminism and its Discontents: Toward a Resolution of the Debate." *Signs: Journal of Women in Culture and Society*, 27(4): 1135–1171. Murphy, Caryle (2003). "Islam and Feminism." *Carnegie Reporter*, 2(3).

[108] A notable exception is Phyllis Chesler, a self-described "right feminist" who regularly criticizes western feminists for "ignoring" the plight of Muslim women. Mona Eltahawy, an Egyptian American Muslim journalist who was publicly assaulted in Tahrir Square in 2012, has also been a vocal crusader against Sharia law throughout the world. Chesler, Phyllis (2005). *The Death of*

the late nineteenth century, there is little political common ground between feminists and Christian conservatives in the twenty-first century. Some feminists have pointed out that many of the strongest anti-Sharia proponents oppose mainstream feminist positions on issues such as reproductive rights and the expansion of state capacity to fight domestic violence.[109] There is an element of nationalist self-congratulation in the discourse of oppressed Muslim women – the suggestion that the United States, unlike the Muslim world, has achieved gender equality – that is used to silence critics of American patriarchy rather than to win their support.

Despite the occasional and qualified successes of anti-Muslim politics at the state level, at the national level the government has remained committed to suppressing popular Islamophobia. Even Peter King's Homeland Security Committee hearings into Islamic radicalization paid substantial lip service to anti-Islamophobia. Democratic committee members attacked the legitimacy of the proceedings because of the way they singled out Muslims, and Republicans were forced into a defensive posture of having to constantly reaffirm their respect for the Muslim community at large. In the words of Georgia's Representative Paul Broun, "I don't think anyone on this side of the aisle is an Islamophobe."[110] In 2012, Obama's chief counter-terrorism adviser John Brennan ridiculed a request by five Republican House members that the federal government investigate Muslim infiltration.[111] President Obama has continued his predecessor's rhetorical trope of distancing Islamic terrorist groups from "real" Islam, including declarations that the group calling itself the "Islamic State" in Syria and Iraq is not Islamic (and "certainly not a state").[112]

For the national state, countering Islamophobia and appearances of Islamophobia remains as much a foreign policy imperative as a necessity for domestic political order. Ever since the *Satanic Verses* controversy began in 1989, western governments have been aware of the potential for real or perceived insults to Islam to incite violence.[113] When Danish newspaper

Feminism. New York: Palgrave MacMillan. Eltahawy, Mona (2012). "Why Do They Hate Us? The Real War on Women is in the Middle East." *Foreign Policy*, May/June 2012.

[109] Hammer (2013), pp. 126 and 141–142.

[110] Stanley, Tiffany (2011). "The King's Speech." *The New Republic*, March 11.

[111] The representatives were Michele Bachmann (R-Mn), Trent Franks (R-Az), Louis Gohmert (R-Tx), Tom Rooney (R-La), and Lynn Westmoreland (R-Ga). Of particular concern to them was Hilary Clinton's aide Huma Abedin, whom they believed might have had family ties to the Muslim Brotherhood. This claim originated in a report by Frank Gaffney's Center for Security Policy. Terkel, Amanda (2012). "Michele Bachmann's Muslim Brotherhood Claims Dismissed By Top Counterterrorism Official." Huffington Post, August 8. www.huffington-post.com/2012/08/08/michele-bachmann-muslim-brotherhood-john-brennan_n_1756865.html, last accessed June 19, 2015.

[112] See the transcript of Obama's televised address on his plans to combat ISIS in Syria, available at: www.cnn.com/2014/09/10/politics/transcript-obama-syria-isis-speech/, last accessed March 1, 2015.

[113] In 1989 Ayatollah Khomeini issued a *fatwa* calling for British novelist Salman Rushdie's death because of his insulting depiction of the Prophet Muhammad in his novel *The Satanic Verses*.

Jyllands-Posten published deliberately inflammatory cartoons of Muhammad in 2005, a global wave of anti-western protests and riots claimed more than 200 lives.[114] Similarly lethal protests followed the release of an American YouTube trailer for an amateur film titled *Innocence of Muslims* which reportedly depicted Muhammad as "womanizer, homosexual and child abuser" (the actual film never appeared).[115] In both cases, most violence took place in Muslim-majority countries, with deaths resulting from clashes between protesters and police. The Muhammad cartoons controversy had a long and violent afterlife. In 2015 two gunmen with links to al Qaeda killed eleven staff at the satirical Paris magazine *Charlie Hebdo*, which had reprinted the *Jyllands-Posten* cartoons in 2006 and had published more cartoons of Muhammad in 2011 and 2012.[116]

Violent anti-western protests in the Muslim world, often directed against governments seen as complicit in American domination, cause strains between the United States and governments in Muslim-majority countries. As the United States has become increasingly dependent on Muslim allies in the war on terror, the government's commitment to free speech has been rhetorically balanced by pleas for prudence and sensitivity toward Islam. George W. Bush declared of the Muhammad cartoons "we find them offensive, and we understand why Muslims would find them offensive." While the State Department defended the rights of the Danish newspaper to publish the cartoons, it also issued the statement that "anti-Muslim images are as unacceptable as anti-Semitic images, as anti-Christian images, or [mockery of] any other religious belief."[117] In 2012, Barack Obama declared before the United Nations that *Innocence of Muslims* was "crude and disgusting … an insult not only to Muslims, but to America as well." He also reiterated that the United States did not and would not ban blasphemy, regardless of the offense it provokes: "The strongest weapon against hateful speech is not repression, it is more speech."[118]

The U.S. government is particularly sensitive to Islamophobic acts that might have consequences for American troops or diplomatic personnel.

Rushdie survived and Iran lifted the *fatwa* in 1998, but in the meantime it was linked to several other killings, attempted killings and bombings. See Helm, Leslie (1991). "Translator of 'Satanic Verses' Slain." *Los Angeles Times*, June 13.

[114] Cohen, Patricia (2009). "Yale Press Bans Images of Muhammad in New Book." *New York Times*, August 12.

[115] Isikoff, Michael (2012). "Man behind anti-Islam film is reportedly Egyptian-born ex-con." NBC News, September 13 2012, available at http://worldnews.nbcnews.com/_news/2012/09/13/13842406-man-behind-anti-islam-film-reportedly-is-egyptian-born-ex-con, last accessed March 1, 2015.

[116] See http://www.bbc.com/news/world-europe-30708237, last accessed March 9, 2015. As a manhunt for the gunmen unfolded, an armed sympathizer and acquaintance from prison killed a police officer and took hostages at a kosher deli in Port de Vincennes, eventually killing four.

[117] Brinkley, Joel and Ian Fisher (2006). "U.S. Says It Also Finds Cartoons of Muhammad Offensive." *New York Times*, February 4 2006.

[118] Available at http://www.mediaite.com/tv/president-obama-condemns-both-disgusting-anti-islam-video-and-mindless-violence-before-the-u-n/, last accessed March 1, 2015.

Innocence of Muslims protests had targeted the US embassy in Cairo, and the State Department initially believed the attacks on the US consulate in Benghazi that killed ambassador Christopher Stevens arose from a protest about the video. In May 2005 there had been lethal riots in Afghanistan following the publication of a *Newsweek* article carrying allegations by Guantanamo detainees that interrogators at the camp had desecrated copies of the Quran.[119] In 2010, Florida Pastor Terry Jones achieved international notoriety when he announced plans on social media to burn Qurans on the anniversary of 9/11. The burning attracted inordinate media coverage and condemnation from the highest levels of the state. General David Petraeus, Commander of US forces in Afghanistan, described the planned action as "precisely the kind of action the Taliban uses and could cause significant problems."[120] President Obama remarked that the event could help recruit "individuals who would be willing to blow themselves up in American cities or European cities," endanger US troops in Iraq, and cause "serious violence in places like Pakistan or Afghanistan."[121] Secretary of State Hillary Clinton said "It's regrettable that a pastor in Gainesville, Florida, with a church of no more than fifty people can make this outrageous and distressful, disgraceful plan, and get, you know, the world's attention, but that's the world we live in right now."[122]

Post 9/11 surveillance and suppression of Islam

While representatives of the state drew distinctions between terrorists who perverted Islam and Muslim citizens who "make an incredibly valuable contribution to our country,"[123] Muslims found the burden was on them to prove they were the "good" kind. Peter King's complaints that Muslims were not doing enough to cooperate with counter-terrorist initiatives ignored the non-cooperative nature of the tactics adopted by the FBI, Department of Homeland Security, and Attorney General's Department. In the months and years following 9/11, these federal agencies proceeded from the assumption

---

[119] Hertzberg, Hendrik (2005). "Big News Week." *The New Yorker*, May 30.

[120] Barnes, Julian E. and Matthew Rosenberg (2010). "Petraeus Condemns U.S. Church's Plans to Burn Qurans." *Wall Street Journal*, September 6.

[121] Reuters News Service (2010). "Obama says planned Koran burning is boosting Qaeda." September 9, 2010. http://ca.reuters.com/article/topNews/idCATRE68820G20100909?sp=true, last accessed June 19, 2015.

[122] See www.cbsnews.com/videos/clinton-quran-burning-does-not-represent-america/, last accessed June 19, 2015.

[123] Quote from a speech by George W. Bush at the Islamic Center in Washington, September 16, 2001. He continued, "Muslims are doctors, lawyers, law professors, members of the military, entrepreneurs, shopkeepers, moms and dads." Zelizer, Julian (2010). "Bush was right: we're not at war with Islam." CNN Opinion, September 13, 2010. ,www.cnn.com/2010/OPINION/09/13/zelizer.bush.muslims/, last accessed June 19, 2015.

that, in Attorney General John Ashcroft's words, the terrorists "live in our communities – plotting, planning and waiting to kill Americans again."[124] The thousands of detentions, mass registrations, and deportations following 9/11 left no doubt that the "communities" to which Ashcroft referred were made up of Arabs and Muslims.

As critics of the PATRIOT act have pointed out, the actual counter-terrorist yield from the federal government's post-9/11 dragnet was pitifully low. David Cole wrote in 2006 that

> Of the 80,000 Arab and Muslim foreign nationals who were required to register after September 11, the 8,000 called in for FBI interviews, and the more than 5,000 locked up in preventive detention, not one stands convicted of a terrorist crime today. In what has surely been the most aggressive national campaign of ethnic profiling since World War II, the government's record is 0 for 93,000.[125]

The Bush Administration boasted more than 400 criminal indictments and 200 convictions in "terrorist-related" cases, which deepened the public perception that there really were terrorists hiding in America's Arab and Muslim communities, but a *Washington Post* investigation found that most of these were for crimes such as immigration fraud, and only 39 involved actual charges related to terrorism.[126] Meanwhile, agencies ignored advice from security policy experts to build more sympathetic alliances with Muslim and Arab communities, despite the frequent usefulness of information that members of these communities supplied to counter-terrorist operations.[127]

However effective the state was in condemning and suppressing popular Islamophobia in the years following 9/11, Muslims felt most threatened during this period by the state itself, not the behavior of the public.[128] Air travel became a site of routine humiliation and denial of service for Muslim men and women at the hands of state agents, contributing in a very visible way to public suspicion of them.[129] In 2014, the Center for Constitutional Rights filed a lawsuit on behalf of Muslims who alleged that FBI agents placed them on the No Fly List when they refused to become informants on their own religious communities. The plaintiffs claimed the FBI had violated the Religious Freedom Restoration Act. In a motion to dismiss the lawsuit, the Justice Department argued "there is no constitutional right not to become an informant" and "it is not clearly established that a request to inform on an individual's American

---

[124] Prepared remarks of Attorney General John Ashcroft at US Mayors Conference, October 25 2001. Quoted in Cainkar, Louis A. (2009). *Homeland Insecurity: The Arab and Muslim Experience after 9/11*. New York: Russell Sage Foundation, p. 110.
[125] Cole, David (2006). "Are We Safer?" *The New York Review of Books*, 53(4).
[126] Eggen, Dan and Julie Tate (2005). "US Campaign Produces Few Convictions on Terrorism Charges." *Washington Post*, June 12, quoted in ibid.
[127] Cainkar (2009), pp. 113–114.
[128] Ibid., p. 116.
[129] Chandrasekhar, Charu A. (2003). "Federal Civil Rights Remedies to Post-9/11 Airline Racial Profiling of South Asians." *Asian American Law Journal*, 10(2): 215–252.

Muslim community imposes a substantial burden on religious exercise."[130] After the initial wave of post-9/11 arrests, detentions, and deportations, Arab and Muslim Americans remained under electronic and telephonic surveillance, the full extent of which is still unknown. A survey of American Muslims found that the overwhelming majority of respondents believed they were being watched online.[131]

The post-9/11 counter-terrorism effort was not limited to federal agencies. Local law enforcement agencies have undertaken their own intelligence-gathering operations, backed by increasing levels of federal funding and coordination.[132] Some of the most egregious abuses of Muslims' civil liberties have taken place at this local level, where officers are often poorly trained for counter-terrorism and unconstrained by the protocols within which federal agents operate. While billions of dollars in federal funds have been made available for police counter-terrorism, responsibility for training has often been turned over to freelancing Islamophobes rather than genuine counter-terrorist experts. Meg Stalcup and Joshua Craze reported in 2011 on the lack of quality control within federally funded training; trainers included have included people with no counter-terrorism background or qualifications, who teach police that terrorists can be recognized by features such as conical beards and headbands.[133]

In 2003 the New York Police Department established its Demographics Unit, with responsibility for identifying "hot spots of radicalization" in New York's Muslim communities. An AP investigation found that the Demographics Unit had infiltrated "hundreds" of mosques and Muslim student groups. It went well beyond its jurisdictional boundaries, in one instance cataloging and photographing every mosque in Newark and taking license plate details outside a mosque in Paterson, New Jersey.[134] The unit targeted second- and third-generation citizens for surveillance based exclusively on their religion, despite Mayor Michael Bloomberg's assertions to the contrary.[135] Those under surveillance included religious leaders who had willingly cooperated

---

[130] Gosztola, Kevin (2014). "In No-Fly List Lawsuit by American Muslims, DOJ Argues 'No Constitutional Right Not to Become an Informant.'" Firedoglake, July 29, 2014, available at http://dissenter.firedoglake.com/2014/07/29/in-no-fly-list-lawsuit-by-american-muslims-doj-argues-no-constitutional-right-not-to-become-an-informant/, last accessed March 1, 2015.

[131] Sidhu, Dawinder S. (2007). "The Chilling Effect of Government Surveillance Programs on the Use of the Internet by Muslim Americans." *University of Maryland Law Journal of Race, Religion, Gender and Class*, 7(2): 375–393.

[132] See Stalcup, Meg and Joshua Craze (2011). "How We Train Our Cops to Fear Islam." *Washington Monthly*, March/April.

[133] Ibid.

[134] Goldman, Adam and Matt Apuzzo (2012b). "Consequences for security as NYPD-FBI rift widens." Associated Press, March 20. www.ap.org/Content/AP-In-The-News/2012/Consequences-for-security-as-NYPD-FBI-rift-widens, last accessed June 19, 2015.

[135] Goldman, Adam and Matt Apuzzo (2012a). "NYPD Docs: 'Focus' scrutiny on Muslim Americans." Associated Press, March 9. www.ap.org/Content/AP-In-The-News/2012/Focus-scrutiny-on-Muslim-Americans, last accessed June 19, 2015.

with the NYPD and who considered themselves partners in building relationships between their mosques and the police.[136] One former police informant, a 19-year-old Bangladeshi American, told of a strategy that involved "creating a conversation about jihad or terrorism, then capturing the response to send to the NYPD."[137] The New York Police Department shut the unit down in 2014. As AP's Goldman and Apuzzo note, "Despite investigations that stretched for years, the Police Department's efforts never led to charges that a mosque or an Islamic organization was itself a terrorist enterprise."[138]

Even "community outreach" programs could serve as surveillance operations for local police, in cooperation with national agencies. In 2009 the St. Paul Police Department submitted a proposal to the Justice Department for an outreach program to the city's Somali community, which would direct young people into police athletic leagues and YWCA programs but also "identify radicalized individuals, gang members and violent offenders who refuse to cooperate with our efforts." The program, which received a $670,000 grant from the Justice Department, was designed to counter the recruitment of youth to al-Shabab, an al Qaeda affiliated Islamist organization that had reportedly attracted more than twenty people from Minnesota to fight with the group in Somalia since 2007. Muslim individuals and organizations who willingly liaised with police for the program were unaware of its intelligence-gathering purpose.[139]

CONCLUSION

Distinctions between "good" and "bad" forms of Islam have long characterized the American state's response to Muslims and the persecution of Muslims.[140]

---

[136] Sullivan, Eileen (2011). "NYPD Spied on city's Muslim anti-terror partners." Associated Press, October 6. www.ap.org/Content/AP-In-The-News/2011/NYPD-spied-on-citys-Muslim-anti-terror-partners, last accessed June 19, 2015.

[137] Goldman, Adam and Matt Apuzzo (2012c). "Informant: NYPD paid me to 'bait' Muslims." Associated Press, October 23. www.ap.org/Content/AP-In-The-News/2012/Informant-NYPD-paid-me-to-bait-Muslims, last accessed June 19, 2015.

[138] Apuzzo, Matt and Joseph Goldstein (2014). "New York Drops Unit That Spied on Muslims." *New York Times*, April 16, 2014, p. A1.

[139] Currier, Cora (2015). "Spies Among Us: How Community Outreach Programs to Muslims Blur the Line between Outreach and Intelligence." *The Intercept*, January 22, available at https://firstlook.org/theintercept/2015/01/21/spies-among-us-community-outreach-programs-muslims-blur-lines-outreach-intelligence/, last accessed March 1, 2015.

[140] As Mahmood Mamdani has argued, it also characterized the global terms of America's "war on terror." "After an unguarded reference to pursuing a "crusade," President Bush moved to distinguish between 'good Muslims' and 'bad Muslims.' From this point of view, 'bad Muslims' were clearly responsible for terrorism. At the same time, the president seemed to assure Americans that 'good Muslims' were anxious to clear their names and consciences of this horrible crime and would undoubtedly support 'us' in a war against 'them.' But this could not hide the central message of such discourse: unless proved to be 'good,' every Muslim was presumed to be 'bad.' All Muslims were now under obligation to prove their credentials by joining in a war against 'bad Muslims.'" Mamdani (2004), ch. 1.

While the state has made efforts to protect "good" Muslims from popular prejudice, it has sought to repress "bad" variants of Islam more ruthlessly than any religious group since the Mormons. This reaction makes sense within the theoretical framework of this book. State actors have seen both Islam and Islamophobia as potential threats to the authority of the American state. Even as it repressed Muslims, the state has sought to maintain a monopoly on that repression, disallowing expressions of anti-Islamic prejudice that may create political disorder.

For immigrant Muslims, like nineteenth-century Catholics and twentieth-century Jews, membership of a world religion has been a double-edged sword. Status as a world religion confers religious legitimacy, and the United States has had to consider the reactions of Muslim co-religionists abroad in its dealings with its own Muslim population. As members of a foreign-originated religion, Muslims have also had to contend with constant suspicions about their loyalty to the United States, especially since 9/11. But, as Mormons and Jehovah's Witnesses also discovered, being a member of a home-grown version of a world religion offers no protection from the same suspicions. The Nation of Islam went even further than these groups in its radical critique of the country that gave birth to it. Only when it softened that critique would the state cease to consider it a threat.

10

Conclusion

To my knowledge, this is the first study to compare the persecution experiences of different religious minorities throughout American history. What can a work of comparative social science add to the many historical studies of persecution focusing on individual religious groups, most of which explore their cases in far more detail than I have been able to do here? In this book I have proposed a theoretical framework to explain variance within and across cases of religious persecution over time. In this concluding chapter, having examined the experiences of numerous religious minorities, I revisit some of the comparative lessons learned from studying these cases together within a single theoretical framework. I consider both the strengths and limitations of this framework, and what future research may either extend its applicability or lead to a different, better theoretical understanding.

Perhaps unconventionally for a conclusion, I will also briefly examine two other cases – MOVE, a small African American sect whose leader and many other members died when Philadelphia police bombed their compound in 1985, and the Branch Davidians of Waco, Texas, whose leader and many followers were killed when federal agents raided their compound in 1993. The point of including these two cases is to show my theory is robust beyond the experiences of well-known religions that survived their persecutory encounters with the state. If anything, it applies even more to these groups, which never achieved the mantle of religious legitimacy and today are defined by their violent endings. They are not often mentioned in mainstream discourse about religious persecution in the United States, which makes them useful for understanding the logic of violent state response from the viewpoint of state actors close to our own time, who did not believe that they were engaging in religious persecution.

Finally, I reflect on how experiences of religious persecution affected the religions involved across the medium and long term. Most of the religions discussed in this book are much more favorably perceived today than they were at the time of their persecution. Our sense of injustice at their persecution is shaped by our contemporary understanding of them as legitimate religions. I consider how these religions themselves changed in response to persecution, and how these changes affected their place in American life.

THEORETICAL OVERVIEW AND COMPARATIVE LESSONS OF THE BOOK

This book has sought to explain the involvement of state actors in religious persecution. When social conflict arises that threatens the safety of unpopular religious minorities, agents of the state may act to protect those minorities, they may allow persecution to take place, or they may actively join the persecution, generally taking a leading role. All three responses, as I show, have occurred throughout American history. Why did the state act to protect some minorities but persecute others? While non-state actors have certainly been capable of inflicting great damage and distress on religious minorities, I have argued from the outset that it is most important to explain the actions of the state. The involvement of the state largely determines the intensity and duration of the persecution, as well as the final outcome of it. Religious minorities without the protection of the state, or facing its active hostility, must often change substantially in order to survive.

None of the cases in this book are simple instances of "persecution" or "non-persecution." All the minorities discussed in this book have faced persecutory threats at different points in American history. However, the state responses to those threats were different, and so were the experiences of each group. Moreover, those responses changed over time. I have argued that the state response depends on the perceptions of state actors of threats to political order. If state actors – from the president to police officers – believe a religious minority poses a threat to the political order on which their authority rests, they will persecute that minority or allow it to be persecuted. If they believe that persecution itself poses a greater threat to political order, they will act to protect the persecuted minority. The differences in experiences of persecution, both over time for a single group and compared to other groups, can be explained by the factors that contribute to the threat perceptions of state actors.

As the case studies have shown, the stories of how state actors come to see religious groups as threats are very complex. But rather than just focus on the things in each case that caused antagonism between minorities and broader society – Mormon polygamy, Jehovah's Witnesses' refusal to salute the flag, or the Nation of Islam's black particularism – we can also look for broader, recurrent causal processes that determined whether state actors would see these antagonisms as a greater threat to political order than the persecution that followed. These causal processes allow us to explain historical patterns which are striking but which themselves have little explanatory value, such as the fact that Mormons, Jehovah's Witnesses, and the Nation of Islam all originated in the United States.

The perceived legitimacy of each group as a religion has had great causal importance in nearly every case. Respect for religious freedom has long been part of the self-conception of Americans, and state actors generally see religious freedom as part of the political order they are defending. Only rarely does a state actor, such as the Brooklyn judge who jailed anti-war Bible Students in 1918, openly condemn religion. In order to persecute a religious minority, state actors must believe they are not violating religious liberty; often, this means not believing the group in question is a real religion.

From its beginnings, many Americans pronounced Mormonism a fraud. Newspapers declared it was a scheme to enrich to Joseph Smith, and charged that he was using his control over his followers to build a political and military power base that was incompatible with American democracy. These widely held suspicions about Smith made it simple for state governments to side with anti-Mormon antagonists in their conflicts with him. State actors would later recognize Mormonism as an actual religion, but saw polygamy as a scheme to aggrandize and gratify Mormon leaders at the expense of helpless women, not a practice grounded in religious belief that was worthy of the protection of the First Amendment. Similarly, the federal government during the Second World War understood Jehovah's Witnesses were motivated by religious belief, but would not acknowledge the legitimacy of their religious reasons for refusing to contribute to the war effort. The FBI explicitly told its operatives that the Nation of Islam was not a genuine religion, but a dangerous, anti-white political movement. Even George W. Bush's and Barack Obama's pronouncements that terrorist groups are not "real Islam," derided by critics as hypersensitive political correctness, have the purpose of drawing the boundaries of religious legitimacy. They effectively warn that the state will not tolerate certain forms of religion, and followers of those forms of religion cannot expect the Constitution to protect them.

The causal force of religious legitimacy helps explain why the state has targeted home-grown American religions while usually protecting world religions and their adherents. Judaism and Catholicism have been recognized as legitimate religions in America since the revolution, their status assured by their longevity and global presence. Even Christians who held Jews responsible for killing Christ, or Protestants who believed the Vatican was trying impose priestly despotism on America, could not deny that Jews and Catholics were religious enemies. No state actor could sanction the persecution of these groups without capsizing the principle of religious liberty. It was far easier to deny the religious legitimacy of groups with only a few thousand members, founded only decades previously. The exceptionalist belief that America was a Godly land did not make Americans accept claims that other Americans were prophets.

Another causally important factor was the broader political context of religious persecution. The success of persecution depended to some extent on the political identities of the persecutors. The anti-Mormon coalition consisted of, at various points, newspaper editors, "gentiles" in heavily Mormon areas, the Republican Party, and suffragette groups. While they were not necessarily supporters of the political status quo, these groups were certainly supporters of the established political order. Many of them wanted to bring political institutions more faithfully in line with that order, including enclaves of Mormon government that they regarded as aberrant. The persecution of Jehovah's Witnesses was led by the American Legion, an organization that enjoyed high social status and that was committed to protecting that status. The Nation of Islam experienced harassment at the hands of none other than the exalted Federal Bureau of Investigation. The state was willing to tolerate and support persecutory campaigns when they were instigated by actors who identified strongly with the existing political order.

Persecution that incurred the wrath of the state had a far more anti-establishment character. Anti-Catholic organizations were drawn to secretive, esoteric rituals, effectively mimicking the qualities that made Catholicism suspicious to many Americans in the first place. In electoral politics in American cities, Know-Nothings were often hard to distinguish from street gangs, and city authorities violently suppressed them as such. Unlike other political parties of the mid-nineteenth century, Know-Nothings could not capture the state when they captured government. For the brief period in which they commanded legislative majorities at the state level, they encountered immovable institutional resistance to their agendas.

Anti-Semitism in the twentieth century was even more politically marginal. Prejudice against Jews was widespread, but elites were content to practice social discrimination without institutionalizing it at the level of government. With the exception of a few luminaries such as Henry Ford and Charles Lindbergh, anti-Semitism was the political ideology of people on the losing side of industrialization. Jews to them were scapegoats for the misdeeds of banks, factory owners, and politicians. The Ku Klux Klan of the mid-1920s attempted to make anti-Semitism politically respectable, along with a raft of other Protestant prejudices including anti-Catholicism. But by the end of the decade the Klan, which was never as high-status as it pretended to be, was collapsing under the weight of scandal and anti-Semitism was without allies in either party. By the time the Nazis were threatening Europe the FBI was keeping files on known anti-Semites, including even the sainted Lindbergh.

Islamophobia in the twenty-first century has never quite attracted the same stigma as anti-Semitism. Anti-Islamic legislative measures have occasionally found mainstream political sponsorship at the state or local level. Federal officials, however, regard popular expressions of Islamophobia as dangerous. As well as posing the danger of violent civic disorder, public Islamophobia in America risks alienating citizens and governments of the Muslim world, further entrenching perceptions of the United States as a crusader power. The United States has long depended on the support of

Muslim allies such as Saudi Arabia, and these alliances have only become more urgent with the war on terror.

A final causal variable I have identified throughout the book is the ability of religious minorities, or their antagonists, to control the boundaries of conflict. When facing victimization at the local level, religious minorities have often appealed to higher authorities for intervention. Within the theoretical framework of this book, this is a predictable strategy. It is at the national level that state actors are most concerned with protecting individual rights such as freedom of religion, which they perceive as fundamental components of the national political order. At local levels, state actors are more concerned with a political order that protects social cohesion and regional economic interests, both of which may appear threatened by an unpopular or disruptive religious minority.

Jews in the Department of the Tennessee successfully petitioned President Lincoln to prevent their expulsion from the region, ordered by General Ulysses S. Grant. Lincoln was reportedly appalled by this treatment of Jews, of which he had been unaware, and immediately revoked the expulsion order after meeting with Jewish delegates. Jehovah's Witnesses found it much harder to mobilize higher authorities to their defense. The problem they faced was qualitatively different: they did not face a single tormentor under the direct authority of the national executive, but a dispersed wave of civic violence aided by the indifference or hostility of local officials. While figures such as Solicitor General Francis Biddle were concerned about attacks on Witnesses, there was little they were prepared to do about it while those attacks remained non-lethal and were almost never reported on, except in outraged affidavits written by Witnesses themselves. Given the other pressures of the time, anti-Witness violence was simply not threatening enough to warrant an extensive response from the Justice Department.

In some cases the situation was reversed; local antagonists of religious minorities would appeal to federal authorities for help, arguing that those minorities were becoming a threat to national political order. This occurred in cases where the antagonists were themselves a local minority, or felt in danger of becoming one. Anti-Mormons in Utah, such as the publishers Salt Lake City's *Anti-Polygamy Standard*, ultimately succeeded in bringing about a federal intervention that briefly delivered political power to them in Utah while Mormons were disfranchised. Here they were following the example of earlier anti-Mormons, such as those in Missouri who mobilized the state militia in the 1830s to drive Mormons out of the counties where they were close to becoming a majority. Anti-Catholic nativists, on the other hand, received no help from the federal government. To achieve their goal of taking Catholic immigrants out of municipal politics, nativists needed the cooperation of the federal government on immigration and naturalization policy. The federal government, promoting the westward growth of the United States, had no interest in an agenda that restricted either immigration or the rights of immigrants.

This theoretical framework, and the causal mechanisms I propose, cannot explain everything that has happened to religious minorities, nor every decision made by state officials. They do, I suggest, represent a significant advance in our understanding of the religious minority experience in the United States, allowing us to consider separate incidents of religious persecution as part of the same political phenomenon, driven by the recurring logic of state response to threats to political order. The cases I have examined, however, do not represent the whole universe of religious minority experiences in the United States. By choosing cases of well known, surviving minorities, I run the risk of not being able to explain qualitatively different cases, in which persecution was so severe that the state actually destroyed the religions in question. To test the robustness of my theory against this broader range of cases, I briefly turn to two examples of religions that did not survive their violent encounters with the state and today exist only as minimal remnants. This book would not be complete without a discussion of MOVE and the Branch Davidians.

NON-SURVIVING CASES: MOVE AND THE BRANCH DAVIDIANS

MOVE

MOVE, originally known as the "Christian Movement for Life," is a difficult organization to classify. Never numbering more than a few dozen people, it began in Philadelphia in 1972 under the leadership of the charismatic, semi-literate Vincent Leaphart, who changed his name to John Africa. MOVE was initially part of a constellation of black power movements in American cities in the 1970s, though it had some white members, and Leaphart's first advocate was Donald Glassey, a white community college professor who transcribed his philosophies into the book that became MOVE's "bible," *The Teachings of John Africa*. The most distinctive feature of John Africa's revolutionary philosophy was his "back to nature" revolt against technology, which he believed held back black people and humanity more broadly. He urged radical simplicity to break the shackles of "the system," which included shunning electricity, meat, cooked food, and clothing for children.

John Africa's followers, who also took the surname "Africa," lived under his guidance in a ramshackle commune in Philadelphia's Powelton Village neighborhood. They regarded his teachings as the "absolute truth," in the words of one MOVE member, and another wrote in his notebook that although it had not been confirmed or denied, it had been "clearly spelled out" that John Africa was the messiah. They attributed miracles to him, or at least to his teachings.[1] MOVE's lifestyle and aggressive proselytism put the group in constant conflict with their neighbors and city authorities. Their

---

[1] Anderson, John and Hilary Hevenor (1987). *Burning Down the House: MOVE and the Tragedy of Philadelphia*. New York: Norton, p. 7.

unsanitary commune attracted vermin and insects, and a large number of unvaccinated dogs added to the health risks (MOVE despised veterinarians and zoos). Neighbors claimed that MOVE members neglected their children, who went mostly unclothed and uneducated. At all hours of the day, loudspeakers transmitted John Africa's teachings and obscene denunciations of those who rejected them or who complained. Massive unpaid bills to the city mounted for utilities and back-taxes. In 1976, the group displayed to horrified reporters the body of an infant they claimed had been killed in a clash with police.[2]

The group only sporadically claimed the mantle of being a "religion," and that was usually when asserting its rights against city authorities. In May 1977, when MOVE members armed with inoperable rifles engaged in a standoff with police, the group issued a statement that "We are not a bunch of frustrated, middle-class college students, irrational radicals or confused terrorists. We are a deeply religious organization totally committed to the principle of our belief as taught to us by our founder, John Africa. We are not looking for trouble. We are just looking to be left alone."[3] During John Africa's trial for weapons offenses in 1981, an ATF agent testified he had likened his role within MOVE to that of the Pope within Catholicism.[4] MOVE's self-definition was far from consistent, and the city authorities and media also had difficulty finding a stable description for the group. Philadelphia's 1986 MOVE Commission report stated "By the early 1980s MOVE had evolved into an authoritarian, violence-threatening cult."[5]

MOVE was certainly an affront to civic authority in the most fundamental of ways. "Self-defense" was one of the tenets of John Africa's teachings, which necessitated the gathering of weapons and a hostile stance toward the police. By 1978, their stockpiles of illegal weapons and nonpayment of bills gave the Rizzo Administration sufficient reason to cut off utilities to the Powelton Village commune and force an eviction using heavily armed police. The result was a shoot-out on August 8 that left an officer dead, for which nine MOVE members would be convicted of murder despite their claims he had been killed by friendly fire. Three police officers who savagely beat a fleeing MOVE member, Delbert Africa, were later acquitted of assault charges.[6]

The fatal confrontation in 1978 set the stage for an even bloodier eviction seven years later. MOVE had by this time re-established its headquarters on Osage Avenue in West Philadelphia. Mayor Rizzo, who had a reputation for racism and authoritarianism, was long gone and the city had its first black mayor, Rizzo's nemesis Wilson Goode. But MOVE's relationship with the city was as bad as ever, as the group had recreated the antagonistic conditions of the

---

[2] Ibid., pp. 9–14.
[3] Quoted in Wagner-Pacifici, Robin (1994). *Discourse and Destruction: The City of Philadelphia versus MOVE*. Chicago: University of Chicago Press, p. 30.
[4] Ibid., p. 37.
[5] Ibid., p. 32.
[6] Anderson and Hevenor (1987), pp. 22–47.

Powelton Village commune. Philadelphia police continued to harbor a hatred of the group that was further inflamed by the 1981 conviction of Mumia Abu-Jamal, a black nationalist and early MOVE supporter, for the murder of officer Daniel Faulkner. In 1984, neighbors and police had observed the group constructing what appeared to be a wooden bunker on the roof of their row house. In May 1985 a residents' group announced it could "no longer co-exist" with MOVE and demanded that numerous outstanding warrants on MOVE members be served. District Attorney General Ed Rendell relayed rumors that MOVE had wired neighboring houses with explosives, and Mayor Goode authorized a tactical eviction.[7]

On May 12 Philadelphia Police evacuated the surrounding neighborhood in preparation for the forcible eviction of MOVE. On the morning of May 13 police armed with semi-automatic weapons surrounded MOVE's block on Osage Avenue and demanded that the adult members inside surrender. When the group did not respond, they assaulted the row house with tear gas and water from mounted fire hoses. This led to an exchange of gunfire that lasted several hours, in which police used 10,000 rounds of ammunition. Late in the afternoon, state police decided to eliminate the wooden bunker on the roof by dropping two pounds of C–4, a military explosive, onto the roof from a helicopter. Police Commissioner Gregore Sambor instructed Fire Commissioner William C. Richmond to "let the fire burn" in order to destroy the bunker, a decision that would later be blamed for one of the most traumatic events in the city's memory. The ensuing blaze killed eleven members of MOVE inside the house: John Africa, five other adults, and five children. There were two survivors, Ramona Africa and 13-year-old Birdie Africa. The fire spread and destroyed sixty other houses.

The MOVE incident remains notorious in Philadelphia and little known outside it, though Jason Osder's 2013 documentary *Let the Fire Burn* may help memorialize the event for a national audience.[8] The city's 1986 MOVE Commission resulted in no criminal charges but subjected the city and police leadership to heavy criticism for their handling of the episode, and resulted in the payment of tens of millions of dollars in compensation to survivors, their children, and their neighbors. Despite the deep unpopularity of MOVE with Philadelphians, almost nobody at the time or since has attempted to justify the city's response. Ramona Africa, spokesperson of MOVE's surviving remnant, continues to campaign for the release of imprisoned members and maintains "We weren't accused of anything that would warrant what this government came at us with."[9]

---

[7] Ibid., pp. 78–85.
[8] The documentary is constructed entirely from archival footage. It contains several instances, mostly from the taped proceedings of the MOVE Commission, in which surviving members and ex-members claim they were practicing a religion.
[9] Fagone, Jason (2014). "Birdie Africa: The Lost Boy." *Philadelphia Magazine*, February 27.

The Branch Davidians

The Waco siege of 1993, which resulted in the deaths of four federal agents and eighty-three members of the Branch Davidian sect, attracted much more attention than the MOVE killings. The sheer scale of the violence, the white and Christian identities of the victims, and the importance of the event to right-wing narratives of government threat have ensured Waco remains in the memory of the public and of state actors. The lessons of the siege have arguably shaped a far more cautious approach by law enforcement agencies toward armed standoffs involving ideational groups. There is less need to recount the well-known details of the Branch Davidian case, but some key facts are worth recalling.

The Branch Davidians at the time of the siege were widely depicted as an exotic cult, but they began in the 1920s and 1930s as a splinter group from Seventh-day Adventists, a group with more than 700,000 adherents in America in 1993.[10] The history of the group was shaped by a number of succession crises and schisms, which ultimately led to Vernon Howell, who changed his name to David Koresh, gaining control of the group in Mount Carmel, Texas, in 1981. To establish his authority, Koresh had to deal with a challenge from George Roden, the son of the previous leader, who regarded himself as the natural successor and who also owned the Mount Carmel property. Roden forced Koresh and his followers from Mount Carmel and attempted to discredit Koresh, who claimed to be a prophet, by disinterring the corpse of a church member and inviting Koresh to resurrect her. The dispute between Roden and Koresh over church possessions led to a gunfight in 1987, after which Koresh was charged with attempted murder but found not guilty, cementing his leadership at Mount Carmel.[11]

The Sheriff's Department of McLennan County closely monitored the Branch Davidians after failing to convict Koresh in 1989. In 1992 the Bureau of Alcohol, Tobacco, and Firearms began a formal investigation into the Davidians' stockpiling of weapons, based on information received from McLennan County.[12] As in the MOVE conflict, the most important trigger for state action was the accumulation of arms, an activity that directly threatened the authority of the state as the legitimate monopolist of violence. This was not, however, the only factor. Koresh, like John Africa, was a charismatic leader whose authority extended to every aspect of his followers' lives. Former members of the group told authorities that Koresh practiced both

---

[10] A series of articles in the *Waco Tribune-Herald* in March 1993 had a major role in shaping public and state perceptions of the Branch Davidians as an abusive cult. The first of these articles took pains to point out that the Seventh-day Adventist Church denied any connection with the group. See England, Mark and Darlene McCormick (1993). "The Sinful Messiah." *Waco Herald-Tribune*, March 3, 1993. On Seventh-day Adventist adherents, see http://www.thearda.com/Denoms/D_1108.asp, last accessed June 19, 2015.

[11] Shaw (2009), pp. 863–864.

[12] Ibid., p. 869.

polygamy and sexual relations with minors at Mount Carmel, raising alarms familiar from history about the relationship between charismatic authority and sexual servitude. Alleged violations of children, the citizens who require the most protection, were even more effective for compelling a response from the state than the alleged imprisonment of women had been for earlier groups. Throughout the siege that followed, child abuse allegations featured prominently in the state's justification of its actions.[13]

Acting on weapons charges, the ATF raided the Davidians' Mount Carmel compound on February 28, 1993. The Davidians were aware of the impending raid and were armed and ready to fight; four federal agents and six Davidians were killed in this encounter. The fact that the Davidians fought back with lethal force, as MOVE had done, is what sealed their fate. Faced with the killings of agents of the state, the state could be counted on to act with decisive force to reassert its authority. Around 700–800 armed personnel from various agencies, led by the FBI, surrounded the remote compound for 51 days, attempting to extract Koresh and the Davidians through negotiation and sleep deprivation tactics. During this period Koresh talked to negotiators in deeply religious terms that became increasingly unintelligible and dangerous-sounding to the FBI. Jayne Seminare Docherty has argued that negotiations failed because of an inability to recognize divergent perceptions of reality on the part of the FBI and Koresh.[14] The authorities developed fears that Koresh was planning a Jonestown-style mass-murder–suicide, despite Koresh's claims to the contrary. Religious scholars warned a violent end was not inevitable, but the FBI's siege tactics increased the likelihood that the Davidians would interpret events in apocalyptic terms.[15]

US Attorney General Janet Reno, responding to the FBI's mounting frustration, authorized an assault on the compound with the approval of President Clinton. On the morning of April 19 the FBI attacked the compound with tanks, grenade fire, and tear gas. At around noon, three fires began that would destroy the building and lead to the deaths of most of those inside. The Justice Department's report on the conflagration found the Davidians had lit the fires, and "the compound residents had sufficient time to escape the fire, if they so desired."[16] Davidian survivors heavily dispute this

---

[13] See Ellison, Christopher G. and John P. Bartkowski (1995). "'Babies Were Being Beaten': Exploring Child Abuse Allegations at Ranch Apocalypse." In Stuart A. Wright (ed.), *Armageddon in Waco: Critical Perspectives on the Branch Davidian Conflict*. Chicago: University of Chicago Press, pp. 111–149.

[14] Docherty, Jayne Seminare (2001). *Learning Lessons from Waco: When Parties Bring Their Gods to the Negotiation Table*. Syracuse: Syracuse University Press.

[15] Tabor, James (1995). "Religious Discourse and Failed Negotiations: The Dynamics of Biblical Apocalypticism at Waco." In Stuart A. Wright (ed.), *Armageddon in Waco: Critical Perspectives on the Branch Davidian Conflict*. Chicago: University of Chicago Press, pp. 263–281.

[16] United States Department of Justice (1993). *Report to the Deputy Attorney General on the Events at Waco, Texas, February 28 to April 19, 1993*. Section XIII.D.3. www.justice.gov/publications/waco/wacothirteen.html, last accessed June 19, 2015.

version of events, claiming the attack started the fire and caused structural damage that blocked exits.[17]

Like the MOVE killings, the siege of Waco is often remembered as a tragic but unjustifiable mistake on the part of state actors.[18] The event was given a long afterlife in public memory by the 1995 Oklahoma City bombing, which targeted a building housing the ATF and other federal agencies. The bombing killed 168 people; its culprit, Timothy McVeigh, claimed it was in retaliation for deaths at Mt. Carmel and Ruby Ridge. He had chosen the date of the bombing, April 19, because it was the two-year anniversary of the end of the Waco siege.[19] As in the MOVE case, the subsequent public understanding of the consequences of Waco obscures the fact that public hostility toward the Davidians ran high during the siege, and few in the political mainstream would have denied the state was within its rights to "do something" about them.[20]

Do these cases fit?

The cases of MOVE and the Branch Davidians support the overall logic of this book. State actors were highly responsive to demands from civil society – MOVE's neighbors, and organized groups of former Davidians – that they take action against these groups. A difference between these and most other cases is that the state itself, rather than civil society, was the sole perpetrator of violence against these groups. State actors had all the justification they needed to engage in repressive violence. Both groups stockpiled weapons, antagonized local authorities, and ignored the state's demands. In both cases, the state saw these groups solely in terms of the threat they posed to public order and properly constituted authority. There was little if any consideration of the religious dimensions of MOVE, and federal agents saw the Branch Davidians' religiosity as an aggravating factor in the danger they posed. In each case, the decision to remove both groups forcibly was a tactical one for state actors, given the nature of the threat at hand. They did not foresee that their actions would themselves come to be seen by the public as massive violations of American political order – killing citizens, violating religious freedom, and undermining public trust in government.

---

[17] Kelly, Dean M. (1995). "The Implosion of Mt. Carmel and Its Aftermath: Is It All Over Yet?" In Stuart A. Wright (ed.), *Armageddon in Waco: Critical Perspectives on the Branch Davidian Conflict*. Chicago: University of Chicago Press, pp. 358–378.

[18] See, e.g., Gladwell, Malcolm (2014). "Sacred and Profane: How not to negotiate with believers." *The New Yorker*, March 31 2014, pp. 22–28.

[19] Vidal, Gore (2001). "The Meaning of Timothy McVeigh." *Vanity Fair*, September.

[20] The media played an important role in supporting the state's narrative about the threat posed by Koresh and the Davidians. See Richardson, James T. (1995). "Manufacturing Consent about Koresh: A Structural Analysis of the Role of Media in the Waco Tragedy." In Stuart A. Wright (ed.), *Armageddon in Waco: Critical Perspectives on the Branch Davidian Conflict*. Chicago: University of Chicago Press, pp. 153–176.

These relatively recent cases conform to the historical logic of state response to religious minorities outlined in this book. However, there is another major difference, and that is in how these groups are perceived now. If we rarely call these cases of "religious persecution," it is because MOVE and the Davidians are hardly ever recognized as entities worthy of the respect that a liberal democratic society accords to the term "religious minorities." Observers were, and are, horrified by the fates of these groups, violently extinguished close to our own time. But neither group achieved, or is likely to be retrospectively given, the mantle of religious legitimacy. The Davidians will probably always be described as a "cult," MOVE as something even less legitimate than that. In ordinary language use "persecution" denotes an unambiguously bad activity, and in religious terms we tend to reserve it for the experiences of religions with whom we can at least respectfully disagree. We do not think of persecution as including police actions whose logic we can understand and maybe even sympathize with. Given that law enforcement officers had died in earlier confrontations with both groups, it is hard not to apportion at least some of the blame for what happened to the groups themselves, and especially their charismatic leaders.[21] All of this makes it less likely that we would refer to the violent destruction of these groups by the state as "persecution."[22]

This difference, however, affirms a central point of my argument. In this book we have seen that religious persecution has never looked like religious persecution to the state actors involved in it. It can always be justified in the name of preserving public order, public safety, democracy, community cohesion, wartime unity, national security, even religious freedom itself. State actors have often not been sure whether the group they are targeting is a real religion – which, as I have repeatedly stressed, is itself a causal factor in religious persecution. At the times most of the actions in this book occurred, the label of "persecution" was only used by the persecuted group itself and would not gain broader currency until decades later, when the group was so entrenched that the prospect of the same thing happening again was

---

[21] There is still a live debate over who was to blame for the conflagration at Waco. See, e.g., Wessinger, Catherine (2009). "Deaths in the Fire at the Branch Davidians' Mount Carmel: Who Bears Responsibility?" *Nova Religio: The Journal of Alternative and Emergent Religions*, 13(2): 25–60.

[22] Even the most sympathetic scholarly treatments stop short of calling these cases of "religious persecution," or do so only in a very oblique way. In the introduction to *Armageddon at Waco*, Stuart Wright notes: "The holocaust at Mt. Carmel represents a tragic episode in the history of sectarian religion in America. It belies some of our deepest and most sacred convictions about the sanctity of religious freedom and tolerance for individual differences and beliefs. We should find it odd that a nation founded by religious sectarians (Puritans attempting to escape religious persecution at the hands of the state) should itself so easily forget the lessons of history." Wright, Stuart A. (1995). "Another View of the Mount Carmel Standoff." In Stuart A. Wright (ed.), *Armageddon at Waco: Critical Perspectives on the Branch Davidian Conflict*. Chicago: University of Chicago Press, p. xvii.

unimaginable. The "persecution" label may never gain widespread use in cases of religions that did not survive.

DIRECTIONS FOR FUTURE RESEARCH

Future research will hopefully either extend the use of my theoretical framework or replace it with something better. Here I will briefly outline three potential limitations of this study that can act as starting points for further research. One potential limitation is that I have proposed a logic of state action and a series of causal mechanisms that do not vary over time. As I suggest in the previous sections of this chapter, the calculus for state actors has remained the same throughout American history, and the same recurring causal mechanisms have influenced their decision-making. The American state, however, has certainly changed, and there is a large body of scholarship on American political development that explains these changes. Different parts of the state have developed new capacities over time, often at the expense of other parts of the state. How might these changes in capacity affect the way the state treats religious minorities, in ways I have not explored?

I will leave it to others to offer a properly developmental account of the state's treatment of religious minorities. One possibility is that the state has become increasingly assertive of its status as the sole monopolist of violence. In most of the later cases in this book – the Nation of Islam, the Branch Davidians, and Muslims after 9/11 – the federal government was itself the principal antagonist. There was a great deal of antagonism toward these groups from within civil society, especially in the case of Muslims. But the state has jealously guarded its exclusive right to take forceful action against these groups, as Chapter 9 demonstrates in the post-9/11 context. One of the three main state responses I identify in this book – allowing civil society to persecute – may have disappeared from the state's repertoire as its coercive capacities have increased. Even if local authorities tolerated the kind of civic violence that afflicted Jehovah's Witnesses in the 1940s, we might expect a far more effective federal response now, empowered by better technology, larger budgets, and decades of civil rights legislation.

Another limitation of this study is that I have restricted it to the United States. My original reason for doing so was because I was interested in what seemed a distinctly American puzzle: why a country that so venerates religious freedom has allowed the persecution of some religious minorities while protecting others. This is, however, part of a broader class of puzzles about when liberal democracies engage in repressive actions that seem to violate democratic norms.[23] Would my theoretical framework about the state's relationship with religious minorities apply beyond the United States? In my theoretical construction I have conceived of "the state" in general, rather than specifically

---

[23] See, e.g., Davenport (2007).

American terms. I have argued that however much the American state has differed from the centralized Weberian model, it has retained the core element of monopolizing coercive control over territory, and it has endowed actors at different territorial levels with the authority to exercise that control. The basic logic I propose – that the state response to religious persecution depends on actors' perceptions of relative threats to political order – should be portable beyond the United States.

There would of course be significant differences between the United States and other countries. Some of these differences could be easily translated into causal variables in a cross-national study, such as the degree of federalism. But the most significant variance would be in the nature of the political order state actors see themselves as defending, and the role of religion in that order. Authoritarian states, for example, are generally less preoccupied with individual rights and more aligned toward goals such as national cohesion. Religion may either bolster or endanger authoritarian goals. Authoritarian regimes may be completely anti-religious in nature, they may rely on the support of a dominant religious group for political legitimacy, or they may follow any number of configurations between those two poles. Russia and China, often identified in US State Department reports as persecuting states, have undergone complex negotiations with religious groups over their roles in society.[24] While the overall treatment of religion is very different in those countries, it would be possible to study variance in the treatment of religious minorities within each country using the same framework I have used for the United States.

There are great differences too within the universe of democratic countries. Nearly all Westphalian democracies are essentially secular, but they have very different conceptions of what a secular political order entails.[25] Ahmet Kuru characterizes the dominant American ideology as "passive secularism," in which the state allows religion to play a visible role in the public sphere. The Netherlands, though quite institutionally different, is another example of a passive secular order (as is my own country of Australia). Kuru contrasts this with the "assertive secularism" found in France, Mexico, and Turkey, in which the state takes an active role in minimizing religion in the public sphere.[26] In an assertive secular regime, state actors may be far more sensitive to the threats that religion poses to secular political order; it may also be the case that members of major world religions, not just heterodox minorities, would be

---

[24] See Koesel, Karrie (2014). *Religion and Authoritarianism: Conflict, Cooperation, and the Consequences.* New York: Cambridge University Press.

[25] See Monsma and Soper (1997); Hurd (2008); Bosco (2014); and Kuru, Ahmet T. (2009). *Secularism and State Policies toward Religion: The United States, France, and Turkey.* New York: Cambridge University Press.

[26] Kuru (2009), ch. 1. Kuru's study explores the ideological struggles within three countries over which form of secularism will prevail. In Turkey, assertive secularism faces a strong challenge from pro-Islamic conservatives.

less likely to support a political order that actively excludes them from public life. The logic of state response may be the same across Westphalian democracies, and indeed across authoritarian states, but the causal factors affecting that response would be very different.

A final limitation is that this study is only about the American state's treatment of religious groups. Is there anything inherent about religious minorities that should make the state treat them differently from other minorities? In this book I have not attempted to extend my theoretical framework to the experiences of racial, ethnic, sexual, or political minorities, though the religious minorities in this book do overlap with all those categories at different points. I believe the framework can, and hopefully will, be extended. In all of these categories there are groups which either state or non-state actors have considered "subversive," actual, or potential threats to political order. And, as in the religious category, there have been disagreements between state and non-state actors over how best to respond to the subversive threat, to the point where state actors have sometimes considered civic "counter-subversives" the greater threat. Wherever this dynamic exists, my framework may have some explanatory use.

There certainly are some features of the religious category of minorities that may make it unique in causally important ways. It is the oldest category of minority in the Westphalian system of states, the first around which there was a discourse of protection of rights. It is particularly salient in the United States, where the Constitution at least nominally protected the basic rights of religious minorities in a way it would not for other minority groups until after the Civil War, or much later than that in some cases. This was why, in the 1920s, Noble Drew Ali believed that African Americans could escape persecution by transforming their racial identity into a religious one. For these reasons, the question of legitimacy – whether a group can be considered part of this category – has arguably been much more urgent for religious minorities than it may be for other types of minorities. Another unique feature of religion, mentioned in Chapter 1, is that it invokes sources of authority outside of and above the state. This gives all religions subversive potential. All religions must decide how to reconcile holy and temporal obligations when they come into conflict, and they may do so in a way that either supports or undermines state authority. These two features of religion have played important roles in all the cases under investigation in this book.

But these differences do not make religious minorities so unique that they should change the basic logic of how states deal with them. Other types of minorities also strive for recognition from the state, bringing with it legal protection and a defense against stigmatization. Other types of minorities are also characterized by multiple or divided loyalties, making them targets of state or non-state counter-subversives. Above all, the fates of all minority groups are decided by processes of political struggle and accommodation, not by native membership of fixed categories. Conflict between a minority group and the state

235

is never only about the minority and its characteristics; it is also about the broader context of political order. Future work on how the state relates to minorities must continue to take into account not just the perceived threat minorities pose, but also the perceived threat of their antagonists.

CONCLUSION: RELIGIOUS PERSECUTION AND RELIGIOUS CHANGE

The Amish would have appeared to be prime candidates for persecution during the First and Second World Wars. Not only did they refuse to be drafted, they spoke German as their first language. Jehovah's Witnesses were considered "fifth column" suspects on the basis of far flimsier connections to the enemy. But the Amish, like the Brethren and the Quakers, were known as historic "peace churches," whose pacifism on the American continent went back to the Revolutionary War (or to conflicts with Native Americans, in the case of the Quakers). The visible distinctiveness of the Amish – their separate language, archaic dress, and self-imposed rural isolation – if anything made their pacifism less threatening, because they were clearly not attempting to spread resistance to war as a political doctrine. Perhaps most importantly, the peace churches were prepared to negotiate alternative service arrangements with the state, which Jehovah's Witnesses were not.[27]

For religious groups that encounter and survive persecution, the experience often plays a critical role in collective memory. This collective memory shapes their understandings of temporal authority and their strategies for negotiating with it. Anabaptist groups, including the Amish and Mennonites, brought with them to America copies of *Martyrs' Mirror*, an illustrated book documenting the lives and deaths of Anabaptists and other Christians persecuted by European states while observing the doctrine of non-resistance. Donald Kraybill posits the Amish posture of "courteous disregard for the affairs of the state" is derived in part from the historical experience of violent persecution.[28] This has allowed Anabaptists in the United States to act as loyal dissidents, able to depart radically from political consensus without being seen as a threat to political order.

It can take religious minorities a long time to develop practices that allow them to simultaneously dissent from and defer to secular authority. Mormons faced the prospect of institutional destruction before subjugating their most contentious theological principle to the imperative of obeying the law. Wilford Woodruff, the fourth president of the church, understood that "I have arrived at the point in the History of my life as President of the Church of Jesus Christ of Latter Day Saints where I am under the necessity of acting for the Temporal

[27] Keim, Albert M. (1993). "Military Service and Conscription." In Donald B. Kraybill (ed.), *The Amish and the State*. Baltimore: Johns Hopkins University Press, pp. 43–64.
[28] Kraybill, Donald B. (1993). "Negotiating With Caesar." In Donald B. Kraybill (ed.), *The Amish and the State*. Baltimore: Johns Hopkins University Press, pp. 3–20.

Salvation of the Church."[29] The Nation of Islam also confronted the likelihood of financial and organizational ruin before Elijah Muhammad began a search for new allies in the Muslim and secular worlds, paving the way for his son to realign the Nation with orthodox Islam and American patriotism.

But religions cannot simply be persecuted into obedience. Jehovah's Witnesses under the leadership of Judge Rutherford expected persecution, and Rutherford even welcomed it. In the 1941 *Yearbook of Jehovah's Witnesses*, Rutherford described the public violence that Witnesses had suffered during the previous year, explaining the Lord had said to his faithful followers and servants that at the time of the second coming, "Ye shall be hated of all nations for my name's sake." (Matt. 24:9) He extolled the positive role that persecution played in the Witness experience:

> Although daily suffering cruel persecution at the hands of religious fanatics, Jehovah's Witnesses are not in the least bit discouraged or dismayed. On they joyfully go performing their God-given commission. They know that the persecution they suffer is indisputable proof that they are the children of God and that nothing can befall them except by the permission of almighty God and that all things shall work together for the ultimate good of them because they love God and are called according to his purpose.[30]

Statements such as this suggest Witnesses rejoiced in persecution, and actively brought it on themselves as a way of proving their righteousness. But the Witnesses' affidavits show that for most of them the experience of persecution was anything but "joyful," and they devoted considerable efforts to ending it. However much they despised the American state, Witnesses (including Rutherford) wanted its protection. As noted earlier, Witnesses pursued a relentlessly legalistic strategy, believing the law would ultimately be on their side. By 1946 a slew of Supreme Court cases had secured the rights of Witnesses to refuse the flag salute and proselytize. But Witness tactics slowly began to change after 1942, when Rutherford died and was succeeded by Nathan Knorr.

The Knorr-led Witnesses underwent a period of quiet reform after the Second World War. Once again, a war they thought was the beginning of the end times had finished, and once again their leader had died during the war, all without any sign of Armageddon. Membership growth was stagnant between 1942 and 1947. Knorr sought to expand and reshape the Witnesses in light of the fact that their work was evidently not over. Now the Witnesses' wartime conflict with the state was finished, the group sought to make peace with civil society. According to Joseph Zygmunt, "a tone of accommodative restraint began to

---

[29] From Wilford Woodruff's journal, 1890, quoted in Gedicks, Frederick Mark (1992). "The Integrity of Survival: A Mormon Response to Stanley Hauerwas." *DePaul Law Review* 42(1): 167–173.

[30] Watch Tower Bible and Tract Society (1941). *Year Book Of Jehovah's Witnesses, 1941*, pp. 46–47.

pervade the sect's evangelistic operations on the American scene." Witnesses were now instructed to refrain from making offensive attacks on other religions while proselytising, and Witness literature began to discuss religious difference without vehement condemnation of established churches.[31]

The Witnesses also "depoliticized" their image, no longer attacking the state or secular organizations in their literature. This new approach to the state and secular power culminated in the 1966 reversion to Russell-era doctrine on "higher powers." Rutherford had held that the only higher power to which Witnesses owed allegiance was God; under Russell, and now Knorr, they were required to defer to secular authority provided it did not conflict with God's law, accepting it as part of the "divinely permitted" earthly system. Zygmunt argues these changes significantly reduced tension between Witnesses and society, and also resulted in an accelerated growth rate after 1947, reaching 100,000 members by 1950 and 500,000 members by 1975.[32] The experience of persecution certainly contributed to the changes the Witnesses made, but they could only make those changes after persecution ended.

Orthodox Muslims in the United States today face an entirely different dilemma. Since they originally arrived in the United States, orthodox Muslims have been a politically loyal group. They have never challenged the prevailing political order, and during the Cold War they were regarded as part of the fabric of American religiosity that was needed to defeat communist ideology. That American Muslims are loyal citizens has remained the "official" line after 9/11, often repeated by government officials from the president downwards. Muslim leaders and ordinary adherents constantly reaffirm this loyalty, and there is little more they can do to demonstrate it. Yet the state's own actions reveal that it regards Muslim communities as potential threats, Muslim citizens as potential terrorists, and Muslim religious institutions as incubators of anti-American radicalism. Unlike a contentious sect led by an authoritative prophet, American Muslim communities cannot announce a sudden doctrinal change to allay suspicions about their loyalties. They must live with those suspicions for as long as the discourse of an open-ended crisis in American national security continues.

Mormons, Jehovah's Witnesses, and the Nation of Islam are all seen very differently now from how they were at the time of their persecution. Mormons may be routinely mocked in popular culture, and many Americans do not regard them as Christians, but few question their legitimacy as a religion.[33] People may not welcome visits from door-knocking Jehovah's Witnesses, but

[31] Zygmunt (1977), p. 48.
[32] Ibid., pp. 48–49.
[33] In the 2012 American National Election Study, which took place amid Mitt Romney's bid for the presidency, around 44% of survey respondents answered that Mormonism "is a Christian religion," while 42% said it is "not a Christian religion." Data is available at www.electionstudies.org/studypages/anes_timeseries_2012/anes_timeseries_2012.htm, last accessed March 2, 2015.

no mainstream media outlet today would describe them as a "freak cult." Mormons and Jehovah's Witnesses are now among the world's fastest growing religions;[34] in the United States there are currently more than six million Mormons and one million Jehovah's Witnesses.[35] While maintaining their distinctiveness from mainstream Christianity, both groups have undergone processes of assimilation into American life that have reduced the tension between their members and broader society.[36] Mormons in particular have come to embody many positive American stereotypes.[37]

The Nation of Islam, after its reconstitution by Louis Farrakhan, remains a smaller and more marginal group. In 2007 the *New York Times* reported an estimated membership of about 50,000, "with an ardent following in prisons, where the emphasis on black identity and the struggle against racism ... have a pervasive appeal."[38] The future identity of the Nation of Islam is uncertain; Louis Farrakhan, now in his eighties, reportedly began integrating the Nation with the Church of Scientology in 2012.[39] Nevertheless, the Farrakhan-era Nation of Islam achieved a distinctive cultural salience, especially through music, that went well beyond Farrakhan's hard-core following. The Nation, and the splinter group Nation of Gods and Earths (Five Percenters) played a major role in the politicization of hip-hop, influencing Public Enemy, Eric B. and Rakim, Ice Cube, the Wu-Tang Clan, and numerous other commercially successful artists. In 1996, Ted Swedenburg observed "Islamic rap is no marginal cultural phenomenon, but has firmly implanted itself at the *center* of US mass culture. One week last September, for instance, *three* of the Top Ten albums in the Billboard charts were by rap groups with Islamic affiliations."[40]

In 1989 Public Enemy's iconic Spike Lee-directed video for "Fight the Power" took the form of a boisterous political rally marshaled by the Fruit of Islam, the Nation's paramilitary bodyguard. Zaheer Ali noted signs of a revival

---

[34] Stark, Rodney (2005). *The Rise of Mormonism*. New York: Columbia University Press; Stark, Rodney and Laurence R. Iannaccone (1997). "Why the Jehovah's Witnesses Grow so Rapidly: A Theoretical Application." *Journal of Contemporary Religion*, 12(2): 133–157.

[35] Data available from the Association of Religious Data Archives, see http://www.thearda.com/ Denoms/D_1117.asp and http://www.thearda.com/Denoms/D_1107.asp, last accessed March 2, 2015.

[36] Mauss (1994); Zygmunt, Joseph F. (1977). "Jehovah's Witnesses in the U.S.A., 1942–1976." *Social Compass*, XXIV, 1977/1: 45–57.

[37] Amy Chua and Jeb Rubenfeld include Mormons in their treatise on high-status American minorities, pointing to the prominence of Mormons in business and politics and their higher than average levels of education and wealth. Chua, Amy and Jeb Rubenfeld (2014). *The Triple Package: How Three Unlikely Traits Explain the Rise and Fall of Cultural Groups in America*. New York: Penguin.

[38] MacFarquhar, Neil (2007). "Nation of Islam at a Crossroads as Leader Exits." *New York Times*, February 26.

[39] Gray, Eliza (2012). "The Mothership of All Alliances." *The New Republic*, October 5.

[40] Swedenburg, Ted (1997). "Islam in the Mix: Lessons of the Five Percent." Paper presented at the Anthropology Colloquium, University of Arkansas, February 19 1997. Available at http://comp. uark.edu/~tsweden/5per.html, last accessed March 9, 2015.

of the hip-hop connection with the NOI in 2014, when bestselling artist Jay Z appeared at the Brooklyn Hip-Hop festival flanked by Fruit of Islam personnel. "With their clean-shaven appearance, dark suits, white shirts and bow ties with matching pocket squares," writes Ali, "the FOI project a particular kind of black male cool, which remains one of the most valuable commodities in hip-hop culture. And unlike other expressions of black male cool, this one is difficult to appropriate outside the black community."[41]

All three of these groups remain proudly outside the American mainstream, yet enjoy a degree of acceptance from it. This could only happen after the state stopped persecuting them. In the classic Tocquevillean model of America, civil society mediates relations between the individual and the state. The state, however, also has a mediating role between different groups in civil society. However much the United States has achieved Jefferson's "wall of separation" between religion and the state, the state remains the ultimate – if haphazard – arbiter of religious legitimacy in a country that values religious faith deeply. That legitimacy is a valuable prize for any new religion. It is not given to everyone.

---

[41] Ali, Zaheer (2014). "Is It Nation of Islam Time Again in Hip-Hop?" *The Root*, July 19. Available at www.theroot.com/articles/culture/2014/07/jay_electronica_puts_hip_hop_s_noi_ties_center_stage.html, last accessed March 2, 2015.

Sources and bibliography

PRIMARY SOURCES

Throughout this book I have made use of numerous primary historical sources. In the course of my research I examined thousands of primary documents, mostly newspapers, congressional records, and affidavits. I cite many of these sources in the text of the book itself, while others remain as background information. For the three chapters in which I made most use of primary sources (Chapters 3, 4, and 6), I will briefly describe how I located and used these sources, listing the most important. Although Chapter 9 also includes what could be called primary historical material – stories from newspapers and websites from 2001 to 2015 – given the recency of these documents, I do not include them here. Readers can seek them out in the footnotes.

Chapter 3: Joseph Smith and the rise of Mormonism

To examine reactions to Joseph Smith by his contemporaries, I used the America's Historical Newspapers database to search for references to Smith, Mormons, and the Book of Mormon. When that avenue was exhausted, I found Dale Broadhurst's online archive, "Uncle Dale's Readings in Early Mormon History," an invaluable source of newspaper articles that even the AHN database did not contain. Located at www.sidneyrigdon.com/dbroadhu/artindex.htm, I recommend this as a starting point for any scholar interested in media reactions to early Mormonism. Among the newspapers I used in my research, not all of which I cited in this chapter, are the following:

Baltimore Sun
Boston Courier
Connecticut Courant
Daily Commercial Bulletin and Missouri Literary Register
Eastern Argus
Evangelical Magazine and Gospel Advocate (Utica, NY)
Farmer's Cabinet (Amherst, NH)
Farmer's Gazette (Barre, MA)

Haverhill Gazette
Hudson River Chronicle (Sing Sing, NY)
Manchester Guardian
New Hampshire Gazette
New Hampshire Sentinel
New Orleans Picayune
Ohio Atlas
Ohio Statesman
Philadelphia Mirror
Portsmouth Journal and Rockingham Gazette
Rhode Island American
Richmond Enquirer
Salem Gazette
Sentinel and Witness (Middletown, VT)
U.S. Telegraph (Washington, DC)
Vermont Chronicle
Waldo Patriot (Belfast, ME)
Warsaw Signal
Weekly Herald (New York, NY).

Chapter 4: The federal response to Mormonism

In this chapter, where I examined the vote on the Edmunds Bill in Congress, I relied mainly on Volume 11 of the *Congressional Record*, which recorded the 47th Congress. In this chapter I also made use of the *Anti-Polygamy Standard*, published in Salt Lake City, Utah, in the early 1880s.

Chapter 6: Mass violence against Jehovah's Witnesses, 1940–1942

In this chapter I used a range of primary sources, the most important of which were sworn affidavits by Jehovah's Witnesses describing the violence they endured. The American Civil Liberties Union encouraged Witnesses to write these affidavits and send them to the Justice Department, and also send copies to the ACLU. The affidavits are preserved in the American Civil Liberties Union Papers, which I accessed on microfilm at the University of Michigan library ("American Civil Liberties Union: The Roger Baldwin Years [1917–1950]"). The affidavits are in the state correspondence section of the papers, found mainly between volumes 2200 and 2500. I used several hundred of these affidavits to construct my dataset of violent incidents. Among the affiants whose writing I quote directly in the chapter are:

Mae Armstrong, John R. Barnes, Harry Barwig, Robert Barwig, Otto Bauer, William Baumgartner, Eugenia Buzalski, Roy Crabb, R.L. Drummond, Jerome Fain, Lane Hare, J.W. Jones Anton Kadjzik, Emil Koch, A.M. Mellander, Mike Mesarik, Ernest Miller, David Nalepinski, Edmond M. Perrenoud, Ray Rose, Allan D. Weaver, Read A. Wilkinson.

I also used the ProQuest Historical Newspapers database to search for accounts of Witness persecution in major national newspapers. Newspapers I used in this chapter include the *Chicago Tribune*, *Los Angeles Times*, *New York Times*, and *Washington Post*.

SECONDARY BIBLIOGRAPHY

Abdel-Masek, Kamal (ed.) (2000). *America in an Arab Mirror: Images of America in Arabic Travel Literature.* London: Palgrave MacMillan.

Abrahams, Ray (1998). *Vigilant Citizens: Vigilantism and the State.* Cambridge: Polity Press.

Adams, Peter (2014). *Politics, Faith, and the Making of American Judaism.* Ann Arbor: University of Michigan Press.

Adorno, T.W., Else Frenkel-Brunswik, Daniel J. Levinson, and R. Nevitt Sanford (1950). *The Authoritarian Personality.* New York: Harper and Row.

Aldrich, John (2011). *Why Parties? A Second Look.* Chicago: University of Chicago Press.

Alexander, Thomas G. (1986). *Mormonism in Transition: A History of the Latter-Day Saints, 1890–1930.* Urbana and Chicago: University of Illinois Press.

Allen, Jr., Ernest (1996). "Religious Heterodoxy and Nationalist Tradition: The Continuing Evolution of the Nation of Islam." *The Black Scholar*, 26(3/4): 2–34.

Allport, Gordon W. (1958). *The Nature of Prejudice* (abridged). New York: Doubleday.

American Civil Liberties Union (1936). *How Goes the Bill of Rights: The Story of the Fight for Civil Liberty, 1935–1936.* New York: American Civil Liberties Union.

Anbinder, Tyler (1992). *Nativism and Slavery: The Northern Know Nothings and the Politics of the 1850s.* New York: Oxford University Press.

Anderson, Gary M. and Robert D. Tollison (1998). "Celestial Marriage and Earthly Rents: Interests and the Prohibition of Polygamy." *Journal of Economic Behavior and Organization*, 37(2): 169–181.

Arato, Andrew (1981). "Civil Society against the State: Poland 1980–81." *Telos*, 23–47.

Arrington, Leonard (1958). *Great Basin Kingdom: An Economic History of the Latter-Day Saints.* Cambridge: Harvard University Press.

(1985). *Brigham Young: American Moses.* Urbana and Chicago: University of Illinois Press.

Arrington, Leonard J. and Davis Bitton (1979). *The Mormon Experience.* London: George Allen & Unwin Ltd.

Asbury, Herbert (1933). *The Barbary Coast: An Informal History of the San Francisco Underworld.* New York: Alfred A. Knopf.

Bailyn, Bernard (1968). *The Ideological Origins of the American Revolution.* Cambridge: Harvard University Press.

Balogh, Brian (2009). *A Government Out of Sight: The Mystery of National Authority in Nineteenth-Century America.* New York: Cambridge University Press.

Barbalet, Jack, Adam Possamai, and Bryan S. Turner (eds.) (2011). *Religion and the State: A Comparative Sociology.* London: Anthem Press.

Barrett, James R. (1992). "Americanization from the Bottom Up: Immigration and the Remaking of the Working Class in the United States, 1880–1930." *Journal of American History*, 79(3): 996–1020.

Beam, Alex (2014). *American Crucifixion: The Murder of Joseph Smith and the Fate of the Mormon Church.* New York: PublicAffairs.

Becker, Gary (1981). *A Treatise on the Family.* Cambridge: Harvard University Press.

Beckford, James (1975). *The Trumpet of Prophecy: A Sociological Study of Jehovah's Witnesses.* New York: John Wiley and Sons.

Belknap, Michal R. (1987). *Federal Law and Southern Order: Racial Violence and Constitutional Conflict in the Post-Brown South.* Athens: University of Georgia Press.

Beneke, Chris (2006). *Beyond Toleration: The Religious Origins of American Pluralism.* New York: Oxford University Press.

Bennett, David H. (1995). *The Party of Fear: The American Far Right from Nativism to the Militia Movement.* New York: Vintage.

Bensel, Richard Franklin (1984). *Sectionalism and American Political Development 1880–1980.* Madison: The University of Wisconsin Press.

  (2000). *The Political Economy of American Industrialization, 1877–1900.* Cambridge: Cambridge University Press.

Benyon, Erdmann Doane (1938). "The Voodoo Cult among Negro Migrants in Detroit." *The American Journal of Sociology,* 43(6): 894–907.

Berg, Thomas C. (1994). "What Hath Congress Wrought – An Interpretive Guide to the Religious Freedom Restoration Act." *Villanova Law Review,* 39(1): 1–70.

Berman, Sheri (1997). "Civil Society and the Collapse of the Weimar Republic." *World Politics,* 49(3): 401–429.

Bernstein, Elizabeth (2010). "Militarized Humanitarianism Meets Carceral Feminism: The Politics of Sex, Rights and Freedom in Contemporary Antitrafficking Campaigns." *Signs: Journal of Women in Culture and Society,* 36(1): 45–71.

Biggers, Jeff (2012). *State Out of the Union: Arizona and the Final Showdown over the American Dream.* New York: Nation Books.

Billington, Ray Allen (1952). *The Protestant Crusade, 1800–1860.* New York: Rinehart & Co., Inc.

Blalock, Hubert M. (1967). *Toward a Theory of Minority-Group Relations.* New York: Capricorn Books.

Bloom, Harold (1992). *The American Religion.* New York: Simon and Schuster.

Bordin, Ruth (1981). *Woman and Temperance.* Philadelphia: Temple University Press.

Bosco, Robert M. (2014). *Securing the Sacred: Religion, National Security, and the Western State.* Ann Arbor: University of Michigan Press.

Bradley, Martha Sonntag (1993). *Kidnapped from That Land: The Government Raids on the Short Creek Polygamists.* Salt Lake City: University of Utah Press.

Brekus, Catherine A. and W. Clark Gilpin (eds.) (2011). *American Christianities: A History of Dominance and Diversity.* Chapel Hill: University of North Carolina Press.

Brinkerhoff, Merlin B. and Marlene M. Mackie (1986). "The Applicability of Social Distance for Religious Research: An Exploration." *Review of Religious Research,* 28(2): 153–154.

Bromley, David G. (ed.) (1998). *The Politics of Religious Apostasy: The Role of Apostates in the Transformation of Religious Movements.* Westport: Greenwood.

Bromley, David G. and Lewis F. Carter (eds.) (1996). *The Issue of Authenticity in the Study of Religions.* Greenwich: JAI Press.

Bronner, Stephen Eric (2000). *A Rumor about the Jews: Reflections on Antisemitism and the Protocols of the Learned Elders of Zion.* New York: St. Martin's Press.

Brown, Richard (1975). *Strain of Violence: Historical Studies of American Violence and Vigilantism.* New York: Oxford University Press.

Buice, David (1988). "A Stench in the Nostrils of Honest Men: Southern Democrats and the Edmunds Act of 1882." *Dialogue: A Journal of Mormon Thought,* 21(3): 100–113.

Bushman, Richard L. (2005). *Rough Stone Rolling: A Cultural Biography of Joseph Smith.* New York: Knopf.

Cainkar, Louis A. (2009). *Homeland Insecurity: The Arab and Muslim Experience after 9/11*. New York: Russell Sage Foundation.

Cannon, Donald Q. (2007). "In the Press: Early Newspaper Reports on the Initial Publication of the Book of Mormon." *Journal of Book of Mormon Studies*, 16:2.

Capozzola, Christopher (2002). "The Only Badge Needed Is Your Patriotic Fervor: Vigilance, Coercion and the Law in World War I America." *The Journal of American History*, 88(4): 1354–1382.

Carpenter, Daniel (2000). "State Building Through Reputation Building: Coalitions of Esteem and Program Innovation in the National Postal System, 1883–1913." *Studies in American Political Development*, 14: 121–155.

Chambers, Simone and Jeffrey Kopstein (2001). "Bad Civil Society." *Political Theory*, 29(6): 837–865.

Chandrasekhar, Charu A. (2003). "Federal Civil Rights Remedies to Post-9/11 Airline Racial Profiling of South Asians." *Asian American Law Journal*, 10(2): 215–252.

Chesler, Phyllis (2005). *The Death of Feminism*. New York: Palgrave MacMillan.

Chin, Gabriel (1998). "Segregation's Last Stronghold: Race Discrimination and the Constitutional Law of Immigration." *UCLA Law Review*, 46(1).

Chua, Amy and Jeb Rubenfeld (2014). *The Triple Package: How Three Unlikely Traits Explain the Rise and Fall of Cultural Groups in America*. New York: Penguin.

Churchill, Robert H. (2009). *To Shake Their Guns in the Tyrant's Face: Libertarian Political Violence and the Origins of the Militia Movement*. Ann Arbor, MI: University of Michigan Press.

Cohn, Norman ([1967] 1996). *Warrant for Genocide: The Myth of the Jewish World Conspiracy and the Protocols of the Elders of Zion*. London: Serif.

Corbould, Clare (2009). *Becoming African Americans: Black Public Life in Harlem, 1919–1939*. Cambridge: Harvard University Press.

Curtis IV, Edward E. (2002). *Islam in Black America: Identity, Liberation and Difference in African-American Islamic Thought*. Albany: State University of New York Press.

Dahl, Robert (1961). *Who Governs? Democracy and Power in an American City*. New Haven: Yale University Press.

Davenport, Christian (2007). *State Repression and the Domestic Democratic Peace*. New York: Cambridge University Press.

　(2014). *How Social Movements Die: Repression and Demobilization of the Republic of New Africa*. New York: Cambridge University Press.

Davis, Darren (2007). *Negative Liberty: Public Opinion and the Terrorist Attacks on America*. New York: Russell Sage Foundation.

Davis, David Brion (1960). "Some Themes of Counter-Subversion: An Analysis of Anti-Masonic, Anti-Catholic and Anti-Mormon Literature." *The Mississippi Valley Historical Review*, 47(2): 205–224.

Dinnerstein, Leonard (1995). *Antisemitism in America*. New York: Oxford University Press.

Disha, Ilir, James C. Cavendish, and Ryan D. King (2011). "Historical Events and Spaces of Hate: Hate Crimes against Arabs and Muslims in Post-9/11 America." *Social Problems*, 58(1): 21–46.

Dizard, Jan E., Robert M. Muth, and Stephen P. Andrews (eds.) (1999). *Guns in America: A Reader*. New York: NYU Press.

Docherty, Jayne Seminare (2001). *Learning Lessons from Waco: When Parties Bring Their Gods to the Negotiation Table*. Syracuse: Syracuse University Press.

Dochuk, Darren (2011). *From Bible Belt to Sun Belt: Plain-Folk Religion, Grassroots Politics, and the Rise of Evangelical Conservatism*. New York: Norton.

Dohen, Dorothy (1967). *Nationalism and American Catholicism*. New York: Sheed and Ward.

Drakeman, Donald (2007). "'Everson v. Board of Education' and the Quest for the Historical Establishment Clause." *American Journal of Legal History*, 49(2): 119–168.

Driggs, Kenneth David (1988). "The Mormon Church-State Confrontation in Nineteenth-Century America." *Journal of Church and State*, 30(2): 273–289.

Dueck, Colin (2010). *Hard Line: The Republican Party and U.S. Foreign Policy since World War II*. Princeton: Princeton University Press.

Duffield, Marcus (1931). *King Legion*. New York: Jonathan Cape and Harrison Smith.

Dunn, Elizabeth and Chris Hann (eds.) (1996). *Civil Society: Challenging Western Models*. London: Routledge.

Eaton, Alison H. (1996). "Can the IRS Overrule the Supreme Court?" *Emory Law Journal*, 45: 987–1034.

Ekiert, Grzegorz and Jan Kubik (1999). *Rebellious Civil Society: Popular Protest and Democratic Consolidation in Poland, 1989–1993*. Ann Arbor: University of Michigan Press.

Elliff, Nathan (1945). "Jehovah's Witnesses and the Selective Service Act." *Virginia Law Review*, 31(4): 811–834.

Ellis, Mark (1994). "J. Edgar Hoover and the 'Red Summer' of 1919." *Journal of American Studies*, 28(1): 48–49.

Ellis, Richard J. (2005). *To The Flag: An Unlikely History of the Pledge of Allegiance*. Lawrence: University Press of Kansas.

Eltahawy, Mona (2012). "Why Do They Hate Us? The Real War on Women is in the Middle East." *Foreign Policy*, May/June 2012.

Ernst, Carl W. (ed.) (2013). *Islamophobia in America: The Anatomy of Intolerance*. New York: Palgrave MacMillan.

Evans, Peter B., Dietrich Rueschemeyer, and Theda Skocpol (eds.) (1985). *Bringing the State Back In*. New York: Cambridge University Press.

Farr, Thomas F. (2008). *World of Faith and Freedom: Why International Religious Liberty is Vital to American National Security*. New York: Oxford University Press.

Feldman, Stephen M. (ed.) (2000). *Law and Religion: A Critical Anthology*. New York: New York University Press.

   (2003). "Religious Minorities and the First Amendment: The History, the Doctrine, and the Future." *Journal of Constitutional Law*, 6(2): 223.

Fennell, William G. and Edward J. Friedlander (1936). *Compulsory Flag Salute in Schools: A Survey of the Statutes and Examination of Their Constitutionality*. New York: American Civil Liberties Union.

Fine, Gary A. (2007). "The Construction of Historical Equivalence: Weighing the Red and Brown Scares." *Symbolic Interaction*, 30(1): 27–39.

Fine, Gary A. and Terence McDonnell (2007). "Erasing the Brown Scare: Referential Afterlife and the Power of Memory Templates." *Social Problems*, 54(2): 170–187.

Fisher, Louis (2002). *Religious Liberty in America: Political Safeguards*. Lawrence: University Press of Kansas.

Flake, Kathleen (2004). *The Politics of American Religious Identity.* Chapel Hill: University of North Carolina Press.

Fleisher, Michael L. (2000). *"Sungusungu:* State-Sponsored Village Vigilante Groups among the Kuria of Tanzania." *Africa,* 70(2): 209–228.

Fluhman, J. Spencer (2012). *"A Peculiar People": Anti-Mormonism and the Making of Religion in Nineteenth-Century America.* Chapel Hill: University of North Carolina Press.

Foley, Michael W. and Bob Edwards (1996). "The Paradox of Civil Society." *Journal of Democracy,* 7(3): 38–52.

Foner, Eric (1970). *Free Soil, Free Labor, Free Men: The Ideology of the Republican Party before the Civil War.* New York: Oxford University Press.

(1988). *Reconstruction: America's Unfinished Revolution, 1863–1877.* New York: Harper Collins.

Fox, Jonathan (2004). "Counting the Causes and Dynamics of Ethnoreligious Violence." *Totalitarian Movements and Political Religions,* 4:3, 119–144.

(2008). *A World Survey of Religion and the State.* New York: Cambridge University Press.

Freeman, Steven M. (1992). "Hate Crime Laws: Punishment Which Fits the Crime." *Annual Survey of American Law,* 1992/1993: 581–586.

Fryer, Roland G. and Steven D. Levitt (2012). "Hatred and Profits: Under the Hood of the Ku Klux Klan." *Quarterly Journal of Economics,* 127(4): 1883–1925.

Gans, John A. (2011). "America 2012: Duelling Exceptionalisms." *Survival: Global Politics and Strategy,* 53(3): 169–186.

Gardell, Mattias (1996). *In the Name of Elijah Muhammad: Louis Farrakhan and the Nation of Islam.* Durham: Duke University Press.

Gary, Brett (1999). *The Nervous Liberals: Propaganda Anxieties from World War I to the Cold War.* New York: Columbia University Press.

Gedicks, Frederick Mark (1992). "The Integrity of Survival: A Mormon Response to Stanley Hauerwas." *DePaul Law Review* 42(1): 167–173.

Gellerman, William (1938). *The American Legion as Educator.* New York: Bureau of Publications, Teachers College, Columbia University.

Gerlach, Larry R. (1982). *Blazing Crosses in Zion: The Ku Klux Klan in Utah.* Logan: University of Utah Press.

Gerstle, Gary (1997). "Liberty, Coercion and the Making of Americans." *Journal of American History,* 84(2): 524–558.

GhaneaBassiri, Kambiz (1997). *Competing Visions of Islam in the United States.* Westport: Greenwood Press.

Gibson, Edward L. (2012). *Boundary Control: Subnational Authoritarianism in Federal Democracies.* New York: Cambridge University Press.

Gill, Anthony (2008). *The Political Origins of Religious Liberty.* New York: Cambridge University Press.

Givens, Terryl L. (1997). *The Viper on the Hearth: Mormons, Myths, and the Construction of Heresy.* New York: Oxford University Press.

Glock, Charles Y. and Rodney Stark (1966). *Christian Beliefs and Anti-Semitism.* New York: Harper and Row.

Godoy, Angelina Snodgrass (2006). *Popular Injustice: Violence, Community and Law in Latin America.* Palo Alto: Stanford University Press.

Goluboff, Risa (2007). *The Lost Promise of Civil Rights*. Cambridge: Harvard University Press.

Gordon, Sarah Barringer (1996). "The Liberty of Self-Degradation: Polygamy, Woman Suffrage and Consent in Nineteenth-Century America." *The Journal of American History*, 83(3): 815–847.

(2003). *The Mormon Question*. Chapel Hill, University of North Carolina Press.

Grant, Colin (2008). *Negro with a Hat: The Rise and Fall of Marcus Garvey and His Dream of Mother Africa*. London: Jonathan Cape.

Grim, Brian J. and Roger Finke (2011). *The Price of Religious Freedom Denied: Religious Persecution and Conflict in the 21st Century*. New York: Cambridge University Press.

Grimsted, David (2003). *American Mobbing, 1826–1861: Toward Civil War*. New York: Oxford University Press.

Grzymala-Busse, Anna (2012). "Why Comparative Politics Should Take Religion (More) Seriously." *Annual Review of Political Science*, 15: 421–442.

Gualtieri, Sarah M.A. (2001). "Becoming 'White': Race, Religion, and the Foundations of Syrian/Lebanese Ethnicity in the United States." *Journal of American Ethnic History*, 20(4): 29–58.

(2009). *Between Arab and White: Race and Ethnicity in the Early Syrian American Diaspora*. Berkeley: University of California Press.

Gusfield, Joseph (1972). *Symbolic Crusade: Status Politics and the American Temperance Movement*. Urbana and Chicago: University of Illinois Press.

Haddad, Yvonne Yazbeck (ed.) (1991). *The Muslims of America*. New York: Oxford University Press.

Hamburger, Philip (2001). "Illiberal Liberalism: Liberal Theology, Anti-Catholicism, and Church Property." *Journal of Contemporary Legal Issues*, 12: 693–726.

Hamburger, Philip (2002). *Separation of Church and State*. Cambridge: Harvard University Press.

Harper, Steven C. (2006). "Dictated by Christ: Joseph Smith and the Politics of Revelation." *Journal of the Early Republic*, 26(2): 275–304.

Hartz, Louis (1955). *The Liberal Tradition in America*. New York: Harcourt Brace.

Henry, Patrick (1981). "'And I Don't Care What It Is': The Tradition-History of a Civil Religion Proof-Text." *Journal of the American Academy of Religion*, 49(1): 35–47.

Herzog, Jonathan P. (2011). *The Spiritual-Industrial Complex: America's Religious Battle against Communism in the Early Cold War*. New York: Oxford University Press.

Hesse, Hans (ed.) (2001). *Persecution and Resistance of Jehovah's Witnesses during the Nazi Regime 1933–1945*. Chicago: Edition Temmen.

Higham, John (1965). *Strangers in the Land: Patterns of American Nativism 1860–1925*. New York: Atheneum.

Hill, Marvin S. (1980). "Cultural Crisis in the Mormon Kingdom: A Reconsideration of the Causes of Kirtland Dissent." *Church History*, 49(3): 286–297.

(2005). "Carthage Conspiracy Reconsidered: A Second Look at the Murder of Joseph and Hyrum Smith." *Journal of the Illinois Historical Society*, 97(2): 107–134.

Hoekema, Anthony A. (1963). *The Four Major Cults: Christian Science, Jehovah's Witnesses, Mormonism, Seventh-day Adventism*. Grand Rapids: William B. Eerdmans Publishing Company.

Hoffmann, Karen S. (2000). "Presidential Character in the Nineteenth Century." *Rhetoric and Public Affairs*, 3(4): 661.

Hofstadter, Richard ([1964] 1996). *The Paranoid Style in American Politics and Other Essays*. Cambridge: Harvard University Press.

Horowitz, David A. (1999). *Inside the Klavern: The Secret History of a Ku Klux Klan of the 1920s*. Carbondale and Edwardsville: University of Southern Illinois Press.

Huntington, Samuel P. (1968). *Political Order in Changing Societies*. New Haven: Yale University Press.

Hurd, Elizabeth Shakman (2008). *The Politics of Secularism in International Relations*. Princeton: Princeton University Press.

Hutchison, William R. (2003). *Religious Pluralism in America: The Contentious History of a Founding Ideal*. New Haven: Yale University Press.

Iannaccone, Laurence R. (1998). "Introduction to the Economics of Religion." *Journal of Economic Literature*, XXXVI: 1465–1496.

Ingalls, Robert P. (1987). "Lynching and Establishment Violence in Tampa, 1858–1935." *The Journal of Southern History*, 53(4): 541–570.

Issel, William (2009). *For Both Cross and Flag: Catholic Action, Anti-Catholicism, and National Security Politics in World War II San Francisco*. Philadelphia: Temple University Press.

Jenkins, Philip (2003). *The New Anti-Catholicism: The Last Acceptable Prejudice*. New York: Oxford University Press.

John, Richard (1995). *Spreading the News: The American Postal System from Franklin to Morse*. Cambridge: Cambridge University Press.

Jones, Richard Seelye (1946). *A History of the American Legion*. Indianapolis: Bobbs-Merrill.

Joyce, James (1922). *Ulysses*. Paris: Shakespeare and Company.

Junn, Jane (2007). "From Coolie to Model Minority: U.S. Immigration Policy and the Construction of Racial Identity." *Du Bois Review: Social Science and Research on Race*, 4(2): 355–373.

Kalkan, Kerem Ozan, Geoffrey C. Layman, and Eric M. Uslaner (2009). "'Bands of Others'? Attitudes toward Muslims in Contemporary American Society." *Journal of Politics*, 71(3): 847–862.

Karabel, Jerome (2006). *The Chosen: The Hidden History of Admission and Exclusion at Harvard, Yale and Princeton*. New York: Houghton Mifflin.

Katz, Jacob (1980). *From Prejudice to Destruction: Anti-Semitism, 1700–1933*. Cambridge: Harvard University Press.

Kaya, Ilhan (2004). "Turkish-American Immigration History and Identity Formations." *Journal of Muslim Minority Affairs*, 24(2): 297.

Kersch, Ken (2004). *Constructing Civil Liberties: Discontinuities in the Development of American Constitutional Law*. New York: Cambridge University Press.

Key, Valdimer Orlando (1943). "The Veterans and the House of Representatives: A Study of a Pressure Group and Electoral Mortality." *Journal of Politics*, 5(1): 27–40.

  (1949). *Southern Politics in State and Nation*. New York: Alfred A. Knopf.

Kilde, Jeane Halgren (2011). "The Park 51/Ground Zero Controversy and Sacred Sites as Contested Space." *Religions*, 2: 297–311.

Kim, Carrie Jean (2003). *Bitter Fruit: The Politics of Black-Korean Conflict in New York City*. New Haven: Yale University Press.

Kinder, Donald R. and Allison Dale-Riddle (2012). *The End of Race? Obama, 2008, and Racial Politics in America*. New Haven: Yale University Press.

Kirkpatrick, Jennet (2008). *Uncivil Disobedience: Studies in Violence and Democratic Politics*. Princeton: Princeton University Press.

Kleppner, Paul (1970). *The Cross of Culture: A Social Analysis of Midwestern Politics, 1850–1900*. New York: Free Press.

Koesel, Karrie (2014). *Religion and Authoritarianism: Conflict, Cooperation, and the Consequences*. New York: Cambridge University Press.

Korn, Bertram W. (1961). *American Jewry and the Civil War*. Cleveland and New York: Meridian Books.

Kowalewski, David (1991). "Counterinsurgent Vigilantism and Public Response: A Philippine Case Study." *Sociological Perspectives*, 34(2): 127–144.

Krasner, Stephen (1984). "Approaches to the State: Alternative Conceptions and Historical Dynamics." *Comparative Politics*, 16(2): 223–246.

Kull, Steven (2011). *Feeling Betrayed: The Roots of Muslim Anger at America*. Washington: Brookings Institution Press.

Kuru, Ahmet T. (2009). *Secularism and State Policies toward Religion: The United States, France, and Turkey*. New York: Cambridge University Press.

Kutulas, Judy (2006). *The American Civil Liberties Union and the Making of Modern Liberalism, 1930–1960*. Chapel Hill: University of North Carolina Press.

Lake, Marilyn and Henry Reynolds (2008). *Drawing the Global Colour Line: White Men's Countries and the International Challenge of Racial Equality*. Cambridge and New York: Cambridge University Press.

Lee, Martha (1996). *The Nation of Islam: An American Millenarian Movement*. Syracuse: Syracuse University Press.

Leepson, Marc (2005). *Flag: An American Biography*. New York: St. Martin's Press.

Levi, Margaret (1988). *Of Rule and Revenue*. Berkeley: University of California Press.
  (1997). *Consent, Dissent and Patriotism*. New York: Cambridge University Press.

Lindblom, Charles (1977). *Politics and Markets*. New York: Basic Books.

Lipset, Seymour Martin, and Earl Raab (1970). *The Politics of Unreason: Right Wing Extremism in America, 1790–1970*. New York: Harper and Row.

Liska, Allen E. (1992). *Social Threat and Social Control*. New York: SUNY Books.

López, Ian Haney (2006). *White By Law: The Legal Construction of Race*. New York: NYU Press.

Lyman, Edward L. (1986). *Political Deliverance: The Quest for Utah Statehood*. Champaign: University of Illinois Press.

MacDonnell, Francis (1995). *Insidious Foes: The Axis Fifth Column and the American Home Front*. New York: Oxford University Press.

Mamdani, Mahmood (2004). *Good Muslim, Bad Muslim: America, the Cold War, and the Roots of Terror*. New York: Pantheon Books.

Manwaring, David (1960). *Render unto Caesar: The Flag Salute Controversy*. Chicago: University of Chicago Press.

Marable, Manning (2009). "Racializing Obama: The Enigma of Post-Black Politics and Leadership." *Souls: A Critical Journal of Black Politics, Culture and Society*, 11(1).

Marr, Timothy (2006). *The Cultural Roots of American Islamicism*. New York: Cambridge University Press.

Martin, Walter (1996). *The Kingdom of the Cults*. Minneapolis: Bethany House Publishers.

Marvin, Carolyn and David W. Ingle (1999). *Blood Sacrifice and the Nation: Totem Rituals and the American Flag*. New York: Cambridge University Press.

Mashaw, Jerry (2012). *Creating the Administrative Constitution: The Lost 100 Years*. New Haven: Yale University Press.

Mason, Patrick Q. (2011a). "God and the People: Theodemocracy in Nineteenth-Century Mormonism." *Journal of Church and State*, 53(3): 349–375.

  (2011b). *The Mormon Menace: Violence and Anti-Mormonism in the Postbellum South*.

Mauss, Armand (1994). *The Angel and the Beehive: The Mormon Struggle with Assimilation*. Champaign: University of Illinois Press.

Mayhew, David (1974). *Congress: The Electoral Connection*. New Haven: Yale University Press.

McAlister, Melani (2001). *Epic Encounters: Culture, Media and U.S. Interests in the Middle East, 1945–2000*. Berkeley: University of California Press.

McMahon, Kevin J. (2004). *Reconsidering Roosevelt on Race*. Chicago: University of Chicago Press.

McVeigh, Rory (2009a). "Power Devaluation, the Ku Klux Klan, and the Democratic National Convention of 1924." *Sociological Forum*, 16(1): 1–30.

  (2009b). *The Rise of the Ku Klux Klan: Right-Wing Movements and National Politics*. Minneapolis: University of Minnesota Press.

Michlic, Joanna Beatta (2006). *Poland's Threatening Other: The Image of the Jew from 1880 to the Present*. Lincoln: University of Nebraska Press.

Mickey, Robert W. (2014). *Paths Out of Dixie: The Democratization of Authoritarian Enclaves in America's Deep South, 1944–1972*. Princeton: Princeton University Press.

Milkis, Sidney M. and Jesse H. Rhodes (2007). "George W. Bush, the Republican Party, and the 'New' American Party System." *Perspectives on Politics*, 5(3): 461–488.

Miller, William Lee (1986). *The First Liberty: Religion and the American Republic*. New York: Knopf.

Moghadam, Valentine M. (2002). "Islamic Feminism and Its Discontents: Toward a Resolution of the Debate." *Signs: Journal of Women in Culture and Society*, 27(4): 1135–1171.

Monsma, Stephen V. and J. Christopher Soper (1997). *The Challenge of Pluralism: Church and State in Five Democracies*. Lanham: Rowman and Littlefield.

Moore, Deborah Dash (2004). *GI Jews: How World War II Changed a Generation*. Cambridge: Harvard University Press.

Moore, R. Laurence (1986). *Religious Outsiders and the Making of Americans*. Oxford: Oxford University Press.

Morone, James A. (1998). *The Democratic Wish: Popular Participation and the Limits of American Government* (revised edition). New Haven: Yale University Press.

Morone, James A. (2003). *Hellfire Nation: The Politics of Sin in American History*. New Haven: Yale University Press.

Moseley, Charles (1972). "Latent Klanism in Georgia, 1890–1915." *Georgia Historical Quarterly*, 56(3): 365–386.

Murphy, Caryle (2003). "Islam and Feminism." *Carnegie Reporter*, 2(3).

Nettl, J.P. (1968). "The State as a Conceptual Variable." *World Politics*, 20(4): 559–592.

Newton, Merlin Owen (1995). *Armed with the Constitution: Jehovah's Witnesses in Alabama and the U.S. Supreme Court, 1939–1946.* Tuscaloosa: University of Alabama Press.

Newton, Michael (2001). *The Invisible Empire: The Ku Klux Klan in Florida.* Gainesville: University of Florida Press.

Niemi, Richard G. and Jane Junn (1998). *Civic Education: What Makes Students Learn.* New Haven: Yale University Press.

Noll, Mark A. and Luke E. Harlow (eds.) (2007). *Religion and American Politics: From the Colonial Period to the Present.* Oxford: Oxford University Press.

Novak, William (1996). *The People's Welfare: Law and Regulation in Nineteenth-Century America.* Chapel Hill: University of North Carolina Press.

O'Dea, Thomas F. (1957). *The Mormons.* Chicago: University of Chicago Press.

O'Reilly, Kenneth (1982). "A New Deal for the FBI: The Roosevelt Administration, Crime Control, and National Security." *The Journal of American History*, 69(3): 638–658.

Olson, Mancur (1993). "Dictatorship, Democracy and Development." *The American Political Science Review*, 87(3): 567–576.

Oney, Steve (2003). *And the Dead Shall Rise: The Murder of Mary Phagan and the Lynching of Leo Frank.* New York: Random House.

Parker, Christopher S. and Matt A. Barreto (2013). *Change They Can't Believe In: The Tea Party and Reactionary Politics in America.* Princeton: Princeton University Press.

Parsons, Stanley B., William W. Beach, and Michael J. Dubin (1986). *United States Congressional Districts and Data, 1843–1883.* Westport: Greenwood Books.

Pauley, Bruce F. (1992). *From Prejudice to Persecution: A History of Austrian Anti-Semitism.* Chapel Hill: University of North Carolina Press.

Pencak, William (1989). *For God and Country: The American Legion, 1919–1941.* Boston: Northeastern University Press.

Penton, M. James (1976). *Jehovah's Witnesses in Canada: Champions of Freedom of Speech and Worship.* Toronto: MacMillan of Canada.

  (1997). *Apocalypse Delayed: The Story of Jehovah's Witnesses.* Toronto: University of Toronto Press.

Peters, Shawn Francis (2000). *Judging Jehovah's Witnesses.* Lawrence: University Press of Kansas.

Philpott, Daniel (2007). "Explaining the Political Ambivalence of Religion." *American Political Science Review*, 101(3).

Pierce, Bessie Louise (1933). *Citizens' Organizations and the Civic Training of Youth.* New York: Charles Scribner's Sons.

Pipes, Daniel (1983). *In the Path of God: Islam and Political Power.* New York: Basic Books.

Platvoet, Jan G. and Arie L. Molendijk (1999). *The Pragmatics of Defining Religion: Contexts, Concepts and Contests.* Leiden: Brill.

Poll, Richard (1993). "Thomas L. Kane and the Utah War." *Utah Historical Quarterly*, 61(2): 112–135.

Prashad, Vijay (2000). *The Karma of Brown Folk.* Minneapolis: University of Minnesota Press.

Preston, Andrew (2012). *Sword of the Spirit, Shield of Faith: Religion in American War and Diplomacy*. New York: Knopf.

Puar, Jasbir K. and Amit S. Rai (2004). "The Remaking of a Model Minority: Perverse Projectiles under the Specter of (Counter)Terrorism." *Social Text*, 22(3): 75–104.

Pulzer, Peter G.J. (1964). *The Rise of Political Anti-Semitism in Germany and Austria*. New York: Wiley.

Putnam, Robert (2000). *Bowling Alone*. New York: Simon & Schuster.

Putnam, Robert D. and David E. Campbell (2010). *American Grace: How Religion Divides and Unites Us*. New York: Simon & Schuster.

Quinn, D. Michael (1985). "LDS Church Authority and New Plural Marriages, 1890–1904." *Dialogue*, 18(1).

Reed, Betsy (ed.) (2002). *Nothing Sacred: Women Respond to Religious Fundamentalism and Terror*. New York: Thunder's Mouth Press.

Remnick, David (1998). *King of the World: Muhammad Ali and the Rise of an American Hero*. New York: Vintage.

Ribuffo, Leo P. *The Old Christian Right: The Protestant Far Right from the Great Depression to the Cold War*. Philadelphia: Temple University Press.

Richardson, James T. (1991). "Cult/Brainwashing Cases and Freedom of Religion." *Journal of Church and State*, 33: 55–74.

(1993). "Definitions of Cult: From Sociological-Technical to Popular-Negative." *Review of Religious Research*, 34(4): 354.

Robbins, Thomas (2001). "Combating 'Cults' and 'Brainwashing' in the United States and Western Europe: A Comment on Richardson and Introvigne's Report." *Journal for the Scientific Study of Religion*, 40(2): 169–175.

Roelofs, Mark (1992). The Prophetic President: Charisma in the American Political Tradition. *Polity*, 25(1): 1–20.

Rogin, Michael (1975). *Fathers and Children: Andrew Jackson and the Subjugation of the American Indian*. New York: Knopf.

(1987). *Ronald Reagan, the Movie: and Other Episodes in Political Demonology*. Berkeley: University of California Press.

Rogowski, Ronald (1974). *Rational Legitimacy: A Theory of Political Support*. Princeton: Princeton University Press.

Rosenbaum, H. Jon and Peter C. Sederberg (eds.) (1974). "Vigilantism: An Analysis of Establishment Violence." *Comparative Politics*, 6(4): 541–570.

(1976). *Vigilante Politics*. Philadelphia: University of Pennsylvania Press.

Rosenblum, Nancy (1998). *Membership and Morals: The Personal Uses of Pluralism in America*. Princeton: Princeton University Press.

Rumer, Thomas A. (1990). *The American Legion: An Official History*. New York: M. Evans & Company, Inc.

Rutherford, Joseph F. (1926). "Introduction" in *Year Book of the International Bible Students Association*. Brooklyn: International Bible Students Association.

Sarna, Jonathan D. (2012). *When General Grant Expelled the Jews*. New York: Schocken.

Sartre, Jean-Paul ([1948] 1995). *Anti-Semite and Jew: An Exploration of the Etiology of Hate*. New York: Schocken Books.

Schattschneider, E.E. (1960). *The Semisovereign People: A Realist's View of Democracy in America*. New York: Holt, Rhinehart and Winston.

Schlozman, Kay Lehman (1984). "What Accent the Heavenly Chorus? Political Equality and the American Pressure System." *The Journal of Politics*, 46(4): 1006–1032.

Schwartz, E.A. (2002). "The Lynching of Robert Prager, the United Mine Workers, and the Problems of Patriotism in 1918." *Journal of the Illinois State Historical Society*, 95(4): 414–437.

Schwille, John and Jo-Ann Amadeo (2002). "The Paradoxical Situation of Civic Education in Schools: Ubiquitous and Yet Elusive." In Steiner-Khamsi, Gita, Judith Torney-Purta and John Schwille (eds.) *New Paradigms and Recurring Paradoxes in Education for Citizenship: An International Comparison*. Bradford: Emerald Publishing Group, pp. 105–136.

Sehat, David (2011). *The Myth of American Religious Freedom*. New York: Oxford University Press.

Shaw, Brent D. (2009). "State Intervention and Holy Violence: Timgad/Paleotrovsk/Waco." *Journal of the American Academy of Religion*, 77:4.

Shulman, George M. (2009). *American Prophecy: Race and Redemption in American Political Culture*. Minneapolis: University of Minnesota Press.

Sidhu, Dawinder S. (2007). "The Chilling Effect of Government Surveillance Programs on the Use of the Internet by Muslim Americans." *University of Maryland Law Journal of Race, Religion, Gender and Class*, 7(2): 375–393.

Skocpol, Theda (1997). "The Tocqueville Problem: Civic Engagement in American Democracy." *Social Science History*, 21(4): 455–479.

Skocpol, Theda, Marshall Ganz, and Ziad Munson (2000). "A Nation of Organizers: The Institutional Origins of Civic Voluntarism in the United States." *The American Political Science Review*, 94(3): 527–546.

Skowronek, Stephen (1982). *Building a New American State: The Expansion of National Administrative Capacities, 1877–1920*. Cambridge: Cambridge University Press.

Smith, Rogers (2003). *Stories of Peoplehood: The Politics and Morals of Political Membership*. New York: Cambridge University Press.

Somit, Albert and Joseph Tannenhaus (1957). "The Veteran in the Electoral Process." *Journal of Politics*, 19(2): 184–201.

Sparrow, James (2011). *Warfare State: World War II Americans and the Age of Big Government*. New York: Oxford University Press.

Stansell, Christine (2010). *The Feminist Promise: 1792 to the Present*. New York: Simon and Schuster.

Stark, Rodney (1997). *The Rise of Christianity*. San Francisco: HarperSanFrancisco. (2005). *The Rise of Mormonism*. New York: Columbia University Press.

Stark, Rodney and Laurence R. Iannaccone (1997). "Why the Jehovah's Witnesses Grow so Rapidly: A Theoretical Application." *Journal of Contemporary Religion*, 12(2): 133–157.

Stark, Rodney and William Sims Bainbridge (1985). *The Future of Religion: Secularization, Revival, and Cult Formation*. Berkeley: University of California Press.

Stein, Stephen J. (1992). *The Shaker Experience in America*. New Haven: Yale University Press.

Stein, Stephen J. (ed.) (2012). *The Cambridge History of Religions in America: Volume II, 1790 to 1945*. New York: Cambridge University Press.

Stewart, Charles and Barry Weingast (1992). "Stacking the Senate, Changing the Nation: Republican Rotten Boroughs, Statehood Politics, and American Political Development." *Studies in American Political Development*, 6(2): 223–271.

Stroup, Herbert Hewitt (1945). *The Jehovah's Witnesses*. New York: Columbia University Press.

Telhami, Shibley (2013). *The World Through Arab Eyes: Arab Public Opinion and the Reshaping of the Middle East*. New York: Basic Books.

Theiss-Morse, Elizabeth (2009). *Who Counts as an American? The Boundaries of National Identity*. New York: Cambridge University Press.

Theoharis, Athan (1985). "The FBI and the American Legion Contact Program, 1940–1966." *Political Science Quarterly*, 100(2): 271–286.

Tilly, Charles (2003). *The Politics of Collective Violence*. New York: Cambridge University Press.

Tischler, Barbara L. (1986). "One Hundred Percent Americanism and Music in Boston during World War I." *American Music*, 4(2): 164–176.

Turner, John G. (2012). *Brigham Young, Pioneer Prophet*. Cambridge: The Belknap Press of Harvard University Press.

Wade, Wyn Craig (1987). *The Fiery Cross: The Ku Klux Klan in America*. New York: Simon and Schuster.

Walker, Ronald W., Richard E. Turley, Jr. and Glen M. Leonard (2008). *Massacre at Mountain Meadows*. New York: Oxford University Press.

Wallace, Max (2005). *The American Axis: Henry Ford, Charles Lindbergh, and the Rise of the Third Reich*. New York: MacMillan.

Wallis, Roy (1982). "The Social Construction of Charisma." *Social Compass*, 29(1): 25–39.

Weber, Max (1947). *The Theory of Social and Economic Organization*. Translated by A.M. Henderson and Talcott Parsons. Glencoe, Illinois: The Free Press.

Wilson, Stephen (1982). *Ideology and Experience: Antisemitism in France at the Time of the Dreyfus Affair*. Rutherford: Fairleigh Dickinson University Press.

Wood, Elisabeth Jean (2003). *Insurgent Collective Action and Civil War in El Salvador*. New York: Cambridge University Press.

Woodward, C. Vann ([1938] 1963). *Tom Watson, Agrarian Rebel*. New York: Oxford University Press.

Wright, Stuart A. (ed.) (1995). *Armageddon in Waco: Critical Perspectives on the Branch Davidian Conflict*. Chicago: University of Chicago Press.

X, Malcolm (1965). *The Autobiography of Malcolm X, As Told to Alex Haley*. New York: Random House.

Young, Kimball (1954). *Isn't One Wife Enough?* New York: Holt.

Zablocki, Benjamin and Thomas Robbins (2001). *Misunderstanding Cults: Searching for Objectivity in a Controversial Field*. Toronto: University of Toronto Press.

Zygmunt, Joseph F. (1977). "Jehovah's Witnesses in the U.S.A., 1942–1976." *Social Compass*, XXIV, 1977/1: 45–57.

Index